Get the eBook FREE!

(PDF, ePub, Kindle, and liveBook all included)

We believe that once you buy a book from us, you should be able to read it in any format we have available. To get electronic versions of this book at no additional cost to you, purchase and then register this book at the Manning website.

Go to https://www.manning.com/freebook and follow the instructions to complete your pBook registration.

That's it!
Thanks from Manning!

100 C++ Mistakes
and How to Avoid Them

RICH YONTS

MANNING
SHELTER ISLAND

For online information and ordering of this and other Manning books, please visit www.manning.com. The publisher offers discounts on this book when ordered in quantity.

For more information, please contact

>   Special Sales Department
>   Manning Publications Co.
>   20 Baldwin Road
>   PO Box 761
>   Shelter Island, NY 11964
>   Email: orders@manning.com

Manning Publications Co.
20 Baldwin Road
PO Box 761
Shelter Island, NY 11964

Development editor:	Doug Rudder
Technical editor:	Matt Godbolt
Review editor:	Radmila Ercegovac
Production editor:	Kathy Rossland
Copy editor:	Christian Berk
Proofreader:	Keri Hales
Technical proofreader:	Abel Sen
Typesetter:	Tamara Švelić Sabljić
Cover designer:	Marija Tudor

ISBN 9781633436893
Printed in the United States of America

brief contents

contents

10   *Exceptions and resources*   *250*

11   *Functions and coding*   *285*

preface

Learning C++ is mainly about applying its language features in an environment to solve specific problems. Teaching C++ in a college environment differs from mentoring a junior developer in a work environment, yet the language is the same. Think of C++ as the common language (pun intended) that developers speak at the lowest level. Design patterns, conventional use, problem domain specifics, and company processes are higher levels of communication. These higher levels are the most critical; Alan Turing demonstrated that any single computer can compute a solvable problem that any other computer can, differing only in approach and time. Likewise, any language can solve a computational problem that C++ can solve.

This thought is not meant to criticize C++ (or any other language) in any way, only to establish that, in a business that uses C++, that fact is of almost no consequence to the overall direction of the company and the problems it solves. Your skill at becoming a seasoned developer is of much greater importance than your (simple?) knowledge of a specific programming language.

With all that said, why this book about C++? Earlier, we established that you will be introduced to an environment that uses C++. Given your interest and skills in the language, you will have the opportunity to apply your knowledge and skills in solving problems that the company cares about. You will be using C++ to do that work. Therefore, knowing how to identify some of the mistakes that are common in C++ gives you the ability to mitigate them and, more importantly, not repeat them. Having to work in a code base that uses specific approaches narrows your opportunity to use C++ in its most expressive and proper way. For example, many string-handling solutions use C idioms, such as `strcat`, `strstr`, and `strcpy`. If this is common practice, you may feel inclined, even pressured, to use the same, although these functions should be avoided in preference to C++ approaches.

C++ is a very flexible language, allowing a programmer to do anything made possible by their machine. Many more modern languages abstract away much of the details and complexity of the machine. Notable exceptions are Go and Rust. C++ unapologetically provides the lowest level of detail for manipulating machine characteristics. This approach makes it a compelling language for working with low-level details.

However, this flexibility and granularity come at a cost. One cannot program C++ with the "looseness" of Python or Java. For example, C++ provides no default garbage collector to manage memory and resources. The developer must handle these details themselves. Numerous mistakes are made around resource management, which can significantly impact program performance and correctness. It seems appropriate to quote the *Spider-Man* (2002) movie, in which Uncle Ben warns, "With great power comes great responsibility." This quote should have originated with C++.

My interest in C++ began with C-Front, Dr. Bjarne Stroustrup's C++-to-C transpiler. I had already learned and used C, and I'd struggled to get on a project that would use C++. Finally, those projects came along in the late 1980s, when the workstation revolution occurred. Then came Java, around 1995, which abruptly ended my C++ journey. I later picked up projects using C++ in the early 2020s. Concurrently, I was teaching programming at the university level and was able to instruct many C++ classes.

In both venues, I began seeing weaknesses, a prevalence of classical C++ issues and idioms, and far too little modern C++; most textbooks barely mention its modern features. Hence, sharing my blunders and discoveries in book form arose. My hope is that students and practitioners will be encouraged to tackle existing code, armed with some background of how much of it got there—warts and all—and how to improve it. If they can avoid these pitfalls, they are well ahead of where many of us started.

acknowledgments

In a 1624 prose work by English poet John Donne, it was stated that "no man is an island." We all are interconnected in several ways. Writing a book exposes those interconnections as few other enterprises do.

I wish to acknowledge the Manning editorial and support staff, especially Doug Rudder and Michael Stephens. These gentlemen allowed me to create and bring to fruition a concept, kept me on track, cleaned up my messes, and were genuinely pleasant to work with. Several other team members did their jobs so well that attention was never drawn to them. That does not diminish their effectiveness; it proclaims their professionalism. To the unsung heroes, thanks.

My technical editor, Matt Godbolt, was very supportive and thorough. Matt Godbolt is a C++ developer with a passion for striking the balance between readable, maintainable code and high-performance solutions. His sharp eyes detected several mistakes, inconsistencies, and opportunities for improvement. Any remaining errors are my fault.

Thanks as well to all the reviewers: Abe Taha, Abel Sen, Abir Qasem, Aldo Biondo, Andre Weiner, Dmitri Nesteruk, Doyle Turner, Frances Buontempo, Francesco Basile, Ganesh Harke, Greg Wagner, Ivan Čukić, Jialin Jiao, John Donoghue, John Villarosa, Juan José Durillo Barrionuevo, Juan Rufes, Keith Kim, Leon Pfletschinger, Luke Kupka, Marcus Geselle, Michael Wall, Narendra Merla, Ofek Shilon, Piotr Jastrzebski, Rajat Kant Goel, Richard Meinsen, Ronaldo Scarpate, Ruud Gijsen, Saboktakin Hayati, Sachin Handiekar, Shantanu Kumar, Shawn Smith, Simone Sguazza, Srinivas Vamsi Parasa, Sriram Macharla, Stanley Anozie, Stefan Turalski, Timothy Jaap van Deurzen, Troi Eisler, and Walt Stoneburner. Your suggestions helped make this a better book.

My family was supportive throughout the entire process. My wife, Kim, helped keep me on task with sympathetic words. My children were always jazzed that their dad was writing a book and encouraged me by keeping me positive about the process (and so many others).

Finally, my talents, education, work experience, and much more have been given to me by a gracious Father. One cannot repay such debt; one can only bask in it, be grateful, and try to pass it on (James 1:17).

about this book

C++ is a multiparadigm language that has existed for much of the computing era. It started as a better C—that is, *C with classes*—and has become an international standards-based language in active development. At the time of this writing, the C++20 standard was published, the C++23 standard was out for final review, and the C++26 standard was being formed. C++ is used in projects ranging from very small to very large by inexperienced to highly experienced developers and applies to most areas of software development.

An estimated tens of billions of lines of C++ code are currently running in production environments. Numerous teams and millions of developers from different backgrounds have written this code over decades. Each developer has their own view of what proper programming models look like, what good C++ code is, and which development methodologies should be used.

This volume of code produced by these developers varies considerably in its correctness, readability, effectiveness, and performance. Much of the code is imperative in paradigm; some is object-oriented, and a small amount is functional. Some code was written by novices, much more by experts, though not necessarily experts in C++ design and implementation. A large amount of this code was written before the first C++ standardization effort in 1998. Code written after that time might conform to one of the standards but often looks like a prestandardized form.

This book focuses on several problems when writing programs in C++. Modern C++ is considered to have started with the C++11 standard. The large installed base of pre-modern (or classical) C++ code makes understanding these issues relevant and their remediation critical. After reading this book, programmers should be better able to identify and correct the problems discussed. Further, mistakes that are not discussed should be easier to identify and fix. Thinking through issues should make any developer more attuned to some of the nuances of the language and the development process.

Who should read this book

Regardless of the code's origins, standard, paradigm, and skill level, someone must actively maintain it. New features must be added, existing features must be modified or enhanced, bugs must be fixed, and inefficiencies must be mitigated. Mistakes are rampant in the code base, yet the programs are running and producing meaningful results.

The reader is assumed to be relatively new to the world of C++ development, likely coming from a background of personal learning, college training, or other programming languages. Most developers get few, if any, chances to write a completely new project from scratch; therefore, the reader will likely work mostly with legacy code. Your task will be developing new features and resolving existing problems in a code base of thousands or millions of lines of older code.

Your challenge will be to learn how to code C++ in such an environment. C++ is rarely developed in an open environment, where the developer gets to make all decisions. This environment differs from learning to code in C++ because the company or team sets various guidelines, style guides, naming conventions, and other parameters. Further, the code base establishes acceptable architectural patterns, naming conventions, usage guidelines, and solutions for common problems. If much of this responsibility sounds like everything but actual C++ coding, your instincts are correct.

How this book is organized: A road map

The mistakes in part 1 of *100 C++ Mistakes and How to Avoid Them* represent a misuse of C++, where the developer can improve code and techniques by opting for many of the more recent language and Standard Template Library features. Chapter 2 focuses on classes and data types, emphasizing class design and smart pointers. Chapter 3 covers general programming pitfalls and language features that may need to be utilized more. Chapter 4 focuses on more recent changes to the C++ language and several techniques that make common problems more manageable.

Given its historical roots in the C language, the mistakes in part 2 of the book represent problems that creep into modern C++. Many of these mistakes can be modernized to developers' great benefit. Chapter 5 focuses on habits and practices that silently worm their way into C++, even though there are better approaches. Chapter 6 focuses on poor practices that early C++ programming popularized and remain in several current code bases.

The mistakes in part 3 represent problems commonly found in legacy code bases, for which the developer lacks recourse to modern techniques. Several problems can be improved upon, and the code quality can be enhanced. Chapter 7 focuses on the problem of good class design and several problems with building robust ones. Chapter 8 focuses on additional details associated with good class design and problems that can unexpectedly cause the design to falter. Chapter 9 focuses on several operations classes provide and that can inadvertently cause difficulties if not done well. Chapter 10 focuses on system resource handling and several problems that arise when this is done poorly. Chapter 11 focuses on problems that stem from using functions and parameters. Chapter 12 focuses on problems that arise in general coding using premodern C++.

About the code

This book contains many examples of source code both in numbered listings and in line with normal text. In both cases, source code is formatted in a `fixed-width font like this` to separate it from ordinary text. Sometimes code is also **in bold** to highlight code that has changed from previous steps in the chapter, such as when a new feature adds to an existing line of code.

In many cases, the original source code has been reformatted; we've added line breaks and reworked indentation to accommodate the available page space in the book. In rare cases, even this was not enough, and listings include line-continuation markers (➥). Additionally, comments in the source code have often been removed from the listings when the code is described in the text. Code annotations accompany many of the listings, highlighting important concepts.

You can get executable snippets of code from the liveBook (online) version of this book at https://livebook.manning.com/book/100-c-plus-plus-mistakes-and-how-to -avoid-them. The complete code for the examples in the book is available for download from the Manning website at https://www.manning.com/books/100-c-plus-plus -mistakes-and-how-to-avoid-them.

liveBook discussion forum

Purchase of *100 C++ Mistakes and How to Avoid Them* includes free access to liveBook, Manning's online reading platform. Using liveBook's exclusive discussion features, you can attach comments to the book globally or to specific sections or paragraphs. It's a snap to make notes for yourself, ask and answer technical questions, and receive help from the author and other users. To access the forum, go to https://livebook.manning .com/book/100-c-plus-plus-mistakes-and-how-to-avoid-them/discussion. You can also learn more about Manning's forums and the rules of conduct at https://livebook .manning.com/discussion.

Manning's commitment to our readers is to provide a venue where a meaningful dialogue between individual readers and between readers and the author can take place. It is not a commitment to any specific amount of participation on the part of the author, whose contribution to the forum remains voluntary (and unpaid). We suggest you try asking the author some challenging questions lest his interest stray! The forum and the archives of previous discussions will be accessible from the publisher's website as long as the book is in print.

about the author

RICH YONTS is a senior software engineer at Teradata and a longtime software engineer using C++, Java, and Python. Rich held several technical and leadership roles during his 10 years at IBM. He has deep experience on large code bases and considers himself a student and a teacher of C++.

about the cover illustration

The figure on the cover of *100 C++ Mistakes and How to Avoid Them*, titled "L'Infirmier," or "The Nurse," is taken from a book by Louis Curmer published in 1841. Each illustration is finely drawn and colored by hand.

In those days, it was easy to identify where people lived and what their trade or station in life was just by their dress. Manning celebrates the inventiveness and initiative of the computer business with book covers based on the rich diversity of regional culture centuries ago, brought back to life by pictures from collections such as this one.

C++: With great power comes great responsibility

This chapter covers

- Insight into the origin of C++ programming mistakes
- Four analytical categories of proper code
- An approach to detecting and resolving programming mistakes
- Encouragement to take on the daunting task of correcting mistakes

As a C++ programmer, you have a daunting task: writing and supporting thousands—or millions—of lines of code. Fortunately, *daunting* is not the same as *impossible*! Learning from your mistakes and, more importantly, from the mistakes of C++ developers who have gone before you will prepare you to handle almost any situation you're likely to encounter. Supporting C++ is a long-haul process, and you won't master the language or the code base in just a few months. Dealing with frustration is a constant problem for developers in any language, often because of past decisions that have proven to be questionable or poor. Look for the good, the smart, and the elegant choices in others' code, and you will soon be making the same choices in yours.

This book analyses 100 mistakes you'll likely see (or make yourself) in modern and legacy C++ code. We aim to turn these mistakes into valuable insight you can use to create and maintain a cleaner, more efficient code base. Understanding the approach and fixes for each mistake should prepare you to find and resolve them—or avoid making them in the first place. Let's get started!

1.1 Mistakes

Mistakes are common in any code base, and they can come from a variety of sources. Over many years, C++ coders have studied countless applications to discover mistakes: wrong or outdated coding practices, flaws in the language, poor application designs, and inefficient tools. And we've found ways to make things better! Development methodologies have been invented to address development failures, and language features have been added to address shortcomings.

Typical C++ code bases have many opportunities for improvement. Code written a year or a decade ago will use practices and language features that were popular and available at the time. As time has passed, newer approaches have been added, and mismatches between the designs have become apparent. This advancement in knowledge and technique has only sometimes been translated into improvement of existing code. Technical debt has accumulated, and inconsistencies have multiplied. These problems must be supported, modified, updated, and debugged.

Not all programmers get to redesign or rewrite large amounts of code. Business goals rarely advocate improving existing code when new code or features can be implemented. However, the debt incurred by poor choices and practices affects new development. This technical debt is often manifested as brittle code that is hard to change and challenging to integrate new code into. Rather than choosing an either/or approach, where old code is largely fixed or neglected, the closest approach to the ideal is discovering and resolving frequently appearing patterns.

1.1.1 A quick example

For example, in Mistake 57, a broad range of warnings will be listed if a complete product build is made and the resulting output is studied. When the compilation output is analyzed, specific warnings will show up repeatedly. One option is to focus on a particular compiler warning and fix it across all or most of the code base. The following code shows a minimal test case where the address warning `-Waddress` was discovered in three ways.

The code in listing 1.1 is incorrectly trying to

- call a function without using the syntactically necessary parentheses
- test the returned value from a function call
- compare two object values

Listing 1.1 A code example with compiler warnings

```
int cleanup() {
    return 0;
}

int main() {
    cleanup;

    if (!(cleanup)) {
        ...
    }
    const char* message = "Hello, world";
    if (message == "Hello, world") {
        ...
    }
    return 0;
}
```

An attempted function call without parentheses is just an address, and no code is executed; fix by adding parentheses.

An attempted use of returned value. The function address is used, which is always true (nonzero), negation makes it always false (zero), and the code body never runs; fix by adding parentheses.

Comparison of one const pointer to a different const pointer, which is always false (mismatches); fix by using strcmp type function or C++ strings to compare pointed-to values.

The code base from which these warnings came had these problems resolved as part of other work. If this approach is chosen, communicate to other developers and reviewers that you intend to improve the code over time. It is better to solicit the cooperation of other team members to assist in this process. Be warned: some fixes are not trivial but certainly look that way. Proceed with caution, restraint, and adequate testing. Restraint must be exercised so that you do not try to fix too many problems simultaneously (despite the temptation) but use a slow and steady pace to resolve a manageable number of problems simultaneously.

Another option is to fix multiple problems within one code file. If you are working on that file to modify code already, it is easy to resolve the other problems selectively. As with the previous approach, proceed carefully.

1.2 Anatomy of a mistake

Each mistake discussed in this book stands alone. In the real world, some mistakes will affect other code. This interconnectedness makes diagnosis and resolution more difficult. Our approach eliminates this complication, at the risk of presenting an incomplete view of a mistake's broader influence. Most chapters introduce an overarching concept for the mistakes included. Some mistakes appear in multiple chapters, as they are more broadly applicable. This situation reveals the cross-cutting nature of many C++ features; a feature or mistake rarely affects only one thin slice of that language. Each mistake is analyzed according to four prioritized characteristics that involve development and execution.

1.2.1 Correctness

One important category of mistakes is *correctness*, which measures whether the code solves its intended problem without errors. Ultimately, code can be a disaster by any other measure, but if it is correct, we can be confident that the problem is solved. The most elegant and academically sophisticated code may look appealing, but it needs to be correct. The rule of thumb is to write the code to solve the problem precisely while introducing no unwanted side effects. In many cases, the reality is not this clean, but it is a worthy goal.

> **NOTE**   In several cases, incorrect code can result in undefined behavior (UB). Consider UB a highly offensive vulgarity, and learn to avoid UBs at all costs (play the *Shaft* theme song here). A UB is a program operation that the language standard does not define, leading to unpredictable results, crashes, or security vulnerabilities. The compiler can handle a UB in *any* manner, including optimizing it away.

1.2.2   Readability

A second category is *readability*, which measures how the developer communicates their intentions for the code to another developer. Each developer has their own style, but it should be improved if it interferes with clear, concise communication. Consider generally available or team-oriented style guidelines. The rule of thumb is to write the code for another developer's consumption (the compiler does not care), express yourself so that someone else understands your thought process clearly and quickly, and conform to any mandatory style guidelines. More sophisticated developers tend to write elegant code; this is natural but can cause difficulty for less-skilled developers.

1.2.3   Effectiveness

Effectiveness measures whether developers have used language features designed for specific purposes to save development time. The compactness of expression and adept usage of certain features is at the heart of effectiveness. The time needed to solve a problem is directly related to programmer productivity and often indirectly associated with correctness. A rule of thumb is to use the correct feature for its intended purpose.

1.2.4   Performance

Finally, *performance* is about choosing the best approach, algorithm, data structure, or means of solving a problem that works well with hardware. This aspect is the hardest to get right, since intuition often needs to be corrected about what makes the most performant code. Profiling tools should be used to discover actual bottlenecks and hotspots.

This characteristic is the most academically rigorous of the four factors. Choosing the correct algorithm for a problem is often the best first approach, and it takes some computer science knowledge to select the proper one. The rule of thumb is understanding the computational cost of various approaches or algorithms and choosing the best solution to solve the problem efficiently.

1.3   Learning from our mistakes

Any author hopes they have correctly assessed an audience's needs and helped close gaps in the existing literature. After reading this book, you will be able to detect these and other mistakes; understand why they are problems; know how to resolve them; and, in so doing, avoid making similar mistakes.

1.3.1 Noticing mistakes

Awareness is the first step toward better programming. I have had students who got a glazed look in their eyes when I explained an example. These students were trying to wrap their heads around the concepts, but the breakthrough was yet to happen. To ease their pain, I often say that I do not expect them to develop these concepts alone. I show and explain the examples to sensitize them to specific problems, recognize them, and then see how to solve them.

To any degree that I have expertise, it is because of those who taught me and showed me examples. While I am knowledgeable and might appear clever, I must learn continually (like everyone else). Pattern recognition is critical to growth; we have tools to deal with a problem once we notice a familiar pattern. This book will help you recognize and resolve mistakes in existing code, rather than perpetuate them.

1.3.2 Understanding mistakes

Recognizing a mistake is a critical step, but to understand its nature, we must learn to better understand why it is a mistake. Some of our longtime best practices are no longer considered optimal today. Programming follows the scientific model; we propose solutions, use them, and evaluate their effectiveness. Sometimes, we win; sometimes, we lose.

No one should be surprised at this progression; it is how we all learn. When we make a mistake, we can fill in gaps in our knowledge (or lack thereof). This filling touches other areas, and we expand our knowledge and understanding of relationships between programming features. I want to communicate that every mistake can be an intellectually and emotionally driven opportunity to improve. Failure only occurs when we quit or refuse to learn. This book will help you understand why a particular approach to coding is a mistake.

1.3.3 Fixing mistakes

Fixing mistakes is the real reason for a book like this. While fixing mistakes is essential, it is only one step in a more extensive process. Without the accompanying recognition and understanding of why the mistake is a problem, we are little more than mechanical units modifying source code (hypothetically, a monkey could be trained to do the same).

We want to fix mistakes because we understand why they are problematic. This understanding is beneficial when on a programming team. We all make mistakes, but finding and fixing them before they are pushed to production will ensure a much better experience for the developers, clients, and company. This book will help you learn how to fix and prevent writing mistakes yourself.

1.3.4   Learning from mistakes

Detecting, understanding, and fixing mistakes is essential for good code; however, more can be gained from the process. As one's experience grows, other problematic programming code will be easier to analyze. Pattern detection and comprehension position one to discover other mistakes and problems. This can be considered similar to working out at the gym—it trains the body for various sports without necessarily focusing on any specific one.

Your knowledge of these mistakes will make you a helpful resource to others, both during development and code reviews. As you share your knowledge, you will be helping others grow and develop similar skills.

This book will help prepare you to contribute to others beyond your current capability.

1.4   Where we'll find mistakes

Any experienced C++ developer will tell you there are far more than 100 types of mistakes that can be made in C++. The mistakes I've chosen are some that I have experienced, studied, or otherwise been affected by. Consider this list as my top 100; a different author would correctly have chosen another top 100. They fall roughly into the following categories.

1.4.1   Class design

C++ was designed to bring the object-oriented paradigm to the popular C language. The development of classes is an exercise of defining new data types that the compiler understands and manipulates as if they were built-in types. The developer is entirely responsible for determining what the new classes represent, how they are handled, and their meaning.

The compiler ensures the language rules are followed but places few constraints on the newly created data type. This freedom is a breeding ground for mistakes. Rather than having the language be more restricted, developers need to understand and mitigate these problems.

1.4.2   Program implementation

Programming, in general, has several areas where poor design or implementation can cause difficulties. C++ is flexible, so these areas must be understood to improve or prevent mistakes. Some of the errors in this part could be classified as class design. Since these problems are more generally applicable, they are categorized under this heading. The proper application of language features is essential to producing quality software.

1.4.3   Library problems

A programmer's code is often a tiny part of the overall program. Numerous libraries and functions within them are used throughout a program. Further, some language features allow a more general approach to solving problems. Templates, for example, can solve a family of related problems by describing a general solution and letting the compiler write the final code.

Library functions provide extensive functionality that would be tedious, time-consuming, and error-prone to write ourselves. Correct usage of these functions allows a developer to write significant problem-solving functionality without requiring themselves to implement supporting code. However, misunderstanding how to use this code properly can cause significant problems.

1.4.4 *Modern C++*

One of the goals of C++ is to ensure significant backward compatibility as the language evolves. This value allows modern compilers to compile legacy code. However, this approach does not imply that older code is written well or ideally. As the language has evolved, some of the mistakes and problems from the past have been mitigated, and better solutions have been incorporated.

Many of these improvements allow a programmer to write more correct, resilient, and simple code that does the same work as before. Often, these improvements affect one or more of the elements of mistakes: correctness, readability, effectiveness, and performance. The price we must pay for this improvement is to study the new features and understand how they can positively affect our thinking and coding.

1.4.5 *Old standards and usage*

Code written before these new features were added obviously cannot gain their benefits. Program statements written after the features were added may not take them into account, resulting in code that is functionally older, less expressive, and likely buggier. For example, C++-style strings mitigate significant problems with C-style strings, but a programmer must use C++-style strings to gain the explicit benefit and avoid some likely errors.

1.4.6 *Lost expertise and misguided training*

As experienced C++ developers are lost to attrition, newer developers will be hired to fill those positions. These developers must understand older, perhaps poorer, and more challenging program code. This situation is exacerbated by the incomplete training in modern C++ that many academic institutions provide. Some of the most current C++ textbooks provide examples and give advice that is still premodern, ineffective in the field, and out of touch with development best practices.

Some mistakes are due to premodern approaches, others are due to poor pedagogy, and still others are due to invalidated former best practices. Regardless of the origin of these mistakes, becoming sensitized to them, the problems they raise, and some possible solutions should help any C++ developer produce correct, readable, effective, and performant code.

1.5   *A word about organization*

The book is laid out in reverse chronological order, where modern C++ problems are dealt with first. We then consider transitional problems that affect both modern (C++11 and later) and premodern C++ (C++98 and C++03). Finally, we'll look at premodern C++, where many legacy code bases are limited in using modern methodology.

The code in this book is based mainly on code written before the C++11 standard (a nice mix of C++98 and C++03). The compiler used to generate code is the GNU C++ toolset (11.3.0), running on an Ubuntu installation (22.04 LTS on Windows Subsystem for Linux [WSL] 2). This compiler version was chosen for simplicity and stability on this platform. Later versions already exist and will continue to be released. Any of these can detect the problems and coding flaws discussed in this book. Using an older compiler version might yield different results.

Business constraints will likely require some readers to compile at C++98 and miss all the wonderful opportunities for modern C++ features. It is sad but true; most of my code base is limited to C++03, since the business optimizes for stability. Getting the operating system and tools team to vet later versions has proceeded slowly and agonizingly.

While many of the following mistakes are found in classical C++ (pre-C++11), the first several addressed are in modern C++. A modern programmer will benefit from these, so they are presented earlier.

Later in the book, problems and their solutions were solved using only classical C++. Some of these problems will appear in more modern code, but modern techniques should be used where applicable. Problems discussed later in the book address situations in which the programmer cannot use modern compilers—sad but true. Knowing how to resolve these problems is critical when using constrained technology. Note that the See Also section in each Mistake can include cross references between related modern and classical mistakes and solutions, where appropriate.

Summary

This book can help in your effort to do the following:

- Understand the causes behind some common C++ programming mistakes.
- Identify common programming mistakes found in many existing installed and running C++ code bases.
- Analyze code for its correctness, readability, effectiveness, and performance.
- Know where and how to change code to resolve these common mistakes.
- Write better code that avoids these mistakes and uses modern approaches when applicable.
- Teach others about the problems you have learned, the problems encountered, and some solutions to these problems.

Part 1

Modern C++

A key aspect of modern C++ is its disciplined approach to robust classes and type management. Classes in C++ have evolved beyond simple data containers to become fundamental components of robust software infrastructure. Effective dynamic memory management through smart pointers reduces memory leaks and dangling pointers. By adopting advanced class design techniques and utilizing modern type features, developers can create resilient and adaptable structures, paving the way for more reliable applications.

Modern C++ brings new programming tools, such as lambda expressions, range-based loops, and contextual keywords, promoting concise and precise code writing. Recognizing and integrating these underutilized features into everyday coding can significantly reduce errors and inefficiencies commonly associated with outdated methodologies. By transitioning from traditional to contemporary techniques, developers can tackle modern software challenges with increased confidence and creativity, ensuring their code is correct and future-proofed for ongoing development.

Better modern C++: Classes and types

2

This chapter covers

- Move semantics
- Supplied class members
- Range-based for loops
- Smart pointers

With the advent of the C++11 standard, several changes were added to enhance language features, improve the Standard Template Library (STL), increase performance, and simplify syntax and expressiveness. Although not described in this book, significant improvements were added for concurrency, including threads and tasks, error detection, chronological and calendar enhancements, and compile-time computations.

The language features introduced in C++11 provide substantial advantages. The `auto` keyword enables type inference, simplifies code, and enhances readability and effectiveness. Range-based `for` loops simplify iteration over collections, enhancing code clarity and reducing potential errors. The `nullptr` literal enhances safety by distinguishing between null pointers and the integer zero.

The STL enhancements introduced in C++11 offer significant benefits. The addition of smart pointers facilitates safe memory management and a reduction in memory leaks. Move semantics streamline resource handling, increasing performance by reducing unnecessary copying. New containers enrich data structure options, improving flexibility and efficiency in data handling. Lambda expressions permit concise and expressive code, increasing readability and effectiveness.

The performance benefits introduced enhance program efficiency and resource utilization. Rvalue references enable more efficient handling of temporary objects, minimizing unnecessary overhead. These improvements lead to faster execution times and more efficient resource management, enhancing the overall performance of a C++ program.

The simplified syntax and expressiveness enhancements in C++11 foster more readable and writeable code. Lambda expressions enable inline function definitions, improving code clarity and reducing the need for auxiliary functions. Variadic templates offer flexibility in handling variable numbers of template arguments, enabling more generic and reusable code. Range-based `for` loops provide a more intuitive syntax for iterating over containers. These improvements enable developers to write more expressive, efficient, and flexible code, ultimately improving quality.

Most of these improvements are discussed in this and the following two chapters. Significant improvements and enhancements are not covered but can be found in numerous books, classes, and internet searches. The breadth of enhancements in the C++11 standard is well worth studying, as they provide a basis for the C++17 and C++20 standards, where enhancements, additions, deprecations, removals, and new language features are added. C++ is far from dead and keeps improving as time marches on.

Modern C++ does not prevent a developer from making mistakes, but it supports several features that make them more difficult. For example, range-based `for` loops are immune to off-by-one errors. The advantages noted in the following mistakes are new features designed to improve the language to address classic mistakes. While several features have been added, even a tiny subset significantly benefits the development process. Some of these features are discussed in the following list of problems. There are many more than will be discussed here, but the features covered in this chapter address some of the most essential features that address limitations in premodern C++.

2.1   *Mistake 1: Failing to use move semantics*

This mistake focuses on performance. Transferring information from one area to another can be expensive because the data is usually copied, resulting in two (or more) versions of the data.

PROBLEM

Often, data must be created or built in one place and analyzed or manipulated in another. Copying data from one place to another can be inefficient, since the data is duplicated. Copying small amounts of data seems innocuous, but large volumes of data will cause problems, especially if done frequently.

If multiple entities must own the data, it is shared. Large groups of shared data can usually be implemented by passing around copies of pointers, allowing various pieces of code to access the data without copying any of it. Fairly often, the data is owned exclusively. Passing pointers around for this kind of data can be dangerous, since pointers are inherently a sharing mechanism. Modern C++ offers unique ownership smart pointers for this situation.

It is common to find data that is uniquely owned and managed by value, not by pointer. Consider the code in listing 2.1, where a TextSection is created and initialized in one instance and later passed to another. The p1 object exclusively owns the Text-Section, and the ownership and data are "transferred" to p2; at least, this is the intent. The result is that a single copy of the data is owned by p2, but this path is costly. Notice that the source object's data and headers are destroyed, preserving the unique ownership requirement but breaking the common practice of passing a const reference for the source.

> **Listing 2.1 A uniqueness-preserving assignment operator with heavy cost**

```cpp
class TextSection {
    // assume a clever implementation
};

class Page {
private:
    TextSection* headers;
    TextSection* body;
public:
    Page(TextSection* h) : headers(h), body(new TextSection()) {}
    Page(Page& o);
    ~Page() { if (body) delete body; }
};

Page::Page(Page& o) {
    if (this == &o)
        return;
    body = new TextSection(*o.body);
    delete o.body;
    o.body = 0;
    headers = o.headers;
    o.headers = 0;
}

int main() {
    Page p1(new TextSection());          An assignment operation
    Page p2 = p1;            ◄─────────  with unanticipated behavior
    return 0;
}
```

ANALYSIS

A copy of the data is owned by p2, which is not the original data. This situation results in two copies and the time needed to duplicate it. If the data were extensive, the time to copy could be considerable. The copy constructor destroys the copied data, reducing the number of copies to one, but it cannot minimize the copying cost. The effort to transfer ownership is commendable but could be more efficient. What is needed is a means of transferring the data without copying it.

SOLUTION

Modern C++ provides a new type of reference called an *rvalue* reference (I think of them as "right references"), which refers to a value on the right-hand side of an operator. An rvalue is the source for an assignment; it cannot be its target. This means the right-hand side can be modified despite not being an assignment target. Temporaries are also rvalues, so it makes no sense to modify them, but stealing their values is legitimate. The new syntax is to include a doubled reference character (&&) to indicate move semantics.

The language provides for adding a move constructor and a move assignment operator. These new features are meant to preserve exclusive ownership when a resource is transferred from source to target and add the benefit of moving the data, not copying it. Because the target owns the transferred data after the move, it should be invalidated in the source to prevent incorrect access, as shown in the following listing.

Listing 2.2   A uniqueness-preserving assignment operator with negligible cost

```
class TextSection {
    // assume a clever implementation
};

class Page {
private:
    TextSection* headers;
    TextSection* body;
public:
    Page(TextSection* h) : headers(h), body(new TextSection()) {}
    Page(const Page& o) : headers(o.headers), body(new
        TextSection(*o.body)) {}
    Page(Page&& o) : headers(o.headers), body(o.body) {
        o.headers = nullptr;
        o.body = nullptr;
    }
    ~Page() { delete body; }
};

int main() {
    Page p1(new TextSection());
    Page p2 = std::move(p1);
    return 0;
}
```

A move-capable copy constructor

The source resources are reassigned to target.

The source resources are invalidated.

This looks slightly odd but correctly has move semantics.

A move means the source object releases its contents to the destination object. Some implementations use a swap function to move the source data to the target and the target data to the source. Since the data is reassigned, the source object can no longer have its original data, but having the target's data is usually acceptable. If a swap operation is not used, the best approach is to ensure all moved data in the source is rendered null and void.

In cases where the source object is not destroyed, its previous data must not be accessible under any circumstances. We all know what *can* go wrong *will* go wrong, and often, this is true at the most embarrassing time. Therefore, neutralize the data in the source object to prevent inadvertent use after moving it. This can usually be achieved by setting pointers to `nullptr` (or 0).

Another nice feature is that when the move constructor and assignment operator are provided, the compiler makes every reasonable effort to use them whenever possible. The developer does not have to decide when they can be used. The standard copy constructor and assignment operator will be used when the source is an *lvalue* (an assignable value on the left-hand side of the operator).

The `std::move` function template is critical for proper movement. The industry buzzphrase about it is, "Move doesn't move." How, then, is it vital? Move converts lvalues into rvalues, which makes them eligible for move semantics. If this is not done, a standard assignment will occur, not a move assignment. With the copy and move operators, a class can provide for shared assignment (or construction) or exclusive assignment (or construction), which makes the semantics much cleaner.

RECOMMENDATIONS

- Add move constructor and assignment operators to a class for exclusive transfer of ownership of resources.
- Expand the *big 3* (copy constructor, assignment operator, destructor) to the *big 5* by including the move constructor and move assignment operator.

SEE ALSO

- See Mistake 47 for a discussion of the big 3 (destructor, copy constructor, and assignment operator).
- See Mistake 54 for a discussion about preserving semantics.
- See Mistake 62 for problems with exclusive ownership, which can be resolved using `unique_ptrs`.
- See Mistake 8 for a discussion about `unique_ptrs` themselves.

2.2 *Mistake 2: Using empty exception specifications*

This mistake concerns effectiveness; performance; and, briefly, readability. Exception specifications tell the compiler which exceptions a function can throw.

PROBLEM

Exception specifications have been deprecated since 2011, as their effectiveness and performance never realized their promise to make a developer's life easier. They were complicated, and they confused matters so much that modern C++ deprecated them in the C++11 specification and removed them completely in the C++17 standard. Peruse

P0003R5 (https://mng.bz/N1mE) for the whole story. However, one idea stemming from exception specifications is still appropriate and meaningful.

Exceptions are a brilliant way to separate normal functional flow from error handling. This flexibility comes at a cost, as should be expected. Copious use of exceptions is as frowned upon as failing to use them. Instead, one must strike a reasonable balance that provides explicit error handling and good performance. Many functions do not throw any exceptions; therefore, they should not be penalized with checks to handle any potential exceptions at run time. Exception specifications had one case where a `throw()` was specified, meaning the function would throw nothing. This goal of this specification was to boost performance. With the removal of specifications, this approach was also lost.

The proposal to remove exception specifications acknowledged the value of `throw()` and argued not to delete the functionality but transform it. The C++11 standard added a new operator that effectively does the equivalent of the empty throw specification. The `noexcept` operator was introduced to mean the same as an empty throw, allowing the compiler to perform optimizations to remove run-time exception checking. The following code demonstrates the premodern C++ approach to convincing the compiler to eliminate unnecessary exception checking.

Listing 2.3   Functions communicating premodern nonthrowing behavior

```
const double pi = 3.1415927;
struct Circle {
    double radius;
    Circle(double r) : radius(r) {}
    double perimeter() const throw() { return 2 * pi * radius; }
    double area() const throw() { return pi * radius * radius; }
};

int main() {
    Circle c(3);
    std::cout << "perimeter " << c.perimeter() << ", area " << c.area() << '\n';
    return 0;
}
```

An attempt to optimize because no exceptions are thrown

ANALYSIS

Listing 2.3 shows the premodern approach. Its intent is good but will cause warning messages in modern C++. It does not emit an error because the proposal to remove exception specifications argued that an empty `throw()` should be considered equivalent to a `noexcept(true)` specification. The parameter is an expression that, if evaluated as `true`, the compiler is confident that the function will not throw any exception; ensure your code does not trick the compiler.

A word of caution is necessary: if a `noexcept` marked function happens to lie and throw an exception, the infamous `terminate` function is called, which immediately terminates the program, and no stack unwinding (no destructor calls!) will be performed.

The developer must tell the truth because the compiler will punish undefined (unexpected exceptions) behavior.

SOLUTION

Listing 2.4 updates the previous listing to the modern approach, replacing the empty throw() specification with a new language keyword: noexcept. There is very little change necessary to properly communicate the intent of a function not to throw any exceptions; therefore, updating code should prove simple. Remember that this works only for empty exception specifications.

Listing 2.4 Functions communicating modern nonthrowing behavior

```
struct Circle {
    double radius;
    explicit Circle(double r) : radius(r) {}
    double perimeter() const noexcept { return 2 * std::numbers::pi * radius; }
    double area() const noexcept { return std::numbers::pi * radius * radius; }
};

int main() {
    Circle c(3);
    std::cout << "perimeter " << c.perimeter() << ", area " << c.area() << '\n';
    return 0;
}
```

> A better attempt to optimize, since no exceptions are thrown

A constructor that takes one parameter is called a *conversion constructor*. The code in listing 2.4 can convert a double value to a Circle value. When the compiler looks for such transformations, it determines whether a constructor or conversion operation is available and uses the best fit if one or more are found. However, this behavior is only sometimes wanted.

> **NOTE** Modern C++ has provided the explicit keyword to prevent single-parameter constructors from being used in implicit conversions. Sometimes, implicit conversion behavior is desired, but usually, uncontrolled conversion constructors should be limited. The explicit keyword added to the constructor prevents the compiler from using it to do conversions. Think carefully about this, and refer to the See Also section for further details.

RECOMMENDATIONS

- Change throws() to noexcept to modernize code.
- Ensure functions that say they will not throw an exception don't.

SEE ALSO

- See Mistake 68 for a discussion about conversion constructors and gives a view of when and why to use the explicit keyword.
- See Mistake 80 for a discussion of problems with old-school exception specifications.

2.3   *Mistake 3: Not using override on derived virtual functions*

This mistake affects effectiveness and, slightly, readability. Implementing virtual functions in derived classes provides a way to customize inherited behavior. Misnamed derived virtual functions are enough of a problem that the standardization committee agreed to provide the means for the compiler to help prevent them.

PROBLEM

Classes containing virtual functions are meant to be inherited from. The virtual keyword signals this intent. Virtual functions implemented in derived classes allow behavior modification (or complete replacement) in the base class. This approach is the heart of polymorphic behavior.

The base and derived classes may be far apart in large code bases. Knowing whether a method is virtual can be challenging if the distance is significant. Derived classes do not have to duplicate the virtual keyword in their function declarations; the compiler figures this out. However, this duplication is a reasonable means of documenting that a given method is virtual. But this documentation fails to explain where the most-base class version of the virtual method is, leaving the developer the task of scouring the hierarchy to figure it out.

Listing 2.5 shows a quick and happy attempt to slip in some functionality late Friday evening. The code compiles, the developer is happy, and the code ships. Regrettably, the next week, the client complains that the Square objects are not working correctly. The developer is surprised because everything "looked good."

Listing 2.5   **Code that looks good and compiles without bugs**

```cpp
struct Shape {
    std::string type;
    explicit Shape(const std::string& t) : type(t) {}
    virtual double area() const { return 0; }
};

struct Square : public Shape {
    double side;
    Square(double s) : Shape("square"), side(s) {}
    double aria() const { return side*side; }        ◄──┐ There can be
};                                                      │ typos for a song.

const static double pi = 3.1415927;
struct Circle : public Shape {
    double radius;
    Circle(double r) : Shape("circle"), radius(r) {}
    double area() const { return pi * radius * radius; }
};

int main() {
    Square s(2);
    Circle c(2);
    std::vector<Shape*> shapes;
    shapes.push_back(&s);
```

```
        shapes.push_back(&c);
        for (int i = 0; i < shapes.size(); ++i)
            std::cout << shapes[i]->area() << '\n';
        return 0;
}
```

ANALYSIS

The problem with the code is simple: the developer made a typographical error. The compiler was happy to add the new function to the class, since no syntactical errors were made. The developer should have noticed that successful compilation does not imply a proper redefinition of a virtual method.

Misnamed derived class virtual functions are not syntactically wrong—at least not for the reason of the misnaming! The compiler merely sees and compiles a new method like any other nonvirtual method added to the class. The fact that the developer meant to redefine a virtual function is of no concern.

SOLUTION

The C++11 standard added a new keyword, called `override`. The problem of misnamed virtual functions was prevalent enough that something had to be done to help avoid it. This new keyword is added after the parameter list of a method that should be a redefinition of a virtual method. In this case, if the compiler sees a method with the `override` keyword that does not match a virtual method in some base class, it emits an error. This keyword is not required, but it achieves two significant feats. First, it documents that this class redefines a virtual method, enhancing readability. Second, the compiler verifies that the method redefined a known virtual method—typos are errors, not new methods.

The code in listing 2.5 would not compile with the keyword added after the aria method. When the compiler choked, the developer could see the error; after a few keystrokes, the problem was resolved. Friday evening beers never tasted so good.

A tangential point: `override` is technically a contextual keyword, not a regular one. It is a *keyword* only in specific contexts (e.g., following a method's parameter list). In other contexts, it is a valid (but not recommended!) *identifier*. This distinction was made, since `override` exists as an identifier in many existing code bases. That was very kind of the standardization committee (who probably supported some of those code bases).

Listing 2.6 Using `override` to ensure correct virtual function naming

```
struct Shape {
    std::string type;
    Shape(const std::string& t) : type(t) {}
    virtual double area() const { return 0; }
};

struct Square : public Shape {
    double side;
    Square(double s) : Shape("square"), side(s) {}
    double area() const override { return side*side; }    ◀──┐  Adds an override to get
                                                              │  the compiler to verify
                                                              └─ virtual function names
```

```
};

struct Circle : public Shape {
    double radius;
    Circle(double r) : Shape("circle"), radius(r) {}
    double area() const override { return
        std::numbers::pi * radius * radius; }
};

int main() {
    Square s(2);
    Circle c(2);
    std::vector<Shape*> shapes;
    shapes.push_back(&s);
    shapes.push_back(&c);
    for (auto& shape : shapes)
        std::cout << shape->area() << '\n';
    return 0;
}
```

◄——— **Adds an override to get the compiler to verify virtual function names**

RECOMMENDATIONS

- Use the override keyword to document the intent of redefining an inherited virtual method.

- Use override to have the compiler enforce proper naming of the intended redefinition and its base class naming of the method.

- Remember that override is a contextual keyword; however, refrain from using it elsewhere if possible—it can make comprehension more complicated.

2.4   *Mistake 4: Writing simple or hiding unwanted supplied class members*

This mistake affects effectiveness and readability. When a class is defined, some members will be automatically supplied by the compiler if not written by the developer.

PROBLEM

The compiler easily handles a simple class with no developer-written members that handle construction, copying, and assignment. What the developer does not supply, the compiler will automatically generate. Usually, this is helpful, and the provided versions do what is necessary; developers must write their versions when the automatically supplied methods are incorrect or insufficient.

The compiler will not generate a default constructor if any constructor is supplied. If the copy constructor, move constructor, or destructor is written, none of these will be automatically generated. Further, if certain members should not be provided, a simple approach is to make them private with no implementation.

The flip side of this problem is that some developers write many of these supplied members when not explicitly needed. The developer wrote a simple Container class that provides some basic functionality. Further, it was decided that copying was OK, but assignment was not. Therefore, the following code supplies a default (required) and copy constructor and hides the assignment operator.

Listing 2.7　A simple class with a written default constructor

```
class Container {
private:
    std::vector<int> values;
    Container& operator=(const Container& o);          Hidden away, so no one
public:                                                can write an assignment
    Container() {}
    Container(const Container& o) values(o.values) {}
    void add(int n) { values.push_back(n); }
};

int main() {
    Container c1;                    The copy constructor
    c1.add(42);                      is called.
    Container c2(c1);
    // c2 = c1;                       Assignment would
    return 0;                         be an error.
}
```

ANALYSIS

The code works but is more challenging to write and read than necessary. Constructors and assignment operators are typically public members, so hiding them in the private section feels awkward. Further, this approach does not communicate well what is intended for the default constructor or the assignment operator—one must be familiar with the pattern to understand it. If the class is slightly more complicated than this example, the code in the default constructor takes more effort.

SOLUTION

A better approach, which documents the intent well, is to use the =delete and =default keywords. The =delete keyword states that the member is intentionally omitted; therefore, it cannot be used. The =default keyword states that the compiler should generate a member that behaves in a default manner as it understands the semantics. The value of this usage is that the class can change its implementation without affecting any client code, assuming the changes are clear to the compiler. The best reason is that the developer communicates the intent of these members.

Listing 2.8　A simple class with defaulted and deleted members

```
class Container {                                  The compiler knows what it is doing.
private:                                           Let it write the default constructor.
    std::vector<int> values;
public:                                                          There is no need to
    Container() = default;                                       hide the operator in
    Container(const Container& o) : values(o.values) {}          shame; the compiler
    Container& operator=(const Container& o) = delete;           prevents its use.
```

```
        void add(int n) { values.push_back(n); }
};

int main() {
    Container c1;
    c1.add(42);
    Container c2(c1);
    // c2 = c1;        ◄──────┘ Assignment is an error.
    return 0;
}
```

RECOMMENDATIONS

- Use =delete to eliminate members so that the functionality is removed.
- Use =default to let the compiler generate the member, saving time and eliminating a source of potential errors.

SEE ALSO

- See Mistake 62 for an old-school approach to hiding methods.

2.5   *Mistake 5: Not using in-class initializers*

This mistake focuses on readability, and it may improve effectiveness slightly. Many languages allow the initialization of instance variables in a class definition; C++ did not until C++11.

PROBLEM

Most developers find it handy to write constructors with default values. These values are often meaningful, so the only reason to supply them is if the default value is incorrect for a specific instance.

Typically, a developer would use a default value in the constructor's parameter list, as shown in listing 2.9. This approach works well but has a readability problem. Assume multiple constructors were in the class and there were many instance variables. Some of these constructors would default rarely changing values, but the reader might need help determining a given instance variable's value. The code in listing 2.9 is easy to read, but consider how it would look in a class with four, five, or more parameters. As an example, see how easy it is to read this code where several parameters are defaulted:

```
Demo(int n=0, double d=1.0, double e=0.0, double f=10.5, bool b=false) :
n(n), d(d), e(e), f(f), b(b) {}
```

Defaulting values should be limited to a readable and comprehendible list; too many parameters suggest an overly responsible class that should be refactored into multiple data types. The following code does not make this mistake, yet it still needs to be easier to read.

Listing 2.9 Using default values in the parameter list

```
class Complex {
private:
    double real;
    double imag;
public:
    Complex(double r=0, double i=0) : real(r), imag(i) {}    ◄──  Using defaulted
    double getReal() const { return real; }                        parameters
    double getImag() const { return imag; }
};

int main() {
    Complex c1;
    Complex c2(3);
    Complex c3(-2, -2);
    return 0;
}
```

ANALYSIS

While everything is fine with this code, readability is somewhat impaired when multiple constructors are provided. Further, the more code that's written, the more probable a bug will be introduced. If parameters with default values mismatch across two or more constructors, the reader will find it challenging to decide on the proper value for instance variables.

SOLUTION

Modern C++ offers an alternative that does not depend on default parameter values. Considering the clarity some other languages provide for default values, C++ added in-class initializers. Each instance variable declared in the class can have a default value assigned to it, either by using the assignment operator or the braced initialization form, called *uniform initialization*. This form prevents ambiguity and automatic narrowing conversions and is more consistent. It is a best practice to use this for initializations.

Listing 2.10 Using in-class initialization for readability

```
class Complex {                           │ Uses in-class initialization
private:                                  │ with assignment operator
    double real = 0;          ◄───────────┘
    double imag{0};           ◄─────┐ Uses in-class initialization with
public:                             │ braced initialization
    Complex() {}
    Complex(double r, double i) : real(r), imag(i) {}
    double getImag() const { return imag; }
};

int main() {                                                  This will not work; it is
    Complex c1;            ◄─────┘ Uses default values        ambiguous which member the
    // Complex c2(3);         ◄───────────────────────────────value is intended to initialize.
```

```
        Complex c3(-2, -2);
        return 0;
}
```

If a constructor is supplied a value for the in-class initialized variable, the supplied value is used for initialization. If no value is provided, the in-class value is used.

RECOMMENDATIONS

- Choose in-class initialization to localize the default values for an instance variable.
- Use default values in the constructor parameter list only if using classic C++.

2.6   *Mistake 6: Overusing index-based loops*

This mistake affects effectiveness and readability, and it can negatively influence performance. Indexing over containers using loops is a common idiom. However, this traditional approach is more complicated than necessary.

PROBLEM

Frequently, developers must iterate over a container to access each element. Historically, this has been accomplished by creating a loop control variable starting at the first index and incrementing monotonically (increasing by one) each time through the loop. The last index is always the length of the container minus one. Listing 2.11 demonstrates a generic sum function that takes a vector of values and returns their sum. Let's assume these are test scores, and the average (mean) will be computed afterward. There is nothing special about the loop; it is a general solution to indexing over a container. What could be simpler?

Listing 2.11   Using index values to iterate over a container

```
template <typename T>
T sum(const std::vector<T>& values) {
    T sum = (T)0;
    for (int i = 0; i < values.size(); ++i)          ◄─────  The traditional
        sum += values[i];                                    index-based approach
    return sum;
}

int main() {
    std::vector<int> values;
    for (int i = 0; i < 10; ++i)
        values.push_back(10*i + i);              ◄─────
    std::cout << sum(values) << '\n';
    return 0;
}
```

ANALYSIS

The code in listing 2.11 works and reflects most loops in current code bases. For its traditional implementation, it takes a bit of writing to achieve and focuses on implementing loop mechanics; it does not focus on the problem. Even if one is intimately familiar with the solution, it reads awkwardly. Anywhere extra keystrokes are necessary, the opportunity to introduce an error increases. Further, for those unfamiliar with the idiom, there is the temptation to code the continuation test as

```
i<=values.size()
```

We know this is incorrect. It feels correct intuitively but is an off-by-one error.

SOLUTION

Modern C++ has provided the range-based `for` form for simplifying this familiar pattern. Rather than using the regular `for` statement, the range-based `for` removes the continuation and update sections and modifies the initialization part. Read the colon as "in," as in, "For (each) element in values, do something," where "something" is the loop body.

The mechanics of the loop are simple. Declare a variable that gets assigned the value of each container element in sequence. The value is assigned from the element at index zero, then one, and so on, until the last element, just like the indexed approach. Each iteration of the loop copies the element to the variable. The variable can be modified in the loop, but since it is a copy, the modification does not affect the element value in the container. Consider this loop to be read-only semantics. If you need to modify element values, use a reference type for the variable.

The fact that the element values are copied means if the element type is a class, the copy constructor will be called each time—this likely is much more expensive than necessary. It is better to make the variable a reference of the element type. In this case, only the location of the data is copied, minimizing the volume of data. Use the `const` keyword unless the loop is expected to modify the element. For numeric types, as shown in listing 2.12, the reference is likely excessive; this is demonstration code, so bear with the oddity. When the element type is a class, this approach is highly performant. A pointer variable can be used in some cases, but the reference form eliminates the need for pointer syntax, improving readability.

Listing 2.12 Using range-based `for` values when iterating over a container

```
template <typename T>
T sum(const std::vector<T>& values) {        Uses an initializer to get the
    T sum {};                                correct zero form for the type
    for (const T& value : values)
        sum += value;                        The range-based for
    return sum;                              loop is simple to use.
}

int main() {
    std::vector<int> values;                 The index-based for
    for (int i = 0; i < 10; ++i)             loop feels clunky.
```

```
        values.push_back(10*i + i);
    std::cout << sum(values) << '\n';
    return 0;
}
```

RECOMMENDATIONS

- Use the range-based `for` statement to eliminate much of the coding tedium of traditional index-based loops.
- Remember that the element value is copied to the variable, making the loop inherently read-only.
- If an element copy is expensive, use a reference variable that minimizes data movement.

2.7 *Mistake 7: Failing to use nullptr*

This mistake deals with readability and, to a slight degree, effectiveness. The NULL macro was inherited from C, but a better approach in premodern C++ was to initialize pointers with a zero.

PROBLEM

Listing 2.13 shows a simple model of a `Student` class that includes a few instance variables. One of these instance variables is initialized to the zero value. Further, since the code needs instance pointers, we see their initialization with an assignment to the zero value. Reading the literal zero can be confusing because that value is used in multiple contexts.

Listing 2.13   An admixture of the zero value

```
struct Student {
    std::string name;
    int id;
    double gpa;
    Student(const std::string& name, int id, double gpa) : name(name),
            id(id), gpa(0) {
        if (gpa < 0)
            throw std::invalid_argument("gpa is negative");
    }
};

int main() {                              Better than the NULL macro
    Student* sammy = 0;          ◄─────   but not quite as obvious
    Student* ginny = 0;
    Student* gene = 0;
    sammy = new Student("Samuel", 0, 3.75);
    ginny = new Student("Virginia", 1, 3.8);
    gene = new Student("Eugene", 2, 0);
    return 0;
}
```

ANALYSIS

Initializing a pointer to the zero value is the best approach, and premodern C++ must signify a pointer that does not represent an existing object. However, the literal zero is not a pointer, and it can cause momentary confusion. While many developers are familiar with this usage, it is harder to read than the frowned-upon NULL macro. At least the macro stands out as a *pointer* concept (although it probably is not in most implementations). The compiler is smart enough to take the integer literal value and do the right thing with the pointer.

SOLUTION

However, modern C++ provides `nullptr`, a literal value representing a null value, specifically for a pointer. Its most significant advantage is its clarity of intention; its purpose is easy to understand and grasp quickly. The zero value does not have this ease-of-use characteristic.

Another distinct advantage of this literal is that the compiler cannot confuse it with a function parameter of type `int`. A previous mistake demonstrated this confusion; consult the See Also section for further elucidation.

Listing 2.14 Clarifying pointers with `nullptr`

```
struct Student {
    std::string name;
    int id;
    double gpa;
    Student(const std::string& name, int id, double gpa) : name(name),
            id(id), gpa(0) {
        if (gpa < 0)
            throw std::invalid_argument("gpa is negative");
    }
};

int main() {
    Student* sammy = nullptr;
    Student* ginny = nullptr;
    Student* gene = nullptr;
    sammy = new Student("Samuel", 0, 3.75);
    ginny = new Student("Virginia", 1, 3.8);
    gene = new Student("Eugene", 2, 0);
    return 0;
}
```

This is better than the NULL macro and more apparent than the zero value. What's not to like?

RECOMMENDATIONS

- Use `nullptr` to initialize pointers that are not immediately initialized to a valid object.
- Assign a pointer to `nullptr` immediately after it has been deleted to prevent use-after-free errors.

SEE ALSO

- See Mistake 76 for a discussion about memory leaks where `nullptr` can be used effectively.
- See Mistake 77 for a general solution to deleting dynamic resources.
- See Mistake 28 for a deeper discussion of that macro and its misuse.
- See Mistake 8 for an excellent place to use `nullptr`.
- See Mistake 9 for another place to use `nullptr`.

2.8   *Mistake 8: Not using unique_ptrs for exclusive ownership*

This mistake affects correctness and enhances readability. The RAII pattern should manage dynamic resources but might require writing several management classes. Premodern C++ offered the `auto_ptr` option, which was deprecated due to its proneness to errors and later deleted.

PROBLEM

Exclusive ownership of dynamic resources is essential to keep track of unique resources. Such resources cannot be copied because doing so would leave the source and the target representing the single resource. The reference that owns and manages the resource is uncertain at this point. Furthermore, it leaves the possibility that both might attempt to manage it by modifying or deleting it; the latter might result in a double delete error. The first `delete` will work properly, but the second one takes the program into the fantasy land of undefined behavior where anything can happen—plead with the compiler for a crash.

The following code shows a simple case of managing a unique dynamic resource. Since the resource is created in one place and is manipulated in another, its pointer value must be passed around. Although the code is written sequentially, read it as if the lines were separated by other code, causing enough distraction that the flow is nonobvious—like so many real-world projects!

Listing 2.15   A botched attempt at managing an exclusive resource

```
struct Buffer {
private:
    int* data;
public:
    Buffer() : data(new int[10]) {}
    ~Buffer() { delete[] data; }
};

int main() {
    Buffer* b1 = new Buffer();          Oops! Exclusive resources should
    Buffer* b2 = b1;                     not be copied or assigned.
    if (b1)
        delete b1;
    if (b2)                              This seems reasonable; this
                                         was the original owner.
```

```
        delete b2;
    return 0;
}
```
← ┌─────────────────────────
  │ **This seems unreasonable;**
  │ **this was the second owner.**

ANALYSIS

The problem is that the developer meant to create the dynamic resource in one place and then transfer it to another owner later. However, as with many well-intended ideas, the code needs to implement this better. Since the pointer is copied, it becomes shared, not exclusive. The fact that the original owner `b1` deletes the resource seems sensible but overlooks the attempted ownership transfer. The deletion by `b2` would make sense if the transfer of ownership had been correctly done. Still, since the resource has already been deleted, this attempt causes undefined behavior, transporting the program into the "Twilight Zone" of operations.

The `Buffer` structure is designed reasonably and should manage its dynamic resource correctly, since it has implemented the RAII pattern. However, it could be improved, as will be shown.

SOLUTION

The problem with using raw pointers to manage dynamic resources is the complexity of managing the pointers themselves under normal and exceptional conditions. The RAII pattern was designed to deal with this situation but requires a new implementation with every dynamic resource. The `auto_ptr` attempt recognized this problem and tried to provide a general solution; however, this poor effort caused significant problems and made for strange code.

Modern C++ has provided the `std::unique_ptr` for exclusive ownership. This template is well-designed and will work as expected under all conditions. The code in listing 2.16 demonstrates its use with a pointer and an array (`auto_ptr` could not handle arrays). The internal data of the `Buffer` class uses the array form and lets the `unique_ptr` manage its dynamic data. This class does not need a user-written destructor to handle the array deletion.

The `std::make_unique` function template (see listing 2.16) is preferred to using `new`. It has more exception safety, is more straightforward, avoids raw pointers, and is more performant—sometimes, you can have it all!

In the transfer of ownership, the code uses the `std::move` function template. While this may appear to move the object from one owner to another, it does not—in other words, "move doesn't move." What `std::move` does is cast a left-hand (lvalue) reference to a right-hand (rvalue) reference. An rvalue reference is often a temporary value that is not addressable, holds a value, and is copied to the receiving entity, before being discarded if it its temporary. The `move` operation makes the source entity effectively discardable in terms of ownership. The compiler will notice when an assignment (or copy) of an rvalue entity is being used and invoke move semantics. The value is moved from source to target, leaving the source (conceptually) empty and drained of value. Some implementations use swap to transfer the values, leaving the source with the target's former values. In any case, the source entity should not be used unless reinitialized. It's better, I think, to consider a moved-from entity inaccessible and unusable. This approach is much easier to reason about.

Listing 2.16 Implementing exclusive ownership using `unique_ptr`

```
struct Buffer {
private:
    std::unique_ptr<int[]> data;          The array form
public:
    Buffer() : data(std::make_unique<int[]>(10)) {}   The array form's
};                                                    initialization

                                          The pointer form and using
                                          the preferred make_unique
int main() {                              function template
    auto b1 = std::make_unique<Buffer>();
    auto b2 = std::move(b1);
    return 0;                 Transfer, not copy or assignment,
}                             of ownership, using the move
                             function template
```

The solution offered in listing 2.16 is much cleaner, although it may take a bit of practice to master. This approach's value is more efficient and cleaner than anything that came before it. Notice the use of the `auto` keyword for specifying the type of `b1` and `b2`. Since the compiler can deduce their type unambiguously, it is more effective than specifying the exact type yourself.

RECOMMENDATIONS

- Refuse to use raw pointers for any dynamic resources; in general, use `unique_ptr` for any pointer except shared resources.
- Use `unique_ptr` for exclusive ownership, remembering that an assignment will transfer the resource from the source to the target, leaving the source unusable.
- Prefer `unique_ptr` for efficiency and simplicity; using `shared_ptr` is more expensive.

SEE ALSO

- See Mistake 76 for the motivation of using RAII patterns with dynamic resources.
- See Mistake 77 for an explanation of using this resource management pattern.
- See Mistake 78 for an explanation of why raw pointers are a poor choice for dynamic resources and `auto_ptr` is not a good choice for resolving these problems.
- See Mistake 1 to better understand the performance benefits of move semantics.
- See Mistake 9 for a discussion of shared ownership of dynamic resources.

2.9 *Mistake 9: Not using shared_ptrs for shared ownership*

This mistake deals primarily with correctness and effectiveness. Shared pointers are more expensive than raw pointers, and readability will likely be enhanced once the method is understood.

PROBLEM

Several data structures require working with dynamically allocated entities, arranged in various ways. These dynamic resources are best managed using RAII, but knowing when and who should delete the resource is complicated when multiple references to an entity are necessary.

Listing 2.17 is typical of our developer, who learned to use pointers in a college class. Therefore, the results for implementing a *double-ended queue* (deque) would be like this effort. The code works well enough, but using raw pointers is discouraged when managing entity resources. If a mistake is made, resource leaks are inevitable. Further, the need to manage carefully is elevated in applications where exceptions are thrown.

Listing 2.17   A deque using raw pointers

```
class Node {
public:
    Node(int value) : data(value), prev(NULL), next(NULL) {}
    int data;
    Node* prev;
    Node* next;
};

class Deque {
private:
    Node* front;
    Node* back;
public:
    Deque() : front(NULL), back(NULL) {}
    ~Deque() {                              ◄──  A mandatory destructor
        while (front != NULL) {                  for eliminating remaining
            Node* temp = front;                  dynamic entities
            front = front->next;
            delete temp;
        }
    }
    void push_front(int value) {
        Node* newNode = new Node(value);
        if (front == NULL)
            front = back = newNode;
        else {
            newNode->next = front;
            front->prev = newNode;
            front = newNode;
        }
    }
    void push_back(int value) {
        Node* newNode = new Node(value);
        if (back == NULL)
            front = back = newNode;
        else {
            newNode->prev = back;
            back->next = newNode;
            back = newNode;
```

```
            }
        }
        void pop_front() {
            if (front != NULL) {
                Node* temp = front;          ◄──────────┐   Two references
                front = front->next;                    │   to a single node
                if (front != NULL)
                    front->prev = NULL;
                else
                    back = NULL;
                delete temp;         ◄──┐   Deletes expired
            }                           │   entities
        }
        void pop_back() {
            if (back != NULL) {
                Node* temp = back;   ◄──────────────────┘
                back = back->prev;
                if (back != NULL)
                    back->next = NULL;
                else
                    front = NULL;
                delete temp;         ◄──┘
            }
        }
    }
};

int main() {
    Deque deque;
    deque.push_front(3);
    deque.pop_front();
    return 0;
}
```

ANALYSIS

To place a node in or remove one from the deque requires at least two pointers to reference the node. Several pointers may refer to a single node if other pointers are used (e.g., an indexed queue). Raw pointers provide a simple means for multiple pointers to refer to a single node, but that sharing complicates the node's management.

There are several places where the deletion of nodes is required. Each required place must be correctly coded, or a significant opportunity exists for resource leaks. The destructor and these individual deletion points are a cognitive burden because the developer must solve two problems. First, the deque must be designed and coded correctly. Second, resource management is mandated as support for the deque. This approach is more complex and distracting than necessary.

SOLUTION

Removing the need to manage dynamic resources solves one of the two problems, leaving time and attention to deal with the other. The modern C++ approach is to use std::shared_ptrs to manage the resources. Whenever possible, use std::make_shared instead of the new keyword. The shared pointer uses the RAII pattern and is designed to be used when two or more references are made to a single resource. The `std::shared_ptr` manages the resource by keeping track of the count of references held to the resource. The count increases for each copy or assignment and decreases for each shared pointer that goes out of scope. When the count reaches zero, the resource is deleted. Therefore, no user-written management code is required. Sweet!

Bittersweet is the actual flavor. The `std::unique_ptr` is cheap and should be used for any resource that does not need sharing. The `std::shared_ptr` is not cheap and should be used only when sharing is required. First, shared pointers (see listing 2.18) are larger than unique pointers, since a count variable must be maintained. Second, the management of the count variable takes extra cycles. Therefore, only use these smart pointers when necessary, preferring unique pointers when possible.

Listing 2.18 A deque using shared pointers

```cpp
class Node {
public:
    Node(int value) : data(value) {}
    int data;
    std::shared_ptr<Node> prev;          The shared_ptr is
    std::shared_ptr<Node> next;          implicitly initialized.
};

class Deque {
private:
    std::shared_ptr<Node> front;
    std::shared_ptr<Node> back;
public:                                           The destructor and
    Deque() : front(nullptr), back(nullptr) {}    deletes are unnecessary.
    void push_front(int value) {
        std::shared_ptr<Node> newNode = std::make_shared<Node>(value);
        if (front == nullptr)
            front = back = newNode;
        else {
            newNode->next = front;
            front->prev = newNode;
            front = newNode;
        }
    }
    void push_back(int value) {
        std::shared_ptr<Node> newNode = std::make_shared<Node>(value);
        if (back == nullptr)
            front = back = newNode;
        else {
            newNode->prev = back;
            back->next = newNode;
            back = newNode;
        }
    }
    void pop_front() {
        if (front != nullptr) {
            front = front->next;
            if (front != nullptr)
```

```
                        front->prev = nullptr;
                    else
                        back = nullptr;
                }    #B
            }
        void pop_back() {
            if (back != nullptr) {
                back = back->prev;
                if (back != nullptr)
                    back->next = nullptr;
                else
                    front = nullptr;            The destructor and
            }                                   deletes are unnecessary.
        }
    };

    int main() {
        Deque deque;
        deque.push_front(3);
        deque.pop_front();
        return 0;
    }
```

Another nice feature of std::shared_ptr is that they do not need explicit initialization; they are initialized to nullptr when constructed, saving the developer the effort.

A problem arises when using smart shared pointers—the possibility of circular references, where one entity refers to another using a shared pointer, and vice versa. A *shared pointer* keeps track of the number of references to its shared entity. The count increases for each construction of a shared pointer referring to it, and it decreases for each destruction of a shared pointer. If the count reaches zero, the shared resource is deleted; however, it may never reach zero in circular references, resulting in a resource leak.

The code in listing 2.18 could easily be transformed into a doubly-linked list susceptible to circular reference problems. If you face this situation, consider using a std::weak_pointer to break the circularity. A *weak pointer* works like a shared pointer, except it does not share ownership of the resource. This type of pointer must be converted to a std::shared_ptr before dereferencing. If the conversion succeeds, a valid pointer is created; if it fails, the conversion returns a shared pointer initialized to nullptr.

While the code demonstrates a deque, the Standard Template Library offers its own excellent version, called std::deque. Use this deque, and avoid writing your own, unless you want to illustrate using shared pointers!

RECOMMENDATIONS

- Remember that using smart pointers eliminates the need to manage dynamic resources and allows the focus to remain on the problem being solved.
- Use std::shared_ptr whenever dynamic resources require multiple references; remember to break circular references using a std::weak_ptr.

- Be sure to convert `std::weak_ptr` before dereferencing.
- Prefer to use `std::unique_ptr` in most cases.

SEE ALSO

- See Mistake 78 to learn why it's best to prefer smart pointers.
- See Mistake 8 for a discussion on smart pointers.

Better modern C++:
General programming

3

This chapter covers

- Uniform initialization
- Enhanced if statements
- Tuples
- Structured binding

In the dynamic landscape of C++ programming, coding practices are often shaped by deeply ingrained habits, influencing our problem-solving approaches. However, as we navigate the intricacies of traditional loops, selection statements, and variable initialization techniques, it becomes evident that adherence to tradition only sometimes guarantees readability or effectiveness. While these familiar approaches may initially seem intuitive, they often conceal correctness, readability, and overall code efficiency challenges.

As C++ builds upon the foundational principles of its predecessor, C, it has introduced new initialization techniques and data aggregation methods. This evolution brings forth its own set of complexities. The array of initialization methods can result in cognitive overload and inconsistencies across source files within a code base. Similarly, the reliance on structures or classes for aggregating diverse data types can prove cumbersome, mainly when simplicity is paramount. Although Standard Template Library templates offer an alternative solution, they, too, present challenges, potentially hindering code readability and effectiveness.

This chapter discusses several mistakes to uncover common pitfalls in C++ programming, shedding light on underlying problems and providing insights into better coding approaches. By addressing these mistakes, we can enhance our coding habits and understanding of the complexities of C++ language and STL features. The goal, as always, is for developers to improve their code by refining their practices and embracing more efficient and maintainable coding techniques.

3.1   *Mistake 10: Failing to use if with initialization*

Depending on the reader, this mistake positively affects effectiveness but might negatively affect readability in some cases. The `for` loop uses statement-scoped initialization, but historically, `if` statements could not.

PROBLEM

A container of values needs to be searched for a key value. Historically, an indexed loop would be created and used to index over each value until it either finds the key or exhausts the container. It is better to use the supplied algorithms in the Standard Template Library. A typical approach is shown in the following code. It is expected to write or use a function to search and return a Boolean value indicating whether it was found; this can be done in the conditional. The if statement uses the returned value to select between two options. In this case, a Boolean is not returned, but an iterator is. The iterator needs to be tested to determine whether it is valid.

Listing 3.1   A typical index-based search for a key value

```
int main() {
    std::vector<int> values;
    for (int i = 0; i < 10; ++i)
        values.push_back(i*2);
    int key = 4;
    std::vector<int>::iterator it =
        std::find(values.begin(), values.end(), key);      ← Determines whether
                                                              the key was found
    if (it != values.end())                 ←
        std::cout << key << " was found\n";
    else                                                   Tests the iterator to decide
        std::cout << key << " was not found\n";            the correct behavior
    return 0;
}
```

ANALYSIS

The code necessary to set up a search, for the search itself, and handle the result returned from the search is verbose and heavy on keywords and structure. While all of this is necessary, it could be more convenient. It feels like coding in C (except for the handy vector!).

SOLUTION

Modern C++ has enhanced the if statement to permit initialization, limiting any variables to the statement much like the for statement. This feature is called an if statement with initializer. It is significant since it takes fewer lines of code and does not introduce a variable that might be accidentally reused later in the function. Further, the logic is contained in the conditional, allowing the reader to see it in context more clearly.

The following code demonstrates finding the key value within the initializer. This code further demonstrates using a Standard Template Library algorithm for the search. The iterator variable is declared and initialized before the semicolon—this is the initializer section. The conditional code following the semicolon detects whether the iterator refers to the end (key not found); if not, the key value was found. The conditional value determines the execution path taken in the rest of the statement.

Using an if statement with initializer is more compact and more expressive than traditional if statements. They are also gentle segues when using some functional languages.

Listing 3.2 Using `if` statement with initializer to search for a key value

```
int main() {
    std::vector<int> values;
    for (int i = 0; i < 10; ++i)
        values.push_back(i*2);
    int key = 4;
    if (auto it = std::find(values.begin(),
            values.end(),key); it != values.end())    ◄──  Initializes the
        std::cout << key << " was found\n";                 iterator and decides
    else                                                    if the key was found
        std::cout << key << " was not found\n";
    return 0;
}
```

RECOMMENDATIONS

- Use an if statement with initializer to reduce the number of code lines necessary to set up a decision.
- Remember that variables should be in scope only as far as they are used, never beyond that point; the significant benefit of the if statement with initializer is to limit the variable's scope, which is always a good thing.

SEE ALSO

- See Mistake 13 for an argument against writing common algorithms, since the Standard Template Library has already provided a good set.

3.2   *Mistake 11: Not using type inference for variables*

This mistake affects effectiveness. Readability is often enhanced as well, but that information is opaque when a developer wishes to know the exact data type being used.

PROBLEM

Old habits die hard. The code in the following listing shows a very typical approach to an indexed loop and a selection statement that tests the results of a search. Traditional use of these mechanisms has drilled their form into our brains, making them second nature. However, tradition does not always imply correctness.

Listing 3.3 A typical index-based loop and test variable

```cpp
int main() {
    std::vector<int> values;
    for (int i = 0; i < 10; ++i)          ◄──── A typical index-based loop
        values.push_back(i*2);                   with loop control variable
    int key = 4;
    std::vector<int>::iterator it =
        std::find(values.begin(), values.end())  ◄──── The data type is correct,
    if (it != values.end())                             but is it intuitive?
        std::cout << key << " was found\n";
    else
        std::cout << key << " was not found\n";
    return 0;
}
```

ANALYSIS

Many traditional approaches to solving everyday problems, such as loops and variable types, reflect the primitive state of languages. Compilers used to be less adept at interacting with the developer and depended on a static approach to declaring variables—the compiler either ratified or rejected the developer's choice. The index-based loop is so typical that it does not even draw attention, yet its loop control variable is technically wrong.

Indexes for a container always start at zero and increase up to, but do not include, the container's length. Negative values are incorrect in this context, yet an `int` variable models positive, zero, and negative values. An integer cannot be the correct data type if we are being pedantic. The variable used to test the result of the `find` algorithm requires us to understand both the container, its element, and its iterator types—three pieces of knowledge to keep track of. Worse, these facts have nothing to do with the problem being solved; they are overhead. Overhead negatively affects effectiveness and influences expressiveness.

SOLUTION

Modern C++, following the lead of other more-modern languages, provides compilers with more intelligence and flexibility. Since the compiler ultimately knows whether a data type is correct, it can use that knowledge to determine the ideal type and insert it into the code. Listing 3.4 addresses the two previously mentioned problems.

First, the compiler determines a valid type for the loop control variable—ideally, it will be unsigned. Still, since its initializer is a zero, it will be inferred as `int`. Not only would being unsigned give twice the range, but it also precludes any negative index values. Mathematically, it is the correct type; the actual type is `size_t`, often implemented as an `unsigned long` or `unsigned long long`. It is guaranteed to represent the size of any object, so use it with confidence. Using `auto` and letting the compiler determine its specific type is better.

Second, the complexity of a type can distract from the problem being solved and introduce other subtle bugs. The ability of the compiler to determine the proper data type offloads this complexity and prevents the introduction of oddities. Using the `auto` keyword capitalizes on the compiler's ability to deduce the correct data type and, better, lets it add that information to the code. The developer focuses on the problem being solved, and the language handles the housekeeping, which is synergistic—each does what it is best at.

Listing 3.4   Using `auto` to let the compiler deduce correct types

```
int main() {
    std::vector<int> values;
    for (auto i = 0; i < 10; ++i)              ◄─┐  The compiler always chooses
        values.push_back(i*2);                   │  the correct data type for the
    int key = 4;                                 ┘  loop control variable.
    if (auto it = std::find(values.begin(),
            values.end(), key); it != values.end())  ◄─┐  Lets the compiler figure out
        std::cout << key << " was found\n";              │  the exact type, resulting in
    else                                                 ┘  less for us to remember
        std::cout << key << " was not found\n";
    return 0;
}
```

The `auto` keyword has one caveat: countdown loops are somewhat tricky. The following code shows a simple approach to displaying elements in reverse order.

Listing 3.5   A subtle misuse of `auto`

```
int main() {
    std::vector<int> values;
    for (int i = 0; i < 10; ++i)
        values.push_back(i*2);
    for (auto i = values.size() - 1; i >= 0; --i)   ◄─┐  Implements the
        std::cout << values[i] << '\n';                 ┘  loop in reverse
    return 0;
}
```

When this code is run on my system, it crashes, due to a segmentation fault. Why? Remember that `size_t`, the deduced type for the loop control variable, is `unsigned`. Is there any unsigned value that is not equal to or greater than zero? No. Therefore, when `i` becomes zero, its next value is the maximum value of the data type—certainly well outside the container's boundary. This case is most easily solved by making the data type `int` instead of `auto`. In this case, `size_t` is wrong; this is one of those subtle errors that can be introduced by type deduction. No standard will change this, due to the stability and backward compatibility of the application binary interface (ABI). Oh well.

Another subtle problem that affects performance occurs when `auto` is used to deduce the type of a value in a case like this:

```
auto name = student->getName();
```

The `name` variable is a copy of the student's name, but a reference would be better. The reference is an alias of the `std::string` representing the student's name, not a copy of it, saving a call to the copy constructor. The code would look like this:

```
auto& name = student->getName();
```

This distinction also occurs when using `auto` to deduce the loop control variable in a range-based `for` loop. The variable is always a copy of the element. While this encourages read-only characteristics for the elements, it can be inefficient if the element type is larger than a pointer. This code demonstrates the preferred way of iterating over a list of `students`:

```
for (auto& student : students) …
```

RECOMMENDATIONS

- Use `auto` for many variable declarations.
- Templates can benefit significantly from using the `auto` keyword.
- Use references liberally with `auto` where data types are larger than a pointer, to prevent copying.
- The developer rarely needs to know the exact type—when they do, it should be spelled out.

SEE ALSO

- See Mistake 10, which demonstrates better scoping for test variables.

3.3   *Mistake 12: Using typedef*

This mistake affects both readability and effectiveness. Type aliases are commonly used to define a new data type from an existing one. The new type is more expressive of the type's purpose and increases readability.

PROBLEM

The code in listing 3.6 uses a `typedef` to define a new type that better expresses a concept. That concept is a function that takes two integers and returns one. `Math-Function`'s type is a function pointer so that conforming functions can be assigned and called like any function. What is not apparent is that the alias name is embedded in the definition. This situation is neither obvious nor intuitive.

Listing 3.6   Using a `typedef` to alias a type

```
typedef int (*MathFunction)(int, int);

int add(int a, int b) {
    return a + b;
}

int sub(int a, int b) {
    return a - b;
}

int main() {
    MathFunction f = add;
    std::cout << "Result of addition: " << f(5, 3) << std::endl;
    f = sub;
    std::cout << "Result of subtraction: " << f(5, 3) << std::endl;
    return 0;
}
```

Defines a new type from a function form

Assigns to a variable of the new type

ANALYSIS

The awkwardness of the alias definition is inherited from C. C++ still supports this technique and retains its oddball syntax. If the new type were to be based on a built-in type (e.g., an `int`), the readability would still be strange, as the source type precedes the target type, which is the opposite of what we intuitively expect. For example, defining an alias `age` as an unsigned integer would be

```
typedef unsigned int age;
```

SOLUTION

Modern C++ introduced the `using` keyword, which goes a long way toward uncomplicating aliasing types. This keyword follows a more intuitive approach, where the alias name is on the left-hand side and its definition is on the right-hand side. The assignment operator leads one to think of the alias as assigned from the definition, much like a regular arithmetic assignment, enhancing the readability. Further, writing the alias is more effective, since it follows an intuitive syntax.

The following code is almost identical to listing 3.6; the alias definition is the only difference. This similarity suggests two things: first, using an aliased type is the same as a `typedef` version, and second, there is no reason to continue using `typedef` aliases.

Listing 3.7   Using `typedef` to alias a type

```
using MathFunction = int (*)(int, int);

int add(int a, int b) {
    return a + b;q
}
```

The type name is distinct from its definition.

```
int sub(int a, int b) {
    return a - b;
}

int main() {                                    The usage is the same.
    MathFunction f = add;
    std::cout << "Result of addition: " << f(5, 3) << std::endl;
    f = sub;
    std::cout << "Result of subtraction: " << f(5, 3) << std::endl;
    return 0;
}
```

If the alias is based on a built-in type (e.g., an `int`), the readability is enhanced, since it is natural. For example, one would define an alias `age` as an unsigned integer like this:

```
using age = unsigned int;
```

Now, a note from your professionals: do not use the global inclusion

```
using namespace std;
```

in your code (at the top of the source file). Most textbooks and many online teachers ignore this advice, using this global inclusion apparently to avoid having to code such difficulties as

```
std::cout << …
```

The `std` (standard) namespace is rather large and includes many identifiers. If global inclusion is used, the chances of your code having an identically named identifier are high. Guess which one the compiler will use? I don't know either. The potential for conflicts and ambiguity is significant and might result in undefined behavior—who needs that? Debugging these situations is no easy task; you deserve your sleep.

RECOMMENDATIONS

- Always code the `using` keyword instead of a `typedef`; there is no case where this is disadvantageous.
- Replace `typedef` with `using` in any code that uses them.
- Remember that the code's readers are worth the effort.
- Avoid the global `using namespace std;` inclusion in your code.

3.4   *Mistake 13: Writing common algorithms*

This mistake concerns effectiveness and readability, and correctness is improved. Writing several algorithms in each project we work on is standard practice; it inhibits the practice of code reuse.

PROBLEM

When developers become adept at writing several standard algorithms, they tend to write them for each project, duplicating the code and effort. Many of these are simple enough, so very little time is consumed—muscle memory can be helpful in these cases. The following code demonstrates a couple of frequently written algorithms. Neither of these is difficult or time-consuming, and little thought is put into them. They work and satisfy the program's requirements. What more needs to be said?

Listing 3.8   Two typical, quickly written algorithms

```cpp
template <typename T>
T sum(const std::vector<T>& values) {       ◄─────┐ A nice, general sum
    T total = (T)0;                                │ function that is fast to write
    for (auto val : values)
        total += val;
    return total;
}


template <typename T>
bool find(const std::vector<T> values, T key) {   ◄─────┐ A nice, general find function
    for (auto val : values)                              │ that is fast to write
        if (val == key)
            return true;
    return false;
}

int main() {
    std::vector<int> v { 1, 2, 3, 4, 5, 6, 7, 8, 9, 10 };
    std::cout << sum(v) << '\n';
    if (find(v, 4))
        std::cout << "the key 4 was found\n";
    else
        std::cout << "the key 4 was not found\n";
}
```

ANALYSIS

Most developers become accustomed to doing things a certain way each time, forming many ingrained habits over time. Many habits are helpful, but in this case, they hinder effectiveness. Each algorithm needs about seven lines of code to make it general and well-formatted. However, in many cases, some simplifications improve the developer's ability to focus only on their problem, not the structures needed to solve subproblems, such as sum and find.

SOLUTION

Often, the best code, with the fewest bugs, is one you do not write. Fewer lines of code mean fewer opportunities to make errors. Unsurprisingly, developers are more effective when they aren't tasked with writing housekeeping and overhead code, instead focusing on their main problem. Listing 3.9 shows Standard Template Library code in the `algorithm` and `functional` headers. Learning to use these versions takes some time, but they are simple once understood.

An incidental time-saver also included in this solution is the uniform initialization syntax, which makes simple vectors very easy to write (notice the absence of `push_back` calls). The See Also section points to further information about this subject.

Listing 3.9   Two library functions that need not be written

```
int main() {
    std::vector<int> v { 1, 2, 3, 4, 5, 6, 7, 8, 9, 10 };
    std::cout << std::accumulate(v.begin(), v.end(), 0) << '\n';
    auto it = std::find(v.begin(), v.end(), 4);
    if (it != v.end())
        std::cout << "the key 4 was found\n";
    else
        std::cout << "the key 4 was not found\n";
}
```

A nice, general sum function that does not have to be written

An excellent, general find function that does not have to be written

Standard algorithms are already written and debugged for a developer's use. Learn to lean on them, knowing that if you want correctness and performance, these will meet your needs. Further, their use is simple and makes coding much faster.

RECOMMENDATIONS

- Use Standard Template Library algorithms for most problems; they are remarkably flexible and effective.
- Remember to focus on the programming problem, not subsidiary problems. This will increase your satisfaction.

SEE ALSO

- See Mistake 11 for a discussion about the `auto` keyword.
- See Mistake 14 for further discussion on using uniform initialization.

3.5   *Mistake 14: Not using uniform initialization*

This mistake improves correctness, readability, and effectiveness; in some cases, it also influences performance. There are many ways to initialize variables, each offering advantages and disadvantages; however, these approaches must be more consistent.

PROBLEM

C++ uses the same techniques to initialize variables that it inherited from C. However, in certain cases, C++ goes beyond the limits of C to introduce other forms of initialization. Several approaches have been introduced, with none of them quite doing what the others do in the same way. The net result is that C++ code has multiple ways of initializing variables, and it adds a cognitive load to keep track of each in its proper context. Remember, programming minds are supposed to focus on the problem being solved and use the language to express the solution—keeping track of language details adds an unnecessary burden, and inconsistency dilutes effectiveness.

The following code is a simple case of initializing a vector of integers. Premodern C++ had no other means of doing this, resulting in extra code to set up the problem. Humbug!

Listing 3.10   Typical initialization of container and simple variable

```
int main() {
    std::vector<int> v;
    for (int i = 0; i < 10; ++i)          A loop can be used for
        v.push_back(i);                    consistently computed values.
    v.push_back(33);                      Inconsistent values require
    v.push_back(42);                      a separate insertion.
    int count = v.size();
    std::cout << "the vector has " << count << " elements\n";   Initialization
    return 0;                                                    through
}                                                                assignment
```

ANALYSIS

If all you have is a `push_back`, then as you might guess, every initialization problem looks like a `push_back` problem. This situation demonstrates the impetus for C++ to add other means for initialization; the code is clunky and requires a lot of effort to do a simple task. Several other examples could be shown, but this one serves the purpose.

SOLUTION

There are several reasons to use uniform initialization; the most appealing is its consistency, which makes it understandable and applicable in all contexts. Especially for containers, the ability to use uniform initialization is outstanding. The code in listing 3.11 demonstrates this use for a vector and a standalone variable. When initialization values are placed within the braces, it quickly becomes the preferred approach, although it takes a few tries to understand.

Uniform initialization uses braces to enclose the initialization value. The vector uses this approach, and the count variable does as well. This uniformity makes programming much easier as the developer becomes more adept. Weaning off other methods may take time, but the result is worth the effort.

Listing 3.11   Uniform initialization of a container and simple variable

```
int main() {
    std::vector<int> v {0, 1, 2, 3, 4, 5, 6, 7, 8, 9, 33, 42};
    auto count {v.size()};
    std::cout << "the vector has " << count << " elements\n";
    return 0;
}
                                    Uniform initialization of a
                                    variable (simple variable)

                                    Uniform initialization of a
                                    container (compound variable)
```

Uniform initialization uses one form to initialize any variable. This consistency makes reading and writing code more manageable.

There are other advantages to using this approach, including the following:

- Consistency across different variable types
- Excludes narrowing conversions—`doubles` do not silently initialize `ints`, for example
- Complex data structures are easily initialized (look into designated initialization for more on this)
- Initializer list support for constructors and containers

RECOMMENDATIONS

- Uniform initialization can be used to initialize any variable, even complex ones.
- Once understood and used, this approach is consistent and simple.

3.6 *Mistake 15: Failing to use emplacement*

This mistake focuses on performance. Adding large or complex elements to containers can be more expensive than necessary.

PROBLEM

Containers such as vectors should be preferred when managing collections of objects. Typically, an object is created and copied to the container, as shown in listing 3.12. Creating the object costs a constructor, and copying its contents into the container's element costs another; if the copy assignment operator is used, it still costs about the equivalent of a constructor call. Temporaries can be expensive, but this cannot be helped. Using Standard Template Containers necessitates this two-step process.

Emplacement aims to create an object in a specific memory location. A local variable is allocated on the runtime stack; dynamically created entities are allocated on the heap. The programmer does not influence these variables' location, only ensures they exist. Emplacement, on the other hand, lets the developer specify where an object is created.

The following code demonstrates a typical pattern of creating entities and adding them to a vector. Typically, when an entity is created, it costs a constructor call. When adding the entity to a vector, the vector copies it into its element, costing another constructor call.

Listing 3.12 Creating and adding elements to a container

```
class Resource {
private:
    std::string name;
    int instance;
    static int handle;
public:
    Resource(const std::string& n) : name(n), instance(++handle) {}
```

```
        int id() const { return instance; }
};
int Resource::handle = 0;

int main() {
    std::vector<Resource> resources;
    resources.push_back(Resource("resource 1"));
    resources.push_back(Resource("resource 2"));
    for (int i = 0; i < resources.size(); ++i)
        std::cout << resources[i].id() << '\n';
    return 0;
}
```

◀─── **Creates a temporary, and then copies it to the vector's element**

ANALYSIS

Creating the `Resource` object requires a constructor call. To add the entity to the vector, the container is forced to do a copy or assignment to transfer the contents of the source object to the target container element. This approach is the only way to achieve this functionality. Yet doubling the cost of creating an entity seems wrong. Oh well, that's life.

SOLUTION

Modern C++ changed the rules a bit to circumvent the notion that two-stepping the insertion of objects in a container is too expensive, which is correct in some cases. As in listing 3.12, the instance is created only to be inserted into the container; it is not used otherwise. When this is the case, the object can be constructed directly in the container's element, rather than copied into it, as shown in listing 3.13. Emplacement uses a single constructor to create the entity in the vector element's location. This technique shaves off one of the constructor or assignment calls, enhancing performance. It's also worth noting that defining a move constructor and move assignment operator permits placing noncopyable objects into a container.

Listing 3.13   Creating elements directly in a container

```
class Resource {
private:
    std::string name;
    int instance;
    static int handle;
public:
    Resource(const std::string& n) : name(n), instance(++handle) {}
    int id() const { return instance; }
};
int Resource::handle = 0;

int main() {
    std::vector<Resource> resources;
    resources.emplace_back("resource 1");
    resources.emplace_back("resource 2");
    for (int i = 0; i < resources.size(); ++i)
```

◀─── **Creates an object in the vector's element**

```
        std::cout << resources[i].id() << '\n';
    return 0;
}
```

Not every class can use this technique. If objects are noncopyable or nonassignable, the compiler will complain loudly when the code is compiled. However, the compiler will purr if these objects define move semantics. Objects in a container may have to be moved or copied during container management. For example, if a vector must grow, the elements of the former vector must be copied to the new vector. Therefore, emplacement is only for some data types.

RECOMMENDATIONS

- Consider using emplacement when objects are not used independently of the container.
- Remember that containers of pointers (preferably smart ones!) may be preferable to containers of values.

SEE ALSO

- See Mistake 42 for comments on using only values or pointers as container elements.

3.7 Mistake 16: Failing to use tuples

This mistake focuses on effectiveness. Creating structures or classes to hold heterogeneous or multiple values distracts from the developer's focus on problem-solving.

PROBLEM

A typical problem is aggregating multiple, often heterogeneous, data types into a unit for easier manipulation. Typically, a `struct` or `class` is used, which requires the developer to create code to define the aggregation. This approach has worked for years, but in the case of plain old data (POD) in particular, it is often overkill, primarily when the structure is used in only a few places.

Listing 3.14 results from the developer needing to model three attributes of a student—name, age, and grade point average. The developer must also define several similar classes to carry other aggregate groups, increasing the number of structures and using different data types. One distinct advantage of this approach is that access to the POD is done by field name—more on that later.

Listing 3.14   Defining simple PODs as structures

```
struct Student {
    std::string name;                    ◄──┐   Overhead in defining
    int age;                                │   a simple POD
    double gpa;
    Student(const std::string& n, int a, double g) : name(n), age(a), gpa(g) {}
};
```

```
// other well-defined PODs
struct Employee {};
struct Teacher {};
struct Admin{};

int main() {                                                      POD initialization
    Student s("Susan", 23, 3.85);         ◄────────────────┘
    std::cout << "student " << s.name << ", " << s.age << " years old, carries a "
        << s.gpa << '\n';              ◄─────────────┐
    return 0;                                        │  POD use
}
```

ANALYSIS

Each aggregate defines a new data type, and each instance variable and its data type must be defined. It is easiest to have a constructor to initialize the instance. Access to each variable is done by the instance variable name, which is a natural and effective means. However, the duplication of similar code and the burden of writing each new POD makes this approach tedious and error-prone. Further, understanding the data types is diluted by the quantity of code, the distance between their definitions, and the repetition of similar parts.

SOLUTION

As shown in listing 3.15, the `using` keyword is added to simplify the creation of the data type name and its definition—this is the modern C++ means of the C-based `typedef` keyword. The See Also section calls out another mistake that addresses it.

The key in this code is the `tuple`. The `std::tuple` template provides a means for declaring a structure with multiple instance variables of differing types by enumerating their types; they have no user-supplied names. This difference in the structure minimizes naming and coding. The initialization of an instance looks precisely like the structure version but without having to provide a constructor—another time and clutter savings device.

The final difference is a negative; accessing the fields is not done by name but by index. Each instance variable is indexed in specification order, starting at index zero. Given an index, the `std::get` function template helps determine which field to access; however, the See Also section points to a better means of accessing values, called *structured binding.*

Listing 3.15   Defining simple PODs as tuples

```
using Student = std::tuple<std::string, int, double>;    ◄──────────┐
                                                          A low-overhead means
// other well-defined PODs                                of defining a POD
// using Employee = std::tuple<...>;
// using Teacher = std::tuple<...>;
// using Admin = std::tuple<...>;

int main() {
    Student s("Susan", 23, 3.85);         ◄────────────┘  POD initialization
```

```
    std::cout << "student " << std::get<0>(s) << ", " << std::get<1>(s)
        << " years old, carries a " << std::get<2>(s) << '\n';
    return 0;                                                    POD use
}
```

The `std::tuple` template provides a compact and useable means for defining data aggregates when a class's full semantics is unnecessary; this approach particularly applies to PODs. Templates can be used to generalize tuples further. For example, this alternate approach could be used to define and use a `Student`:

```
template <typename T1, typename T2, typename T3>
using Student = std::tuple<T1, T2, T3>;
```

And its initialization would be

```
Student<std::string, int, double> s("Susan", 23, 3.85);
```

Access to the fields remains the same.

There is one significant caveat here: if a `Student` and an `Employee` are defined identically, they are the same type. Any function or container that takes such a `Student` can also take an `Employee`—this is not the Liskov Substitution Principle but a severe design flaw. Consider carefully how these are used.

As a final comment on using tuples differently, when a function needs to return multiple values, consider using the `std::tuple` template. This application would be a great reason to consider templates with the `using` keyword. Output parameters should be replaced with tuples to enhance readability.

RECOMMENDATIONS

- For simple structures, typically PODs, use the `std::tuple` to simplify coding and ease of reading.
- Consider templatizing tuples for more generic use.
- Return multiple values using a tuple.

SEE ALSO

- See Mistake 85 for a discussion that prefers returning a structure to using output parameters.
- See Mistake 12 for an explanation of taking advantage of the `using` keyword; it simplifies creating new data types when used as in Mistake 16.
- See Mistake 17 for a means of accessing tuple values in an elegant manner.

3.8 *Mistake 17: Not using structured binding*

This mistake focuses on readability and effectiveness. Tuples are convenient templates to pass or return multiple values without requiring as much effort as structures or classes; accessing their values takes more work to write and read.

PROBLEM

The example from Mistake 16 showed the code in listing 3.16 to eliminate writing structures or classes and lean on a `std::tuple` template. The simplicity of this approach is its most significant appeal. However, the function template `std::get` must be used when accessing the values. This code is awkward to write and read, which causes some concern about its usefulness. It is valuable because of its simplicity, but it makes ugly code.

> **Listing 3.16   Using the function template to extract tuple values**

```
using Student = std::tuple<std::string, int, double>;

int main() {
    Student s("Susan", 23, 3.85);
    std::cout << "student " << std::get<0>(s) << ", " << std::get<1>(s) <<
        " years old, carries a " << std::get<2>(s) << '\n';
    return 0;
}
```
Uses the std::get template function with indexing

ANALYSIS

The `Student` tuple is easy to initialize. Its initialization looks like a constructor call to a class the developer would write. We are lured into thinking that this simplicity will continue; however, access to the fields proves otherwise. A tuple's fields are laid out in definition order. Since they have no names, the only option for access is that the `get` function uses index values. This approach works well, but the disconnect between a field's "name," a concept in the developer's mind, and the index is jarring.

SOLUTION

The flexibility of a `std::tuple` template is marred by its excessive and disconnected method of accessing its fields. It would be easy to make a mistake in coding the proper index value or later rearrange the fields and forget the access functions already coded.

Structured binding decomposes a tuple or other object with public data members into individual values. Some languages call this *destructuring*. The syntax is simple: start with the `auto` keyword, add brackets, and add a variable for each data member. Then, assign the tuple instance to it. The following code shows an example that demonstrates the ease of using structured binding. It may require more keystrokes than using the `get` template function, but the benefit of having a named variable makes up for the few extra keystrokes, if any.

> **Listing 3.17   Using structured binding to extract tuple values**

```
using Student = std::tuple<std::string, int, double>;

int main() {
    Student s("Susan", 23, 3.85);
    auto [name, age, gpa] = s;
    std::cout << "student " << name << ", " << age <<
```
Uses structured binding to decompose a tuple

```
        " years old, carries a " << gpa << '\n';
    return 0;
}
```

◄――― **Uses variable names instead of index values**

Structured binding has a significant correctness and readability problem if the order of fields in a structure changes. The names of the variables in listing 3.17 become out of sequence with the fields if they have been rearranged. For example, if `age` and `gpa` are rearranged in the structure, the variable names will have the wrong values. If the rearrangement is such that the types are convertible, the code in listing 3.17 works (no compiler or runtime errors), but the values will be incorrect. Therefore, take care to ensure the structure fields and the structured binding variables remain in harmony.

RECOMMENDATIONS

- Use structured binding to decompose PODs and simple structures or classes.
- Remember that the object must have public data members for structured binding to work.

SEE ALSO

- See Mistake 85 for a discussion about preferring `std::pair` to output parameters.
- See Mistake 16 for a more general discussion of preferring `std::tuple` over `std::pair`.

Better modern C++:
Additional topics

This chapter covers

- Improvements in text formatting
- Regular expressions
- Lambdas
- Variadic templates
- Portable filesystem code

Modern C++ has expanded the range and depth of functionality available for developers. Many areas have improved, and well-designed and articulated recommendations have entered the standard. This chapter is a very sparse sampling of a few features that make everyday programming simpler, more correct, and easier to read.

Almost any C++ developer would benefit from these additional topics but argue that some crucial aspects have been overlooked. This assessment is correct, since there are too many nifty features to enumerate. However, consider this effort a starting point in a general approach to picking up some handy improvements.

Text handling has improved, using the not-yet-implemented-everywhere format header. Parsing text by writing your code is fraught with complexity and errors, but regular expression functionality simplifies developers' lives.

A concern for addressing functional programming concepts has motivated the Standard Committee to adopt ranges and better interaction with defined-on-the-spot functions, called *lambdas*. Entire volumes have been written on lambdas, but a hint of their use will hopefully whet your appetite to learn and use them. Ranges implement the Linux concept of filters (commonly used with the pipe symbol: |), where the output of one becomes the input of the next, and these are composed into very powerful pipelines.

Filesystem code has traditionally been developed for a specific platform. For cross-platform code, some conditional compilation mechanism is used to select the correct platform-dependent code. Modern C++ offers an abstraction over these distinctions that permits a single unit of code to work on any platform. Finally, readability is greatly enhanced with new features for defined mathematical constants (e.g., pi), using a thousand separator to comprehend many-digit literal numbers more quickly, and user-defined literal values that enhance readability and are helpful in unit conversions.

4.1 Mistake 18: Not using variadic templates

This mistake affects effectiveness and readability. Varying length parameter lists is natural for many problems, but handling them adds overhead and complexity.

PROBLEM

Variadic parameter lists are common enough that the C language provided a means for handling them long ago. C++ inherited this approach (see the See Also section), but it has proven problematic. C++ provides a cleaner means for handling this situation but not without its complexities and overhead. Listing 4.1 bundles parameters into a container and passes the container to the sum function (this can be better solved using the std::accumulate algorithm). There are no special function calls (e.g., va_list), and handling the container is straightforward. This solution is templatized to handle any type where the addition operator makes sense. However, this benefit comes at a cost: the developer must create the container, package the parameters into it, and pass it as an argument to the function. All this effort is incidental to solving the problem; it is only a necessary housekeeping effort to package data. Reading this code requires splitting one's attention, focusing on both problem-solving and overhead.

Listing 4.1 Using a vector to implement a variadic parameter list

```
template <typename T>
T sum(T initial, const std::vector<T>& vals) {        Chooses a templatized
    T sum = initial;                                  form for greater flexibility
    for (int i = 0; i < vals.size(); ++i)
        sum += vals[i];
    return sum;
}

int main() {                                   Creates a container
    std::vector<int> intvalues;
    for (int i = 1; i < 10; ++i)               Populates the container
```

```
        intvalues.push_back(i);
    std::cout << sum(0, intvalues) << '\n';          ◀──────── Finally, solves the problem
    std::vector<double> doublevalues;
    for (int i = 1; i < 4; ++i)
        doublevalues.push_back(i);
    std::cout << sum(5.0, doublevalues) << '\n';
    return 0;
}
```

ANALYSIS

The solution shown in listing 4.1 is recommended in a previous section (see the See Also section), which leaves a significant problem for developer effectiveness but opens an opportunity for improvement. The programmer is responsible for building a structure with the list of values to be processed. The construction of this structure is pure overhead; it is not part of the problem being solved but a necessary step to aggregate values into a usable form. The more code not directly focused on the problem, the less effective the developer is, and the greater the opportunity is to make errors. Further, it is boring.

SOLUTION

Modern C++ provides an excellent way to use a recursive approach to solving this problem. The idea is to provide varying-length argument lists to a general template function. The template parses the variadic parameter lists into pairs in the form of the first and the remaining parameters. Recursion occurs on the remaining parameters, pasted into the aforementioned pair. This continues until the last parameter stands alone without any remaining parameters. A second template function that takes one parameter is written; this is a specialization of the general template. A significant advantage of templates is that they are evaluated at compile time, saving runtime costs.

Listing 4.2 shows these two template functions. The specialization (or base) template is straightforward; it takes one parameter and returns it. The recursive (or general) template is also simple. Each parameter pair is the left-most parameter and a variadic parameter pack of the remaining parameters. The current template is (conceptually) pushed on a stack, and its remaining parameters become the parameter list for the next recursive call to the template. This template call separates the parameter list into the left-most parameter and its remaining parameters. The specialized template is called when the remaining parameters contain precisely one parameter. Then the stacked template calls are (conceptually) popped with their single parameter, and the function call is built from each parameter.

To achieve this templatized variadic pattern, first, write the base case, and then, write the recursive case. That's it! When the compiler parses the function calls, it looks for a sum function that can handle multiple parameters. It will discover the template with the single parameter and the variadic pack. It knows to keep calling that template version if it can produce parameter pairs (left-most and remaining). When a single parameter is left, the variadic template is not applicable. The compiler will choose the sum template with a single parameter. Without that base case function, this technique would not work. But it does, and it does so splendidly.

Listing 4.2 Using a templatized variadic parameter list

```
template <typename T>  // base case
T sum(T t) { return t; }

template <typename T, typename... Pack>  // general (recursive) case
T sum(T t, Pack... remaining) { return t + sum(remaining...); }

int main() {
    std::cout << sum(3, 4) << '\n';
    std::cout << sum(3, 4, 5) << '\n';
    std::cout << sum(3, 4, 6, 7) << '\n';
    return 0;
}
```

> Solves the problem
> in its natural form

Consider using fold expressions (C++17 and later) for a stretch goal. The templates in listing 4.2 can be condensed into

```
template <typename T, typename... Pack>
T sum(T t, Pack... remaining) {
    return (t + ... + remaining);
}
```

RECOMMENDATIONS

- Use templates with variadic packs to cleanly handle variable length parameter lists.
- Avoid premodern C++ means for dealing with variadic parameter lists.

SEE ALSO

- See Mistake 40 for a discussion on variable length parameter lists.

4.2 Mistake 19: Using global namespace enums

This mistake affects effectiveness and readability and can have a subtle but significant influence on correctness. Enumerations allow developers to name literal values to enhance readability symbolically, but they must be coded properly and cleanly.

PROBLEM

Variables and constants can be used to name concepts, such as colors. For example, an integer constant can be assigned some value that maps to red or blue. Unless the developer is careful, this mapping can be sufficiently arbitrary that the reader may need clarification, primarily when multiple entities in a group are used. The C++ language provided a means for simplifying this, using enum constants. A named entity within an enumeration can represent a possible value among a set.

Enumerated constants are implemented as integers, so they are easily translatable to and from integers. This fact may sound powerful, but it often makes very little sense.

Listing 4.3 shows an integer variable representing a color being assigned the value of 2. What does that mean?

Our developer is working on a problem dealing with automobiles and their interactions. Cars and traffic lights have colors. It makes sense to enumerate the colors so that symbolic names can be used. The compiler assigns values to these constants by default, and changes (i.e., addition, deletion, or rearrangement) are automatically accounted for. However, our developer ran into some problems. The following code shows a (shabby) attempt at modeling the color attribute of automobiles and traffic lights.

Listing 4.3   Problematic global namespace enumerations

```
enum TrafficColor {                    The red traffic light is entered
    Green,                             into the global namespace.
    Yellow,
    Red                               The index defaulted to
};                                    1 in both enumerations.

enum PaintColor {
    Gray,
    White,
    Black,
    Paint_Red,                         You cannot reuse the exact enumeration
    Blue,                              name; it must be modified.
    Paint_Yellow,
    Paint_Green
};

int main() {
    int color = 2;                     Assigning and using an
    switch (color) {                   int for an enumeration
    case Red:
        std::cout << "we have a red one\n";
        break;
    case Blue:
        std::cout << "we have a blue one\n";
        break;
    case Yellow:
        std::cout << "we have a yellow one\n";
        break;
    default:
        std::cout << "we have a white one\n";
        break;
    // case White:                     Duplicate index value within
    };                                 enumerations—cannot be defined
    return 0;
}
```

ANALYSIS

Enumeration constants reside in the global namespace. This namespace is where every declared symbol lives if not contained in a specific namespace. The developer discovered several problems using enum constants, as shown listing 4.3.

First, as noted, all constants are in one namespace, making duplicate values an error. The effort to rename the paint color shows how a developer must weaken the meaning of the symbol's name to get around this problem.

Second, since integers are backing the constants, any code that mixes two enum sets runs the risk of having multiple conflicting values so that they are ambiguous or an error. The switch statement cannot have two cases where the enumeration constant value is identical, such as Yellow for TrafficColor and White for PaintColor (each is assigned the same value; in this case, it is 1). Other logic likely would confuse which of the two colors is intended.

Third, a variable to which a color is assigned can be assigned an arbitrary integer value. This example assigns two to the color. The developer must work hard to communicate clearly what the assignment means. It needs to be clarified in the example which enumeration constant with the value of 2 is intended.

Finally, the backing integer variable cannot know if a value is out of bounds. The variable could be assigned a negative or a value bigger than the largest valid constant value. Neither the reader nor the program would know what was meant. Worse, the code might continue to run but handle the incorrect assignment unexpectedly or erroneously (more of that undefined behavior business).

SOLUTION

Modern C++ comes to the rescue! Enumerations can now be encapsulated in a class namespace. This declutters the global namespace, allowing duplicated constant names in separate namespaces. Although the backing variable type is an integer, the code cannot assign an integer value to the variable, since the assignment must be within the set of enumerated values for that class. Any attempt to assign a value out of bounds is prevented, simply because there would be no legitimate constant out of bounds and no illegitimate value can be assigned.

The following code shows the use of an enum class, isolating all defined values into one class with no conflict with another. Constants of one class (and namespace) cannot be assigned to another variable, preventing some of the previously described problems.

Listing 4.4 Separate namespace enumerations

```
enum class Traffic {          A namespace bounded
    Green,                     enumeration
    Yellow,
    Red
};

enum class Paint {            A different namespace
    Gray,                     bounded enumeration
    Black,
    White,
    Red,
    Blue,
    Yellow,
    Green
```

```
};
int main() {
    auto color = Traffic::Yellow;
    switch (color) {
    case Traffic::Red:
        std::cout << "we have a red light\n";
        break;
    case Traffic::Yellow:
        std::cout << "we have a yellow light\n";
        break;
    case Traffic::Green:
    default:
        std::cout << "we have a green light\n";
        break;
    };

    Paint can = Paint::Blue;
    switch (can) {
    case Paint::Red:
        std::cout << "we have a red cube\n";
        break;
    case Paint::Yellow:
        std::cout << "we have a blue cube\n";
        break;
    case Paint::White:
        [[fallthrough]];
    default:
        std::cout << "we have a white cube\n";
        break;
    };
    return 0;
}
```

Uses auto for the data type, which is deduced from the initialization value

A different enumeration literal than the literal in the other class with the same name

Eliminates warnings for intentional fall-through behavior

The [[fallthrough]] annotation documents intentional cases of fall-through behavior where the break keyword is not used. The switch statement is fraught with opportunities to make mistakes, so use every available technique to prevent bugs. Don't forget the statement-ending semicolon (;) after the final closing brace (}).

Enumeration classes isolate values into one namespace and prevent arbitrary values from being assigned to a class variable. The problems with the classic enum are resolved and disambiguated, using this important feature. If the type of the underlying representation of the enum class needs to be specified, it can be done by extending from a basic type:

```
enum class Traffic : uint8_t {
    ...
};
```

RECOMMENDATIONS

- Change global enum definitions to enum classes to eliminate the described problems.

4.3 *Mistake 20: Not using new formatting functionality*

This mistake affects effectiveness and readability, and in some cases, it affects correctness. Formatting output well is an art form. It is a rare case where C-style formatting has a few distinct advantages compared to C++'s clunky approach.

PROBLEM

C offered a helpful—albeit dangerous—solution for fine-grained output text formatting. The `printf` family of functions provided a format specifier with any readable text and embedded directions for formatting variables. The specifier used special characters to denote where a variable would be inserted, followed by a list of variables or expressions. However, problems arose when format specifier variable placeholders did not match the variable type. The compiler did no checking to ensure that the types matched the specifiers nor that the number of variables was equal to the number of specifiers. In other words, correct behavior is difficult to accomplish, and undefined behavior is always surprising.

Let's assume we are modeling a school. One essential data type in this example is `Student`. Naturally, once we have a student, we want to know their name, age, and GPA. To print these out, a format specifier should include three placeholders, one for each property. The code must ensure the placeholders are correctly defined for the property's data type and the arguments are in the correct order. The following code demonstrates a clean example with no wonkiness. Most developers are very familiar with this approach.

Listing 4.5 Using `sprintf` for fine-grained formatting functionality

```cpp
struct Student {
    std::string name;
    int age;
    double gpa;
    Student(const std::string& n, int a, double g) : name(n), age(a), gpa(g) {}
};

int main() {
    Student dinah("Dinah", 26, 3.3);
    char buffer[256];
    sprintf(buffer, "%s is a student aged %d carrying a gpa of %.2f",
        dinah.name.c_str(), dinah.age, dinah.gpa);    ◄──
    std::cout << buffer << '\n';
    return 0;
}
```

Understandable formatting (but with all sprintf dangers)

ANALYSIS

While this code is correctly written, swap a few format specifiers or variables around during a maintenance session for some surprising behavior (again, undefined). Almost any variation will compile cleanly, which is a red flag. One cumbersome problem is that the `%s` specifier wants a `char*`, not a `std::string`. It is simple to fix, but there is one more thing to address that removes the focus from the problem and reorients it to housekeeping.

Classic C++ gave us the `std::stringstream` template, which works with the `operator<<` to do most output very cleanly (primarily numeric values to string values). A different mistake recommends this solution in many cases; however, string streams become overly awkward when the formatting gets more complicated.

The following code offers a solution to the this problem, but it is highly doubtful that it reads any more clearly—perhaps it is worse. Its most significant benefit is that there is no way to get undefined behavior from incorrectly specifying variables; the underlying character stream will properly format whatever data type is used.

Let us add a new requirement: the student's GPA must be formatted in such a way that it always has a leading digit, a decimal point, and two trailing digits—no one brags by saying, "I have a 3.8 GPA," when, in fact, their GPA is 3.85. Further, for reports, the GPA needs to have both trailing digits for consistency and column alignment. The school administration is adamant about this requirement; they do not want to manually align a GPA of 4 and one of 3.85—they want 4.00 and 3.85. So two trailing zeros must be added to a GPA of 4, and one trailing zero is also necessary to ensure a GPA of 3.5 is output as 3.50. As the following code shows, the requirement is more straightforward to specify than implement in code. Getting the `gpa` variable to pad with trailing zeros properly is a chore, and a bit of frustrating research was necessary for the solution. It ain't as obvious as it might seem.

Listing 4.6   Using `stringstream` for fine-grained formatting functionality

```
struct Student {
    std::string name;
    int age;
    double gpa;
    Student(const std::string& n, int a, double g) : name(n), age(a), gpa(g) {}
};

int main() {
    Student dinah("Dinah", 26, 3.3);
    std::stringstream str;
    str << dinah.gpa;
    std::string gpa_str(str.str());
    str.str("");
    str << dinah.name << " is a student aged " << dinah.age << " carrying a
    gpa of "
        << gpa_str << std::setw(4 - gpa_str.size()) << std::setfill('0') << "";    ◄
    std::cout << str.str() << '\n';
    return 0;                                                      Complicated formatting
}                                                                      for little result
```

SOLUTION

Modern C++ offers a slick solution that combines all of the ease of specification of a `printf` family function with the type safety of a string stream. Listing 4.7 demonstrates the same form as a `printf` family function by using { } as a placeholder and a list of variables or expressions following the format specifier. The benefit of using this approach is that the output is well represented, and the placement of the variables is prominent. Better, however, is the fact that the compiler figures out the data type and does the conversion to a string automatically and with type safety. The ability to fine-tune a variable's output harkens back to the C-style approach but with more uniform usage. Admittedly, it takes a bit of experimentation to grasp these symbols and their interaction, but it is not difficult. The result is that the output formatting is straightforward to read without any problems with type mismatch. The requirement for two trailing digits is now satisfied in a simple manner. The school's requirement for the leading digit, decimal point, and two trailing digits is specified by the column width (4) and the padding character (0). Therefore, a GPA of 4 will be output as 4.00; a GPA of 3.5 will be output as 3.50; and a GPA of 3.85 will be output as 3.85. In all cases, the columns are consistently lined up and padded as necessary.

> **NOTE** The `std::format` functionality part of the `format` header is available on limited compilers. The C++20 standard defined the functionality, but some compilers still need to implement it. I had to download Ubuntu 23.10 and install its GCC compiler suite (version 13+) to obtain this functionality. Clang and MSVC have already implemented it, so you might be lucky.

Listing 4.7 Using `std::format` for fine-grained formatting functionality

```
struct Student {
    std::string name;
    int age;
    double gpa;
    Student(const std::string& n, int a, double g) : name(n), age(a), gpa(g) {}
};

int main() {
    Student dinah("Dinah", 26, 3.3);
    std::cout << std::format("{} is a student aged {} carrying a gpa of
    {:0^4}", dinah.name, dinah.age, dinah.gpa) << '\n';    ◄─── sprintf-like
    return 0;                                                     functionality with
}                                                                 type-safe behavior
```

RECOMMENDATIONS

- Use `std::format` to get the benefits of `printf`-style functions without the sneaky problems they introduce.

- String streams are more type safe than `printf`-style functions, but they also make fine-grained formatting more awkward.

- Some compilers do not yet implement `std::format` functionality; check whether yours does.

- C++23 offers a `std::print` and `std::println` to simplify coding output statements; it is consistent with languages that use a similar form (e.g., Java and Python).

SEE ALSO

- See Mistake 36 for a discussion about the problems using this family of functions.

4.4   *Mistake 21: Not using ranges with containers*

This mistake affects effectiveness significantly. The developer's approach to writing code that maps, filters, or reduces data is often verbose and tedious, with much of the code concentrated on housekeeping chores.

PROBLEM

Data containers represent an efficient and compact means for handling sequences of values. Vectors are an excellent choice, since they are easy to use, flexible, and powerful. However, the code necessary to use them essentially requires completing housekeeping tasks that detract from the developer's focus on the problem being solved. Range-based `for` loops are a significant move toward more functional programming and hint at the possibility of using data streams.

Our developer must take a sequence of values, transform all negatives to their absolute value, eliminate odd values, and sum the remaining values. Listing 4.8 is a straightforward approach to doing this work and represents a common approach to dealing with sequences. The first two loops could be compacted into one, but the operations would be more obscure. Doing one functional aspect at a time is more straightforward but with reduced performance. As always, I prefer readability to performance in most cases.

Listing 4.8   Several independent functions on a value sequence

```
int main() {
    std::vector<int> vals { 42, 3, 7 -9, 0, 22, 23, -7, 22 };

    for (auto v : vals)                          Transforms negative values into
        if (v < 0)                               their positive counterparts
            v = -v;

    std::vector<int> evens;                      For simplicity, creates
    for (const auto v : vals)                    a new container
        if (v % 2 == 0)
            evens.push_back(v);                  Filters out negative values

    int sum = 0;
    for (const auto v : evens)                   Sums all values in the
        sum += v;                                second container

    std::cout << sum << '\n';
    return 0;
}
```

ANALYSIS

The code performs the functionality the developer was required to implement. It is simple and obvious what is happening, how it is intended to work, and what the result means. However, the duplication of loops suggests that something better should be used. Unfortunately, there are few options. Compacting the first two loops is possible but negatively effects readability. The second container also feels awkward. Modifying a vector in place correctly is challenging; a second vector is used to keep things clean and correct. This affects performance, too.

SOLUTION

The advantage of data sequences is that they can be processed as streams. The `cin` and `cout` objects use this approach. File input and output follow the data stream model. This model is compelling, and its approach should be used where possible. The overhead of using them is reduced, and the code necessary to manipulate them is minimized. C++ has introduced the ranges header with ranges and views to manipulate value streams. These reduce code to a bare minimum, especially when using lambdas.

A distinct advantage of ranges is that functions are composable. This means the functions can be invoked one after another in a sequence. A simple analogy is the Linux filter programs used in the command line or scripts. The output of the first filter function is fed into the following filter function as its input; its output becomes input for the following filter function and so on. Frequently, this composition of filters is called a *pipeline*, which is a beneficial and meaningful term.

The following code introduces three essential functional forms for handling data streams:

- Mapping
- Filtering
- Reduction

It is important to understand this second usage of the word *filter*. The Linux example represents a traditional name; in the context of ranges, it means a type of functionality. They are related but are not equivalent. The code in listing 4.9 demonstrates the composition of two functions, the absolute value and even predicate.

Mapping is a function that takes each element of the input stream, performs a function on the element, and produces another element that is placed into the output stream. This functionality is a one-to-one production—each input value produces exactly one output value. The `std::views::transform` range adapter is supplied with a function that maps or transforms the input value to an output value. The following code calls the `abs` function to convert any negative values into their positive counterparts. Positive values are unmodified, demonstrating that a transformation may not affect a value but pass it through. Each value is mapped to its absolute value.

Filtering is a function that takes each element of the input stream and determines whether that element should be passed onto the output stream. It takes a predicate that determines inclusion or rejection. A *predicate* is a function that returns a Boolean value.

If the returned value is `true`, the element is retained; if the returned value is `false`, the element is rejected (eliminated). The code in listing 4.9 filters out odd values, retaining only even values. This functionality is a one-to-one or one-to-none production; either the value or nothing is kept. The `std::views::filter` range adapter is supplied the predicate function to determine element inclusion or exclusion. Each value is filtered out or left in based on the predicate's return value. Peruse the See Also section for a discussion of lambdas.

Finally, reduction is a function that takes each element of the input stream and performs some operation on it, contributing to producing a single resultant value. The function uses each element from the input stream to develop the final value. A typical example is summing. The code in listing 4.9 adds the filtered values to arrive at their sum. This functionality is a many-to-one production—each input element contributes to the final, single value. The `std::accumulate` function template takes iterators for the first and last elements and an initial value (zero for summing). All input values are reduced to their sum.

The C++ ranges and range adapters are powerful but have yet to reach the performance levels offered by other languages. The `accumulate` function cannot be composed with the result of the mapping and filtering functionality, since the developer must supply the beginning and ending iterators. Therefore, a second container must be created to hold the results of the pipelined stream values. In the future, an accumulate-style range adapter may be developed. Several functional languages provide many composable functions, which are a pleasure to work with.

Listing 4.9   Composed functions on a value sequence

```
int main() {
    std::vector<int> vals { 42, 3, 7 -9, 0, 22, 23, -7, 22 };        Creates a stream,
                                                                    absolutizes values,
                                                                      filters out odds,
    auto evens = vals                                                  and stores in a
        | std::views::transform([](int x) { return abs(x); })          new container
        | std::views::filter([](int x){ return x % 2 == 0; });
    auto sum = std::accumulate(evens.begin(), evens.end(), 0);

                                                                    Sums values in the
    std::cout << sum << '\n';                                        second container
    return 0;
}
```

RECOMMENDATIONS

- Ranges can significantly decrease the overhead of traditional container-processing code.
- Where possible, process containers using ranges and range adapters to ease writing and simplify reading the code.
- Remember that not all range-oriented functions are composable in pipelines.
- Functional programming is powerful, and pipelines can be used to transition toward that paradigm.

- See Mistake 6 for a discussion on dissuading the use of the traditional approach of index-based loops.

- See Mistake 13 for a discussion on using Standard Template Library algorithms instead of rewriting them.

- See Mistake 23 for a discussion on using lambdas.

4.5   Mistake 22: Writing nonportable filesystem code

This mistake affects readability and effectiveness. Filesystems vary across platforms, and developing code to interact with them can be complex, obscure, and nonportable.

PROBLEM

Many programs must access the filesystem to input and output data for configuration, processing, documenting results, or other purposes. Over the years, the code needed to implement this has grown in complexity and functionality. A significant problem with this progression is that different platforms have moved in different, incompatible directions.

Writing a program that needs to check the existence of a file and create it if it does not exist is straightforward until one considers the complexity of the platform's filesystem. The developer needs to write a simple program to check for a file's existence; create it, if necessary; and output a line of text. The program is required to be operable on both Windows and Linux. While writing the functionality for either system is simple enough, writing it for both is complex. Two approaches present themselves: preprocessor directives and separate source files. The first approach is not demonstrated, but several code bases use this technique. The code in listings 4.10 and 4.11 demonstrate the second approach of using separate files. Windows file handling depends on several platform-specific functions and constants.

Listing 4.10   Creating and populating a file: Windows

```
#include <windows.h>              ◀─────┐ Windows-specific include file

void createFileIfNotExists(const std::string& filename) {
    std::wstring wideFilename = std::wstring(filename.begin(), filename.end());
    if (GetFileAttributesW(wideFilename.c_str()) == INVALID_FILE_ATTRIBUTES) {
        HANDLE hFile = CreateFileW(wideFilename.c_str(), GENERIC_WRITE, 0,
        NULL, CREATE_NEW,                    ┌─ Windows-specific constants
        FILE_ATTRIBUTE_NORMAL, NULL);   ◀────┘
        if (hFile != INVALID_HANDLE_VALUE) {      ◀────┘ Windows-specific usage
            std::wcout << L"File created: " << wideFilename << std::endl;
            const wchar_t* content = L"Hello, world!\r\n";
            DWORD bytesWritten;
            WriteFile(hFile, content, wcslen(content) * sizeof(wchar_t),
                &bytesWritten, NULL);
            CloseHandle(hFile);
        } else
```

```
            std::cerr << "Error creating file: " << filename << std::endl;
    } else
        std::wcout << L"File already exists: " << wideFilename << std::endl;
}
```

Uses wcerr when using wide-character streams

```
int main() {
    createFileIfNotExists("example_file.txt");
    return 0;
}
```

Linux has its share of platform-specific functions and constants, which differ from those used in Windows. This difference is what makes cross-platform handling difficult and error-prone. A programmer specializing in one platform will emit caustic expletives about the wisdom of the other's developers.

Listing 4.11 Creating and populating a file: Linux

```
#include <unistd.h>
#include <fcntl.h>
```
Linux-specific include files

```
void createFileIfNotExists(const std::string& filename) {
    if (access(filename.c_str(), F_OK) == -1) {
        int fd = open(filename.c_str(), O_CREAT | O_WRONLY, S_IRUSR
            | S_IWUSR | S_IRGRP |S_IROTH);
        if (fd != -1) {
            std::cout << "File created: " << filename << std::endl;
            const char* content = "Hello, world!\n";
            write(fd, content, strlen(content));
            close(fd);
        } else
            std::cerr << "Error creating file: " << filename << std::endl;
    } else
        std::cout << "File already exists: " << filename << std::endl;
}

int main() {
    createFileIfNotExists("example_file.txt");
    return 0;
}
```

Linux-specific constants

Linux-specific usage

ANALYSIS

A common approach is using preprocessor directives, which optionally include or exclude code based on the platform. All the code is contained in one source file, and any variations are separated by platform and enabled by #ifdef directives. This has the advantage of simplifying the build process. A single source file is straightforward to write and build; however, duplicating code with optional inclusion is often more challenging to read.

The second approach demonstrated here is to use separate files and determine which is included in the build process by some platform-specific macros or other techniques.

The simplicity of having all the code for one platform in one source file makes reading easier but complicates building.

The main problem is that cross-platform code rarely exists for platform-specific operations, such as filesystem manipulation. Once again, our developer must spend significant time dealing with bugs that do not directly affect the problem being solved but are housekeeping details that, while essential, are typically a pain to manage.

SOLUTION

Modern C++17 has provided a standard set of functions that apply to a filesystem on any conforming platform. The commonality permits straightforward writing of code that performs filesystem functionality in a general manner. The code in listing 4.12 reworks the previous code examples into one general form applicable to Windows and Linux. This solution removes the need for conditional compilation using preprocessor directives or multiple source files to isolate the platform-specific code. Several error-checking tests are performed, since filesystems are notoriously badly behaved under stress (but rarely during development).

Listing 4.12 Creating and populating a file: General

```
namespace fs = std::filesystem;                      A handy way to alias a namespace for simpler
                                                     usage; fs in code aliases std::filesystem
void createFileIfNotExists(const
     std::string& filename) {                        General code that works on
  fs::path filePath = filename;                       both Windows and Linux
  if (fs::exists(filePath)) {
      std::cout << "File already exists: " << filePath << std::endl;
      return;
  }                                                         Time of checking
  std::ofstream file(filePath);
  if (!file) {
      std::cerr << "Error creating file: " << filePath << std::endl;
      return;
  }
  if (!file.is_open()) {
      std::cerr << "File cannot be opened: " << filePath << std::endl;
      return;
  }
  std::cout << "File created: " << filePath << std::endl;
  file << "Hello, world!\n";
}                                                      Time of use

int main() {
    createFileIfNotExists("example_file.txt");
    return 0;
}
```

The generalization of filesystem functionality into a standard header allows developers to focus on solving the problem using filesystem primitives. The simplified abstraction of the filesystem provides all essential functionality in a way that is removed from any specific system. The directive specifies an alias; this form can be used in several contexts (e.g., templates). Here, it simplifies writing `std::filesystem` before the `path` variable and `exists` function; they can be specified with just the `fs` alias and the scope resolution operator (`::`). Nifty!

The code in listing 4.12 has one significant caveat: the example is meant only for single-threaded environments. Concurrency adds complexity, which is not demonstrated in the code. The problem is that another thread could have deleted, updated, or otherwise affected the file's characteristics between the time of checking (TOC) and the time of use (TOU). Naturally, this problem is called *TOCTOU*; it represents a race condition that can trip up the unwary developer.

RECOMMENDATIONS

- Use the new filesystem functionality for file and directory handling.
- Where possible, update existing code to use the new functionality.
- Remember to check for errors after accessing the filesystem; while the code is easier to write, errors still present problems.

4.6 *Mistake 23: Writing excessive standalone functions*

This mistake focuses on both readability and effectiveness; however, there might be a short, steep learning curve to navigate. One-off and infrequently-called functions tend to clutter source code and make finding them distracting.

PROBLEM

Let us assume a case where a developer writes code to manage a typical school in the United States. Several students are attending, and each must be in the database. As with any organization of more than one person, ranking or sorting must be done. Our developer has requirements for ranking students by name, age, and GPA.

The list of students is maintained in a container, for ease of handling. Therefore, some means must be used to iterate over the container and determine the preferred order. Modifying the order within the container is acceptable to keep things simple.

The developer writes three standalone functions to implement the ranking based on the given criteria. The code base is much larger than one can keep in mind. These new functions must be placed somewhere, so they are defined in a file among many other codes, and elsewhere, these functions are invoked to perform their behavior. The following code shows this situation.

Listing 4.13 Several standalone functions

```
class Student {
private:
    std::string name;
    int age;
    double gpa;
public:
    Student(const std::string& n, int a, double g) : name(n), age(a), gpa(g) {}
    std::string getName() const { return name; }
```

```cpp
    int getAge() const { return age; }
    double getGpa() const { return gpa; }
};

// assume lots of code

bool by_name(const Student& s1, const Student& s2)
    { return s1.getName() < s2.getName(); }
bool by_age(const Student& s1, const Student& s2)
    { return s1.getAge() < s2.getAge(); }
bool by_gpa(const Student& s1, const Student& s2)
    { return s1.getGpa() < s2.getGpa(); }

void output_by_student_name(const std::vector<Student>& s) {
    for (int i = 0; i < s.size(); ++i)
        std::cout << s[i].getName() << '\n';
    std::cout << '\n';
}

// assume even more code

int main() {
    std::vector<Student> s;
    s.push_back(Student("Susan", 23, 3.85));
    s.push_back(Student("James", 24, 3.35));
    s.push_back(Student("Annette", 25, 3.75));
    s.push_back(Student("Wilson", 26, 3.8));

    std::sort(s.begin(), s.end(), by_name);
    output_by_student_name(s);

    std::sort(s.begin(), s.end(), by_age);
    output_by_student_name(s);

    std::sort(s.begin(), s.end(), by_gpa);
    output_by_student_name(s);
    return 0;
}
```

Several functions buried in code, used only once

Functions called but no hint of parameters or implementation

ANALYSIS

The naming of the functions results in an easy-to-remember handle to describe their behavior. However, when mixed into other code, their implementation is challenging to keep track of and becomes another thing to remember. Because the definition and call sites are far removed from each other, the developer must remember its implementation details to understand the site's expected behavior fully.

Now, let's make a big assumption: our developer recently had the opportunity to study functional programming. An idea sprang to their mind, thinking that these functions could be reworked into a more functional approach. A new requirement came in, and the developer thought it was the prime opportunity to try creating a functor.

A *functor* is a structure (or class) that implements operator(). This operator has various names, but we will call it the *apply operator* (following functional terminology). The apply operator is a normal function that does a behavior—in this case, determining the maximum element. To implement this, a `Maximum` structure is created to communicate its intent. Its apply operator is implemented to find the maximum value in a vector. Think of the term *apply* in the sense that a function is applied to data; perhaps, this feels backward, but it is the functional way of thinking. Conventional imperative programming thinks more of passing data to a function and performing its behavior; functional programming thinks of impressing or applying a function to data—a more data-centric model.

The code in listing 4.14 shows two implementations of determining the maximum value. The first was what the developer came up with after creating a functor. The instantiation of the functor creates a function object `f`. The application of the function object `f` to the data is achieved conventionally; a parameter list follows the function object, and a result (if any) is returned. The developer's team lead offered another approach, which is shown below the developer's code. The team lead suggested a lambda to simplify the code, eliminate a named functor and its instantiation, and let the reader see the behavior at the call site.

Listing 4.14   Demonstrating an in-place function definition

```
template <typename T>
struct Maximum {                                    Defines the function object
    T operator()(const std::vector<T>& vals) {      class (the functor)
        T max = vals[0];
        for (const auto& v : vals)                  Defines the apply operator
            if (v > max)
                max = v;
        return max;
    }                                               Instantiates the function
};                                                  object class, making a
                                                    function object
int main() {
    std::vector<int> v {3, 9, 6, 2 -1, 0, 8};       Applies the function object
    Maximum<int> f;                                 to the data; invokes the
    std::cout << f(v) << '\n';                       apply operator

    auto max = std::accumulate(v.begin(), v.end(), v[0],
        [](auto a, auto b){return std::max(a, b); });    Uses a numeric algorithm
    std::cout << max << '\n';                            with a local maximum
    return 0;                                            lambda function
}
```

SOLUTION

The team lead demonstrates one of the strengths of lambdas, which is its ability to define a behavior exactly where it is needed. This approach eliminates the scrolling back and hunting for function definitions and the awkwardness of defining functors. The code in listing 4.15 demonstrates the original three functions for ranking students by name, age, or GPA. In this example, the behavior is defined at the point of its use, clearly communicating what is being done. Admittedly, the first few times take longer to write and read, but lambdas become idiomatic and automatic once understood.

Since lambdas are function objects, they can be assigned to a variable, and that variable is passed at the call site. This approach is demonstrated by where GPA ranks students.

> **Listing 4.15 In-place function definitions (lambdas)**

```
class Student {
private:
    std::string name;
    int age;
    double gpa;
public:
    Student(const std::string& n, int a, double g) : name(n), age(a), gpa(g) {}
    std::string getName() const { return name; }
    int getAge() const { return age; }
    double getGpa() const { return gpa; }
};

// assume lots of code

void output_by_student_name(const std::vector<Student>& s) {
    for (int i = 0; i < s.size(); ++i)
        std::cout << s[i].getName() << '\n';
    std::cout << '\n';
}

int main() {
    std::vector<Student> s;
    s.push_back(Student("Susan", 23, 3.85));
    s.push_back(Student("James", 24, 3.35));
    s.push_back(Student("Annette", 25, 3.75));
    s.push_back(Student("Wilson", 26, 3.8));

    std::sort(s.begin(), s.end(),
        [](const Student& s1, const Student& s2){
            return s1.getName() < s2.getName(); });      ← Defines the function
    output_by_student_name(s);                              where it is needed

    std::sort(s.begin(), s.end(),
        [](const Student& s1, const Student& s2){
            return s1.getAge() < s2.getAge(); });       ←
    output_by_student_name(s);

    auto f = [](const Student& s1, const Student& s2) {    Defines the function
        return s1.getGpa() < s2.getGpa(); };              ← just before it is needed
    std::ranges::sort(s, f);                            ←
    output_by_student_name(s);                             Uses ranges and passes the
    return 0;                                              function object as a parameter
}
```

The sorting for the GPA was done slightly differently for name and age. It shows an alternative approach using the ranges API. It is more compact, more readable, and simpler to write. So why wait to start using ranges?

Lambdas are broadly applicable; they shine when one-off and infrequently called functions are distractingly hard to find and remember in the context of the code being written or studied. Lambda functions offer the opportunity to define a function exactly where needed, relieving the developer and maintainer of the need to hunt for its implementation.

Generally, lambdas are best when their functionality is used once; if called several times, assign the lambda to a variable. Of course, the benefits of defining the function where it is needed are lost; as with almost everything, the tradeoff of competing values must be considered.

Recommendations

- Use lambdas for simple, infrequently called functions; the documentation they provide dramatically increases understanding without overloading short-term memory.
- Consider adding lambdas where existing code makes use of simple functions.
- The Standard Template Library has several functions that can be used instead of writing your implementations (e.g., `std::max_element` and `std::less`, `std::sort`).
- Consider using the ranges API to simplify coding and ease reading. The programmer does not have to specify the `begin` or `end` iterators; the range figures this out—just supply the container and a function.

4.7   *Mistake 24: Using awkward constants*

This mistake affects readability, effectiveness, and to a degree, correctness. Constants are essential, but expressing them often leads to difficult-to-read code, truncated values, and inflexible use.

Problem

Many programs must define constants or use functions that convert units by a constant amount. Traditionally, a `#define` or a `const` definition can be used to specify the name and value of a constant or a function, which we use to convert a value from one unit type to another.

The following code shows three examples of using defined constants. The first is the number of seconds in one year (assuming a non-leap year, for simplicity). However, this definition has a problem: it is 10 times too large.

Listing 4.16 Traditional use of constant values

```
const int SEC_PER_YEAR = 315360000;        ◄────    Is this correct, or is
                                                    this 10 times too large?
const double pi = 3.1415927;               ◄────
struct Circle {                                     Stunted approximation
    double radius;
    Circle(double r) : radius(r) {}
    double perimeter() throw() { return 2 * pi * radius; }
```

```
        double area() throw() { return pi * radius * radius; }
};

int main() {
    Circle c(3);
    std::cout << "perimeter " << c.perimeter() << ", area " << c.area() << '\n';

    double rads = 90 * pi / 180;
    std::cout << "90 degrees is " << rads << " radians\n";

    std::cout << "There are " << SEC_PER_YEAR << " seconds in a year\n";
    return 0;
}
```

An inflexible approach, only good for 90 degrees

ANALYSIS

It is easy to make a mistake when defining the first constant. The developer had difficulty distinguishing the number of zeros, and an extra one was erroneously added. The second is the truncated value of `pi`. The developer wrote a reasonable approximation for many uses, which is relatively imprecise given what the data type can represent. Finally, converting 90 degrees to radians is inflexible—it works for only 90 degrees. A function would have been better.

SOLUTION

Modern C++ provides relief for all three of these problems. The value of `pi` will be addressed first. Rather than the developer creating some approximation, the `numbers` header defines this value and several others. The system architecture is considered for these values, and the best value is chosen; there is no need to handwrite them again.

The definition of the seconds per year is improved using a thousand separator. The apostrophe separates a constant value into groups that approximate how they are read in books or articles. Commas are already defined as operators, so a similar symbol was chosen. Using it simplifies counting the number of zeros (in this case) and makes errors much more apparent.

Finally, converting degrees to radians uses user-defined literals (UDL). The `operator""` is a function that takes a parameter value and performs a conversion on it. The result is a readable usage that handles any legitimate value.

Listing 4.17 Improved use of constant values

```
constexpr double operator"" _deg_in_rad(long double d) {
    return d * std::numbers::pi / 180;
}

constexpr int SEC_PER_YEAR = 31'536'000;

struct Circle {
    double radius;
    Circle(double r) : radius(r) {}
    double perimeter() noexcept { return 2 *
        std::numbers::pi * radius; }
```

A user-defined literal that does conversions

Nicely separated digits that are easy to read

As good an approximation as the architecture can make

```
        double area() noexcept { return std::numbers::pi * radius * radius; }
};

int main() {
    Circle c(3);
    std::cout << "perimeter " << c.perimeter() << ", area " << c.area()
        << '\n';

    std::cout << "90 degrees is " << 90.0_deg_in_rad << " radians\n";

    std::cout << "There are " << SEC_PER_YEAR << " seconds in a year\n";
    return 0;
}
```

Defining constants is often a necessity. The available modern C++ techniques make code more readable and straightforward to implement.

RECOMMENDATIONS

- Use a thousand separator to break up long sequences of digits.
- Use `operator""` to effortlessly convert one unit to another; a literal can be created for any data type—check out `std::chrono`, which has strongly typed `minutes`, `hours`, and more, demonstrating this powerful concept.
- Use constants defined in the `numbers` header to simplify usage and obtain the best approximations for your system.

4.8   *Mistake 25: Writing pattern-matching code*

This mistake affects effectiveness and correctness but is a negative for readability. Pattern matching in string data is typical; pattern-matching code is laborious and complicated to get just right.

PROBLEM

A frequent problem is the parsing of textual data. Input is entered as string data, and information read from a file is often textual. When the required data type is a string, this works nicely, but in many cases, the text needs to be validated or broken apart into constituent parts. Code that analyzes the data for correct format, contents, or similar is challenging in all but the most straightforward cases. Listing 4.18 demonstrates the validation of an email address. The rule is that a single word (username) is separated by an at sign (@), followed by another single word (domain) separated by a period, followed by another word (top-level domain). The code checks for these two separators and three words, where a word is a single letter or more (just not including at signs or periods). If anything is amiss, the email address is considered invalid.

> **Listing 4.18   Handcoded email validation function (with bugs)**

```
bool isValidEmail(const std::string& e) {
    size_t pos_at = e.find('@');                    ◄─── Parse separator
    if (pos_at == std::string::npos)  // no '@' found
        return false;
```

```
    if (pos_at == 0)  // no first word          ◄──────────────┐  Parse word
        return false;
    size_t pos_period = e.find('.', pos_at);  ◄─────┘  Parse separator
    if (pos_period == std::string::npos)  // no '.' found
        return false;
    if (pos_at + 1 >= pos_period)  // no middle word      ◄──────┐
        return false;
    if (pos_period == e.length() - 1)  // no last word    ◄──────┘
        return false;
    return true;
}

int main() {
    std::cout << isValidEmail("prof@nu.edu") << '\n';
    return 0;
}
```

ANALYSIS

The code determines the presence of characters (any characters, even invalid ones) composing the username, domain, and top-level domain. The at sign and a period must separate these. There is imprecision in this matching, but it correctly parses the form without checking for validity beyond that. Malicious or erroneous code can slip a bad email address past this checking. Imagine enhancing this code to ensure the proper set of letters, digits, and punctuation for the username and, similarly—without punctuation—for the two domain sections. As previously stated, writing your parser is difficult. Further, to understand the code, it is essential to document it heavily with comments. Comments have the nasty habit of becoming stale or wrong after the first maintenance of the code.

SOLUTION

Textual pattern matching was added in modern C++ by including the `regex` header. *Regular expressions* are a type of computing machine, the simplest kind recognized. Usually, they are implemented by a state machine, and each letter (symbol) causes a transition from one state to another. If the pattern matches, it is considered accepted. Listing 4.19 shows that behavior in action. We see five essential parts, starting from the pattern's left and moving to the right:

1 The username, composed of one or more letters, digits, and limited punctuation
2 The at sign separator
3 The domain, composed of one or more letters or digits
4 The period (notice the backslash escape before it)
5 The top-level domain, composed of two or more letters

This parser pattern is more precise than the code in listing 4.17 because it ensures that the top-level domain has at least two letters (technically, a top-level domain could have one character, but none are registered yet; see http://data.iana.org/TLD/tlds-alpha -by-domain.txt for the current list). Also, the username and the domains are validated to include only allowable symbols. This precision makes a significant difference in correctness.

Listing 4.19   Using a regular expression for email validation

```
bool isValidEmail(const std::string& e) {
    std::regex pattern(
        R"([a-zA-Z0-9._%+-][CA}+@[a-zA-Z0-9.-]+\.[a-zA-Z]{2,})");
    return std::regex_search(e, pattern);
}

int main() {
    std::cout << isValidEmail("prof@nu.edu") << '\n';
    return 0;
}
```

A five-section regular
expression for matching
an email address

Another demonstrated feature is a raw string. A raw string starts with `R"(` and is terminated with `)"`. Its purpose is to express—usually a regular expression pattern—without having to escape any characters. A sharp-eyed reader will notice an escaped character in the regular expression; that escape is an essential part of the regular expression. Usually, a period matches a single character (except a new line). It must be escaped to tell the regular expression to match a period.

When escaping (non-raw strings) is needed, the regular expression is even more challenging to read because the pattern must be distinguished from the characters that generally control C++ formatting. A simple example shows the benefit clearly. Assume that a double backslash was being matched. With escape characters, the pattern would be the following:

```
std::string pattern = "\\\\";
```

With a raw string, it would be

```
std::string pattern = R"(\\)";
```

The latter shows precisely what is being matched, and the former buries it in escape characters. Convinced?

Regular expressions are designed to match textual patterns. Their language is complex and takes effort to learn, but developers find that effort well worth the price. Once somewhat understood, a pattern is quick to write, simple to test, and compact in expression. Significantly more power is available using regular expressions. Parts of the matched pattern can be extracted, such as the username or all three portions. Substitution of text with a new value can be achieved using regular expressions.

RECOMMENDATIONS

- It is worth the effort to learn and use regular expressions; it is challenging to ensure the correctness of bespoke textual pattern-matching code.
- Regular expressions are highly expressive but are challenging to read and write; test them thoroughly with every variation of data you can think of.

Part 2

Transitional C++

A significant aspect of transitional C++ is the persistence of C-influenced idioms. While these habits were once nearly indispensable, introducing modern C++ features has rendered them obsolete. Many of these habits are carried into current work, introducing potential inefficiencies and pitfalls to contemporary development. By identifying and replacing these outdated practices with modern alternatives, developers can clean up their code bases and leverage the full capabilities of C++, enhancing both code clarity and effectiveness.

While the legacy of C and early C++ programming still lingers in many code bases, these design choices and paradigms no longer align with best practices. These once-best-in-class approaches need reassessment in light of new techniques and language features. Transitioning from C and early C++ to modern practices involves refactoring code to adhere to current standards resulting in improved maintainability, readability, and efficiency. This modernization effort ensures applications meet today's expectations and performance standards and remain adaptable to future advancements.

C idioms

This chapter covers

- An overview of macros
- Using specific macros
- C-style strings
- Incorrect data types for Boolean values

C was the main predecessor of C++, and its influence is felt across a broad range of projects. Many early adopters of C++ were C programmers looking for a "better C." C++ provided compatibility with C with few exceptions. Those exceptions were necessary for better type checking, correctness, and language consistency.

However, there are many areas where C coding never changed, even after the advent of C++. Many programmers learned styles and techniques in C and carried them forward to C++. The compiler rarely complained about any of these approaches. The resulting code compiled and ran—what more could have been expected? However, this transition did not necessarily mean developers began shedding the C idioms and adopting a C++ approach. Much code was written without regard to new ways of expressing the same intent.

Over the intervening years, C++ and C began to diverge more and more. The C99 standard clarified and standardized C, while picking up a few things from C++; C++ adopted some of the innovations of C. The two languages are still separate, but each has fertilized the other.

The divergence of languages sets up a set of problems and mistakes that characterize C orientation in C++ code. These mistakes are primarily benign because the code works, but the style is more difficult to read and write, and the effort to maintain C-style code is more significant than it should be.

This chapter covers several problems that persist in code bases written in C++ by C developers. Even though a better approach exists, a developer must adopt it to solve these problems. To improve C++ code, it is essential to understand the influence of C and how to correct for common misapplications of its backward compatibility with C. The next chapter continues this theme but focuses on misapplying C++ constructs, often coded under the influence (of C).

5.1   *Mistake 26: Always declaring variables at the top of a function*

This mistake affects correctness, readability, and effectiveness, respectively. C required all variables to be declared at the top of a function; developers usually initialize them there.

PROBLEM

Many languages demand all variables to be declared, and sometimes defined, at the top of a function. This was a concession to the compiler, not the developer's needs, and there are a few problems associated with this practice. First, when all variables are declared at the top of the function, the reader and developer must refer to the top to see the names, remember their meaning, and see where the variable is used. This approach requires a cognitive load that may prove burdensome. Second, the developer must determine the variable's initialization before it is used; for expedience's sake, this initialization is likely to be a simple value (often zero) but does not necessarily reflect the proper value on which later code depends. However, if the programmer takes time to initialize the value correctly, the reader may only understand why much later. Maintenance programmers may need to change this value later, introducing problems. Finally, these initialization values may often appear to be magic numbers; why should 1 be initialized to 0, 1, or an (apparently) arbitrary value?

Listing 5.1 demonstrates some of these problems. The developer needed to initialize the max variable, but with a knee-jerk value of 0, it computes the wrong answer because of this poor initialization. Further, the pos variable is used in the code before the loop and is left with some value. The original code assumed pos would be initialized (somewhere) and used correctly in the loop. A later developer overlooked this undocumented assumption and used the "perfectly good" variable for a different purpose.

Listing 5.1   Declaring variables at the top of the function

```
int maximum(const std::vector<int>& values) {
    int max = 0;
```

The variable is initialized with a poor choice.

```
    int pos;                                    ←── There is no initialization; it is
                                                     assumed this will occur later.
    // assume code here that uses pos ...
    pos = 1;                                    ←── The ending value of some
    // assume more code here...                      computation added later
    for (; pos < values.size(); ++pos)  ←──
        if (values[pos] > max)                   pos is used with the
            max = values[pos];                   assumption that its
    return max;                                  value is meaningful.
}

int main() {
    std::vector<int> values;
    values.push_back(1);
    values.push_back(-2);
    values.push_back(-3);
    std::cout << maximum(values) << '\n';
    return 0;
}
```

ANALYSIS

The separation between the declaration of the variable and its use allows strange things to happen to the variable before its intended use. The pos variable was a good choice for some additional computation, but it was left in a state that was not appropriate for the loop. The initialization of the max variable used a value that is often correct and appropriate, but every problem can use this initial value. Because all the tested values in the vector were negative, none was larger than the wrongly initialized value. This mistake introduces a foreign value not contained in the container as its maximum.

SOLUTION

Consider declaring a variable just before it is used—keep the distance between declaration, definition, and usage as small as possible. In some cases (the for loop), a variable may be declared in the structure's scope, ensuring it is visible only there (modern C++ permits this in if statements).

Initializing variables is an interesting exercise. Many students tend to initialize variables by always using the zero value. In many cases, this is appropriate, but not all. This subset of problems where zero is wrong will cause subtle problems. The maximum function in listing 5.2 demonstrates this by searching for a maximum value in a set of negative values. For some reason, too many developers consider only positive values when they write code. Integer and real numbers have a nasty habit of being negative too often to ignore. Before scanning through a collection of values, a simple initialization approach is to copy the first element's value to the variable and compare other values. This approach ensures the variable is initialized with actual data, not a value the developer assumes. As previously mentioned, initializing with a developer-chosen value may use one that does not exist within the data set, causing a correctness error.

Listing 5.2   Declaring variables at the point of need

```
int maximum(const std::vector<int>& values) {
    // assume code here...
    int max = values[0];
    for (int pos = 1; pos < values.size(); ++pos)
        if (values[pos] > max)
            max = values[pos];
    return max;
}

int main() {
    std::vector<int> values;
    values.push_back(1);
    values.push_back(-2);
    values.push_back(-3);
    std::cout << maximum(values) << '\n';
    return 0;
}
```

Initializes the variable with one of the collection values

Limits the scope of the loop control variable to the loop

Remembering the meaning and value of variables is critical for readability and reasoning about code. Declaring variables exactly where needed and initializing them just before usage simplifies the reader's cognitive load.

RECOMMENDATIONS

- Limit the scope of every variable; when declared, initialize it immediately with a meaningful value.
- Use the ability to declare variables in `for` loop scope and any other constructs that permit this approach (modern C++ has added more opportunities).

SEE ALSO

- See Mistake 10 for the modern C++ answer to variable scope.
- See Mistake 60 for a discussion of this problem in the context of a class.

5.2   *Mistake 27: Depending on macros*

This mistake affects correctness; readability; effectiveness; and, sometimes, performance. Macros are a means to add information to the program source without being directly checked by the compiler. The text of the macro is checked when the affected source is compiled. This implies some mistakes may be unapparent; difficult to debug; and, worst of all, almost always work except in the most critical situations.

PROBLEM

The code in listing 5.3 introduces a few difficulties with C++ macros—many more exist. Often, macros are meant to define literal values by giving them a meaningful name that documents their use in the program.

Another use is to produce function-like structures that document their use. As with most functions, parameters may be needed. The macro can handle parameters nicely, so using them is tempting.

Further, macros can reduce coding effort by defining a significant portion of the repetitive code in one symbol. The following code attempts to minimize the effort required to code a `for` loop by specifying the initialization, continuation, and update sections in one symbol. With all these (apparent) advantages, it might appear alarmist to recommend using them rarely, if ever.

Listing 5.3 Using macros to define, reduce, and add types

```
#define PI 3.1415927
#define SQUARE(n) n * n
#define FOR(a, b) for (i = a; i < b; ++i);
#define FALSE 0
#define TRUE !FALSE

int main() {
    int n = 3;
    std::cout << SQUARE(n) << '\n';
    std::cout << SQUARE(n + (n - 1)) << '\n';
    std::cout << SQUARE(++n) << '\n';

    int i;
    FOR(0, 10)
        std::cout << i << '\n';

    int truth = FALSE;
    ++truth;
    ++truth;

    if (truth == FALSE)
        std::cout << "smooth\n";
    else
        std::cout << "dismay\n";
    return 0;
}
```

Introduces a literal value with no specific type

A function-like construct for easy computation

Reduces coding effort by defining most of a structure but has a bug

Another untyped value

The developer is trying to toggle truth values.

ANALYSIS

The single-most-apparent problem with macros is that they are substituted into the code before any compilation occurs; the preprocessor does a textual substitution where they are found and inserts the literal macro definition at that point. If an error is made in the macro, the compiler will likely find it later and issue some wacky message that is not readily associated with the source code. What is compiled is different from what was written. This situation causes some difficulty during debugging.

The code in listing 5.3 has several problems related to macro use. First, PI has no specific type. It would often default to `double`, which is likely correct; however, this might prove incorrect in rare cases, and the compiler might wrongly determine what is meant.

Second, the SQUARE macro looks good, but danger lurks within. The first invocation squares a value that works correctly. The second invocation falters because the code within the invocation is substituted twice in the macro expansion. What should be 5 × 5 turns out to be 3 + 2 × 3 + 2 because the invocation expressions are not evaluated, merely substituted. The third invocation results in the expression ++n * ++n, where n is 5 after squaring.

Third, the FOR macro has an error. The for loop header ends in a semicolon, meaning there is no loop body (actually, it has a null loop body). Therefore, the code that follows the macro is standalone and is executed just once, not the expected 10 times. Further, note that the loop control variable must be defined before the FOR macro; this must be clear to prevent misunderstanding.

Fourth, the attempt to define a Boolean data type works to a degree; it intends to use only the values of TRUE and FALSE, and the developer demonstrates the expectation of toggling between them. Regrettably, since an int data type represents the Boolean values, incrementing adds 1 to the value; it does not toggle. The expected and actual behavior are mismatched. Using a macro tricks the mind into "seeing" Boolean constraints where the compiler is blissfully unaware of any.

SOLUTION

These errors are resolved using C++ language features, which ensures the compiler is involved at every step and emits an error when usage is wrong. The literal value for PI is defined as a double value. This type is likely correct in most cases, but the developer must confirm. If the compiler finds a mismatch, it will emit an error, and the developer can reevaluate their assumptions. Modern C++ gives us the constexpr form, which mitigates any such problems. These expressions are evaluated during compilation and are guaranteed to be of the correct type.

Second, a new function named square is created. It is built as a template, since it is uncertain what data type is needed. The compiler will deduce the proper parameter type and substitute that type for the parameter and the return type. This approach ensures the correct code is used without implicit type conversions that may affect precision and performance.

Third, the FOR macro is eliminated, and the for loop is used. The macro did not reduce coding much but introduced an odd scope for the loop control variable. Defining the loop control variable in the loop header controls its scope to only the loop, providing better readability and correctness.

Fourth, the oddly implemented Boolean value is replaced with the C++-provided truth type bool. Mistakes in toggling the variable are detected, and errors are emitted, requiring the developer to resolve the bug. The type must be used according to definition, and assumptions must match behavior.

Listing 5.4   Using C++ constructs to replace macro usage

```
const double PI = 3.1415927;          ◄──────    Using named constants
                                                   documents code well.
template <typename T>                 ◄──────
T square(T n) {
    return n * n;                               Templates allow one to infer the
}                                               parameter and return type.

int main() {
```

```
int n = 3;
std::cout << square(n) << '\n';
std::cout << square(n + (n - 1)) << '\n';      Argument expressions are
std::cout << square(++n) << '\n';              evaluated before calling.

for( int i = 0; i < 10; ++ i)                  The scope of the variable
    std::cout << i << '\n';                     is limited to the loop.

bool truth = false;
truth = !truth;                                Toggling of the truth value
truth = !truth;                                is limited to the data type.

if (truth == false)
    std::cout << "smooth\n";
else
    std::cout << "dismay\n";
return 0;
}
```

Several other problems could have been demonstrated, but these are sufficient to suggest that macros are more dangerous than helpful. Plenty of posts on the internet argue macros are fine to use in C++, and within a limited approach, this advice is accurate. However, in reality, macros should not be considered universally safe but, rather, safe to use *sometimes*.

The only place where I agree that using macros is generally appropriate is in those already existing (unfortunate) code bases with conditional compilation requirements. In this case, code varying between one conditional section and another should be excised and placed into functions within a header file. Then, use conditional compilation to select between the functions.

RECOMMENDATIONS

- Limit or eliminate macros to stay safe and produce predictable code.
- Use C++ features that provide the anticipated benefit of a macro; the compiler can error-check these and emit meaningful messages.

5.3   *Mistake 28: Misunderstanding NULL*

This mistake affects readability and, sometimes, effectiveness. Misunderstanding the NULL macro can lead to problems with correctness.

PROBLEM

The general advice is to avoid macros whenever possible. This advice is essential because the NULL macro value and type are uncertain. This code was written on a 64-bit architecture, where the size of a pointer is 64 bits, which is also the size of a long. Your system may have different sizes and a different definition of NULL. The definition in unicode/utypes.h on my system is as follows:

```
#define NULL    ((void *)0)
```

Consider listing 5.5, where NULL is used in two ways, neither of which being obvious. The first overloaded compute function in the following listing takes a long value, while the second takes a long pointer. The first call to compute passes a long initialized to NULL. The obvious choice for the call is to match the first function. The second call passes the NULL value, which should match the second compute function.

Listing 5.5   Misusing NULL in two ways

```
long compute(long n) {  // increment the value
    return ++n;
}

long compute(long* p) {  // increment valid dereferenced pointer value
    if (p)
        return ++*p;
    return 0;
}

int main() {
    long x = NULL;
    long n = compute(x);
    std::cout << n << '\n';
    n = compute(NULL);
    std::cout << n << '\n';
    return 0;
}
```

Uses NULL as an integral zero value, which is bad form

The long value should match the first function.

The NULL pointer should match the second function.

ANALYSIS

The code seems to call the first and then the second function; however, this is incorrect. The first call matches the long value (first function), and the second call also matches the long value (first function). Is this unobvious? The NULL macro reads as "a pointer that references no valid memory object." The code in listing 5.5 uses a definition of NULL that is a long integer value of zero; it is *not* a pointer. But that is part of the problem with this macro; it reads like a pointer and is used as a pointer, yet it is not a pointer. A reader easily can be misled.

Further, different compilers on differing architectures may define NULL differently. Therefore, any "valid" use on one system does not necessarily apply to another. If developers use NULL on their system, they may assume another system will work identically. They would be wrong. NULL has no definitive definition, making it problematic to use consistently. Its natural semantics are incorrect in systems that do not define it as a pointer (C did define it as a pointer). Some implementations define NULL as an integral value of zero, whose size matches a pointer size. But can you be certain without checking?

The very first line of code uses NULL as a zero value. This may seem like a contrived bug that's used exclusively for teaching purposes, but rest assured, this happens often enough that some (perhaps most) compilers detect and warn about this incorrect usage. I have seen this in a code base as an initializer and parameter value where zero was needed—horrible!

SOLUTION

First and foremost, do not use NULL as a slick zero value. Second, be aware that NULL is not a pointer and cannot be used as one. The ideal premodern C++ way to describe a pointer that refers to no valid memory object is to use the zero value. If a developer wants to use NULL to implement a pointer, it must be cast to a pointer of the proper size. The one advantage of using NULL is that it communicates pointer semantics better than the zero value.

Listing 5.6 Using NULL in a better way

```cpp
long compute(long n) {  // increment the value
    return ++n;
}

long compute(long* p) {  // increment the value
    if (p)
        return ++*p;
    return 0;
}

int main() {
    long m = 0;
    long n = compute(m);
    std::cout << n << '\n';
    n = compute((long*)NULL);
    std::cout << n << '\n';
    return 0;
}
```

Uses zero where a zero value is needed

Matches the first function, preserving value semantics

Matches the second function, preserving pointer semantics

The NULL macro clearly states the intent of assigning a pointer, which is the value that states it does not point to any object. However, using the zero value to eliminate the oddities when converting the macro is better.

Modern C++ provides a language keyword to address the shortcomings of the NULL macro or zero value. The following snippet shows how to properly assign a pointer variable to the null value. The nullptr keyword is a pointer literal, so no games are being played or implicit conversions occurring:

```cpp
long* p = new long(42);
...
delete p;
p = nullptr;
```

RECOMMENDATIONS

- Use the zero value to declare a pointer that refers to no valid memory object.
- Avoid using NULL as a zero value anywhere.
- Avoid using NULL as a pointer; it is not one.

SEE ALSO

- See Mistake 7 for an extensive discussion on using this keyword.

5.4   *Mistake 29: Accessing disk files using FILE*

This mistake affects effectiveness and readability. Developers have been using the C FILE object for years, but it is often more complex than preferred.

PROBLEM

Quite often, developers need to open files and read lines of text, and the C FILE object has been used extensively for this purpose in C++ code. The code in the following listing shows a common approach that attempts to open the file; tests if this assumption is accurate; and, if so, proceeds to read the file line by line.

Listing 5.7   Reading lines of text using FILE

```
const int SIZE = 100;                        ◄─── Hopefully, each line will be
int main() {                                      99 characters or less.
    FILE* file;
    file = fopen("data.txt", "r");
    if (!file) {                             ◄─── The first use of
        std::cerr << "Error opening file\n";      negative logic
        return 1;
    }
    char buffer[SIZE];
    while (!feof(file)) {
        if (!fgets(buffer, SIZE, file))      ◄─── Negative logic and,
            break;                                hopefully, a full-line read
        std::cout << buffer;
    }
    return 0;
}
```

ANALYSIS

The code in listing 5.7 works well and achieves the purpose for which it was written. But is it clear? The code uses negative logic in three places: testing for a successfully opened file, testing for the end-of-line condition, and testing whether a line has been read. Negative logic is always more cognitively expensive than positive logic. The load increases when negative logic is nested, as in this example. Further, it is harder to write negative logic. What would seem to be the natural approach must be inverted, and the resultant flow must be held in short-term memory.

Another problem with the code is the line length. The code assumes no line will be longer than 99 characters. Is this a reasonable assumption? No matter what value is used, the likelihood exists that it will either be too small, leading to multiple reads per line, or too large, leading to inefficient memory use.

Although not technically an error, the buffer definition should be one character larger to anticipate the end-of-line character. Assuming a line of text was exactly SIZE characters, the end-of-line character would be read on the next iteration of the loop. This approach is a slight hit to performance because each line should take one read operation. Still, there is no good definition for SIZE; only workable ones exist.

Finally, the FILE object remains open. A long-running program with this bug could negatively affect system resources and, potentially, lead to resource exhaustion.

SOLUTION

These problems can be solved using a C++ std::ifstream object. There is no negative logic in listing 5.8, leading to easier writing and reading. The lack of negative logic means the code reads as straightforward. If the input file is not opened, the test for failure reads naturally.

This solution has no buffer; instead, a std::string object is used. Whatever size is needed for each input line is the length of the line variable. Further, as each line is created, no previous data exists in the string. Buffers were always vulnerable to extra data when partial reads were performed.

The std::ifstream object goes out of scope at the end of the main function. This fact ensures the file will be closed. This is an excellent example of the RAII pattern where a constructor–destructor pair manages a dynamic resource. It is OK to close the stream, but it is unnecessary. This approach simplifies writing and reading. The developer must ensure the automatic destruction is documented; otherwise, it is their best guess as to what happens. The Standard Template Library is excellent in this respect.

Listing 5.8   Reading lines of text using `ifstream`

```
int main() {
    std::ifstream file("data.txt");
    if (file.fail()) {                      ◄──┐ Positive logic makes
        std::cerr << "Error opening file\n";    │ reading and writing easier.
        return 1;
    }
    std::string line;
    while (std::getline(file, line))        ◄──┐ More positive logic and no
        std::cout << line << '\n';              │ overwriting of old data
    return 0;
}
```

The std::ifstream approach is a simple way to read textual data and test the stream for errors that affect its operation. This approach is superior to the FILE* approach, inherited from C.

RECOMMENDATIONS

- Use the std::ifstream and std::ofstream objects to simplify reading and writing data to files.
- Use positive logic where possible.

SEE ALSO

- See Mistake 77 for a discussion of the RAII pattern.

5.5   *Mistake 30: Using integers for Boolean values*

This mistake affects correctness and readability. C did not provide a data type representing Boolean values; C++ added one later. Early code had to use the concept and usually implemented it as an integer.

PROBLEM

Using an integer to capture the value of FALSE and TRUE makes sense; 0 means FALSE, and 1 means TRUE (actually, anything nonzero serves as TRUE). Listing 5.9 suggests this concept and shows some code that uses the idea. Making the definitions constant is essential so that the truth values cannot be changed (George Orwell might protest in support of his concept in *1984*). Naturally, since a Boolean value is implemented as an integer, anything an integer can do, a Boolean variable can as well. This leads to some strange code.

Listing 5.9   Simulating Boolean values in an integer

```
const int TRUE = 1;
const int FALSE = 0;
int main() {
    int truth = FALSE;
    std::cout << "truth is " << (truth ? "real" : "illusory") << "\n";
    ++truth;
    std::cout << "truth is " << (truth ? "real" : "illusory") << "\n";
    truth = 42;
    std::cout << "truth is " << (truth ? "real" : "illusory") << "\n";
    return 0;
}
```

> What would incrementing a Boolean mean?

> What does assigning something other than FALSE or TRUE mean?

Many early programmers discovered that the intent of a Boolean value was better implemented by using an enumeration. This approach limits the operations performed on a variable representing the Boolean value. The following code demonstrates this approach.

Listing 5.10   Simulating Boolean values with an enumeration

```
enum BOOL { FALSE, TRUE };
int main() {
    BOOL truth = FALSE;
    std::cout << "truth is " << (truth ? "real" : "illusory") << "\n";
    truth = TRUE;
    std::cout << "truth is " << (truth ? "real" : "illusory") << "\n";
    return 0;
}
```

> Assignment is limited to FALSE and TRUE.

ANALYSIS

The main problem with representing a Boolean value as any data type other than a Boolean is that of intent. An integer representation permits operations that have no meaning but are legal. The enumeration solution is much better and offers a much more restricted set of operations. The main problem with the enumeration solution is that it is not standard, and not all developers would necessarily implement it this way. The lack of a common understanding makes this otherwise excellent solution less than ideal.

SOLUTION

The C++ language developers recognized the problem with the two aforementioned solutions and added a `bool` data type. It represents a Boolean value that should be clearer in its intent and content. Their intent was right, but the implementation could have been more successful. A `bool` is a data type, but compilers implement `bool`s as integers, which allows for nefarious operations such as those in listing 5.9. The language standard does not define behavior for values other than 0 or 1; anything else is undefined behavior. However, this definition does not prevent misuse. The fact that a separate data type is provided documents the purpose and intent of the variable but does not enforce strict semantics when abused. This situation is one we must accept as it is.

As of C++17, the ability to increment a `bool` variable was removed; this change improves the correctness of the set of operations of the data type. The following code shows the usage of a `bool` variable, which should take only `false` and `true` values. Don't assign anything else, or your readers will think poorly of you—for shame!

Listing 5.11   Using the `bool` data type

```cpp
int main() {
    bool truth = false;
    std::cout << "truth is " << (truth ? "real" : "illusory") << "\n";
    ++truth;
    std::cout << "truth is " << (truth ? "real" : "illusory") << "\n";
    truth = 42;
    std::cout << "truth is " << (truth ? "real" : "illusory") << "\n";
    return 0;
}
```

The `bool` data type must be used per its defined set of operations and represent only Boolean values. Any other use should be avoided.

RECOMMENDATIONS

- Use the provided `bool` data type for truth concepts; it works and documents the intent well.
- Do not assign anything other than the values `false` and `true` to a `bool` variable.
- If possible, compile at C++17 or above for even better `bool` semantics.

5.6   *Mistake 31: Using C-style casts*

This mistake affects correctness and readability with a slight negative hit on effectiveness. However, the preferred casting benefits are well worth the extra keystrokes. The negative hit to effectiveness is intentional; C++-style casts are big, ugly, and hard to write, suggesting they should be used advisedly and carefully.

PROBLEM

There are four primary situations when a cast is necessary:

- Getting around constant limitations
- Reinterpreting underlying data as a new type
- Converting one type into another type
- Downcasting a base pointer to a derived pointer

The C-style cast can complete all four behaviors without causing compilation problems. However, a successful compilation is different from a meaningful compilation. Consider the code in listing 5.12. The first part casts around the character array's constness and allows data modification. The second part considers an integer value to be a sequence of characters. The third is a character array masquerading as a double pointer, which makes no sense (except for those doing marshaling and unmarshaling, who have no meaningful option). The fourth takes a base class object and treats it as a derived object.

Listing 5.12   Using C-style casts prolifically and dangerously

```
struct B {
    virtual int compute() { return 0; }
};
struct D : public B {
    int n;
    D() : n(42) {}
    int compute() { return n; }
};

int main() {
    const char msg[] = "Hello, world";
    char* p = (char*)msg;                            ◄──┐ Bypasses the const nature
    *(p+1) = 'a';                                        │ of the character array
    std::cout << msg << '\n';

    int n = 0x2A2A2A2A;
    char* c = (char*)(&n);                           ◄──┐ Considers an integer as
    for (int i = 0; i < sizeof(int); ++i)                │ a collection of bytes
        std::cout << *(c+i);
    std::cout << '\n';

    std::cout << *((double*)msg) << '\n';            ◄──┐ This has no meaning,
                                                         │ but it compiles cleanly.
    B* b = new B();
    D* d = (D*)b;                                     ◄──┐ A D is a B, but a B
    std::cout << d->compute() << '\n';                   │ may not be a D.

    return 0;
}
```

ANALYSIS

The first problem violates the semantics of the data type and should rarely be done. The compiler does not see a bug by default but can be configured to do so. This "looseness" lets the programmer do whatever they wish with the data.

The second problem is "clever" but usually a stretch; while it works, better types and designs are called for. The third mistake is an abomination, where semantics is completely violated—the two types are incompatible and nontranslatable, yet this code compiles, resulting in undefined behavior. Finally, the fourth problem may have applications (rarely) and is dangerous when done this way. The virtual function in the derived class is not called correctly, and if it were, a nonexistent instance variable would be accessed—undefined behavior!

SOLUTION

Each cast situation demands something more meaningful than a simple C-style cast. Two central problems exist with the C-style cast: first, the programmer's intent needs to be communicated, and second, some conversions need to be clarified. C++-style casts are intentionally long and feel clumsy, but they document intent well and make the developer think twice about using one. Usually, better-designed code can eliminate the need for casts, but in the few cases where they are necessary (expedient?), use the provided versions.

The `const_cast` intentionally subtracts (or adds, if not already constant) the `const`ness of an entity. This cast is often necessary when mixing C and C++ code—use it responsibly.

The `reinterpret_cast` should be used very sparingly. This cast tells the compiler to ignore what it knows about the pointed-to data (its type) and pretend that it is the to cast-to type; it is a case of "pretending." The compiler capitulates to the programmer's wishes but assumes no responsibility for results. Writing and reading binary files with numeric data is a case where this comes in handy. The cast documents the intent well.

The `static_cast` transforms one compatible data type into another. The compiler checks the compatibility of data types; if incompatible, an error is emitted. Of all the casts, this is the most likely to be needed. For example, truncating a double value to an integer is quickly achieved with this cast.

Finally, the `dynamic_cast` transforms a base class pointer or reference to a derived class pointer or reference. If this technique is used, ensure there is at least one virtual method (don't inherit without one!); otherwise, there is no canonical means for storing the class type used for downcasting. The result of the cast is checked at run time, making it possible to compile cleanly yet crash while running. The result of a compatible cast is a pointer, while the result of an incompatible cast is a null pointer; however, developers should be highly reluctant to take this approach. If a reference is cast and fails, an exception is thrown. C++ provides better mechanisms for this, especially inheritance with polymorphic behavior.

Listing 5.13   Using C++-style casts more reservedly and responsibly

```
struct B {
    virtual int compute() { return 0; }
};
struct D : public B {
    int n;
    D() : n(42) {}
    int compute() { return n; }
};

int main() {
    const char msg[] = "Hello, world";
    char* p = const_cast<char*>(msg);
    *(p+1) = 'a';
    std::cout << msg << '\n';

    int n = 0x2A2A2A2A;
    char* c = reinterpret_cast<char*>(&n);
    for (int i = 0; i < sizeof(int); ++i)
        std::cout << *(c+i);
    std::cout << '\n';

    // std::cout << static_cast<double*>(msg) << '\n';
    std::cout << static_cast<double>(n) << '\n';

    B* b = new B();
    D* d = dynamic_cast<D*>(b);
    if (d)
        std::cout << d->compute() << '\n';
    else
        std::cout << "incompatible downcast\n";

    return 0;
}
```

◄─── Assuming this is correct and the intent is well documented

◄─── Another strange case with well-documented intent

◄─── The compiler determines that the types are incompatible.

◄─── A reasonable conversion of types

If it is compatible, the pointer will be valid and NULL (nullptr) if not.

C-style casts and `reinterpret_casts` can be the source of undefined behavior if misused. Consider redesigning the code if you find that casting is necessary. If a cast must be used, do so only when the conversions are as safe as you know how to make them.

RECOMMENDATIONS

- Avoid casting where possible.
- Use a `const_cast` when interfacing C++ code with C functions.
- Check the result of a `dynamic_cast` to ensure that the pointers are compatible.
- Think carefully before using a `reinterpret_cast`; not all architectures represent data in the same way, making the conversion open to differing results; it is easy to stumble into a pit of undefined behavior doing this.

5.7   *Mistake 32: Converting text with atoi*

This mistake focuses primarily on correctness and includes a healthy dose of readability and effectiveness. Keyboard input is always done as a stream of characters; however, these characters have no inherent meaning. In other words, there is no context by which to know what their data type should be. Conversion functions coerce this context.

C provides conversion functions for data types not directly converted by the compiler. The `atoi` function is used to transform C-style strings into integer values. The `sprintf` class of functions reverses the direction, taking numeric data and building corresponding C-style strings.

PROBLEM

The `atoi` function analyzes the C-style string and skips any leading whitespace. Starting with the first nonwhitespace character, it scans for characters consistent with an integer value. These characters include a leading plus or minus sign and base-10 digits. The first character found that does not conform to this pattern is considered the delimiter, and the conversion process ends.

If the input is an empty string or no valid integer-type characters are found, the function quietly returns a 0 value. Consider the following code where an age is input.

Listing 5.14　Innocently inputting text representing an age

```cpp
int main() {
    std::cout << "Enter your age: ";
    std::string input;
    std::cin >> input;

    int age = atoi(input.c_str());          // Converts invalid input and a
                                            // zero value to an integer zero
    std::cout << "On your next birthday, you will be " << age + 1 << " years
    old\n";
    return 0;
}
```

Everything works well, assuming valid digits are entered. However, if invalid input is received, the conversion function fails, which it indicates by returning a 0. If the input happens to be 0, the conversion function also returns a 0. What is missing is the essential knowledge of whether the returned 0 is valid (e.g., the 0 digit was entered) or invalid (e.g., `cat` was entered).

ANALYSIS

The fundamental problem with the `atoi` class of functions is that the 0 return value needs to be clarified. If the user of the code in listing 5.14 happens to be an infant, then the output result is correct. The output result is incorrect if the user stumbles across the keyboard and enters anything aside from digits between 0 and 9.

Adding a test to determine if the value is 0 legitimately involves inspecting each input digit to ensure they are within the valid range. Even if this checking functionality is added, the result is cluttered and difficult to read. Since C++ provides the means to add intelligence to conversion, do so to validate the input. Your users likely will not thank you—better yet, they will refrain from cursing you.

SOLUTION

While there is more than one approach to solving this problem, the simplest solution uses the `stringstream` class to parse string data using the familiar stream with the extraction operator. A benefit of this method is the ability to test the input string stream for a failure, which the `atoi` type functions do not provide.

Listing 5.15   Checked the input for an age

```cpp
int main() {
    std::cout << "Enter your age: ";
    std::string input;
    std::cin >> input;

    std::istringstream is(input);
    int age;
    is >> age;
    if (is.fail()) {
        std::cout << "Invalid input\n";
        return 1;
    }
    std::cout << "On your next birthday, you will be " << age + 1 << " years
old\n";
    return 0;
}
```

Invalid input can be checked for and handled appropriately.

If the `fail` function is not checked, the default behavior is identical to `atoi`—a zero value is returned for invalid data. Check the stream for incorrect data; objects are smart and use their knowledge. Doing so ensures a more correct program. Using the extraction operator allows easy checking for failures to convert text to the anticipated data type. Be sure to check the result of the conversion. C++11 provides the `std::stoi` function for converting C-style or C++-style strings to numeric values and throws an exception for failures. C++17 provides `std::from_chars` to convert text to numbers efficiently and permits checking for errors. To see these options in action, consider the following code listing.

Listing 5.16   Modern checked input for an age

```cpp
int main() {
    std::cout << "Enter your age: ";
    std::string input;
    std::cin >> input;
    int age;

    // C++11
    try {
        age = std::stoi(input);
    } catch (const std::invalid_argument& e) {
        std::cout << "stoi: Invalid input\n";
        return 1;
    }
```

```
std::cout << "On your next birthday, you will be " << age + 1 << " years
old\n";

// C++17
auto result = std::from_chars(input.data(), input.data() + input.size(),
 age);
if (result.ec != std::errc()) {
    std::cout << "from_chars: Invalid input\n";
    return 1;
}
std::cout << "On your next birthday, you will be " << age + 1 << " years
old\n";
return 0;
}
```

RECOMMENDATIONS

- Use input streams, so a failure can be tested.
- Use functions that throw exceptions where possible; they are easy to check.
- Where possible, change calls to `atoi` to some other, smarter solution using C++ functionality.
- If you have access to modern C++, consider the `std::stoi` or `std::from_chars` functions.

5.8   *Mistake 33: Using C-style strings*

This mistake affects readability and effectiveness; in some cases, performance is affected. C-style strings are character arrays whose final character is a zero value, a sentinel value representing the end of the string.

PROBLEM

C had no concept of a *class* or what might be called *smart objects*. Instead, procedural code tended to be filled with specific commands to manage *dumb objects*. Each developer was prone to handling C-style strings in numerous places, often duplicating code and repeating (often via copying and pasting) functionality.

The code in listing 5.17 is one of many possible examples. Older code tends to use C-style strings throughout because of their familiarity. Many functions have `char*` parameters, encouraging their use across the code base.

Consider the following code, where the developer counts a character's occurrences in a C-style string. The code is innocent and does precisely what is needed. It appears performant, clocking in as an O(n) solution. Who would be unhappy with this?

Listing 5.17   Simple search and append algorithms

```
int freq(const char* s, char k) {
    int count = 0;
    for (int i = 0; i < strlen(s); ++i)          ◄─── Linear search through
        if (s[i] == k)                                the string
            ++count;
```

```
        return count;
    }

    char* concat(const char* lhs, const char* rhs) {
        char* buffer = new char[strlen(lhs) + strlen(rhs)];      ◀──┐  Dynamic memory
        strcpy(buffer, lhs);                                         │  allocation—is it
        strcat(buffer, rhs);                                         │  correct?
        return buffer;
    }

    int main() {
        const char* msg = "Hello, world";
        char letter = 'l';
        std::cout << letter << " occurs " << freq(msg, letter) << " times\n";
        const char* msg2 = ", come on in!";
        std::cout << concat(msg, msg2) << '\n';
    }
```

ANALYSIS

For relatively short strings, this approach works well because it is easy to write; however, its performance detriment might be unacceptable for long strings. Use a profiler to show where a better solution is necessary. Analysis of the loop appears to show a linear search, and indeed, it is linear $O(n)$. The algorithm is quadratic $O(n^2)$. Why? C-style strings are dumb; code cannot simply ask the string for information to know their length. Instead, the size must be computed each time it is requested. The loop must calculate the string's length each iteration through the loop; that is, each execution of `strlen` is itself linear $O(n)$, and it is done n times, resulting in a quadratic solution. Thankfully, most compilers will detect this situation and move the `strlen` function outside the loop. However, do not trust the compiler to figure this out for all possibilities. This is one of those cases where knowing the problem leads to a simple solution. However, this approach is not ideal because it still focuses on C-style strings. The code in listing 5.18 improves the performance without really improving the approach.

Any other code not in the loop's scope would have to recalculate the length of the string. If the string-handling code were spread throughout the code base, the length calculation in one place would not benefit others.

Managing the arrays of characters proves difficult, too. One must memorize the distinction between `strcpy` and `strcat` and remember how the null character is handled. One needs to ensure that destination buffers are at least the length of the string plus one for the terminating character. The problem is that the developer must remember and manage all the fine details, most often of which happens correctly. However, undefined behavior occurs in those rare cases where it is bungled. Often, if the destination is too small, the copy or append still appears to work but corrupt data. Nice systems crash (and not all systems are nice).

The string length computation in the `freq` function does not benefit the same calculation in the `concat` function. Further, the dynamic memory obtained in the `concat` function was not freed. This fact might appear innocuous here, but this error affects correctness.

Listing 5.18 Improved search and append algorithms

```
int freq(const char* s, char k) {
    int count = 0;
    int len = strlen(s);
    for (int i = 0; i < len; ++i)
        if (s[i] == k)
            ++count;
    return count;
}


char* concat(const char* lhs, const char* rhs) {
    char* buffer = new char[strlen(lhs) +
        strlen(rhs) + 1];
    strcpy(buffer, lhs);
    strcat(buffer, rhs);
    return buffer;
}


int main() {
    const char* msg = "Hello, world";
    char letter = 'l';
    std::cout << letter << " occurs " << freq(msg, letter) << " times\n";
    const char* msg2 = ", come on in!";
    std::cout << concat(msg, msg2) << '\n';
    delete [] msg;
}
```

◄── **Computes the length once for this function**

◄── **Ensures space for the null terminator**

Solution

C++ provides significant improvements over C-style strings. The problems with them were substantial enough that one of the first major user-written classes, provided since the earliest days of C++, was the `string` class. A C++-style `string` is an intelligent object; a developer can ask it questions and obtain answers. The following code uses this fact in querying a `string`'s length.

Listing 5.19 Using C++ strings to solve detected problems

```
int freq(const std::string& s, char k) {
    int count = 0;
    for (int i = 0; i < s.length(); ++i)
        if (s[i] == k)
            ++count;
    return count;
}


std::string concat(const std::string& lhs, const std::string& rhs) {
    return lhs + rhs;
}

int main() {
    std::string msg = "Hello, world";
    char letter = 'l';
```

◄── **Constant time query of length**

◄── **The developer is not concerned about lengths for data movement.**

```
    std::cout << letter << " occurs " << freq(msg, letter) << " times\n";
    std::string msg2 = ", come on in!";
    std::cout << concat(msg, msg2) << '\n';   ◄──┐  Memory obtained for temporary
}                                                 │  objects is automatically handled.
```

The solution could be better but conforms to the previous code while improving it. A local variable initialized with the string's length is better, but this approach demonstrates the benefit of smart objects. Leaving the string length query in the loop shows that although the function is called n times, the loop's computational cost is $O(n)$. This time characteristic is maintained because querying the length does not trigger a computation of the length. The string determines its length at construction time and stores the result in an instance variable, so the length query is done in $O(1)$ time.

The concatenation of two strings handles the challenge of managing the length of the resulting string by letting the object itself determine the needed memory. The developer does not need to know how the data is handled—does it use a null terminator or not? Further, there is no need to delete dynamic memory, since the string manages its data using the RAII pattern.

RECOMMENDATIONS

- Learn to use C++-style strings wherever sequences of characters are used; the string class is highly optimized and easy to use.
- Eliminate C-style strings where possible and introduce C++-style strings in their place.
- Strings automatically handle dynamic memory; when the string goes out of scope, its destructor is called.

SEE ALSO

- See Mistake 43 for an improved way to index a string instance. This approach works with any container.

5.9   *Mistake 34: Calling the exit function*

This mistake deals with correctness. Using the `exit` function can cause leaks with limited or dynamic resources, affecting a system's stability.

PROBLEM

Assume that our developer is under the burden of following some questionable requirements. The program must crash immediately during payroll processing if a terminated employee is discovered. The developer understood this requirement and remembered that previous C programs immediately used the `exit` call to terminate; therefore, the developer decided to use this technique in the C++ program. Later, after some strange problems, a systems programmer asked the developer why this program was causing system stability problems.

Listing 5.20 Terminating a program with `exit`

```cpp
class Connection {
private:
    int conn;
public:
    Connection(const std::string& name) : conn(0) {
        conn = 1;  // assume: database connection resource is returned
    }
    ~Connection() {
        if (conn)
            conn = 0;  // assume: destroys database connection resource
        std::cerr << "Connection destroyed\n";
    }
};

struct Employee {
    bool isTerminated() { return true; }
    double computePay() { return 42.0; }
};

int main() {
    Connection c("payroll");
    Employee emp;
    if (emp.isTerminated())                    The program must
        exit(-1);                              terminate at this point.
    std::cout << emp.computePay() << '\n';
    return 0;
}
```

ANALYSIS

The program allocates a database connection, processes employees, and crashes when a terminated person is discovered. The program was rerun after cleaning up the database, and it presumably crashed a few more times. At the end of processing, the database is clean, the program runs to completion, and everyone gets paid—happy day! But why the system stability problems? The `Connection` class is the problem. Its constructor accesses a limited resource which the destructor is designed to release. Under normal circumstances, this code works correctly. But as usual, it is during exceptional circumstances that problems rear their ugly heads. The `exit` call forces the program to terminate immediately. `Connection` objects will not be cleaned up, since their destructors cannot run. The dynamic resource is allocated, but nothing uses it—a classic resource leak.

SOLUTION

Resolving this problem takes two steps. First, do not use the `exit` call; instead, throw an exception. Second, wrap the outermost code in a general `try/catch` block whose exception action is to rethrow the exception. Of course, the `catch` clause could be more specific, but in solving this problem, the code's intelligence is limited.

This approach prevents resource leaks because destructors are given a chance to run. When the Connection object goes out of scope, its destructor will return the database connection to the pool, preventing an allocated but unused resource.

Admittedly, the code is awkward, but in many cases, developers find themselves needing to improve the overall structure or implementation. In these cases, "cheap" solutions are necessary, even if the design is poor. Too rarely can developers afford the time and budget required to improve old code—it is a matter of adapting when and where they can and seeking improvements in limited areas. Reality bites, sometimes.

Listing 5.21 Terminating a program with an exception

```
class Connection {
private:
    int conn;
public:
    Connection(const std::string& name) : conn(0) {
        conn = 1;  // assume: database connection resource is allocated
    }
    ~Connection() {
        if (conn)
            conn = 0;  // assume: returns database connection to pool
        std::cerr << "Connection destroyed\n";
    }
};

struct Employee {
    bool isTerminated() { return true; }
    double computePay() { return 42.0; }
};

struct TerminatedEmployee {
    std::string message;
    TerminatedEmployee(const std::string& msg) : message(msg) {}
};

int main() {
    try {
        Connection c("payroll");
        Employee emp;
        if (emp.isTerminated())
            throw TerminatedEmployee("Employee was terminated");
        std::cout << emp.computePay() << '\n';
    } catch (...) {
        throw;                          ◄─────┐  Terminates the
    }                                         │  program at this point
    return 0;
}
```

Exiting a program early is necessary in some cases. When this need arises, ensure that the exit is coded so that all destructors are called before exiting. The program should only exit without cleaning up resources in cases where stack unwinding is not desired (debugging). In this case, be careful not to leak system resources such as sockets, database connections, and similar limited entities.

RECOMMENDATIONS

- Avoid using the `exit` call.
- Throw an exception, catch it generally (or specifically), and rethrow to allow destructors a chance to run.
- Improve what you can where you can; you likely will not get significant opportunities to improve large swathes of code.

SEE ALSO

- See Mistake 74 for a discussion about dynamic resources.
- See Mistake 75 for dangers of terminating a program without cleaning up dynamic resources.
- See Mistake 76 for other cases where dynamic resources can be leaked.
- See Mistake 77 for the ideal pattern to prevent resource leaks.

5.10 *Mistake 35: Preferring arrays to vectors*

This mistake deals with effectiveness and readability; it can affect correctness and, if so, have adverse effects. C provided one built-in data container, which was used extensively. The array is a sequence of elements that can be addressed with one name and distinguished by an index.

PROBLEM

Many programming problems require collections of entities, whether built in or user written. A default constructor must exist if the entity is user written and stored in an array. In some cases, this constructor makes sense, but in many cases, it does not. Meaningless default constructors suggest the design needs to be corrected or completed. Using arrays does not provide an option, however.

When creating a static array, the number of elements must be known at compile time. Many problems do not clearly express the number of elements that must be handled, which means the chosen size is arbitrary. If the developer's guesses are too large, space is wasted; if they are too small, this often leads to crashes—or worse. An excellent choice here is to use dynamic arrays because often, the code can determine the number of elements before needing the container. The developer must remember to manage the container's memory—oh, and dynamic arrays require a default constructor, too.

No matter how many elements the array-based container has, adding one element too many is possible. Using dynamic arrays allows the developer to manage too-short arrays by allocating a larger one and copying over the values. If the array is referenced by other entities, developers often get a nasty surprise, not knowing that the allocated memory has been shifted under its feet.

Finally, try deleting an array element that is no longer needed or valid. All code using the array must know how to determine an invalid (or deleted) element. This problem spreads knowledge across any function using the array and duplicates the effort. Since arrays are dumb objects, there is no way to ask them which elements are valid. The developer must determine a scheme by which individual elements are marked invalid somehow—it may not be evident to readers what this code means or why it is dinking with certain elements. The following code demonstrates a simple case of a static array that forces the `Person` class to contain a bogus default constructor.

Listing 5.22   Static arrays force using a default constructor

```
struct Person {
    std::string name;
    int age;
    Person(const std::string& n, int a) : name(n), age(a) {}
    Person() : name(""), 0) {}
};

int main() {
    Person people[3];                              ◄──────────┐   Each element is
    Person suzy("Susan", 25);                                 │   initialized by calling
    people[0] = suzy;                                         │   the default constructor.
    Person anna("Annette", 32);                               │
    people[2] = anna;                                         │
    std::cout << people[1].name << '\n';                      │
                                                              │
    int count = 5;  // assume this is computed                │
    Person* others = new Person[count];    ◄──────────────────┘
    return 0;
}
```

ANALYSIS

The first array is static; the number of elements must be known at compile time. This example suggests the number of elements was too small. An alternative was tried by allocating a dynamic array after determining the number of elements. In both cases, the default constructor is required, but there are no reasonable default values for the instance variables. Something must be chosen, regardless of its meaning. If four of the five elements were initialized meaningfully, the missing one would still be a "legitimate" `Person` element; however, it would contain illegitimate information, since no person is represented by its data.

SOLUTION

Replacing an array with a vector is almost always the correct choice. Dr. Stroustrup (the inventor of C++) recommends this approach, so I have it on good authority. Even if he had not made such a statement, the reasons for using one are convincing enough on their own.

First, vectors are dynamic; therefore, choosing too few elements is impossible. Using a vector is similar in some ways to an array. An array is used to implement a vector called a *backing array*. The magic occurs when the backing array fills up and has no elements to spare. No crash occurs when a new element is added. The vector will allocate a new, larger backing array; copy the elements from the previous one; and add the new element to the first unused index. The developer only basks in the glow of effortless use, and no user-written memory management code is required to obtain this result. See the third benefit for a caution on extending the backing array too often. Please do not assume vectors cannot be misused or used without consequences; incorrect code can cause an exception—as it should!

Second, elements can be pushed onto the vector without regard for specific index values. If the index is valid, an element can be added. Removing an element removes the element as far as the developer is concerned; there are no awkward flags to set to indicate an invalid element.

Third, if the backing array is reallocated more than a few times, there may be a significant performance setback, due to the number of times the elements are copied. Estimating the number of elements needed and calling the `reserve` function is better. The `reserve` function allocates sufficient memory for that number of elements. A well-chosen value means no reallocations or wasted space is encountered. Even if the guess is wrong, the vector will behave correctly. If the guess is too low, a reallocation will occur; if the guess is too high, there will be wasted space. However, the developer will not have to manage the memory or worry about the vector's mechanics.

The following code improves the array implementation and makes coding smoother and mistake-free. Developers do not get something for nothing; with judicious use, vectors come close to this impossible dream.

> **Listing 5.23 Using a vector to replace awkward arrays**

```cpp
struct Person {
    std::string name;
    int age;
    Person(const std::string& n, int a) : name(n), age(a) {}
};

int main() {
    std::vector<Person> people;
    Person suzy("Susan", 25);
    people.push_back(suzy);
    Person anna("Annette", 32);
    people.push_back(anna);
    std::cout << people[people.size()-1].name << '\n';

    int count = 5;  // assume this is computed
    std::vector<Person> others;
    others.reserve(count);
    return 0;
}
```

RECOMMENDATIONS

- Replace arrays with vectors in most cases.
- Carefully read about and understand the space and time implications of using `vectors`; in many cases, they are trouble-free and have excellent behavior.
- Vectors have many methods available; research them to understand their power and possibilities.

SEE ALSO

- See Mistake 49 for an argument against default constructors in general, especially when applied to arrays.

Better premodern C++

This chapter covers

- Input and output
- Memory allocation
- Variable-length parameter lists
- Iterators

In the evolution from C to C++, the legacy of past programming practices continues to shape the software development landscape. As we transition from examining C idioms in chapter 5, in this chapter, we focus on the persistent influence of entrenched habits within early C++ programming. This chapter considers the subtle yet significant effect of historical continuity on the structure and functionality of C++ code bases.

Despite the advancements introduced by C++, developers grappled with straying from familiar C-oriented constructs and ways of thinking. This inclination toward existing methodologies extended to the selection of library functions, sometimes hindering the use of newer C++ features. Even among those who embraced the latest capabilities of C++, there were uncertainties regarding the most effective use of some of its enhanced features.

The effects of these patterns were seen in several problems that lurk within code bases. This chapter discusses these challenges, offering insights and solutions to several pitfalls and misconceptions. By detecting these problems and understanding their resolution, we can better navigate some of the complexities of C++ programming.

6.1   *Mistake 36: Input and output using scanf and printf*

This mistake focuses on effectiveness, which is closely followed by readability. When scanf and printf type functions are all one has, they must be used. However, they frequently find it challenging to get right and always read awkwardly.

PROBLEM

Many problems require that textual data be input from the keyboard or a file and converted into various data types. The scanf and printf functions use a format specifier to determine the data type. This specifier is usually a single character that symbolically represents the data type. If the wrong specifier is used, it results in undefined behavior. In some cases, the error will be tolerated; in others, a crash happens—or worse. The data will most likely be incorrect if the incorrect specifier does not cause a crash.

Reading the format specifier is only possible if the developer knows its possibilities. Listing 6.1 uses a complex format specifier for the sscanf (string scan) function. The specifier is sometimes more complicated to read than a regular expression, making the reader stop and mentally parse the sections. If any specifier is unknown, developers must discover its meaning and proper use by scouring the internet or other resources for information. This is true of many aspects of programming, not just format specifiers. The point is that anything that causes us to stop our reading and do some research is an opportunity for improvement. Format specifiers are such an opportunity.

Listing 6.1   Using complicated format specifiers to determine conversions

```
int main() {
    const char* str = "3.14159 042 boxes .3";     All input specifications
    double pi;                                     are applied in one
    int cats;                                      operation; are they
    int mice;                                      correct?
    char buffer[5];

    int count = sscanf(str, "%lf%*c%i%s%d", &pi, &cats,    The programmer
        buffer, &mice);                                    must determine the
    if (count != 4)                                        correct number.
        std::cout << "error reading value " << count+1 << '\n';

    printf("%f being eaten by %d cats in %s along with %d mice\n",
        pi, cats, mice, mice);          Text, specification, and variables are
    return 0;                           mixed awkwardly—it contains a bug.
}
```

ANALYSIS

The format specifier has a few oddities that are not obvious. The double variable would intuitively be scanned and converted using a d character, but doing so would result in an error. The `d` character here refers to *decimal*, not *double*. The `f` character represents a floating-point value, which is intuitively the float data type. To read the text into the double variable requires a long floating-point specifier `lf`. We might expect something more straightforward.

Another oddity is that the first integer variable uses the `i` specifier (for integer?), while the second integer variable uses the `d` specifier. The output of the first integer variable turns out to be 34, not 42. The mystery is cleared up by understanding that `d` implies an integer base 10. In contrast, `i` denotes an integer with a base determined by the leading input character of the data (0 for octal, 0x for hexadecimal, and decimal otherwise). In this case, the leading zero means the text is an octal value. As you might imagine, these details are easy to forget.

Finally, the `buffer` variable represents a C-style string and uses the `s` specifier—finally, a specifier with an intuitive meaning! Since the developer knew that the containers were five characters, that number of elements was allocated for the array. Nice, clean, and wrong. The `scanf` type functions transfer the relevant characters into the destination and add a terminating null character. This may be obvious; however, if the `c` specifier were used, that null terminator would not be added. These differences must either be memorized or looked up every time.

The `printf` output suffers from a few problems, too. Its specifiers differ from the `scanf` ones in some cases. In this example, the double variable uses an `f` specifier but not an `lf`, as in the `scanf`. One must remember that. Mixing the output text with specifiers in one string is understandable, but it does introduce some cognitive discontinuity, since the variables are listed after the format string. Reading left to right also requires jumping back and forth from the string to the variables (and their order must be rigidly maintained in mind).

Finally, what might happen if a variable mismatch occurs between the specifier and variable types? The example in listing 6.1 misspecifies `mice` twice; the first should have been `buffer`. What happens when an integer variable is used as the source for a C-style string? Nothing good happens, that's for sure; the dreaded undefined behavior is the correct answer. My system issues a segmentation fault that reminds me gently that something is broken without deceiving me by continuing execution.

These function families are not type-safe, which makes them risky to use. It is too easy to mismatch the intended format specifiers and actual data types. Given these limited error detection abilities, meaningful recovery code is complex.

SOLUTION

The C language gave us `scanf` and `printf` functionality; however, we are programming in C++, which has better options available. Any time character data is moved into or out of a program, a stream should be used. Streams provide the very helpful insertion and extraction operators (`<<` and `>>`, respectively). These operators determine how to convert text to the proper data type (assuming the input data is consistent with the data type) and relieve the developer of needing a data type specifier.

The wrong coding in listing 6.2, where `mice` are output twice, does not cause a runtime error or misrepresent data—the output is incorrect, and there is no erroneous conversion from one type to another, as in listing 6.1. Extracting textual data into the various variables works correctly if the data is consistent but fails when it is inconsistent. The problem with `scanf` was that the input and conversion happened in one fell swoop; if an error occurred, the developer had to determine which conversion failed from the returned value. The detection logic in listing 6.1 is more straightforward than in listing 6.2, but at least the second version gives the developer finer-grained control over error detection.

Listing 6.2 Using types to determine conversions

```cpp
int main() {
    std::istringstream str("3.14159 042 boxes .3");
    double pi;
    int cats;
    int mice;
    std::string buffer;                         The input and conversion work
                                                correctly or set the easily
    str >> pi;                              ◄─── detected fail() function.
    if (str.fail())
        std::cout << "error reading value 1\n";
    str >> cats;
    if (str.fail())
        std::cout << "error reading value 2\n";
    str >> buffer;
    if (str.fail())
        std::cout << "error reading value 3\n";
    str >> mice;
    if (str.fail())
        std::cout << "error reading value 4\n";

    std::cout << pi << " being eaten by " << cats << " cats in " << mice
        << " along with " << mice << " mice\n";   ◄───
    return 0;                                         Conversion is based
}                                                     on the actual data.
```

The integer value `042` is correctly converted to the value 42; the leading zero does not affect its meaning. If the data is truly octal, the input stream can be set to base 8 for the input operation. This code would input and convert `cats` as octal:

```cpp
str >> std::setbase(8) >> cats;
```

RECOMMENDATIONS

- Replace `scanf` and `printf` calls with their better stream-oriented extraction and insertion operators where possible.
- Avoid complicated input and output format strings; they are hard to get right and even harder to read.

6.2 *Mistake 37: Overusing endl*

This mistake centers on performance. Operating systems typically buffer input and output data to minimize input/output (I/O) operations. Misunderstanding buffering can have a significant effect on performance.

PROBLEM

The code in the following listing is straightforward; the loop iterates one thousand times, outputting the loop control variable's value each time. Finally, the termination message is output—simple, right?

> **Listing 6.3   Using `std::endl` indiscriminately**

```
int main() {
    for (int i = 0; i < 1000; ++i)
        std::cout << i << std::endl;              ◄──┐  Outputs into the std::cout buffer
    std::cout << "finished!" << std::endl;          │  and flushes to the device
    return 0;
}
```

ANALYSIS

There are no tricks here! The code works as expected, except it may perform worse than hoped. The simple problem is that `std::endl` outputs the end-of-line character and flushes the output buffer. Fewer I/O operations equate to greater throughput. The `std::cout` stream is a buffering stream that uses fewer I/O operations. Its buffer accumulates the output values and newlines until it is filled and then flushes the buffer as a large block. Using `std::endl` precludes this buffering optimization, since it flushes the buffer regardless of the amount of data it contains. On several systems, various optimizations offset this stark difference for terminal output but not file output, so consider a slightly more nuanced understanding of this analysis.

SOLUTION

If you change `std::endl` to `'\n'`, the buffering works as expected. Remember that in some cases, partially filled buffers should be flushed to complete an I/O operation. The code in listing 6.4 optimizes the buffer filling until all values and newlines are output. Then, the termination message flushes the buffer to ensure any buffered data gets written out, cleanly completing the output operation. In this case, the program terminates after the flush, so it is not strictly needed here; it is generally a good practice to implement it this way.

> **Listing 6.4   Using `std::endl` judiciously**

```
int main() {
    for (int i = 0; i < 1000; ++i)              Outputs into the
        std::cout << i << '\n';          ◄──    std::cout buffer
    std::cout << "finished!" << std::endl;   ◄──┐  Outputs and flushes the
    return 0;                                    │  buffer to the device
}
```

Use buffered output in almost all cases, since it cooperates with the operating system to provide the best performance. If data should be output without buffering, consider the `std::cerr` stream.

RECOMMENDATIONS

- Change `std::endl` to `\n` everywhere feasible to prevent unnecessary buffer flushes.
- When flushing the output buffer is necessary, use `std::endl`.
- If a large amount of data is output, use `\n` for all but the last operation; use `std::endl` for the final operation.
- Consider `std::cerr` for unbuffered output.

6.3   *Mistake 38: Dynamic allocation with malloc and free*

This problem focuses on correctness and, to a lesser extent, effectiveness. Memory allocation has come a long way since C, but that does not mean everyone is on board with the changes.

PROBLEM

C provides the `malloc` and `free` pair of memory allocation and deallocation operators. As with C++ dynamic resource allocation using `new` and `delete`, whatever is obtained with `malloc` should be freed with `free`. It sounds simple, and in many cases, it is. However, C and C++ code can complicate this "simple" process, especially if ownership of resources changes as the object is passed around from function to function.

Listing 6.5 shows two common problems that occur with `malloc` code:

- Incorrect size computation
- Failure to initialize obtained memory

Listing 6.5   Using `malloc` and `free` in an undisciplined manner

```
struct Buffer {
    char* str;
    Buffer(int size) : str(new char[size+1]) { str[0] = '\0'; }
    ~Buffer() { free(str); }
};

int main() {
    double* val = (double*)malloc(sizeof(int));
    std::cout << val << '\n';
    Buffer* buf = (Buffer*)malloc(sizeof(Buffer));
    std::cout << buf->str << ", size " << strlen(buf->str) << '\n';
    free(buf);
    return 0;
}
```

A typo missed by bleary eyes

The dynamic object space is allocated but not initialized.

ANALYSIS

Besides the two `malloc` problems noted previously, the preceding code has at least three additional bugs. First, a dynamic memory block is obtained to hold a double value. Due to late nights and fading caffeine levels, the developer mistakenly requested enough memory for an integer (typically one-half the size of a double value). The compiler is silent about this mismatch, a classic type-safety bug. Any access to the data stored in this too-short block will access data beyond its boundary. I hate the smell of undefined behavior in the morning.

The second problem is found in the creation of the `Buffer` object. This time, the allocated size is correct, but the initialization of the `char*` variable is missing. The constructor should handle obtaining a block of dynamic memory to hold character data and ensure the terminating character is written into the first position. However, this never happens. When `malloc` is called, no constructor is executed, and initialization never occurs.

Third, there is no corresponding free for the `val` variable. The dynamic allocation of the memory is leaked as the main function exits; no destructor or other management entity is watching the memory. In a long-running program, several of these leaks could cause significant problems.

The fourth problem is that while the `buf` object is properly freed, the dynamic memory obtained by the object is not freed. Granted, it was never allocated in this case, but better code would have allocated it, only to leak it as the enclosing entity is freed. The `free` call never calls the destructor, leaving any dynamic resources high and dry.

Finally, there is a mismatch between allocating the `Buffer` object's dynamic memory obtained in the constructor by calling `new` and the destructor's attempt to release it by calling `free`. The behavior of this mismatch is not defined, leaving the poor program (and programmer!) at the mercy of whatever the compiler chooses to do. A much more robust implementation of the `Buffer` class addressing copy and assignment (and move) semantics would mitigate many of these problems.

SOLUTION

The `new` and `delete` operators were not developed just to be contrary. The deficiencies of `malloc` and `free` were sufficient to warrant a new approach.

As shown in listing 6.6, the first problem is handled by `new` to ensure that whatever entity is obtained is the proper type for the receiving variable—no type-safety bugs can slip through. The second problem is handled by ensuring a constructor is called for every allocation. Properly designed code will implement the RAII pattern to ensure the allocation is paired with the proper deallocation. Third, it is still possible to fail to delete a `new` object; the developer must ensure their pairing. The fourth problem is addressed when the destructor is called if it is properly designed (the RAII pattern). Fifth, and finally, no mismatch can occur when only `new` and `delete` operators are used. Mixing `new`/`delete` with `malloc`/`free` is not only bad form, but it can also have severe consequences: more undefined behavior.

Listing 6.6 Using `new` and `free` in a disciplined manner

```
struct Buffer {
    char* str;
    Buffer(int size) : str(new char[size+1]) { str[0] = '\0'; }
```

```
    ~Buffer() { delete[] str; }
};

int main() {
//    double* val = new int;          No longer possible
    double* val = new double;         Type safety is guaranteed.
    std::cout << val << '\n';
    Buffer* buf = new Buffer(25);     The constructor is called.
    std::cout << buf->str << ", size " << strlen(buf->str) << '\n';
    delete buf;
    return 0;                         The destructor is called;
}                                     remember to delete it!
```

The `Buffer` class could delete or hide the copy constructor and copy assignment operator to make its implementation more robust. This is not demonstrated but should always be considered when using dynamic resources. The See Also section points readers to additional discussions on these topics.

RECOMMENDATIONS

- Replace `malloc` calls with `new`, and replace `free` calls with `delete`.

- Remember that every `new` has a corresponding `delete` and that every `new[]` has a matching `delete[]`.

SEE ALSO

- See Mistake 77 for a discussion of the pattern.

- See Mistake 78 for a discussion on leaking resources.

6.4   *Mistake 39: Using unions for type conversion*

This problem focuses on correctness and readability. The compiler understands C++ types, and the programmer's attempts to convert them can blindside the type-checking mechanisms.

PROBLEM

The type-checking system in the compiler is meant to prevent mismatching one type for another. While humans might see little difference between some types, the compiler knows better and prevents many conversions, unless the programmer insists on converting and tells the compiler to back off. This approach works like a charm—the compiler shuts up—but likely leads to bugs that are hard to discover and frustrating to debug.

The code in listing 6.7 works on some systems. It uses a `union` to describe an array of four characters and an integer. The programmer intends to convert integers to characters and output them to a binary file. The union `mixer` simplifies the conversion between a small character array and an integer. An integer is written to the union instance; its value is read in the `write` function call. On my system, this works well.

Listing 6.7   Using a `union` for type conversion

```
static const int bytes_per_int = 4;          An integer is
                                             always four bytes?
union mixer {
    char ch[bytes_per_int];           It is assumed here.
    int n;
};

int main() {
    mixer converter;
    converter.n = 42;
    std::ofstream out("data.txt", std::ios::binary);
    out.write(converter.ch, bytes_per_int);
    return 0;
}
```

ANALYSIS

The `union` reserves four bytes for the character array and overlays it with an integer. This works on systems with four-byte integers, but does it work everywhere? Does it work when the compiler version is changed? Perhaps; the answers are *yes* and *yes*, but do not expect it to work on someone else's system. There is no guarantee that an integer will take four bytes. Of course, the programmer can check this value and hardcode it; however, this solution is nonportable. The `union` does not effectively deal with dynamic memory to automatically adjust the character array to an integer size.

SOLUTION

The fundamental problem with type conversions that are not promotions is that the programmer makes assumptions about the underlying layout of sizes, bits, and bytes. These assumptions mean the code is inherently rigid and nonportable. Programmer-induced conversions are problematic because of these assumptions, but if they must be coded, the compiler should be involved to help where possible.

The `reinterpret_cast` with the compiler-supplied size of the integer shown in listing 6.8 is a better approach. There is no hardcoded size that the programmer must determine and verify; the compiler figures it out for the specific architecture at compilation time.

One of the few places binary streams make sense is where user-defined type conversions, likewise, make sense. The data converted to characters (really, bytes) are never used in the converted form. The corresponding pointer conversion using the `reinterpret_cast` from characters back to the original data type should be reversed exactly to prevent oddities and errors.

Listing 6.8   Using `reinterpret_cast` in a reasonable manner

```
int main() {
    int n = 42;
    std::ofstream out("data.txt", std::ios::binary);
```

```
out.write(reinterpret_cast<const char*>(&n),
    sizeof(n));
return 0;
}
```

The compiler determines the correct size; no assumptions are made.

With all of this said, it is still much better to design the program in a way that does not need user-defined type conversions. Trust the underlying data types and use classes to aggregate different data types. Push the implementation details to the compiler, and work at a higher level wherever possible.

Two other places user-defined type conversions may be required are at the interface boundary of an API and integration with modules from another language. Use the compiler as best you can to assist the conversion effort in these cases. Further, isolate the conversion code into well-documented, small, single-purpose functions that perform the transformations. Check the assumptions of these functions every time the compiler, system level, and architecture change.

RECOMMENDATIONS

- Avoid user-defined, implementation-dependent type conversions where possible.
- Where required, avoid hardcoded assumptions if at all possible; use the compiler to help out.
- Carefully document each place conversation code occurs; make every assumption clear so that maintenance programmers can modify them as needed when inevitable change occurs.

SEE ALSO

- See Mistake 31 for further discussion about `reinterpret_cast` and some of its limitations.

6.5   *Mistake 40: Using varargs for variable parameter lists*

This mistake focuses on correctness and influences effectiveness and readability. Variable argument lists are used when the developer does not know how many parameters a function will require beyond the first few.

PROBLEM

Rather than writing several overloaded functions that take an increasing quantity of parameters, a single function that uses variable arguments (varargs) can be used for any number of parameters. Typically, the function will have one or more named parameters, one of which is the length of the list of parameters. The last parameter is an ellipsis (...), which indicates to the compiler that an unknown number of parameters follow. More technically correct, an unknown number of values follow, but let us not quibble over nomenclature.

Consider the code in listing 6.9. The developer wanted to have one function that would perform the summing of a list of values. For flexibility, the initial starting value is added, just in case the result of a former sum is included (usually, it is zero). The number of values needs to be passed because the function must know how many times to read the value list; the compiler does not automatically determine this. What possibly could go wrong?

The function starts by calling va_list to establish a variable argument list. It initializes the process by calling va_start; then, it iterates over each argument using va_arg; and finally, it cleans up the mess by calling va_end.

This code demonstrates a bug, one that has been observed in production code. The va_start macro needs to know two facts; the first is where the argument list is, and the second is the last-named parameter before the variable arguments. In this case, initial should have been used, not len. While certainly not recommended, this strange approach seems to work (determining why this is the case is left to the curious reader).

Listing 6.9 Using `varargs` for a variable length list of values

```cpp
int sum(int len, int initial, ...) {
    int sum = initial;
    va_list args;
    va_start(args, len);          ◄──── Oops, a bug! But
                                        this is close.
    for (int i = 0; i < len; ++i) ◄──── Accesses each
        sum += va_arg(args, int);       passed value
    va_end(args);
    return sum;
}

int main() {
    std::cout << sum(9, 0, 1, 2, 3, 4, 5, 6, 7, 8, 9) << '\n';
    std::cout << sum(3, 5, 1, 2, 3) << '\n';
    return 0;
}
```

ANALYSIS

The expected sum of the two calls is produced correctly on some systems, but others may experience problems. But consider what might happen if one of the variable argument values was a double or Person instance. The compiler does not type-check the arguments, so these would not cause an error or warning. Effectively, using the C-based varargs turns off any validation, leaving the results to the developer. As should be assumed, mismatched types will cause undefined behavior. Worse, the sum function might return a value that does not disclose its compromising unwillingness to crash.

> **NOTE** The fact that a system has worked as "expected" by no means suggests the code is correct or working as expected. It only means no apparent failure occurred. The advantage of providing such an example is that incorrect programming may appear to work but masks a potentially fatal problem. Do not ignore warnings, wrong techniques, and so on because "nothing seems broken." The demonstrated code is incorrect. This is one of those situations that can suddenly fail when something—anything—in the entire system changes (compiler, platform, solar flares, etc.). Caveat emptor!

SOLUTION

Simply stated, using `varargs` is a bad idea. This conclusion does not mean they always fail to work, but it does mean the developer cannot be protected from mistakes. C had almost no other way to achieve this functionality but had fewer possibilities for type-related problems. C++ makes it quite easy to mess things up in this case. One possible solution is to pass an array of values and remove the `varargs` altogether. The basic functionality of sum would remain after removing the `va_*` macros, but a better solution exists using vectors. Both solutions offer the distinct advantage of preventing data types other than the element type from being added. Therefore, the compiler can achieve type safety. Consider the code in listing 6.10, where a vector is used and the need to pass a length is removed.

Th following code uses a template to increase the flexibility of the element type. The solution adds the flexibility to use an unknown number of values and their type—a lovely little approach.

Listing 6.10   Using vectors for variable length lists

```
template <typename T>
T sum(T initial, const std::vector<T>& vals) {      ◄──── Chooses a templatized form
    T sum = initial;                                        for greater flexibility
    for (int i = 0; i < vals.size(); ++i)
        sum += vals[i];
    return sum;
}

int main() {
    std::vector<int> intvalues;                     ◄──── Chooses a container
    for (int i = 1; i < 10; ++i)                            for greater flexibility
        intvalues.push_back(i);
    std::cout << sum(0, intvalues) << '\n';
    std::vector<double> doublevalues;
    for (int i = 1; i < 4; ++i)
        doublevalues.push_back(i);
    std::cout << sum(5.0, doublevalues) << '\n';
    return 0;
}
```

RECOMMENDATIONS

- Avoid `varargs` if possible; remove and replace them with a better solution.
- Use arrays or, better yet, vectors to achieve the same results with type safety.

SEE ALSO

- See Mistake 18 for a modern C++ approach, which replaces the `varargs` concept, preserves type safety, and can even be fun to use.

6.6   *Mistake 41: Incorrect class initialization order*

This mistake focuses on performance and effectiveness. Initialization lists are a performance enhancement for initializing instance variables.

PROBLEM

The code in listing 6.11 shows an attempt to build an instance from supplied parameters. The full title is the composition of the `title`, `first`, `middle`, and `last` names. Initializing the full title from these in the constructor is reasonable, since all other variables are initialized from the supplied values. In this case, building the title could be accomplished in an accessor. Still, the effort to save the slight performance difference—assuming the title was never accessed—is negligible and forces the developer to write more code. This approach affects readability without providing sufficient benefit.

When the code is run on my system, a `std::bad_alloc` exception is thrown. A developer would fix this error. This result is one possible effect of this problem; your system may behave differently. Regardless, the code has a problem that results in undefined behavior. If, by chance, this code runs on a given system, strange output will likely result, and debugging might prove difficult.

Listing 6.11 Mixing up initialization order

```cpp
struct Person {
    std::string full;
    std::string first;
    std::string middle;
    std::string last;
    std::string title;
    Person(std::string f, std::string m, std::string l, std::string t) :
        first(f), middle(m), last(l), title(t),
        full(title + ' ' + first + ' ' + ' ' + middle + ' ' + last ) {}   ◄───┐
};                                                                              │
                                                    Builds the full title from │
int main() {                                             the individual parts
    Person judge("Hank", "M.", "Hye", "Hon.");
    std::cout << judge.full << '\n';
    return 0;
}
```

ANALYSIS

For the most part, this code is correct, but note the order of declaration for the instance variables and the order of initializing them. The `full` instance variable is declared first, followed by the rest. The programmer has reasoned about this and decided to initialize this instance variable last, since the individual instance variables (seemingly) have been initialized.

The developer made a mistake in this assumption; although the full instance variable seems to be initialized last, the compiler writes code to initialize the variables in declaration order. Therefore, `full` is initialized first, before any of the others. The concatenation of these uninitialized variables causes an exception or other nasty behavior.

After understanding this mandated order, the developer decided to take control of initialization by placing the code in the constructor body. Listing 6.12 shows the result.

Listing 6.12   Pushing initialization to the constructor body

```
struct Person {
    std::string full;
    std::string first;                            Puts all initialization in
    std::string middle;                           the constructor body
    std::string last;                             (poorer performance)
    std::string title;
    Person(std::string f, std::string m, std::string l, std::string t) {
        first = f;  middle = m;  last = l;  title = t;
        full = title + ' ' + first + ' ' + ' ' + middle + ' ' + last;
    }
};

int main() {
    Person judge("Hank", "M.", "Hye", "Hon.");
    std::cout << judge.full << '\n';
    return 0;
}
```

This solution works but needs to be more performant. It may not be obvious, but all instance variables are still initialized using the initializer list form as if the code were

```
Person(std::string f, std::string m, std::string l, std::string t) :
        full(), first(), middle(), last(), title() {}
```

The compiler ensures all class instances are initialized using their default constructor. Therefore, all instance variables are initialized to their default value in the initializer list. After this initialization, the constructor body is executed, and parameter values are assigned to the existing instances. This is twice the cost for each operation (let's not nitpick about the performance difference between a copy constructor and a copy assignment operator). This approach is suboptimal.

SOLUTION

Since the compiler will use the initialization list form for initializing every class-based instance variable (not primitives) in the declaration of this class, if order is important, the ideal approach is to sequence the variables in the order in which they should be initialized. This example is sensitive to order, but this should be avoided whenever possible. If order is not sensitive, choose whatever makes sense (alphabetical, grouping by type, etc.). The following code considers the order and ensures `full` is initialized only after all its component parts are fully initialized.

Listing 6.13   Disciplined use of initialization order

```
struct Person {
    std::string first;
    std::string middle;
    std::string last;
    std::string title;
    std::string full;
```

```
    Person(std::string f, std::string m, std::string l,
            std::string t) :
        first(f), middle(m), last(l), title(t),
        full(title + ' ' + first + ' ' + ' ' + middle + ' ' + last ) {}
};

int main() {
    Person judge("Hank", "M.", "Hye", "Hon.");
    std::cout << judge.full << '\n';
    return 0;
}
```

Reorders variables to ensure component parts are initialized first

RECOMMENDATIONS

- Avoid composite instance variables if possible; if not, order them so that all component parts are initialized first.
- Use initialization lists for all instance variables; if you do not use them, the compiler will generate them regardless.
- Ensure compiler warnings are turned on; this is one of the earliest, most broadly detected problems (consider always using -Wall when compiling).

6.7 *Mistake 42: Adding nonvalue types to containers*

This problem affects correctness. Containers are a preferred alternative to arrays in most cases. However, that fact does not eliminate problems using containers.

PROBLEM

Often, programming problems deal with groups of data that are processed or handled commonly. Arrays are a classic solution for holding and managing individual data elements as a unit; however, they should be used rarely. The Standard Template Library offers several containers that are much smarter than arrays and provide functionality that makes their use worthwhile.

Assume our developer wants to print a list of people at an event. There will be a mix of Persons and Employees, but they all must be listed. The code in listing 6.14 shows the attempt. Because of its ownership semantics, the developer was encouraged to use automatic pointers (auto_ptr) during programming. Boldly marching forward, the code was developed and tested. Its results could have been more encouraging.

Listing 6.14 Misusing a container for polymorphic elements

```
struct Person {
    std::string name;
    Person(const std::string& n) : name(n) {}
    virtual std::string toString() { return name; }
};

struct Employee : public Person {
    double salary;
    Employee(const std::string& n, double s) : Person(n), salary(s) {}
```

```
        std::string toString() {
            std::stringstream ss;
            ss << Person::name << " gets paid " << salary;
            return ss.str();
        }
};

int main() {
    Person p("Sue");
    Employee e("Jane", 123.45);

    std::vector<Person> people;
    people.push_back(p);
    people.push_back(e);
    for (int i = 0; i < people.size(); ++i)
        std::cout << people[i].toString() << '\n';

    std::vector<std::auto_ptr<Person> > persons;
    // persons.push_back(p);  persons.push_back(e);

    std::vector<Person> peeps;
    peeps.push_back(p);
    for (int i = 0; i < peeps.size(); ++i)
        std::cout << peeps[i].toString() << '\n';

    std::vector<Employee> emps;
    emps.push_back(e);
    for (int i = 0; i < emps.size(); ++i)
        std::cout << emps[i].toString() << '\n';
    return 0;
}
```

The polymorphic behavior does not work.

This would not compile; it has differing element types.

Individual vectors solved the problem.

ANALYSIS

The attempt at using a vector of `auto_ptrs` does not compile. The developer commented on this code, hoping to study it later. Since the developer was desperate to get the code working, they wrote separate containers to hold each data type. This approach works but needs to be optimized.

The problem with the single vector is that it holds objects of the base type. Only sufficient room for a base class object is allocated for each element, slicing off the derived class data. This problem also appears when using arrays for the same problem. So much for polymorphic behavior!

The second attempt was to use the newfangled `auto_ptr` type, which exclusively owns the instances within the container. This approach makes sense, but it runs into a brick wall. Only data types that are both copy constructible and assignable can be inserted into containers. The `auto_ptr` type is neither. Because it supports exclusive ownership semantics, instances cannot be added to the vector—so much for newfangled ideas. (Modern C++ has a much better approach than using `auto_ptr`; this type was deprecated, for good reason, in C++11). The developer's final attempt solved the problem; however, without the flexibility of a single container, the solution could be better.

SOLUTION

Containers should contain value types, either primitives, class types not mixed with derived class instances, or pointers (raw pointers in this case). Modern C++ has addressed the raw pointer problem, so this advice should only be used in premodern C++. Raw pointers are chosen as the container's element type to maintain the flexibility that the developer intended, eliminate the slicing problem, and permit copy construction and assignment. The following code shows the solution and exhibits all the developer's preferred behavior.

Listing 6.15 Using a container correctly for polymorphic elements

```cpp
struct Person {
    std::string name;
    Person(const std::string& n) : name(n) {}
    virtual std::string toString() const { return name; }
    virtual ~Person() {}
};

struct Employee : public Person {
    double salary;
    Employee(const std::string& n, double s) : Person(n), salary(s) {}
    std::string toString() const {
        std::stringstream ss;
        ss << Person::name << " gets paid " << salary;
        return ss.str();
    }
};

int main() {
    Person p("Sue");
    Employee e("Jane", 123.45);

    std::vector<Person*> people;
    people.push_back(&p);                          // Each can be added; they
    people.push_back(&e);                          // are the same element type.
    for (int i = 0; i < people.size(); ++i)
        std::cout << people[i]->toString() << '\n';  // Polymorphic
    return 0;                                         // behavior works.
}
```

Containers are beneficial when using polymorphic elements but must be managed correctly. Ensure that base classes add a virtual destructor, since containers copy and delete elements during construction and destruction. Code safety for runtime stability!

RECOMMENDATIONS

- Ensure that anything added to a container is both copy constructible and assignable; classes that eliminate one or both do not qualify for inclusion.
- Containers should hold a value type or a pointer type to prevent slicing or other problems.
- Consider modern C++ improvements if possible.

SEE ALSO

- See Mistake 8 for a discussion of exclusive-ownership pointers.
- See Mistake 9 for a discussion of shared-ownership pointers.
- See Mistake 35 for a discussion regarding the benefit of using Standard Template Library containers.
- See Mistake 57 for a discussion about virtual base class destructors.
- See Mistake 59 for a discussion of the pitfalls associated with slicing elements in a container.
- See Mistake 6 for a discussion of range-based `for` loops.

6.8   *Mistake 43: Favoring indexes over iterators*

This mistake focuses on effectiveness and affects performance. Many programmers are familiar with using indexes to iterate over arrays and apply this approach to containers.

PROBLEM

Developing code that uses arrays channels a developer's thoughts into one approach for iteration. Using indexing in a loop is common and applies to many problems; however, using indexing may unnecessarily constrain one's thinking and cause problems when different containers are used.

Arrays are rarely the best choice for containers. The Standard Template Library supplies several more specialized containers and is of greater utility than arrays. Missing out on these containers artificially limits the developer and causes them to design and rewrite code unnecessarily. Using indexing in preference to iterators can affect performance. The loop's body is often sufficiently large that this effect is negligible—but not necessarily.

Listing 6.16 shows indexing to iterate over a few containers. Only a few helpful containers are included; others work similarly (e.g., `deque`, `list`, and `map`). This absence is not laziness; some of these missing containers cannot be indexed over, making handling them jarringly different from the approach learned from C or in the classroom. Passing arrays to functions has the inconvenience of requiring the number of elements to be passed as an additional parameter. It is easy to get this value wrong, resulting in missed data or access beyond the array's end. Further, the caller becomes responsible for handling details the function should be tasked with. Overall, arrays are generally a poor choice for containers.

Listing 6.16   Indexing over an array in a function

```
double sum(const double* values, int size) {
    double sum = 0.0;
    for (int i  = 0; i < size; ++i)
        sum += values[i];
    return sum;
}
```

```
int main() {
    double vals[] = { 3.14, 2.78, 3.45, 7.77 };
    std::cout << sum(vals, 3) << '\n';
    return 0;
}
```

◄──┐ **Oops! The last index was used, not the count.**

ANALYSIS

Programming in C offered no alternatives to indexing. Plenty of mistakes were made. While mistakes are not an inherent indexing feature, the risk of being off by one was tremendous in C. The main reason was that the developer had to keep track of the list of values and the size and pass those to functions or use them in a loop.

The topic of using arrays, as well as their limitations, is well documented, with plenty of textbooks focusing on the technique. Once drilled into one's muscle memory, using iterators seems awkward and "different." What we learn first is often seen as correct, regular, and effective. Indexing has this effect and is a poor choice in most cases.

SOLUTION

Using iterators is ideal in most situations. First, all Standard Template Library containers use them. Second, they are optimized and often more performant than indexes. Third, the do not allow for off-by-one mistakes. Listing 6.17 demonstrates iterators using various containers. The consistency they offer is important; if one learns how to iterate in one case, others will be similar. This approach should become familiar enough that it becomes muscle memory.

Unlike arrays, STL containers are smart; they know their size and can interact with iterators to start at the first element and iterate to the end. The approach does not need to change based on the container.

Listing 6.17 Using an iterator with a vector

```
double sum(const std::vector<double>& values) {
    double sum = 0.0;
    for (std::vector<double>::const_iterator it = values.begin();
            it != values.end(); ++it)
        sum += *it;
    return sum;
}

int main() {
    std::vector<double> vals;
    vals.push_back(3.14);  vals.push_back(2.78);
    vals.push_back(3.45);  vals.push_back(7.77);
    std::cout << sum(vals) << '\n';
    return 0;
}
```

One might complain that the iterator type in the loop is complex. This is a fair objection; modern C++ offers the ability to make type deductions using the auto keyword, which precludes this complexity by having the compiler deduce the correct type. This is a real time-saver!

To prove the assertion that other containers work the same way, consider listing 6.18, which uses a set. The only changes are the type of container, a set rather than a vector, and a change to add an element to the set, insert instead of push_back. A third set of inserts is added to show that the set eliminates duplicate values.

Listing 6.18   Using an iterator with a set

```
double sum(const std::set<double>& values) {
    double sum = 0.0;
    for (std::set<double>::const_iterator it = values.begin();
            it != values.end(); ++it)
        sum += *it;
    return sum;
}

int main() {
    std::set<double> vals;
    vals.insert(3.14);   vals.insert(2.78);
    vals.insert(3.45);   vals.insert(7.77);          ⟵── Duplicated values
    vals.insert(3.45);   vals.insert(7.77);              are ignored in a set.
    std::cout << sum(vals) << '\n';
    return 0;
}
```

This technique becomes more straightforward as time progresses and benefits a developer by standardizing the approach for iterating over any container. Hopefully, this is enough incentive to stop using arrays!

Modern C++ has introduced three features that simplify or replace coding loops. Peruse the See Also section to learn more about these features.

RECOMMENDATIONS

- Use Standard Template Library containers wherever possible.
- Use iterators over these containers to eliminate off-by-one mistakes; let the data type determine the starting and stopping points.
- Generally, stop using arrays.

SEE ALSO

- See Mistake 6 for a discussion of range-based for loops.
- See Mistake 11 for a discussion of using the auto keyword to simplify determining the types of variables.
- See Mistake 13 for a discussion of using Standard Template Library algorithms to eliminate writing some for loops.
- See Mistake 35 for a strong argument against arrays.

Part 3

Classic (premodern) C++

In software development, grappling with legacy code is an ongoing challenge, particularly for C++ programming. The classic, or premodern, era of C++ is marked by practices developed before modern language features were established, often lacking the safety, efficiency, and simplicity that contemporary features offer. This section delves into these classic coding problems, offering insights and strategies to improve code quality and robustness within the confines of legacy systems.

A critical area of focus is the design and maintenance of class invariants, foundational principles for creating robust and stable applications. Establishing strong class invariants is paramount to ensuring application stability and predictability, yet maintaining these invariants over time, especially as the code base evolves, presents challenges. This section explores past pitfalls and offers guidance on crafting and sustaining class integrity through deliberate design, helping developers shield against the gradual decay of design quality and the improvement of new code.

Additionally, this part addresses concerns regarding class operations, resource management, and function usage. Thoughtful implementation of class operations, such as constructors, destructors, and assignment operators, is crucial for error minimization and performance optimization. Proper handling of exceptions and system resource management is vital in preventing resource leaks and ensuring application reliability. Refining the design of functions and parameters is necessary to avoid inefficiencies in pre-modern C++ practices. Finally, an overarching examination of general coding practices in classic C++ provides developers with a roadmap to enhance the quality and sustainability of their legacy code, ensuring it remains resilient and relevant for future demands.

Establishing the
class invariant

7

This chapter covers

- The class invariant, an essential view of what a class is and does
- Building class behavior from a minimum set of essential functions
- Treating classes as new data types
- Good inheritance design, as seen from the class invariant
- Ensuring classes work correctly and cooperate with the compiler

Classes represent data types. The C++ standardization committee could never anticipate every data type needed; therefore, the language was designed to be extensible. If a new data type is required, a developer can write it by creating a new class.

While writing a class is a simple process, writing a good class is much more challenging to get correct. Over the years, different advice has been given, and numerous problems have been detected. Learning some of these problems helps programmers detect these and similar problems in existing code. Eliminating these problems altogether guides a developer toward better class design.

7.1 *Class invariants enforce proper class design*

A class has a minimum of four essential characteristics. Some academics may suggest others, but these four should be regarded as fundamental:

- Interpretation
- Set of operations
- Range of values
- Memory mechanics

7.1.1 *Interpretation*

The primary characteristic of class invariants is the interpretation of class data. Classes are aggregates of data and functions. The data is the state, and the functions are the behavior of an instance of the class. In this context, an *instance* is used to mean a created occurrence of the class from the program's viewpoint, while an *object* refers to its values stored in memory. What the various component data types mean, in isolation (each datum) and in aggregate (the object), depends on the design of the class. Each value has a specific type, which carries a particular meaning, and each contributes to the overall understanding of the instance.

The class designer must determine what the data means beyond their data type. For example, in a Student class, a std::string could hold a student's name. The data type is std::string with all of its built-in meaning, but in the context of the Student object, the particular value represents something specific to a given student and may have a particular form. Let's say the format looks like this: last name, comma, space, first name. The std::string instance cannot know or enforce such a scheme; therefore, it is up to the class to maintain it. This approach is poor; it would be better to have multiple strings representing each piece of data. This example suggests that good class design can be complex.

The interpretation of the std::string becomes one of the student's last name, some delimiting punctuation, and the student's first name. In aggregate, other data fields will add to the meaning of the Student instance. The result of that instance is a sufficient representation of a particular student in some academic institution. All the data necessary to solve the problem is expected to be modeled in the class and represented in the instance.

7.1.2 *Set of operations*

Manipulating instance data should be limited to the class itself. If external code (client) code can directly use instance data, mistakes or exploitations could quickly occur. Mistakes are inevitable; therefore, access to and modification of the data needs to be controlled. The knowledge of what the values mean (interpretation), what legitimate values are (range of values), and how the values may be manipulated must be controlled to prevent bugs.

The public interface is the set of operations (constructors and functions) a client can use. Making only some of the class members public limits access to the instance and ensures access is done correctly. Other members not considered part of the public interface (protected and private functions and destructors) may exist. Altogether, these functional members are the set of operations. Think of an integer variable. Typical operations include addition, subtraction, multiplication, and division—all things that can be done to and with an integer. Likewise, the public interface is what can be done to and with an instance of the class.

Thinking through the proper set of operations will entail considering several use cases: How do clients use and interact with an instance? A class, by default, will have a few operations available, but usually, these are insufficient for doing anything meaningful. Since the class is written to represent a concept or entity, the developer must provide meaningful behaviors and ways of interacting with its instances.

Class designers and developers determine this set of operations. In designing a good set of operations, the developer should consider the absolute minimum set (basis) of operations that can be made. Other nonbasis operations can be implemented with this minimum set. Good design reduces the number of functions that do computations or manipulations, eliminates duplicated code, minimizes maintenance efforts, and simplifies the class. Discovering the basis for a class takes work, but it is beneficial.

7.1.3   *Range of values*

The range of values is related to the idea of interpretation. Valid values are often bounded on one or both ends. Consider an `unsigned char` variable: it is bounded on the low end by the value 0 and on the high end by the value 255. The nature of a byte determines these bounds. Other data types usually have values in a subrange of the variable's possible values. An integer on my machine is a 32-bit entity with bounds of plus and minus 2.14 billion, but most problems do not need that range. For example, if a person's age were being modeled, the range of values would need to be restricted to nonnegative values, with a possible maximum of 150 (it is tough to say what this maximum value should be).

Assuming a `Student` class has an integer variable called `age`, the possible range of values would be restricted; using an unsigned one would be better. First, valid values would be nonnegative—it makes no sense to have a negative age. Second, the maximum value is challenging to determine and could be arbitrarily set to an unreasonably large value of 200. Perhaps it would be better to ignore the upper range. This range means that no age should fall outside the specified values; the range permits any valid value and precludes every invalid one. Sometimes, ranges are apparent, but other cases prove to be vague.

A well-designed class must enforce the range of values every variable can hold. Thought must be given for each data field and all the data fields in aggregate. Each data field has some vital knowledge about the instance, and they must work together harmoniously and make sense together. For example, consider a `Movie` class, where two dates represent the first date available for viewing and the last date of viewing. Each must maintain a meaningful value (no February 30th) and correctly relate to the other. It would not be correct to have the last viewing date before the first viewing date, even if both dates were well formed.

7.1.4   *Memory mechanics*

The allocation and usage of memory are only an problem for many classes if dynamic resources are used. Usually, the layout of instance variables follows the developer's preference, perhaps arranged by data type or alphabetically. Yet C++ allows developers to determine where and how memory is allocated, if desired. The ability to specify allocators with custom behavior is a powerful, nontrivial tool. The layout of memory depends on data type sizes and alignment. Some types will fall on a 4-byte starting boundary with others on a 2-byte or an 8-byte boundary. If instance variables are defined poorly, some variables will have gaps of unused memory. In today's large-memory-size machines, this is rarely a problem for space considerations, but it can be a problem for machine performance. Depending on the size of an object, it could take two or more cache lines and prove inefficient to move with the extra bytes being wasted. Ideally, little to no extra bytes should be introduced into an object.

7.1.5   *Performance implications*

While not a characteristic of data types, performance is influenced by data type design and implementation. Performance optimization should be one of the last steps in developing a program, not because it is unimportant but because premature optimization may affect correctness and effectiveness. Designing efficient algorithms, data structures, and minimally-sized instances with good layouts is much better. Performance tuning should discover bottlenecks and hotspots and seek to correct those. As many advise, performance must be achieved using proper tools rather than intuition. When necessary, C++ provides mechanisms to optimize memory allocation and object layout. These options may prove significant when used at the correct time and with restraint.

7.2   *Mistakes in class design*

Quite often, class design starts with a relatively pure idea implemented well but then faces the inevitable—change. Changes are usually required because the class is valid but seemingly incomplete. Then, additional changes are needed, the design is compromised, expediency trumps precision, and churn happens. The class rots but still serves a purpose. Code smells—non-ideal techniques or implementations, often due to time constraints or insufficient understanding of the problem space or the code's influence—mount, but time and budget dictate other priorities.

Detecting these problems is often less complicated than determining a solution. Common mistakes can usually be fixed with minimal effect on other parts of the code base. However, these mistakes represent only a (small) subset of existing problems. An entire volume could be written about class design mistakes.

Good class design is fundamental to understanding and maintaining the class invariant. The class represents a data type that must maintain consistency and correctness for the instances to have meaning. Neglecting any invariant aspect exposes the instance to inconsistency and probable failure. Clients expect correctness, and it is our duty as developers to deliver on that expectation.

7.2.1 *The class invariant*

A *class invariant* is a condition that must always hold for an object of a class after the object's construction and between any sequence of method calls on that object. It represents the consistent, valid state of the object and is typically enforced through constructors, destructors, and member functions. Class invariants ensure the integrity and correctness of the object's data throughout its lifetime.

Every class should represent a concept or an entity; a class is a new data type. It describes its concept or entity meaningfully, aggregating other data types, from different classes to primitive types. Good design and understanding the class invariant are two sides of the same coin. The principle of abstraction means, first, that the class reduces the details of the concept or entity to the bare minimum, which is used in defining the class. Second, abstraction means the entire instance can be handled as a unit. This abstraction of an entity or concept is expected to behave meaningfully by client code. The class should avoid surprising its client code by behaving in unexpected ways.

Since the class represents a concept or entity, it must restrict its internal data to specific values that are meaningful to its representation. As previously stated, a `Student` should have a nonnegative `age`. The class is the locus of knowledge about the represented entity or concept. It should not depend on any other class or external data to convey that knowledge. The principle of encapsulation, in part, means that everything the class knows and does should be contained entirely within the class. Client code should be able to interact with or obtain any necessary data from an instance without having to manipulate or query other objects or variables.

These characteristics come with responsibility. The class must ensure all its data members, individually and in aggregate, are legitimate and always make sense as well as that interaction with it is predictable and free from surprises. Further, it must ensure that this sensibility and predictability are never compromised during program execution. This class responsibility is called the *class invariant*. The invariant is a property of an instance that is always true no matter how the instance is initialized or modified. The class must never create instances that do not honor the invariant and protect existing instances from changes that violate the invariant.

The characteristic of correctness is the most important for proper program behavior. If the program code is incorrect, nothing can be guaranteed; no amount of performance can make up for this error, and results are suspect. Maintaining the class invariant is a significant means of ensuring correctness. When a class behaves in a controlled, predictable manner, clients can use it confidently, and its results are meaningful.

Legacy code often has classes designed with something other than the invariant in mind. Tremendous opportunities exist to clean up many current classes. Regrettably, modifications—even those that make the class more predictable and robust—are likely to cause unexpected behavior. As always, ideals and theories must respect reality. The goal is improvement, but the path might be somewhat (or horribly) bumpy.

7.2.2   *Establishing the class invariant*

A class represents a consistent, cohesive concept or entity. The class requirements must specify the bounds for each instance variable separately and in aggregate. The aggregate represents the state of an instance. A significant goal is to ensure the instance's state is consistent. Continuing with the example of a `Person`, if the value of `age` were negative, the meaning of a `Person` would be jeopardized—what would a negative age represent?

Establishing the class invariant is the job of the constructor or constructors; maintaining the invariant is the responsibility of the mutators or other functions that alter state. Every instance variable must be initialized and maintain a meaningful and correct value. Interpretation of the instance depends on it maintaining the invariant. The range of values for a variable's type will likely exceed that of the invariant, so constructors and mutators must ensure no value goes out of range. I have observed code that initializes or sets instance variables to invalid values with accessors used to validate the range and return only meaningful values. If any instance variable represents an invalid value, one must consider the class invariant violated.

The mistakes in this chapter focus on establishing the class invariant; therefore, it focuses on constructors. Mutators are considered separately in the following chapter, where they are required to maintain the class invariant. These two chapters are distinct but must coordinate and work together to keep the class invariant correct.

7.3   *Mistake 44: Failing to maintain the class invariant*

This mistake focuses on correctness and effectiveness within class design and development. Instance variables must be initialized to a value within the boundaries determined by the class. This ensures the object is well defined and valid before it is used.

Mutators modify the state of instance variables. To maintain the class invariant, they must ensure input parameters are checked for values that fall within the acceptable range for that variable. Further, any code in other methods that affects the state of any instance variable must ensure that it does not compromise the invariant. Ensuring the constructors, mutators, and support code maintain the class invariant is essential.

Each constructor is responsible for initializing all instance variables. If any of the values are defaulted, that value must generally make sense and not render the instance invalid if the defaulted value is not later modified. Each mutator must ensure its input parameter value lies within the range of acceptable values and only modify its instance variable in such cases. Suppose the parameter value of either a constructor or mutator is invalid. In that case, the class's behavior must ensure the instance's state conforms to the invariant. In many cases, invalid parameter input should be handled by throwing an exception; in other cases, no modification of the instance variable should occur. This last approach may cause problems with the constructor. Further complications can arise when using a builder or factory pattern. In all cases, the instance variables must be valid before the instance is used.

PROBLEM

A properly coded constructor, or set of constructors, will initialize each instance variable with a meaningful value or not permit the object to be instantiated (i.e., throw an exception). Maintaining the class invariant demands this condition and no less. Every mutator must validate the input parameter and ensure the variable is not updated for invalid values or an exception is thrown. All other methods that affect an instance variable must maintain the class invariant. Difficulties arise when these conditions are not honored, as in listing 7.1.

Many classes have a default, or no-argument, constructor written by the compiler or the developer. Suppose the developer does not provide any constructor for the class. In that case, the compiler will write a default constructor, where each instance variable will be initialized to its zero value for that type if it is called. The conditional part of that statement reveals that whether the default constructor is called depends on how the variable is defined or assigned.

Listing 7.1 A typical textbook structure

```
struct Person {
    int age;
    std::string name;
};

int main() {
    Person p1;
    std::cout << p1.age << " '" << p1.name << "'\n";
    Person p2 = Person();
    std::cout << p2.age << " '" << p2.name << "'\n";
}
```

age prints garbage (undefined) values, and name prints an empty string.

This prints: 0 ''

The compiler provides a no-argument constructor but does not call it in the first case. In the second case, the provided constructor is called, which demonstrates the behavior of initializing primitive (or built-in) variables to their zero value for that type. Instances have their default constructor called in both cases.

The output of the code in listing 7.1 is unpredictable—it is undefined behavior for the age variable. Every byte of memory has some value; the output is whatever value the bytes representing that variable are interpreted as (i.e., garbage!). This leaves us uncertain about this code.

ANALYSIS

Since the constructor's responsibility is to initialize every instance variable, using the first approach causes it to fail in its efforts. If the constructor fails, it cannot maintain the class invariant. Worse, the compiler never complains; the instance variables are whatever undefined values are already in memory, and all seems to work. Undefined behavior will result if the values are used. How the compiler-written default constructor is called depends on the way the instance is set up. If the developer writes a default constructor, it will be called in either case. Therefore, the developer must write a default constructor if needed to maintain the class invariant. For example, this is a possible default constructor:

```
Person() : name("Joey"), age(21) {}
```

But is this a good, meaningful default constructor? This one is simple to write but needs to answer the question of a good default name and age. In more cases than not, the default constructor will cause the class invariant to fail because the instance is initialized with meaningless data—not invalid according to the constraints of the variable types, just meaningless. While the default constructor assigned the name Joey and age 21 to a Person instance, what sense does it make? The client code could later change the values to something meaningful to its problem, but what happens if even one variable of one instance is overlooked? The class invariant cannot be guaranteed.

The developer must write constructors that take more than zero parameters. Client code can create a Person instance and pass a name and an age to a two-argument constructor with reasonable data.

Consider this constructor for the Person structure:

```
Person(const std::string& n, int a) : name(n), age(a) {}
```

The compiler will not supply a default constructor if any constructor is written for the class. Therefore, if a default constructor is also needed, the developer must explicitly include it. Remember, there is a burden for getting the default constructor default values correct for the problem without assuming (or hoping) the client will change them later. The default constructor will violate the constraint if this cannot be done.

Mutators can also violate the class invariant if they are not careful. Consider the following mutator of the age instance variable:

```
void setAge(int a) { age = a; }
```

The age can be set to a negative or unreasonably large value, neither of which makes sense. Restricting the lower bound to nonnegative values solves one end of the range of values, but it is challenging to solve the upper bound truly. What value is the most meaningful largest age?

SOLUTION

Ideally, constructors and mutators work in a coordinated manner. The constructor has the responsibility to establish the class invariant but not necessarily directly initialize each instance variable. If both the constructor and mutator initialize or mutate the same instance variable, they are likely duplicating knowledge. This knowledge should be encapsulated in the mutator. The constructor can call each mutator, passing its initialization parameter value. The mutator validates the parameter value and handles it appropriately. The constructor must ensure the mutator is called to perform initialization, not necessarily initialize the instance variable.

In this case, a default constructor provided by the developer or the compiler would be invalid—no meaningful, correct value can be defaulted for the name or age variables. As tempting as it might be to use a default constructor, avoid them whenever possible, by writing at least one constructor that requires a parameter for each instance variable.

Note that having no default constructor has a negative consequence when using arrays. Defining an array of class instances means the default constructor must be called to initialize each element; in this case, not having a default constructor is an error. Consult the See Also section for further discussion.

Listing 7.2 demonstrates a constructor and mutator working together to initialize an instance with partial age range checking. As a word of caution, `age` gets set twice in this slightly convoluted code, but it is meant to demonstrate limiting the allowed range of values—teachers get to do things like this! Moving the range-checking code to a private validation function and calling it in the initializer and the `setAge` function is a much better approach.

Listing 7.2 Requiring an initialization value for each instance variable

```
struct Person {
    int age;
    std::string name;
    Person(std::string n, int a) : name(n),
        age(setAge(a)) {}                        ◄──── The technique of calling a member
    int setAge(int);                                    function during construction may
};                                                      produce undefined behavior. Keep it
int Person::setAge(int a) {                             simple or choose another approach.
    if (a < 0)
        throw std::out_of_range("age must be non-negative");
    age = a;
    return age;
}

int main() {
    Person annie("Annette", 25);              Throws an out_of_
    Person floyd("Floyd", -1);        ◄────── range exception
}
```

When a function or constructor cannot perform what it is supposed to meaningfully, the best solution is to throw an exception. This approach is different than returning an error return code. The error return code implies that something could not be done due to some erroneous condition, but the object or function is still in a good state. In the case of a constructor, an invalid value cannot be used to initialize an instance variable. The object must not be instantiated if no reasonable default value is available because the variable cannot be initialized. Hence, it is best to throw an exception. An exception forces the caller to deal with the possibility of a nonexistent object. Returning an incorrect return code implies that the object was instantiated and the class invariant held. For invalid data, neither is valid.

> **NOTE** Several solutions throughout the book use the approach of calling a member function in the initializer list. This can produce undefined behavior in some cases. Refer to https://compiler-explorer.com/z/PPes7vPYd for a meaningful example. I use them for simple variables. If the method depends on the state of any other variable, things could go sideways quickly; therefore, use this technique with caution.

RECOMMENDATIONS

- Ensure that a constructor properly initializes each instance variable.
- If available, a constructor should call the instance variable mutator for initialization to prevent duplication of code.
- A mutator should validate the input parameter value before the value is assigned to the instance variable; if the value is improper, throw an exception.
- Throw an exception if the instance cannot be fully and correctly initialized—do not create partially or wrongly constructed objects.
- Avoid default constructors in most cases; if one is needed, write it yourself.

SEE ALSO

- See Mistake 35 for an explanation of how to solve this problem using containers, not arrays.
- See Mistake 49 for a more detailed discussion of using default constructors.
- See Mistake 70 for a further discussion of exceptions in constructors.

7.4   Mistake 45: Not thinking of classes as data types

Built-in C++ data types, such as `int` and `double`, are intuitive, syntactically simple, and performant. When a developer designs a class, these characteristics should be deemed essential. Class design is type design; everything that makes a correct and useful type must be considered. Few other languages provide the flexibility that C++ gives a class designer, but several potential pitfalls must be considered. These include memory allocation and deallocation; object instantiation, initialization, and destruction; overloaded and friend functions; and, especially, the class invariant.

Types determine the set of operations performed by an instance of the class. The need for subtypes often arises, and the proper use of inheritance must be thought through. If the class or type is meant to be a base class, it must define an interface that is meaningful for all subtypes. Care must be taken to ensure the subtypes do not break the class invariant.

Correct and meaningful type design provides an easy-to-use and clearly defined sense to the reader and the developer. Correctness must be paramount to class design, but a strong emphasis must be placed on the readability of the resulting use of instances. Good design also leads to effective use of the type so that the programmer need not compensate for missing or awkward functionality. Finally, good type design considers how an instance may be used in collections or large sets; this affects performance. As always, think through the runtime and space costs to minimize problems associated with poor algorithm selection.

The four main characteristics of a class affect how it is designed, coded, and used. Careful consideration must ensure everyone involved can effectively use the class. Effective use generally comes down to the set of operations the class provides. Design this set to allow a programmer to use it intuitively (as much as possible).

PROBLEM

Listing 7.3 is a contrived example that shows several problems with a poorly considered data type implemented as a class. The programmer thought that by developing a simple `Rational` class, the concept of a rational number could be easily abstracted and used. At first glance, the code looks reasonable, but it contains several bugs disguised as good code. The class is designed to allow `Rational` instances to be added, multiplied, and printed. Yet using this class produces awkward code.

The idea was to perform calculations with rational numbers and output results afterward. A client using this code would see quickly that regular, expected operations are not provided (e.g., the `plus` method instead of the + operator), and usage becomes cluttered and unclear. This unreadable approach also costs developers time, making this attempt both naïve and cognitively expensive.

Listing 7.3 A naïve implementation of the `Rational` class

```
class Rational {
private:
    double num;
    double den;
public:
    Rational() : num(0), den(1) {}
    Rational(double n, double d) : num(n), den(d) { reduce(); }
    void setNumerator(double n) { num = n; }
    void setDenominator(double d) { den = d; }
    double getNumerator() { return num; }
    double getDenominator() { return den; }
    static int gcd(int a, int b) { return a == 0 ? b : gcd(b % a, a); }
    void reduce() {
        int div = gcd(num, den);
        num = (den > 0 ? 1 : -1) * num / div;
        den = abs(den) / div;
    }
    Rational plus(const Rational& o) const {          The poorly named
        int n = num * o.den + den * o.num;            addition operator
        int d = den * o.den;
```

```
        return Rational(n, d);
    }
    Rational times(const Rational& o) const {    ◄────┐  The poorly named
        int n = num * o.num;                           │  multiplication operator
        int d = den * o.den;
        return Rational(n, d);
    }
    void print() { std::cout << num << '/' << den; }   ◄────┐  The poorly named
};                                                            │  output operator

int main() {
    Rational r1(1, 3);
    Rational r2(2, 4);
    Rational r3 = r1.plus(r2);
    r3.print();
    std::cout << '\n';
    Rational(1, 0);
    return 0;
}
```

ANALYSIS

The first thing that stands out in this `Rational` class is its misunderstanding of the nature of rational numbers. By their nature, rational numbers are composed of ratios (hence the name *ratio*-nal, which does not refer to a "sensible" number, as I initially thought). Number theory asserts that the numerator and denominator are integers, not doubles. Following sound mathematical reasoning is essential. Next, consider the final line of code in the main function just before the return. That is an undefined situation, as the denominator is a divide-by-zero problem.

An important question must be asked: Does a rational number ever change? I prefer immutable data; this is a prime example of the principle. Different considerations must be used for a mutable version. Numbers never change; therefore, a rational number, once constructed, should never change its value (but this depends on the problem being solved). Remove the mutators in every place possible. Consider whether obtaining the numerator independently of the denominator makes sense—in this case, probably not. Remove the accessors.

Determine whether a client should be able to call `gcd` or `reduce`. These functions are provided as helpers for the `Rational` class; they should not be part of the public interface—mark them `private`. Finally, determine whether these functions should be inlined; generally, recursive functions are not inlined, but actual results depend on the compiler. By defining them inside the class, they are implicitly inline. Such a method will be implemented as the compiler sees most appropriate. An argument can be made to leave `gcd` implicitly inline, since it is simple and implemented in the class; the compiler will determine its actual case. However, `reduce` is less likely to save any significant overhead by being inlined.

Consider carefully what the `plus` and `times` functions mean. The designer meant for them to be addition and multiplication, but that needs to be communicated clearly. Further, it is unclear whether these functions alter the calling object (`r1` in the case of `plus`) or if they create a new object initialized with the result of the computation. The source code resolves the question, but making the user read the source code significantly affects readability.

That `print` function is well intentioned but needs to be more intuitive. It likely was thought that `std::cout` is the natural—therefore only—stream in which a `Rational` instance's output might be used; this is a naïve and awkward decision. Good design is general in its form, but this design is concrete and inflexible. These three poorly designed functions significantly affect effectiveness, since they are not intuitive and do not follow any other known usage pattern.

Solution

This code is a redesigned version that considers the meaning of a rational number and implements that understanding in code. The `plus` and `times` methods have been reimplemented to use the standard arithmetic `+` and `*` operators. Clients use this to write code that intuitively uses the expected computational symbols. The `print` method has been changed to overload `operator<<` for the `ostream` class. This approach allows the developer to use the standard insertion operator to add data to an output stream—just like all built-in data types. This consistency makes using the code natural and effective.

Listing 7.4 An implementation that provides intuitive use

```cpp
class Rational {
private:
    int num;
    int den;
    static int gcd(int a, int b) { return a == 0 ? b : gcd(b % a, a); }
    void reduce();
    int validate(int v) {
        return v != 0 ? v : throw
            std::invalid_argument("zero denominator");
    }
public:
    Rational(int n, int d=1) : num(n), den(validate(d)) { reduce(); }
    Rational operator+(const Rational& o) const;
    Rational operator*(const Rational& o) const;
    friend std::ostream& operator<<(std::ostream&, const Rational&);
};

void Rational::reduce() {
    int div = gcd(num, den);
    num = (den > 0 ? 1 : -1) * num / div;
    den = abs(den) / div;
}
```

The natural addition operator ◄

```cpp
Rational Rational::operator+(const Rational& o) const {
    return Rational(num * o.den + den * o.num, den * o.den);
}
```

The natural multiplication operator ◄

```cpp
Rational Rational::operator*(const Rational& o) const {
    return Rational(num * o.num, den * o.den);
```

```
}

std::ostream& operator<<(std::ostream& out, const Rational& r) {
    out << r.num << '/' << r.den;
    return out;
}
```
                                                                    **The natural
                                                                    insertion operator**

```
int main() {
    Rational r1(1, 3);
    Rational r2(2, 4);
    std::cout << r1 + r2 << '\n';
    //Rational(1, 0);
    return 0;
}
```

The meaning of a rational number is honored by making the instance variables integers. The helper functions are neatly hidden away for use by the class only. Division by zero is addressed and handled appropriately. Operators are intuitive, and the user knows that addition and multiplication do not affect the calling (or left-hand) object. The insertion operator works like any other, so the user uses it like any other occurrence—significantly improving readability and effectiveness.

There are several problems when thinking about inline versus out-of-line function definitions. Here are some to consider:

- *Performance*—Inline functions can reduce function call overhead by embedding the function code directly at the call site, which might improve performance in frequently called small functions. However, excessive inlining can increase code size and degrade cache performance. Out-of-line functions typically have the overhead of function calls, but they do not increase code size at the call site, which can help maintain better instruction cache locality.

- *Code size*—Inline functions can lead to code bloat if used excessively or with large functions because the code is inserted at each call site. Out-of-line functions help keep the executable file size smaller, since function code is reused rather than duplicated.

- *Debugging and maintenance*—Inline functions can make debugging more difficult, as the function code is replicated at multiple locations, complicating stack traces and debugging efforts. Out-of-line functions centralize the implementation, making them easier to maintain and debug.

- *Compilation dependencies*—Inline functions are often defined in header files, which increases the risk of recompilation of multiple translation units if the inline function is changed. Out-of-line functions are frequently defined in source files, which helps minimize recompilation, as changes to these functions do not affect header files and files dependent on the headers.

- *Encapsulation*—Inline functions are often defined in headers; therefore, the implementation details are exposed, which might not be desirable for encapsulation. Out-of-line functions can hide implementation details in source files, improving encapsulation and separation of interface and implementation.

- *Complexity and readability*—Inline functions are best suited for simple functions, where defining them inline can increase readability by keeping related code together. Out-of-line functions are best for complex functions, where separating the implementation helps to keep the class definition clean and easy to read.

RECOMMENDATIONS

- Remember that implementing a class design is designing a new data type. Using types should be intuitive to anyone who has a basic understanding of their meaning.

- Define symbol-based operators when they accurately communicate the operation's meaning in the data type context. Never use them simply because they "look cool."

- Keep data streams and code design general; do not lock a user into one specific path if possible. This is best done by designing a data type to act close to built-in types' natural operations.

- Use inlining judiciously, thinking through the tradeoffs between inline and out-of-line methods.

7.5   *Mistake 46: Not establishing a basis for methods*

This mistake focuses on correctness and effectiveness. Multiple constructors are often implemented as separate operations, although they duplicate much of the code. Further, computational methods frequently duplicate computational code. This duplication is what should lead to the consideration of determining a basis. Not all duplication means a basis must be determined, but it is a good sign that a basis might be found. A *basis* is a mathematical concept that defines a minimal set of functions—all are essential, and none overlap—from which other nonbasis functions can be implemented. The *don't repeat yourself* (DRY) principle is relevant in this discussion but must serve a more nuanced purpose than is often presented—more on that later.

Differences in implementing multiple constructors or functions can lead to incorrect behavior. Supporting essential code in one place leads to more effective use of a programmer's time and reduces the cognitive load.

This discussion analyzes constructors but applies to methods and standalone functions. The big idea is to reduce the number of behavior implementations to prevent code divergence over time. Things can go wrong quickly when functionality is duplicated and maintained differently.

Often, classes will have multiple constructors that take a different number of parameters. In cases where some information is not provided in the instantiation call, default values will be supplied. In other cases, default behavior will be applied to fill in the gaps in knowledge.

PROBLEM

A quick example may be helpful to better understand the meaning of a basis function. Consider an `integer` class that wraps the built-in `int` type. The four basic mathematical operations are likely sufficiently different from each other that all four would be implemented uniquely. However, careful analysis shows this to be untrue. A subtraction problem `a - b` is mathematically equivalent to `a + -b`. Subtraction can be implemented in terms of addition and negation. Therefore, subtraction does not need to be a separate operation. Multiplication is repeated addition, and division is subtraction repeated—or better yet, repeated addition of a negated value. Therefore, only two basis functions are required to implement these four arithmetic functions—adding two integer values and negating an integer value. The other three operations can be defined in terms of these two.

This idea of operations or functions being implemented in terms of others establishes how to distinguish basis functions and leads directly to implementing them in this way. The characteristic of correctness is ensured by making the computational code in as few places as possible. Other methods implemented in terms of these will work correctly and not duplicate code that might become mismatched as changes occur. The characteristic of effectiveness is maintained by writing the core code once per function and demonstrating its correctness by using it repeatedly in other nonbasis functions.

The `Cylinder` code example (listing 7.5) shows a typical approach when basis functions are not appropriately considered. Its constructors and operations are coded separately and independently. Early in the development of a class, it is easy to assume the code will stay mostly the same in the future. In too many cases, this proves untrue. Implementing these constructors and functions could quickly diverge from each other by adding one or two new requirements. Any divergence affects correctness, readability, and effectiveness.

> **Listing 7.5   Duplicated knowledge in a class**

```
class Cylinder {
private:
    double radius;
    double height;
    double area;
    double volume;
public:
    const double PI = 3.1415927;
    Cylinder() {
        radius = 1;
        height = 1;
        area = PI;
        volume = PI;
    }
    Cylinder(double h) {
        radius = 1;
        height = h;
        area = PI;
```

```
        volume = PI * h;
    }
    Cylinder(double r, double h) {
        radius = r;
        height = h;
        area = PI * r * r;
        volume = PI * r * r * h;
    }
    double getBaseArea() const { return area; }
    double getVolume() const { return volume; }
};
```

Computes area using
the standard formula

Volume is area * height; the
area is computed again.

ANALYSIS

The implementations of these constructors and functions duplicate knowledge. The DRY principle is intended to prevent this situation. However, DRY is often implemented as a "do not repeat code" approach, instead of the more helpful "do not repeat knowledge" approach. Over time, a functional class will be susceptible to new requirements, resulting in added and modified code. These changes are inevitable, and the likelihood of duplication of knowledge increases. Divergence occurs when the replicated knowledge changes in one place but not another. After a while, it is unclear which version is correct.

Each constructor duplicates the initialization of the instance variables, sometimes with default values and others with parameters. This duplication suggests a better way. The code shows a typical pattern that can be refactored into a single helper function. The benefit of the helper function is that all constructors can use it and prevent the duplication of knowledge and code. When new requirements are added, the changes are isolated to the helper, preventing divergence.

SOLUTION

The best way to approach this problem is to understand how functions can be implemented in terms of others and then narrow that set of dependencies to a bare minimum. The constructors should factor out the standard code and place it in a private helper method. This helper method becomes the basis for the constructors implemented in terms of the helper.

The getBaseArea method computes the area of the cylinder's circular base. The volume method computes the area of the cylinder's circular base and then multiplies that by its height. The ability to factor out the common code and make a single area computation determines the necessary basis. In this case, the volume method should be implemented in terms of the basearea method, rather than a helper function.

Method reuse also occurs in class inheritance, where a derived class inherits base class method functionality and adds to it. In many cases, the overriding derived class method can call the base class method as part of its computation and modify it as needed. This approach prevents duplicating the functionality and allows the derived class to benefit from the base class. Adequately designed base class methods should be part of the derived class's basis.

These refactoring steps have been taken in listing 7.6. A helper method called `init` has been created to handle the previous duplication in the constructors.

The `volume` method now uses `basearea` to compute the cylinder's area and multiply that value by height. Volume is implemented in terms of the base area, preventing future divergence when the inevitable changes occur. This example is simplified but typical of the problem this mistake addresses. In straightforward cases, knowledge duplication may not be a problem. However, this problem can be extended to more complicated classes, where knowledge duplication has a greater influence. Do not let simplicity fool you into thinking there cannot be bugs.

Listing 7.6   A minimal set of functions

```
class Cylinder {
private:
    double radius;
    double height;
    void init(double r, double h) {
        radius = r;
        height = h;
    }
public:
    const double PI = 3.1415927;
    Cylinder() { init(1, 1); }
    Cylinder(double h) { init(1, h); }
    Cylinder(double r, double h) { init(r, h); }
    double basearea() { return PI * radius * radius; }      ← Computes the area
    double volume() { return basearea() * height; }         ← Computes the
                                                              volume in
                                                              terms of area
};
```

RECOMMENDATIONS

- Factor out common constructor code into a helper function, which becomes part of the basis set for the class.

- Consider how to implement functions in terms of other basis functions to simplify coding, prevent divergence, and maintain one source of truth for that knowledge.

- Minimize the set of basis functions, ensuring their function does not overlap. When new functions are added, base them on the basis functions and reevaluate if a new basis function is needed.

- Relax this approach if it becomes unwieldy or overly awkward. Remember that principles help minimize technical debt and speed development, but slavish implementation may lead to worse consequences.

- Look for opportunities to rework overridden methods into a basis function or set.

SEE ALSO

- See Mistake 82 for a better way to achieve a mixture of passed and default values in constructors and functions.

7.6   *Mistake 47: Failing to code the big 3*

The primary characteristic affected by resource management is correctness. Incorrect behavior affects the program and may adversely affect more than the program itself (e.g., the system). Most other correctness problems are limited in scope—this mistake can be pervasive, affecting other programs and the system.

The big 3—copy constructor, copy assignment operator, and destructor—are available in every version of C++ and should always be coded when dynamic resources are being used. Missing one or more of these can have an adverse effect on the program.

Many classes have one or more value-based instance variables. Examples include integers or doubles to represent numeric values. Some use `std::string` or, perhaps, `std::vector`. These variables are initialized when the instance is instantiated, used for some time during the program's execution, and then deleted when the instance goes out of scope. These variables are automatically managed and provide no adverse consequence for the developer.

However, those more sophisticated classes use dynamic or limited resources and have variables to represent them. One typical example is pointer-based variables. These variables often represent dynamic memory resources. Similarly, finite resources are often represented by a value-based variable. In this case, the resource represents an instance of some limited system resource that must be managed well. This could include a database connection, a socket, or a file handle. While the instance variables are automatically managed when the instance goes out of scope, the referred-to resources are not automatically managed. This lack of management provides significant opportunities for incorrect behavior. The programmer must be vigilant in these situations and correctly manage resources.

PROBLEM

When a class has dynamic resources, it must manage them correctly. Consider their management part of the class invariant. The class promises to establish, manage, and delete the resources as part of its operations. The example of dynamic memory shows the proper allocation and deallocation steps.

Some client code calls a constructor. A `new` operation occurs in the constructor to obtain dynamic memory, establishing part of the invariant. Other instance methods use this memory, keeping the invariant intact. Finally, as the instance goes out of scope (or is explicitly deleted), its destructor is called to `delete` the memory. When this approach is done well, no memory leaks, no double frees, and no freeing of invalid pointers occur. The program and system stability are ensured.

Another problem arises with dynamic resources that have nothing to do with the constructor and destructor operations. The copy assignment operator has problems that can affect correctness and must be considered carefully. Let's distinguish here between a *copy constructor* and a *copy assignment operator*. A constructor is called when a block of raw memory is obtained when creating an instance. This raw memory can hold anything; its state is undefined. The constructor must initialize raw memory with meaningful data that establishes the class invariant.

On the other hand, the copy assignment operator does not initialize an instance; it mutates an existing instance with values from another initialized instance. Care must be taken to ensure the copy assignment operator handles self-assignment (it should simply return). The copy constructor must obtain a new dynamic resource and initialize its pointer or handle variables relative to that value. The copy assignment operator must do the same but with an additional step. If the target of the copy assignment operator already has the dynamic resource, it must be destroyed in many cases to prevent memory or resource leaks. In some cases, the source instance values can be copied, but this approach needs to be revised in many other cases.

Much of the code in the copy constructor and the copy assignment operator will be duplicated. An opportunity exists to refactor this code into a private helper function both can call. Consideration must be given to the effect of destructors being called to ensure any duplicated destruction code is handled correctly. The RAII pattern demonstrates this paired allocation and deallocation.

Assume a project has been written to manipulate wiki pages. The company assigning the project requires a specific set of headers on each page. A new requirement has been raised for a copy operation to be developed to clone a page as the basis for a new page. The copy constructor is the ideal choice for this operation.

This copy constructor code was added to include the new copy functionality. Unfortunately, the developer did not remember to add the copy assignment operator code.

> **Listing 7.7   A copy constructor that shares unique resources**

```
class TextSection {
    // assume a clever implementation
};

class Page {
private:
    TextSection* headers;                           A dynamic resource
    TextSection* body;
public:
    Page(TextSection* h) : headers(h), body(new TextSection()) {}
    Page(const Page& o) : headers(o.headers), body(o.body) {}
    Page& operator=(const Page&);
};                                          Copying the dynamic
                                            resource pointer; two objects
int main() {                                use one dynamic resource.
    Page p1(new TextSection());
    Page p2 = p1;
    return 0;
}
```

ANALYSIS

The developer needs to address the fact that the copy constructor is using sharing semantics. The headers can be shared, since they are company mandated and not changeable. The body being shared is a problem. The cloned page will have changes made to its body text as part of normal operations. Because it is shared, this will affect the copied-from page. Further, when a `Page` is destroyed by going out of scope, the body `TextSection` in heap memory will be isolated and unreachable, causing a memory leak.

A correct copy constructor must consider that a shallow copy of a pointer implements sharing semantics, which is undesirable for the page body. The cloned page must allocate a new `TextSection` initialized from the copied-from page. Since the body text is a dynamic resource handled by a pointer, the destructor must ensure that when the instance goes out of scope, the dynamic resource is deleted before the instance is destroyed. The addition of the destructor ensures proper destruction is achieved. Finally, since the copy constructor and destructor have been added, it is crucial to ensure the copy assignment operator is also added.

Copy constructors assume the new instance uses raw memory (filled with garbage values). The copy assignment operator assumes the affected instance is correctly constructed and that every instance variable has a legitimate value. The `Page` class shows that copying the source body pointer to the target (a shallow copy) would cause the bug demonstrated in the poorly designed copy constructor. The copy assignment operator must ensure deep copy semantics are used for dynamic resources. It also must ensure any existing dynamic resource is deleted correctly or otherwise handled before the deep copy occurs. The copy assignment operator must add code to delete the existing body before creating a new body.

SOLUTION

Listing 7.8 shows these improvements. The copy constructor assumes no existing dynamic resources, so it allocates a new `TextSection` object. Similarly, the copy assignment operator does the same allocation but first takes care of existing resources by deleting them. Finally, the destructor ensures all dynamic resources are deleted.

This coordination of resources across the big 3 prevents resource leaks, often in the form of memory leaks. It preserves the uniqueness of particular objects, ensuring correctness during the program's operation.

> **Listing 7.8 A uniqueness-preserving copy constructor**

```
class TextSection {
    // assume a clever implementation
};

class Page {
private:
    TextSection* headers;
    TextSection* body;          // A dynamic resource
public:
    Page(TextSection* h) : headers(h), body(new TextSection()) {}
    Page(const Page& o) : headers(o.headers), body(new TextSection(*(o.body))) {}
    Page& operator=(const Page&);
    ~Page() { delete body; }
};
```

A new dynamic resource is created and initialized from the existing copy.

```cpp
Page& Page::operator=(const Page& o) {
    if (this == &o)
        return *this;
    headers = o.headers;
    delete body;
    body = new TextSection(*(o.body));
    return *this;

int main() {
    Page p1(new TextSection());
    Page p2 = p1;
    return 0;
}
```

Modern C++ changes the verbiage from the *big 3* to the *big 5*. The additional two members are the move constructor and the move assignment operator. The advice for the big 3 stays the same but adds the additional move semantics. Listing 7.9 shows the code from listing 7.8 improved with modern move semantics and smart pointers. Notice the use of =default.

Listing 7.9   Adding uniqueness preserving, move construction, and assignment

```cpp
class TextSection {
    // assume a clever implementation
};

class Page {
private:
    TextSection* headers;
    std::unique_ptr<TextSection> body;
public:
    Page(TextSection* h) : headers(h),
body(std::make_unique<TextSection>()) {}
    Page(const Page& o) : headers(o.headers),
body(std::make_unique<TextSection>(*o.body)) {}
    Page& operator=(const Page& o) {
        headers = o.headers;
        body = std::make_unique<TextSection>(*o.body);
        return *this;
    }
    Page(Page&&) = default;              // A modern move constructor
    Page &operator=(Page&&) = default;   // A modern move assignment operator
};

int main() {
    Page p1(new TextSection());
    Page p2 = p1;
    return 0;
}
```

RECOMMENDATIONS

- If any dynamic resources are used in a class, always write the big 3—destructor, copy constructor, and copy assignment operator.

- Remember that constructors are meant to initialize raw memory, and assignment operators are meant to update an existing, already constructed instance. Be sure to handle existing resources properly.

- Ensure that moved-from objects are neutralized so that they cannot be reused until correctly initialized.

SEE ALSO

- See Mistake 1 for a more complete discussion of the additional two constituents of the big 5.

- See Mistake 46 for a discussion on minimizing the number and implementation of methods.

- See Mistake 55 for further details.

- See Mistake 77 to discuss the RAII idiom being followed here.

7.7 *Mistake 48: Using inheritance just for code reuse*

Proper use of inheritance is essential for correctness, readability, and effectiveness. Wrongly used, inheritance introduces anomalies, is hard to read and reason about, and takes extra effort to keep details sorted out.

In the early days of object-oriented programming, inheritance was touted as the silver bullet that would solve all our software engineering problems. The DRY principle was quickly adopted as the poster child to encourage inheritance. Textbooks lauded its use and taught that code reuse was achievable.

The main idea was to write the code once in the base class (*superclass*, if you come from other languages) and reuse that code in derived classes. This promise was inviting, and many of us took the bait. Later, we discovered that our classes could have worked better. We had to write weird code that made exceptions for this class but not that class. We needed to understand the concept of the is-a relationship.

All fairy tales carry some truth, but the fantasy details seem to dim in the light of the real world. The fairy tale of code reuse has dimmed significantly over the years. Textbooks still mention code reuse in the context of inheritance. This suggestion is the worst possible reason for using inheritance. Code reuse is a benefit of inheritance, but it is never a reason for it.

PROBLEM

Inheritance is a great idea and a very powerful technique if used correctly. The derived is-a base class is an is-a relationship between the derived and base class. This relationship is precisely what Dr. Barbra Liskov described in the now-famous *Liskov substitution principle* (LSP). She stated that where an instance of the base type is needed, an instance of a derived type can be substituted. We are working on the concept that classes are data types.

> **NOTE** This mistake discusses only public inheritance. Protected, private, and virtual inheritance are quite different and should not be used for the is-a relationship. These are not addressed in this book.

What may need to be evident in the LSP is that when dealing with a collection of objects, some of the base classes, and various derived classes, we treat them all in a specific way. Each instance is treated as if it were the base class. Remember this mantra: "Everything that the base class knows and does, the derived class knows and does." Of course, this does not mean that everything the base class knows and does is directly accessible to the derived class (private members are inaccessible). In this context, it would be better to state that "every nonprivate thing the base class knows and does, the derived class knows and does directly."

One implication is that only the base class interface can be used in dealing with a collection of objects and subobjects—if a behavior is not defined on the base class, it cannot be invoked on a derived class. A second implication is that the collection often must deal with pointers to the objects, not the objects themselves. Many containers hold objects by value, which is of a fixed size. Attempting to squeeze a (most likely larger) derived object into a base-class-sized space is doomed to disappointment—the copy silently works, but the derived class part of the object is sliced off, leaving only the base class part.

Consider the case of a `Student` class being derived from a `Person` class, shown in the following listing. Everything the `Person` class knows (and does), the `Student` class knows (and does).

Listing 7.10   A simple inheritance hierarchy

```cpp
class Person {
    std::string name;
    int age;
};

class Student : public Person {
    double gpa;
};
```

To understand why a derived class can be substituted for a base class, study figure 7.1. On the left, we see an object of class `Person`, which has two instance variables: a name and an age. The `Student` object on the right derives from `Person` and adds a `gpa` instance variable. The top part of the `Student` looks like a `Person` precisely because a `Student` is-a `Person`. The bottom part of the `Student` is the additional instance variable. Because a `Student` can be considered a `Person` or a `Student`, depending on how it is being accessed, it can behave polymorphically as either.

Josie is a `Person`, and so is Sally. If we have a reference to Sally as a `Person`, everything about the `Person` is accessible. The bottom part is accessible only when we treat Sally as a `Student` because students have `gpa` values. Figure 7.1 also demonstrates why storing Sally in an array of `Person` elements has only space for the base class part; the `Student` part is sliced off, and Sally suddenly becomes only a `Person`—the object loses its `Student`-ness.

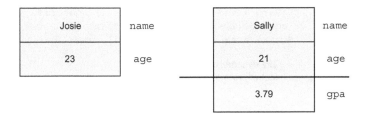

Figure 7.1 `Person` and `Student` **objects showing instance variables and their layout**

ANALYSIS

Polymorphism is the primary reason for arranging classes in a hierarchy. The only other reason would be to reuse code, saving a few keystrokes. However, this reason is an anti-reason; it causes more trouble and awkwardness than it saves.

In the following listing, a base class has the functionality a derived class wants to reuse. However, the derived class fails to be related to the base class by an is-a relationship. This example is designed to show some of the flaws that become apparent—usually later than earlier—when trying to save a few keystrokes by reusing methods when the classes are not closely related.

Listing 7.11 Relating classes by appearance

```cpp
class Square {
private:
    double side;
    double offset;
public:
    Square(double side) : side(side), offset(0) {}        A square can move in
    virtual void move(int n) { offset += n*side; }        a graphics space.
    double getOffset() { return offset; }
    double area() { return side*side; }
};
                                                          A horse can move, but it
class Horse : public Square {                              should be in a different way.
public:
    Horse(double height) : Square(height) {}
};

int main() {
    std::vector<Square*> squares;
    squares.push_back(new Square(1));
    squares.push_back(new Horse(15));                     Casting is likely a bad
    for (int i = 0; i < squares.size(); ++i) {            sign (a code smell).
        squares[i]->move(2);
        Horse* h = dynamic_cast<Horse*>(squares[i]);      This is an awkward
        if (h) {                                          mess; it can get
            std::cout << "Horse moved " << h->getOffset() complicated as
                <<" meters ahead\n";                      more classes are
        } else {                                          added.
```

```
            std::cout << "Square moved to (" << squares[i]->getOffset()
                << ", " << squares[i]->getOffset() << ")\n";
            std::cout << "Square area is " << squares[i]->area() << '\n';
        }
    }
    return 0;                        The dynamic objects are
}                              ◄──── leaked; they should be deleted.
```

First, when a container of these poorly related classes is iterated over, bespoke handling code must be added to ensure that Horse instances do not call the now-meaningless area method. This added burden forces programmers to handle each derived object as a special case, ruining the easy flow of containers of related classes. Further, this special handling might only be added to some newly developed code.

Second, the move method means to move a square to some point n units up and n units right (or vice versa if negative values are used). However, getOffset for a horse means something completely different, and the method name fails to communicate its intent.

Third, a Horse object cannot meaningfully be substituted for a Square object. The Horse instance will have both data fields and inherit the three methods; a Horse object cannot have a legitimate area, nor does it move like a Square. While this example is highly contrived, these essential points of criticism are valid for more "sensible" code running in the field that uses inheritance for code reuse.

SOLUTION

There are two alternatives for resolving this problem. The first is a refusal to code in this manner. Only use inheritance if a derived class is correctly related to its base class and is substitutable in *every* case. The point of reference for this relationship is whether the derived class is always substitutable where a base class instance is needed—again, every time. *Substitutability* means that each data field and behavior is meaningful in the context of the base and derived classes.

This code in listing 7.12 expresses this point better by breaking the vertical inheritance hierarchy and spreading it out horizontally. A program may need Horse and Square objects but not in a directly related way. Each class defines its own set of instance variables (what it knows) and methods (what it does). Both have a move method, but that turns out to be incidental. The more appropriately named getOffset and get-Position methods better communicate the intent of each method. Finally, collections of objects are separated into different containers, which is more intuitive and approximates reality much better.

Listing 7.12   Separation of nonrelated classes

```
class Square {
private:
    double side;
    double offset;
public:
```

```
        Square(double side) : side(side), offset(0) {}
        void move(int n) { this->offset += n*side; }              A square can move
        double getOffset() { return offset; }                     in its own way.
        double area() { return side*side; }
};

class Horse {
    double height;
    double position;
public:
    Horse(double height) : height(height), position(0) {}
    void move(int offset) { position += offset; }                 A horse can move
    double getPosition() { return position; }                     in its own way.
};

int main() {
    std::vector<Square*> squares;
    squares.push_back(new Square(1));                              Keeps squares together
    for (int i = 0; i < squares.size(); ++i) {
        squares[i]->move(2);
        std::cout << "Square moved to (" << squares[i]->getOffset()
            << ", " << squares[i]->getOffset() << ")\n";
        std::cout << "Square area is " << squares[i]->area() << '\n';
    }
    std::vector<Horse*> horses;
    horses.push_back(new Horse(15));                               Keeps horses together
    for (int i = 0; i < horses.size(); ++i) {
        horses[i]->move(10);
        std::cout << "Horse moved " << horses[i]->getPosition()
            << " meters ahead\n";
    }
    return 0;
}
```

The second approach uses a base class that defines only pure virtual functions. Languages like Java provide class-like structures called `Interfaces` with no implementation details (this was loosened in Java 8 and beyond). The idea is to provide an interface declaration of behavior (abstract functions) without implementation. Each derived concrete class implements the interface and must provide a code body for each abstract method. The most significant advantage of using this kind of class is that previously unrelated classes can be related at a more abstract level. However, we must be very careful to ensure these classes *should* be related through that commonality.

In this example, if the problem mainly involved moving objects (assuming it was in a graphics drawing program), it might make sense to relate these two classes by each implementing a typical abstract base class with a single `move` method declared. Be careful not to see patterns where there are none; do not "relate" classes because of a few identical methods or variable names. Focus on semantics (meaning), not grammar (syntax and naming).

For example, the `Square` and `Horse` classes could be related, using a concept called `Moveable`. This concept differs from the technical language feature introduced in

C++20. A `Moveable` object implies that it implements the `move` method, and a container of `Moveable` objects implies that each element can move (but has no other commonality). The following code demonstrates this concept.

Listing 7.13   Using an interface-like class

```
class Moveable {                                  ◄──── A mix-in class that declares
public:                                                 behavior by making
    virtual void move(int) = 0;                         abstract methods
    virtual double getPosition() = 0;
};

class Square : public Moveable {
private:
    double side;
    double offset;
public:
    Square(double side) : side(side), offset(0) {}
    void move(int n) { this->offset += n*side; }  ◄──── Squares can move
    double getPosition() { return offset; }             in their way.
    double area() { return side*side; }
};

class Horse : public Moveable {
private:
    double height;
    double position;
public:
    Horse(double height) : height(height), position(0) {}
    void move(int offset) { position += offset; }  ◄──── Horses can move
    double getPosition() { return position; }            in their way.
};

int main() {
    std::vector<Moveable*> movers;                 ◄──── A collection of Moveable
    movers.push_back(new Square(1));                     objects; these should not be
    movers.push_back(new Horse(15));                     considered squares and horses.
    for (int i = 0; i < movers.size(); ++i) {
        movers[i]->move(2);
        std::cout << "Mover moved " << movers[i]->getPosition() << " units \n";
    }
    return 0;
}
```

When an interface-like class is used, ensure that each method makes sense for the intent and meaning of the idea the class captures. The Liskov substitution principle applies here as strictly as before—anywhere a base class instance is needed, a derived class instance can be correctly and meaningfully substituted.

RECOMMENDATIONS

- Polymorphism should be the primary motivation for inheritance.
- Without polymorphism, the purpose of inheritance degenerates to code reuse.

- Code reuse will cause awkwardness in writing and reading.
- Separate classes that use inheritance for code reuse and write the methods in a relevant way.

SEE ALSO

- See Mistake 45 for a discussion of thinking about classes as data types with the implications of a set of operations and the class invariant.
- See Mistake 50 for a classic example of struggling with arranging an inheritance hierarchy.
- See Mistake 59 for a discussion on how implementing polymorphic behavior on array elements will fail spectacularly.

7.8 Mistake 49: Overusing default constructors

This mistake strongly affects correctness, since it is oriented toward maintaining the class invariant. Readability is affected, since reading code that uses a default constructor says nothing about what the values are initialized to without additional examination.

Ensuring the instantiation of an object maintains the class invariant is the primary responsibility of the constructor. Many classes need specific initialization of instance variables to be in a meaningful state. Default constructors are provided to give a valid (but not necessarily meaningful) value to variables when no initialization values are specified via parameters. If a correct default value cannot be determined, the default constructor will initialize an instance to an inconsistent state. Suppose the class designer expects the developer to fill in those values with meaningful values later. A problem arises if one or more mutators are not called to fulfill this expectation.

PROBLEM

Default constructors may appear more effective, but often this is false. The defaulted values usually must be modified later to add meaningful data, thus complicating effectiveness and readability. Assuming initialized values are changed before the instance is used, performance is slightly affected.

An instance should never have invalid or meaningless data in its state. If default constructors are used, then the class must be designed to have significant default values for a "typical" object that can be used without further modification.

The code in listing 7.14 is somewhat typical but completely nonsensical. Since no programmer-supplied default constructor is given, the compiler provides its default version, which initializes all class instances to their default values. The built-in instances are not initialized at all. Therefore, the `name` will be the empty string (a bizarre name), and the `age` will be undefined (garbage). Meaningful use of such an object can only be achieved if easy-to-forget-to-use setters are invoked to supply meaningful values. Such setters are dangerous without validation, since invalid values can be assigned to instance variables.

Listing 7.14   A default constructor, which leads to meaningless results

```
class Person {
private:
    std::string name;
    int age;
public:
    std::string getName() { return name; }
    int getAge() { return age; }
};

int main() {
    Person p1;
    std::cout << p1.getName() << ' ' << p1.getAge() << '\n';
}
```

No programmer-written default constructor is provided; therefore, the compiler writes one.

A class instance will have its default constructor called.

A built-in instance will not be initialized (it will contain garbage).

The compiler-written default constructor will be called—name will be initialized, but age will not.

Adding an explicit default constructor is no better:

```
Person() : name(""), age(0) {}
```

However, the age instance variable will be initialized, preventing undefined behavior.

ANALYSIS

No business problem is likely to have a person with no name and an age of zero; however, if a default constructor is necessary, this dangerous situation must be allowed to occur. The default values could be changed to Lakshmi and 21, but then, everybody who is defaulted is named Lakshmi and aged 21. This approach gains nothing, and what is worse, it obscures the problem further.

The only meaningful constructor in this case is

```
Person(const std::string& name, int age) : name(name), age(age) {}
```

Here, two parameters are required to create a Person object; the instance variables are initialized with these values, preventing the use of a (likely) meaningless default and eliminating the problem of failing to call a mutator.

The class invariant demands meaningful data in each data member. The default constructor often violates this principle. The default constructor might be an apology for choosing the wrong data structure.

One of the most prominent cases in which the default constructor must be used is when arrays of objects are created. The array is created in this case, and each element is initialized by calling the default constructor. Except in very rare cases, the class invariant is violated for each element.

SOLUTION

As a rule, initializing all instance variables when an object is created is essential to maintain correctness. In a small number of cases, default constructors may be a reasonable approach. Since the initialization data for an element has yet to be determined, the default constructor must be called to initialize the instance variables. Using arrays makes sense in some cases but causes problems. The tradeoff is a small efficiency gain as opposed to correctness. Arrays are typically allocated on the stack (unless they are created using the new keyword). Further, textbooks teach arrays implicitly, granting them primacy in a student's mind. What is learned first is often used first when there is a choice. Due to this problem, vectors should be taught first and used in preference to array in almost all cases.

Vectors use one level of indirection (a pointer) to access the data; therefore, arrays are slightly faster during access. However, the developer must be able to justify the effect on correctness for this small gain. Arrays are typical and frequently used, but their downside can be significant. The better approach is to choose a container that does not insist on default construction.

Listing 7.15 shows a simple example of using an array and a comparable vector. The array uses the default constructor, resulting in a mess. The vector requires using the two-argument constructor for each element, guaranteeing proper (nondefaulted) initialization; the vector requires elements to be copyable. Modern C++ can mitigate default constructors using initialization lists when creating the array, but there is no such luck with premodern C++.

Listing 7.15 Using a vector in preference to an array

```cpp
class Person {
private:
    std::string name;
    int age;
public:
    Person() : name(""), age(0) {}
    Person(const std::string& name, int age) : name(name), age(age) {}
    std::string& getName() { return name; }
    int getAge() { return age; }
};

int main() {
    Person people[2];

    for (int i = 0; i < 2; ++i)
        std::cout << people[i].getName() << " is " << people[i].getAge()
            << '\n';

    std::vector<Person> peeps;
    peeps.push_back(Person("Susan", 21));
    peeps.push_back(Person("Jason", 25));

    for (int i = 0; i < peeps.size(); ++i)
        std::cout << peeps[i].getName() << " is " << peeps[i].getAge()
            << '\n';
}
```

The default constructor is called, leaving each element wrongly initialized.

The number of elements might change, but this value may be overlooked.

Adds any amount of elements to the vector and keeps track of their number

With elements added or removed, this loop always works correctly.

RECOMMENDATIONS

- Resist the urge to add default constructors simply because they are familiar or common; they can be dangerous.

- Think carefully about including a default constructor at all, remembering that unless each instance variable is properly initialized, the object is misleading or invalid.

- Use vectors or other containers in preference to arrays because arrays necessitate the use of default constructors to initialize each element.

- Remember the class invariant and the meaning of defaulted data members—if it is meaningful to have objects default constructed, then do so; if not, avoid using the default constructor.

SEE ALSO

- See Mistake 35 for a discussion of preferring vectors as a default container.

7.9   *Mistake 50: Failing to maintain the is-a relationship*

Readability (or lack thereof) is the primary motivation for this discussion. However, poorly implemented inheritance relationships can adversely affect correctness and will affect effectiveness.

Public inheritance provides the ability to create new classes from existing ones. These newly derived classes must be related to the base class via an is-a relationship. Protected and private inheritance are fundamentally different and will not be discussed in this mistake. When a function has a parameter of (or pointer-to or reference-to) a base class instance, a derived class object will substitute and work as expected. This property is the Liskov substitution principle. Inheritance communicates information to the reader; therefore, to communicate correct and meaningful information, a publicly derived class instance must be substitutable for and behave like a base class instance in all cases.

PROBLEM

As mentioned elsewhere, some textbooks still maintain that inheritance is a nifty means to share code, saving the developer some time. This approach sounds like an effective means to write less code and gain more benefits. However, this advice will paint the unwary developer into a corner (and the painted floor will be lava).

Public inheritance means the base class is a general idea or concept that lends itself to specialization in several ways. For example, consider a Shape class that describes a two-dimensional polygon. Further, assume the program needs to manipulate Circle, Square, and Triangle objects. Since all these are related by the fact that they are Shapes and have typical behavior (e.g., area and perimeter), it makes sense to model these as derived classes of the Shape class. Before doing so, we must consider whether there is any case where a Circle, Square, or Triangle object would fail to satisfy the is-a relationship. The answer is no in this case, but some cases are not nearly so clear or cleanly designed.

In contrast, consider a situation where we have a `Bird` class and wish to derive an `Ostrich` class from it, since ostriches are most definitely birds. This inheritance seems to satisfy the is-a property; however, there is a problem lurking here. We intuitively consider birds to be flying animals, but ostriches are not flyers. Intuition can lead us to make mistakes. The problem being solved determines the proper relationship between classes; sometimes, natural relationships must be minimized or ignored.

Returning to the `Shape` example, one of the most compelling arguments for inheritance, especially public inheritance, is that programs often must treat a collection of related objects in a general manner. The base class interface functions specify the common behavior—that is, why it is the base class. Derived classes may override these functions to provide specialized behavior. If the problem does not require handling collections of related objects, there is likely no need for an inheritance hierarchy.

ANALYSIS

The developer is trying to relate geometric shapes using inheritance because it seems reasonable to handle various classes in a general manner. Therefore, they think a base class with common functions will be used, and derived classes can specialize behavior according to the actual type of the instance. Since a rectangle and a square are very similar, it would be a good idea to derive the square from the rectangle and enforce a more restricted relationship between its height and width.

The `Square` class was developed to share code from the `Rectangle` class, which promises effectiveness, even at a slight loss of readability. However, the desire to share code (read that as the desire to save a few keystrokes) quickly runs aground on the hard rocks of reality. A `Square` seems to be a special case of a `Rectangle` until one realizes that a rectangle whose height and width cannot vary independently is not a rectangle—it simply has a height and width that does not define a proper rectangle. While a rectangle could have identical values for its height and width, this rarity does not justify designing a `Square` as a special case of the `Rectangle`. Rectangles must maintain the ability to have independent height and width properties. This independence is part of the `Rectangle` class invariant for each instance (argue with the geometers if you wish to disagree).

Listing 7.16 Improper inheritance that seems to save coding effort

```
class Rectangle {
private:
    double height;
    double width;
public:
    Rectangle(double h, double w) : height(h), width(w) {}
    double getHeight() { return height; }
    void setHeight(double h) { height = h; }
    double getWidth() { return width; }
    void setWidth(double w) { width = w; }
    virtual void validate() { assert(height >= 0 && width >= 0); }
};

class Square : public Rectangle {
```

Trying to save a few keystrokes leads to this derived class.

```
public:
    Square(double s) : Rectangle(s, s) {}
    void validate() override {
        Rectangle::validate();
        assert(getHeight() == getWidth());
    }
};

int main() {
    std::vector<Rectangle*> shapes { new Rectangle(3, 4),
            new Square(2) };
    for (auto shape : shapes) {
        // guarantee different lengths
        shape->setHeight(shape->getWidth() + 1);      ◄────  A Square instance will
        shape->validate();                                   have differing height
    }                                                        and width values!
    return 0;
}
```

While no problems occur during normal operation of this code, the validate
function exposes the problem. A Square instance must have equal height and width
(by definition), but a Rectangle instance must be free to have different sizes. When
the class invariant is tested, the problem is exposed for what it is—a Square is *not* a
Rectangle (and vice versa), even though they might intuitively "feel" that way.

SOLUTION

Listing 7.17 shows a good use of inheritance. Each derived class can act like a Shape
(the loop in the main function) when needed. Each derived class is related to the other
derived classes via inheritance but represents a different idea. Each class can validate
its class invariant, and finally, each derived class does not deviate from the base class's
interface. Dr. Liskov would be proud.

Rather than starting with Rectangle, this approach starts with an abstract base class
(ideally, where each function is pure; at least one must be) that defines the behavior
of all derived classes. Then, realizing that a rectangle and a square do not have an is-a
relationship derives from the base class. The Rectangle and Square classes are related
as siblings, not incorrectly as a parent and child. Each class can enforce its constraints
on side lengths without affecting the other. Imagine adding a Triangle class into this
mix, which would have even more dissimilar constraints. Adding classes to a properly
ordered inheritance hierarchy does not cause hair-pulling and hacky workarounds.

Listing 7.17   Abstracting the essentials to a base class

```
class Shape {
public:                                     ◄────  The abstract base class
    virtual double area() = 0;                      defines behavior only.
    virtual double perimeter() = 0;
    virtual void validate() = 0;
};
                                                    This class implements the
class Rectangle : public Shape {        ◄────       behavior in its particular way.
```

```
private:
    double height;
    double width;
public:
    Rectangle(double h, double w) : height(h), width(w) {}
    double area() override { return height * width; }
    double perimeter() override { return (height + width) * 2; }
    void validate() override { assert(height >= 0 && width >= 0); }
};

class Square : public Shape {
private:
    double side;
public:
    Square(double s) : side(s) {}
    double area() override { return side * side; }
    double perimeter() override { return side * 4; }
    void validate() override { assert(side >= 0); }
};

int main() {
    std::vector<Shape*> shapes { new Square(2), new Rectangle(3, 4) };
    for (auto shape : shapes)
        shape->validate();
    return 0;
}
```

This class implements the behavior in its idiomatic way, differing from the other class.

Saving a few keystrokes to share code is a dangerous temptation that promises much but delivers disaster. Only when a derived class is-a base class, and therefore substitutable for one in *every* case, can the public inheritance relationship be maintained appropriately. In many actual hierarchies, some code is shared between the derived and base classes, resulting in its reuse, which increases effectiveness. Remember that code reuse (including keystroke savings) is a *benefit* of inheritance, never a *reason* for it.

RECOMMENDATIONS

- Code sharing (reuse) is a benefit of public inheritance, never a reason for it.
- Only use public inheritance when the derived class is correctly substitutable for a base class instance in every case and has meaningfully defined functions for each base class behavior.
- If a real-world behavior does not need to be modeled in the base class, avoid the temptation to implement that behavior, even if intuition suggests it should be modeled. Remove all currently unneeded behavior—this is the *you ain't gonna need it* (YAGNI) principle in action.
- Classes should be related by inheritance because they are related entities and are used in collections where each instance acts like a base class object, perhaps with some specializations of their behavior.

Maintaining the
class invariant

This chapter covers

- How to ensure that the class invariant is
  maintained in program design
- Difficulties that arise from indiscriminate use of
  older object-oriented design advice
- The distinctions between copy constructors and
  the copy assignment operator
- The widespread problem of failing to initialize
  variables of built-in types

After the finishing the hard work of establishing the class invariant discussed in chapter 7, developers must be careful to maintain it. Several aspects of program development provide opportunities for violating the invariant. It's important to become aware of some of these possibilities and be on guard to prevent their use.

There is a possibility of violating the class invariant whenever data is used to initialize or modify a state variable. The flexibility and fine granularity of C++ constructs provide ample opportunity for affecting the data, sometimes in surprising ways. The most obvious place a violation of the invariant can occur is when any state data changes. However, it is only sometimes obvious when this happens. The construction and deletion of objects is a veiled process to some degree yet plays an essential role in establishing the content—hence, the invariance—of an object.

Inheritance offers further opportunities to misuse data and affect the invariant. C++ has strict rules about objects' creation, each part's construction order, and what state data can be used at what point in construction (or destruction). Mistakes in usage can be disastrous. Data copying functions provide a few opportunities to mess up a class instance. Improper usage can be challenging to detect, but the effects can be enormous. Copying has two aspects: shallow and deep; inappropriate usage of these aspects will subtly threaten the class invariantly.

Using arrays and other data containers depends on copying semantics. Their correct use will ensure objects are kept pristine and preserve the meaning of objects' data. The proper use of virtual functions is essential for polymorphism. Further, their proper use is critical for correctly formed objects. The mistakes that can be made in using these functions vary, and each wrong use can adversely affect correct operations, state, or both.

8.1 Maintaining the class invariant

Maintaining the class invariant demands attention to detail and knowledge of some subtle interactions of constructors and virtual functions. The flexibility of the C++ language gives developers extensive freedom to craft specific behaviors, but this flexibility must be well understood and used correctly. Whenever state variables are initialized or modified, there is potential for corruption, and careful attention to some of the more obscure or vulnerable areas is required to prevent these mistakes.

Technically, object construction falls under the establishment of the class invariant. Inheritance is a powerful technique to build a hierarchy of related classes that share standard behavior as defined by the public interface. The construction of derived objects can affect already established invariants by incorrectly using virtual functions or improperly using derived objects in arrays. These mistakes focus on the improper, and perhaps unexpected, use of object-oriented techniques that, if wrongly done, invalidate the class invariant.

8.2 Mistake 51: Writing nonessential accessors

This mistake focuses on correctness, readability, and effectiveness. Nonessential accessors break the knowledge barrier between a class and client code. These unnecessary accessors take time to write but little to maintain; they present an extra cognitive load with little to no benefit.

During the optimistic era of object-oriented programming, many textbooks and writers promoted accessors and mutators for every private instance variable. The popular claim was that every client should have access to every piece of state within an instance. This code dilutes the more essential methods and makes reading and remembering the class much more difficult. The code that followed this advice was littered with accessors that returned a copy of the instance variable value. Such methods break the public/private encapsulation barrier and overly reveal implementation details.

PROBLEM

This approach is a semantic problem in many ways. Where nonessential accessors exist for a variable, the variable and class implementation may be dangerously exposed to the client. Nothing differs between public variables and private variables using simple accessors and mutators. Revealing implementation details of state variables suggests that client code should be responsible for understanding and managing them. This flaw is a direct violation of maintaining the class invariant. Correctness and effectiveness are compromised when modifying the class implementation, since client code likely depends on the class behaving in a certain way that has been exposed.

Another poor practice for accessors is using instance variables to store object states derived from other instance variables. Assume a `Circle` class that computes its area, as shown in listing 8.1. Some legacy code examples define a floating-point variable named `area` initialized in the constructor. A trivial accessor is written to return the calculated value of the `area` instance variable.

Listing 8.1   Class with computed values and trivial accessors

```
class Circle {
private:
    const static double PI;
    double radius;
    double area;
public:
    Circle() : radius(1), area(PI) {}
    Circle(double radius) : radius(radius),         ◀———  Values computed, whether
        area(radius*radius*PI) {}                          they are used or not
    double getArea() const { return area; }       ◀
    double getRadius() const { return radius; }        A trivial accessor that
};                                                     only allows access to
const double Circle::PI = 3.1415927;                   the computed value

int main() {
    Circle c1(3);
    std::cout << c1.getArea() << '\n';
    return 0;
}
```

Nonessential accessors are code bloat. Once an instance has been initialized by its constructor, it is likely that some or many of the instance variables are unnecessary for client access. As mentioned, one consequence of these accessors is that clients may depend on the variable's implementation details, preventing uncomplicated reimplementation. Another result is that clients may assume responsibility for understanding and maintaining the instance's state. This situation violates the class invariant and spreads the class knowledge to code external to the class.

ANALYSIS

Properly written classes reveal only essential state information and not necessarily in the form used in the class. Their public interface defines how the client can access that information but not how it is implemented, whether it is cached or directly computed, or any other implementation details. Clients must not be allowed to depend on implementation details, and it is the class writer's responsibility to prevent this from happening.

The `Circle` class constructs an instance, using the passed-in information for the radius. The accessor gives users an unrestricted view of the `radius` value and its implementation. The `area` method depends on an instance variable being precomputed; its accessor only returns that value.

Gratuitously writing the `radius` accessor should be avoided; in cases when clients need this information, it should be provided. The value needs to be verified with the client code to see if it is required; if so, supply the accessor. Since only the area of the circle seems to be of interest, the calculation of that value is critical but not the radius. But it is there in all its assumed goodness. Before adding the radius accessor, the client requirements should be ascertained. The client already supplied the radius; if it is essential, the client should remember it.

The second problem is the automatic computation of the area. In this case, the client will likely want this information, so precomputing it is a good idea. However, as a habit, precomputing should be deferred to the first (or every) use. If the class were more complex, it would be uncertain whether the area would ever be needed. The machine is called a *computer* because it computes—class designers should work with the machine's intent and let it do its job.

SOLUTION

Nonessential accessors should be removed as a policy. Clients may need these values, but it should not be *assumed* they do. A scan of the code base can reveal if the accessor is used in existing code. If not, remove it altogether. If the accessor is used, determine whether the client code is overstepping its responsibilities by using it. In the example code, the radius would be essential knowledge if the client were a graphics program that needed to draw and arrange circles. If the client were computing the weight of circular paving stones, the radius would be irrelevant; only the area would need to be computed.

Listing 8.2 A class with a computing accessor

```
class Circle {
private:
    const static double PI;
    double radius;
public:
    Circle() : radius(1) {}
    Circle(double radius) : radius(radius) {}
    double getArea() const { return radius*radius*PI; }    ◀── Computes values only when needed
};
const double Circle::PI = 3.1415927;
```

Developers must take a balanced approach that considers computational cost when writing computing accessors. The computation operation will often be inexpensive and can be computed on demand. Supposing the computation is expensive (e.g., uses large amounts of data, accesses a database, or communicates online), its result should be computed as few times as possible. In that case, a better approach is to compute the result only on the first access and then cache the result. Later accesses will quickly access the cached value, mitigating the computational cost.

Since most accessors do not mutate any instance variables, it is best to mark them as const. The compiler will enforce the promise that no values are modified; further, it is good documentation of intent.

RECOMMENDATIONS

- Do not write an accessor until it can be shown that it is essential for client use; essential accessors are necessary.
- Do not maintain an instance variable whose value can be computed unless it is a computationally expensive operation.
- Expensive computation results should be cached for performance reasons.
- Mark accessors const to communicate their immutability.

SEE ALSO

- See Mistake 52 for further discussion about designing, coding, and using trivial mutators.

8.3   *Mistake 52: Providing trivial mutators*

This mistake focuses heavily on correctness and lightly on effectiveness. Many programming textbooks perpetuate an old, familiar anti-pattern. When explaining how to build a class, the authors frequently advise an accessor and mutator for each instance variable. In the early days of object-oriented programming, this was considered a good practice. Current textbook authors tend to carry this forward into their books. Yet this practice often invalidates the class invariant; we need a better approach.

PROBLEM

Let's consider a Circle class that has a single instance variable radius, as shown in the following listing. The constructor initializes the variable, the accessor returns a copy of it, and the mutator modifies it.

> **Listing 8.3   A class with a trivial nonvalidating mutator**

```
class Circle {
private:
    double radius;
public:
    Circle() : radius(1) {}
    Circle(double radius) : radius(radius) {}
    double getRadius() { return radius; }
    void setRadius(double radius) { this->radius = radius; }
};
```

An unrestricted range of values due to no validation checking

```
int main() {
    Circle c1(2);
    std::cout << c1.getRadius() << '\n';
    c1.setRadius(-1);
    std::cout << c1.getRadius() << '\n';
}
```

According to this textbook approach, this is the proper design; however, there are three significant problems:

- Nonvalidated input values
- Insisting that all instance variables be mutable
- Duplicated knowledge between mutators and constructors

Legacy code is replete this pattern. Understanding these problems will help determine when and where to improve your code.

Trivial mutators significantly affect correctness by permitting unrestricted modification of instance variables. Clients should not be responsible for knowing a variable's proper range of values. The class must maintain this part of the class invariant and alert the client of improper values. Readability can be affected by introducing extraneous methods, thus obscuring the important ones. Correctness can be affected by making instance variables mutable. Some classes should not change their instance variables after construction.

Effectiveness is affected by insisting that the developer write unnecessary methods and introducing class-invariant-breaking code. Knowledge of the valid value range is often duplicated between a constructor and mutator, creating an opportunity for divergence. Effective coding seeks to remove and isolate this knowledge duplication in one place.

ANALYSIS

While trivial accessors are distracting but relatively harmless, trivial mutators may be dangerous. A mutator is responsible for maintaining the class invariant that the constructor established. Any wrong value introduced into a class will render the instance inconsistent and possibly contribute to undefined behavior. Therefore, mutators must validate any candidate input value for correctness.

Further, an instance variable may not need to be modified. While our intuition might lean toward changing any and every instance variable, this path is more twisted than it might appear. Before a mutator is written, two essential steps must be taken. First, determine whether the instance variable should be mutable. Second, determine what the range of legitimate values is.

In many cases, the answer to the first question is negative. If so, there is no reason to write a mutator; such a mutator would be dangerous and extraneous. The developer should determine if the radius is properly mutable in the `Circle` class. In this case, it is unlikely; if a circle with a different radius is needed, the client should create a new instance.

For any remaining mutators, carefully consider the proper range of values for the variable. Write validation code to ensure these bounds are met before assigning the parameter value to the instance variable. Consider how to address the problem for parameter values that are out of range. Ideally, throw exceptions when the value is invalid. This is often the best approach, unless project leadership has determined that exceptions should not be thrown. Another option is to ignore the invalid parameter value and do nothing; however, this does not work when the constructor calls the mutator to set the initial value.

SOLUTION

The following code shows a better, but not ideal, approach. It attempts to solve the validation problem by ensuring the constructor and mutator throw an exception when the client passes an invalid value. It does not address the mutability or duplication problem.

Listing 8.4   A class with validation but duplicated knowledge

```
class Circle {
private:
    double radius;
public:
    Circle() : radius(1) {}
    Circle(double radius) {
        if (radius < 0)                                          Duplicated
            throw std::invalid_argument("radius is negative");   knowledge of
        this->radius = radius;                                   valid values
    }
    double getRadius() const { return radius; }
    void setRadius(double radius) {
        if (radius < 0)
            throw std::invalid_argument("radius is negative");
        this->radius = radius;
    }
};

int main() {
    Circle c1(2);
    std::cout << c1.getRadius() << '\n';
    c1.setRadius(-1);
    std::cout << c1.getRadius() << '\n';
}
```

Often, constructors and mutators have code in common. The constructor is responsible for establishing the class invariant, which includes initializing an instance variable's (currently uninitialized) value. The mutator is responsible for modifying the (now initialized) value of the instance variable. This duplication can be eliminated by having the constructor call the mutator. Since both places must maintain the class invariant, knowledge duplication is inevitable. Misreading the don't repeat yourself (DRY) principle might lead one to focus on code duplication; developers should focus on knowledge duplication instead. Range-checking code should be placed in the mutator, and the constructor should call the mutator.

The following code addresses the three previously discussed problems (nonvalidated parameter values, indiscriminate mutability, and duplicated knowledge), resolving each with minimal effort.

Listing 8.5   A class with validation and a single source of knowledge

```
class Circle {
private:
    double radius;
    static double validateRadius(double radius) {        ◄──── Single source of
        if (radius < 0)                                          validation knowledge
            throw std::invalid_argument("radius is negative");
        return radius;
    }
public:
    Circle() : radius(1) {}
    Circle(double radius) : radius(validateRadius(          Code depends on the
        radius)) {}                              ◄──────     knowledgeable source.
    double getRadius() const { return radius; }
    void setRadius(double r) { radius =
        validateRadius(r); }            ◄──────┐
};                                             Code depends on the knowledgeable
                                               source; remove this method if
int main() {                                   immutability is desired.
    Circle c1(2);
    std::cout << c1.getRadius() << '\n';        This throws an exception, alerting
    Circle c2(-1);                      ◄──────  the developer to the problem.
    std::cout << c2.getRadius() << '\n';
}
```

The private `validateRadius` method isolates the knowledge of proper radius values, the constructor initializes the instance variable by referring to this method, and circles with different radii are instantiated separately. Each immutable instance variable must have no mutator; eliminate any existing ones. Completing this step is an exercise in freeing your mind of clutter and your code from unnecessary maintenance costs.

RECOMMENDATIONS

- Make as many instance variables immutable as possible, and eliminate their mutators.

- Validate each input parameter to ensure its value is within the range defined by the class invariant.

- Throw exceptions for invalid values, if possible; otherwise, ignore invalid values.

- Have the constructor and mutator call a common validation method to isolate knowledge to a single place.

- Ensure each instance variable is initialized to a meaningful value.

SEE ALSO

- See Mistake 51 for information about writing nonessential accessors, a companion of this mistake.

8.4   *Mistake 53: Overusing protected instance variables*

This mistake is focused primarily on correctness. The base class establishes and maintains the class invariant but is vulnerable to changes that the derived class makes. The derived class is obligated to honor the base class invariant. Readability is arguably improved, and effectiveness also could be improved.

As a best practice, all instance variables should be private. This approach ensures no external code can access or modify them without being strictly controlled by the class. When inheritance is introduced, derived classes find that base class information they might need is inaccessible. Like client code, derived classes must use base class accessors and mutators. However, this limitation can feel overly restrictive. C++ provides the protected keyword for base classes to permit direct access to these instance variables by derived classes—external code is still prohibited from accessing or mutating these variables. As nice as this relaxation seems, it introduces the possibility (probability?) of violating the class invariant.

PROBLEM

A base class maintains its state by tightly controlling the range of values for each data member. The constructor and mutators should be designed to initialize the class invariant, maintain values within their proper boundaries, and prevent any attempt at an out-of-bounds mutation. Derived classes have direct access to these variables if the base class has made them protected.

The derived class should maintain its class invariant and take pains to honor its base class invariant. Unfortunately, the compiler cannot enforce honoring either invariant; the programmer must make the effort. Further, for a derived class to properly maintain the base class invariant, the developer must possess the external knowledge how to handle base class limits properly. This knowledge already exists in the base class and should not be duplicated in the derived class.

Listing 8.6   Vulnerability of the protected instance variable

```cpp
class Person {
protected:
    std::string name;           The vulnerable
    int age;                    instance variable
public:
                                              Properly validated
    Person(const std::string& name, int age) : name(name) {     and maintains the
        if (age < 0)                                            class invariant
            throw std::invalid_argument("negative age");
        this->age = age;
    }
    std::string getName() const { return name; }
    int getAge() const { return age; }
```

```
};

class Student : public Person {
private:
    double gpa;
public:
    Student(const std::string& name, int age, double gpa) : Person
    (name, age), gpa(gpa) {}
    double getGpa() const { return gpa; }
    void setAge(int age) { this->age = age; }
};

int main() {
    Student jane("Jane", 26, 3.85);
    jane.setAge(-26);
    std::cout << "Jane is " << jane.getAge() << " years old\n";
    return 0;
}
```

Expedience that endangers the base class invariant

ANALYSIS

For derived classes that do not understand or adequately maintain the base class invariant, one or more protected base class variables can be forced into an out-of-range condition without warning. Rejecting invalid values becomes impossible. The Student's setAge method does not restrict parameter values and directly sets the age instance variable; this occurs because that variable is protected, not private.

The designer of the Student class thought it expedient to use the protected variables of the Person base class. The Student programmer decided to add a setAge method, knowing some newer school rules vary based on age and a student could have a birthday during the school year.

The Person class correctly validates the age input value and rejects invalid values. The derived class needed to fully understand the implications of adding the setAge method but failed to do so. Since the base class constructor validates the age, everything initially seems fine. However, the base class does not mutate the age instance variable; hence, there is a need for a shortcut to mutate the variable directly. To properly implement the setAge method in Student, the derived class must duplicate the knowledge about the age base class variable. This duplication of knowledge violates the DRY principle and strains the encapsulation of variables.

SOLUTION

The Person base class is responsible for maintaining its class invariant. Part of this responsibility is handled by the refusal to allow other classes to directly access its instance variables without the protection of some validating logic, as shown in the following listing.

Listing 8.7   Enhancing safety by making instance variables private

```
class Person {
private:
    std::string name;
```

```
    int age;
public:
    Person(std::string name, int age) : name(name) { setAge(age); }
    std::string getName() const { return name; }
    int getAge() const { return age; }
    void setAge(int age) {
        if (age < 0)
            throw std::invalid_argument("negative age");
        this->age = age;
    }
};

class Student : public Person {
private:
    double gpa;
public:
    Student(std::string name, int age, double gpa) :
        Person(name, age), gpa(gpa) {}
    double getGpa() const { return gpa; }
};

int main() {
    Student jane("Jane", 26, 3.85);
    jane.setAge(-26);
    std::cout << "Jane is " << jane.getAge() << " years old\n";
    return 0;
}
```

Not vulnerable to derived class mutation

Properly validated and maintains the class invariant

Must use the base class method with proper validation

The base class correctly validates the age value, which is called from the constructor, a derived class, and client code. The derived class does not need to know anything about a valid age, let alone guarantee one. It delegates that responsibility to its base class, the only class that should know.

This discussion is not meant to imply that protected variables should never be used; there are cases where they already exist, and you cannot alter that fact. However, you can—and must—respect the base class invariant and use its mutators. If the base class cannot be changed and has no validating mutators, write one in the derived class and comment on why. Remember the Liskov substitution principle (LSP); the substitution requirement is not met if the base class mutator does not throw and the derived one does.

If the base class does not intend to expose some of its instance variables to client code, it can provide protected methods for derived classes to use for mutation. These methods ensure the base class remains in control of any changes to its state yet provides an interface for derived classes to mutate state in ways client code cannot.

RECOMMENDATIONS

- Eliminate as many protected variables as possible.

- Always make mutators validate their parameters.

- Understand that the slight awkwardness of derived classes using accessors and mutators is entirely offset by the base class maintaining its class invariant.

- Consider using protected accessors and mutators to provide access that client code is not privileged to use.

- Do not make mutators virtual; they must be implemented only in the owning class.

8.5   *Mistake 54: Mistaking operator= and copy constructor semantics*

This mistake affects correctness and readability. Improper coding of either behavior can adversely affect the class invariant and the suitability of the code.

Copying information from one instance of a class to another occurs routinely. The usual approach for this operation is using the copy assignment operator, but the copy constructor must also be considered. If the semantics of either are misunderstood, it is easy to think of both as doing the same thing and that one is redundant. However, while they are very similar in operation, they differ in meaning.

PROBLEM

When a class is created, the semantics of assignment and copying from an existing object must be considered. If the programmer writes neither a copy constructor nor a copy assignment operator, the compiler provides both by default. If either is provided, the other is automatically generated. See the text at the end of the Solutions section for an explanation of what modern C++ does.

The default implementation for both is to perform a member-wise copy of each instance variable from the source to the target object. In some cases, this is sufficient and the correct operation. However, the developer must still think through the implications. Ignoring them and blithely allowing the compiler to do the heavy lifting is a poor approach.

When using dynamic resources, such as memory, handles, connections, sockets, and others, an alternative to the compiler default approach should be used. The developer must ensure dynamic resources are handled correctly during the copy operation.

The copy constructor is called when a new object is created and is currently uninitialized—it is raw memory, whether stack- or heap-based. The copy assignment operator is called when an existing, initialized target object is overwritten with source object values. The difference is whether the target object is uninitialized or initialized—the meaning subtly differs between the two.

The code in listing 8.8 uses dynamic resources to handle reading files (most of the code is elided) and uses existing file readers as initialization sources. The compiler generously provides its default versions, since the developer did not provide a copy constructor or copy assignment operator. Each of these provided versions uses shallow copy semantics, copying the value from the source instance variable to the target instance variable.

> **Listing 8.8** **Resources handled by default copy constructor and copy assignment operator**

```
class InputReader {
private:
    std::string* filenames;
```

This is a deliberately poor practice for simplicity; the STL provides better means.

```
        int count;
public:
    InputReader() : filenames(new std::string[5]), count(0) {}
    ~InputReader() { delete[] filenames; }
    void addFileName(const std::string& n) {
        if (count == 5)
            throw std::runtime_error("too many files specified");
        filenames[count++] = n;
    }
    int getCount() const { return count; }
    const std::string& operator[](int index) {
        return filenames[index];
    }
};

int main() {
    InputReader ir1;
    ir1.addFileName("statistics.txt");
    InputReader ir2(ir1);
    ir2.addFileName("numbers.txt");
    InputReader ir3 = ir2;
    ir3.addFileName("categories.txt");
    ir1.addFileName("questions.txt");

    for (int i = 0; i < ir1.getCount(); ++i)
        std::cout << ir1[i] << '\n';
    for (int i = 0; i < ir2.getCount(); ++i)
        std::cout << ir2[i] << '\n';
    for (int i = 0; i < ir3.getCount(); ++i)
        std::cout << ir3[i] << '\n';
    return 0;
}
```

The compiler default copy constructor is called using shallow copy semantics.

The compiler default copy assignment operator is called using shallow copy semantics.

ANALYSIS

The first reader adds the statistics.txt file and then is used to initialize the second reader; the second reader adds the numbers.txt file and then is used to initialize the third reader; and the third reader adds the categories.txt file and is expected to have three files to read. The first reader then adds a new file, named questions.txt. The following output shows that things are not working as expected (blank lines added for clarity):

```
statistics.txt
questions.txt

statistics.txt
questions.txt

statistics.txt
questions.txt
categories.txt
Segmentation fault
```

The first reader should be the only one to access questions.txt files; however, the output shows that second- and third-grade readers can also access questions.txt. Since the copy and assignment merely copy the pointer value, each points to the same—shared—data. The `ir2` reader has lost access to the numbers.txt file. When `ir1` adds another file, it believes the array has one valid element. Therefore, when the questions.txt file is added, it becomes the second element in the shared array, overwriting the numbers.txt element.

The default copy constructor and copy assignment operator made a shallow copy of the `filenames` pointer, sharing the array data. Each reader updates the next element independently of the others, causing data corruption. This situation causes unexpected output and dangerously wrong behavior, including a double deletion.

SOLUTION

To get this example to work, a copy constructor and copy assignment operator must be coded to handle the dynamic array of filenames properly. The copy constructor will allocate a new array, perform a copy of any existing elements, and set the count variable.

In the case of the copy constructor, the new instance is uninitialized; therefore, a new dynamic array must be created in the initializer list. The copy of the existing values is done in the constructor body. After this change, the code works correctly and as expected. The copy assignment operator must take a different approach, although much of the functionality will be the same. Since the target object is initialized, it already has its unshared dynamic array, so a new one need not be allocated. It needs only to copy the elements and initialize the count value, as shown in the following listing.

> **Listing 8.9 A properly written copy constructor and assignment operator**

```
class InputReader {
private:
    std::string* filenames;
    int count;
public:
    InputReader() : filenames(new std::string[5]), count(0) {}
    ~InputReader() { delete[] filenames; }
    InputReader(const InputReader& r) : filenames(new std::string[5]),
            count(r.count) {                          ◄─────┐ Allocates a new array and
        for (int i = 0; i < r.count; ++i)                  │ copies elements, not pointer
            filenames[i] = r.filenames[i];
    }
    InputReader& operator=(const InputReader& r) {   ◄───┐ Copies elements,
        for (int i = 0; i < r.count; ++i)                │ not pointer
            filenames[i] = r.filenames[i];
        count = r.count;
        return *this;    }
    void addFileName(const std::string& n) {
        if (count == 5)
            throw std::runtime_error("too many files specified");
        filenames[count++] = n;
```

```
        }
        int getCount() const { return count; }
        const std::string& operator[](int index) {
            return filenames[index];
        }
};

int main() {
    InputReader ir1;
    ir1.addFileName("statistics.txt");         Calls the user-written
    InputReader ir2(ir1);          ◄──────      copy constructor
    ir2.addFileName("numbers.txt");
    InputReader ir3 = ir2;            ◄─────    Calls the user-written copy
    ir3.addFileName("categories.txt");          assignment operator
    ir1.addFileName("questions.txt");

    for (int i = 0; i < ir1.getCount(); ++i)
        std::cout << ir1[i] << '\n';
    for (int i = 0; i < ir2.getCount(); ++i)
        std::cout << ir2[i] << '\n';
    for (int i = 0; i < ir3.getCount(); ++i)
        std::cout << ir3[i] << '\n';
    return 0;
}
```

With these changes, the behavior is corrected. The following output is as expected (blank lines added for clarity):

```
statistics.txt
questions.txt

statistics.txt
numbers.txt

statistics.txt
numbers.txt
categories.txt
```

This copy assignment operator approach may need to be modified for some classes. The code in listing 8.9 shows a case where the array size is identical across all instances. However, assume a class where the array size is different between them. The copy constructor would work the same, since it creates a new array of the same size as the source object. The target object of the copy assignment operator would have a different size array. Since this is the case, the existing array would need to be deleted, and a new one would need to be created based on the source's size and each element copied. Be vigilant, in this case, to destroy the dynamic elements correctly. If the elements are class instances, they likely need to be destroyed. Although it probably will automatically occur, their destructor may need to be called in rare cases. Be sure to understand and deal with this situation.

The code in listing 8.10 shows a variation that addresses this problem, where it is assumed the class added a capacity instance variable representing the maximum array size (which is a superior design to hardcoding the size). This example has a lurking problem; if self-assignment is done, this code will fail. Consult the See Also section for a discussion on this topic.

```cpp
InputReader& operator=(const InputReader& r) {
    if (capacity != r.capacity) {
        delete[] filenames;
        filenames = new std::string[r.capacity];
        capacity = r.capacity;
    }
    for (int i = 0; i < r.capacity; ++i)
        filenames[i] = r.filenames[i];
    count = r.count;
    return *this;
}
```

Modern C++ modifies how default members are generated. If only a move constructor is provided, the compiler will not automatically generate a copy constructor, copy assignment operator, or move assignment operator. If only a move assignment operator is provided, the compiler will not automatically generate a copy constructor, copy assignment operator, or move constructor. Be sure you understand these limitations when expecting the compiler to fill in missing members. The following snippet, which is an addition to the code in listing 8.9, demonstrates both a move constructor and a move assignment operator:

```cpp
InputReader(InputReader&& r) : filenames(r.filenames), count(r.count) {
    r.filenames = nullptr;
    r.count = 0;
}


InputReader& operator=(InputReader&& r) {
    if (this != &r) {
        delete[] filenames;
        filenames = r.filenames;
        count = r.count;
        r.filenames = nullptr;
        r.count = 0;
    }
    return *this;
}
```

RECOMMENDATIONS

- Always think through the mechanics of the copy assignment operator and copy constructor, and decide if member-wise copy is sufficient.
- Remember to handle self-assignment; undefined behavior is possible if ignored.

- Remember that the copy constructor targets uninitialized memory, while the copy assignment operator targets initialized memory.
- Carefully consider how to handle dynamic resources during initialization properly.

SEE ALSO

- See Mistake 47 for understanding that if a destructor is coded, the copy constructor and copy assignment operator should be coded as well.
- See Mistake 55 for information about handling dynamic resources properly.
- See Mistake 65 for advice on handling this case with dynamic resources.

8.6   *Mistake 55: Misunderstanding shallow and deep copy semantics*

This mistake focuses on correctness; other characteristics are unaffected by it. A typical operation assigns the value of one variable to another variable or an object to another object of the same type. The code looks simple for this operation, but some implications will cause incorrect behavior unless understood clearly.

When an object is copied or assigned to another, each data member receives a value that overwrites its existing value. Default copy constructors and copy assignment operators implement a member-by-member copy from source to target. If any member is a pointer, the source and target objects will point to the same memory, thus sharing it. While sharing may be the desired behavior, it often is not and causes significant problems.

PROBLEM

Before the copy or assignment, the class invariant has been established in the source and target objects. After the copy or assignment, the source and target objects should remain consistent with the invariant. However, this may not be true if deep copy semantics are required.

There are two cases to consider: pointers and exclusively owned resources. Mistake 54 explains the first case and recommends techniques for ensuring the invariant remains properly established. The case of exclusive resources is covered in this discussion.

Consider the case where communications channels are being used to transfer messages. Each channel is attached to a different endpoint, perhaps subscribers of fee-based information. The developer realized that since pointers are being used for messages, care should be taken to ensure dynamic resources are not shared. Existing messages are handled correctly, but the use of the unique resources needs to be addressed.

Unique resources are often used as values from a limited set of entities. For example, an office might have three shared printers. Each printer is a unique resource, since only three instances exist, which can be used by only one user at a time. Nondynamically allocated resources might appear to be "just another" value. By default, these values are copied without reservation; however, unique resources must be carefully managed. When a unique resource is copied from one instance to another, it can no longer exist or be used by the source—the resource is transferred to the target.

For a different example, assume a developer wants to transfer existing messages from one channel (presumably, in some error condition on the endpoint) to another and change the attached endpoint. This is essentially a move operation; therefore, they implement the copy assignment operator and carefully manage the dynamic messages. However, when the channel attempts to process Messages, it fails with a bad endpoint, as shown in the following listing.

Listing 8.11 Care is taken for dynamic resources but not for unique resources

```cpp
int createSocket() {
    // assume valid implementation; this is for an example only!
    static int sock_num = 0;
    return ++sock_num;
}

class Message {
private:
    std::string payload;
public:
    Message(const std::string& msg) : payload(msg) {}
    const std::string& getMessage() const { return payload; }
};

class Channel {
private:
    std::queue<Message*> messages;
    int socket;
public:
    Channel(int sock) : socket(sock) {}
    void setMessage(std::string msg) { messages.push(new Message(msg)); }
    int getSocket() const { return socket; }
    std::string getMessage() {
        std::string msg = messages.front()->getMessage();
        messages.pop();
        return msg;
    }
    Channel& operator=(Channel& o) {
        for (int i = 0; i < messages.size(); ++i)
            messages.pop();
        for (int i = 0; i < o.messages.size(); ++i) {
            messages.push(o.messages.front());
            o.messages.pop();
        }
        socket = o.socket;          ◀──┐ The socket is now shared
        return *this;                  │ between source and target.
    }
};

int main() {
    Channel one(createSocket());
    Channel two(createSocket());
    two = one;
    std::cout << one.getSocket() << ' ' << two.getSocket() << '\n';
}
```

ANALYSIS

The pointers in the source queue use the element's message value to construct a new `Message` instance (not a great design; it's just an example). A transfer of the pointer directly would result in a problem, since the call to `pop` removes the element from the source queue and calls that element's destructor—the pointer would refer to deleted memory. The socket resource is copied as is, leaving two objects sharing (neither owning) the resource. Since the socket is not a pointer, it is easy to overlook this fact and assume a straight copy is sufficient.

The copy operation copies the socket value from source to target, but the source object must not keep a copy of the resource. Accidental use of the resource by the source object could cause undefined, incorrect, or unexpected behavior in the system; however, it is assumed the socket represents a failed endpoint. In this case, the copy would likely leave the target with a nonoperational socket, perpetuating the problem the assignment was supposed to resolve.

Exclusive resources require an understanding of their copy behavior. The fact that the resource is exclusive means only one object at a time should own it. Transferring the resource from one object to another means the source must lose any reference to the resource. The unique resource may have to be recreated in a case like this. Be certain to understand which approach is being used and to address it appropriately.

SOLUTION

The most straightforward approach is to ensure the exclusive resource variable is set to an invalid or default value, depending on the class invariant for the data member. A pointer should be nulled out (the specific method depends on your C++ version), and value type variables should have a clear and detectable zero value, meaning no resource is allocated. The change is small, but its influence is large.

Listing 8.12 **Transferring dynamic and unique resources**

```cpp
int createSocket() {
    // assume valid implementation; this is for an example only!
    static int sock_num = 0;
    return ++sock_num;
}

class Message {
private:
    std::string payload;
public:
    Message(const std::string& msg) : payload(msg) {}
    const std::string& getMessage() const { return payload; }
};

class Channel {
private:
    std::queue<Message*> messages;
    int socket;
public:
```

```
Channel(int sock) : socket(sock) {}
void setMessage(std::string msg) { messages.push(new Message(msg)); }
int getSocket() const { return socket; }
std::string getMessage() {
    std::string msg = messages.front()->getMessage();
    messages.pop();
    return msg;
}
Channel& operator=(Channel& o) {
    for (int i = 0; i < o.messages.size(); ++i) {
        messages.push(new Message(o.messages.front()->getMessage()));
        o.messages.pop();
    }
    socket = createSocket();
    o.socket = 0;
    return *this;
}
};
```

A unique version of the endpoint

The source endpoint is invalid, cannot be shared, and clears it up if invalid.

```
int main() {
    Channel one(createSocket());
    Channel two(createSocket());
    two = one;
    std::cout << one.getSocket() << ' ' << two.getSocket() << '\n';
```

RECOMMENDATIONS

- Ensure dynamic resources are appropriately handled and not shared between instances.

- Ensure unique resources are moved from source to target and that the source is set to its zero value. NULL is a common C idiom, but size mismatches between its definition and the resource type may occur. Modern C++ has the nullptr keyword for assigning pointers to the null value.

- Be sure that the zero value assigned to a value data member does not invalidate the class invariant; if zero is a legitimate value, choose another to represent the invalid value.

SEE ALSO

- Mistake 54 explains problems associated with confusing initialization semantics.

8.7   Mistake 56: Failing to call base class operators

This mistake focuses on correctness. The other characteristics are not appreciably affected by this mistake.

Inheritance refers to the definition of new classes from existing ones, allowing collections of related objects to be treated uniformly. Each class in the hierarchy adds a data part to the combined derived class. Objects of the derived class are a composite of these data parts. *Polymorphism* is the runtime ability to treat these derived classes as base classes yet behave as the derived class. The respective class constructors, destructors, and operators must correctly manage the individual data parts of each class in the hierarchy. The correct operation of the copy assignment operator is easy to overlook.

PROBLEM

Each part of a composite object (a derived class instance) must implement each relevant operator properly. Constructors and destructors are frequently mentioned in this context, since it is difficult to code a constructor without reference to its base class constructor. The proper operation of operators in this context should be more frequently mentioned and understood.

Consider the following inheritance hierarchy between a person and a student. Student derives from Person because a student is a person, yet student is more than a person. The developer of the Student class is careful to implement code that addresses the specialized knowledge in that class but might overlook similar knowledge in the base class. The instance variables in the base class are private and inaccessible to the derived class; therefore, the derived class cannot adequately copy those values.

Listing 8.13 shows a copy operation from one instance to another. This example is somewhat contrived, but rest assured that this type of operation frequently occurs with unnamed variables, such as vector or array elements, and happens without the obvious warning signs of copying Thelma to Louise, as seen in the following listing.

> **Listing 8.13   A derived class copying its data but disregarding its base class**

```
class Person {
private:
    std::string name;
public:
    Person(const std::string& name) : name(name) {}
    const std::string& getName() { return name; }
};

class Student : public Person {
private:
    double gpa;
public:
    Student(const std::string& name, double gpa) : Person(name), gpa(gpa) {}
    Student& operator=(const Student& o) {
        if (this == &o)
            return *this;
        gpa = o.gpa;          ◄──────   Student instance variables are
        return *this;                    correctly copied, but Person
    }                                    instance variables are not.
    double getGpa() const { return gpa; }
};

int main() {
    Student thelma("Thelma", 3.85);
    Student louise("Louise", 3.75);

    louise = thelma;
    std::cout << thelma.getName() << ' ' << thelma.getGpa() << '\n';
```

```
        std::cout << louise.getName() << ' ' << louise.getGpa() << '\n';
}
```

The result of this problem is evident from its output:

```
Thelma 3.85
Louise 3.85
```

ANALYSIS

When we finish creating the `louise` object, it isassigned to the `thelma` object. Now, we have two `thelma` values, each associated with a different variable name because of the assignment operation on the `louise` instance. The assignment caused no compilation or run-time problems, so the code worked as expected. However, notice that the `louise` object still maintains its name of Louise but with Thelma's `gpa`—for a student, this might be the best of all worlds. For our programming integrity, it is not.

The derived class defined the copy assignment operator to ensure the `gpa` of the parameter was copied to itself; this code works as expected. However, the `name` field in the base class also needed to be correctly copied. It is private in `Person`, and therefore, `Student` cannot copy it—this is easy to overlook. The copy operation works as expected only if the copy assignment operator definition is removed from the code. There is something different between the default copy assignment operator and our defined version.

The default copy assignment operator written by the compiler ensures the base class copy assignment operator is called before it does the member-wise copy of the data fields of the derived class. This tiny, yet critical, fact is essential for proper operation. Because a derived object is a composite of all base classes and the derived class, when a copy or assignment of one piece of the composite is attempted, it must ensure every piece has its copy or assignment operation performed.

SOLUTION

This problem can be easily resolved once it is understood. The updated code in listing 8.14 makes the assignment operation perform correctly. The copy assignment operator ensures the base class version is called first, and then it proceeds with its copy behavior. The copy assignment operator ensures its base class copy assignment operator is called and passes the parameter as an argument to ensure that all instances higher in the hierarchy are handled. The theme established by the construction order of objects is once again manifested: the base class always constructs, copies, or assigns first, followed by the same operation in the derived class.

Listing 8.14 The derived class properly considering its base class

```cpp
class Person {
private:
    std::string name;
public:
    Person(const std::string& name) : name(name) {}
```

```
        const std::string& getName() { return name; }
};

class Student : public Person {
private:
    double gpa;
public:
    Student(const std::string& name, double gpa) : Person(name), gpa(gpa) {}
    Student& operator=(const Student& o) {
        if (this == &o)
            return *this;
        Person::operator=(o);          The call to the base class copy
        gpa = o.gpa;                   assignment operator occurs first.
        return *this;
    }                                  Copies the derived class
    double getGpa() const { return gpa; }    instance variables afterward
};

int main() {
    Student thelma("Thelma", 3.85);
    Student louise("Louise", 3.75);

    louise = thelma;
    std::cout << thelma.getName() << ' ' << thelma.getGpa() << '\n';
    std::cout << louise.getName() << ' ' << louise.getGpa() << '\n';
}
```

RECOMMENDATIONS

- If any operator is defined in a derived class, ensure the implementation includes a call to the equivalent base class operator before performing any data movement operation.

- Keep in mind that the order for constructors and operators must follow a rigid pattern of most-base class first to most-derived class last, while destructors reverse this order.

SEE ALSO

- See Mistake 57 for a discussion on overlooking the destructor in inheritance hierarchies.

8.8   *Mistake 57: Failing to use virtual destructors in polymorphic base classes*

This mistake focuses on correctness. The difference between correct and incorrect implementation likely does not affect readability, effectiveness, or performance (if it does, it depends on the compiler's implementation).

Constructors must be thought through carefully, as proper initialization of instance variables is essential to maintain the class invariant. Likewise, careful thought must be given to destructors. C++ gives the developer the power and responsibility of class design. Consideration must be given to the class to determine if it should use inheritance, be inherited from, or be a standalone data type.

PROBLEM

Standalone classes are the easiest to plan for. This does not mean the design is necessarily easy; it only means things are more straightforward without inheritance, and you have more control. The design of a base class influences the design of a derived class. Mistakes made higher in the inheritance hierarchy can cause anguish to developers of derived classes. There may be little you can do about this other than program defensively and consider exceptional cases. However, if you are writing a base class, you must consider not only your type but all subtypes—the behavior of your base class will affect every derived one.

If a class is designed to be a base class, it should conform to some rules. One of these is that a base class should provide a virtual destructor, since it should have at least one virtual function. Said backward, do not provide virtual destructors without having any virtual functions. A class should not contain virtual methods, unless it is intended to be a base class; therefore, every base class should provide a virtual destructor.

C++ surprises us when deleting derived objects when using a base class pointer or reference. Polymorphic behavior is only possible using pointers or references, so this approach must be used. Pointers and references do not imply heap-based objects, but that is a very common use case. So what is the catch? Try deleting a derived class using a base class pointer or reference. It seems all should be fine, but the results are anyone's guess; worse, it is undefined behavior.

The code in listing 8.15 has a base and a derived class that uses a dynamic resource. The destructor of the base class is not defined as virtual. The main function creates a dynamic `Square` object and assigns it to a `Shape` pointer. After using the derived object, it is deleted.

Listing 8.15 Base class without a virtual destructor

```cpp
class Point {
private:
    double x;
    double y;
public:
    Point(double x, double y) : x(x), y(y) {}
};

class Shape {
private:
    Point* location;
public:
    Shape(double x, double y) : location(new Point(x, y)) {}
    ~Shape() { delete location;  std::cout << "~Shape\n"; }
    virtual double area() const = 0;
};

class Square : public Shape {
```

> **Nonvirtual destructor, which only seems correct** → (points to `~Shape()` line)
>
> **A virtual method intended for polymorphic behavior** → (points to `virtual double area() const = 0;` line)

```
private:
    double* side;
public:
    Square(double side, double x, double y) : Shape(x, y),
        side(new double(side)) {}
    ~Square() { delete side;  std::cout << "~Square\n"; }
    double area() const { return *side * *side; }  // looks weird
};

int main() {
    Shape* s = new Square(2.5, 0, 0);  // place at origin
    std::cout << s->area() << '\n';
    delete s;          ◄────────  Deletes the base class part
    return 0;                      of the object but not the
}                                 derived class part
```

The output of this code is

```
6.25
~Shape
```

This demonstrates that the base class destructor ran but leaked the dynamic side value—your results may differ.

ANALYSIS

The output from the main function shows that only the Shape destructor was called. Regardless of the awkward design of both classes, the fact that the Square destructor was not called demonstrates a memory leak.

A base class should have at least one virtual function, since only virtual functions can participate in polymorphic behavior. Otherwise, inheritance is probably being used for code reuse. A base class with no virtual destructor may seem to be properly designed, since it works. When the derived object is manipulated through the base class pointer, it all works as expected. That is, it works until the destruction of the object occurs. The behavior goes wonky but is something not likely to be noticed. This situation depends entirely on how the compiler implements this feature; debug and release versions may differ as well.

The destruction of the derived class through the base class pointer will likely delete only the part that defines the base class. The destructor of the base class will be called and perform its duties. The base class does not know (nor should it) that a derived class portion of the object should be deleted. The net result likely is that the derived part becomes a memory leak. This situation is undoubtedly a problem but will probably avoid significant problems in short-running programs—which is deceptive behavior. However, the problem becomes far more likely to affect operations when the derived class has dynamic resources, such as database connections, file handles, or other unique or constrained resources.

SOLUTION

The fix is simple: always provide a virtual destructor for base classes with one or more virtual functions. Further, do not have base classes without virtual methods or classes with virtual methods that are not base classes. The order of construction is always the most-base class down the inheritance hierarchy to the most derived class. By contrast, destruction order is from the most-derived class up the hierarchy to the most-base class—the opposite of construction. The base class must be constructed first because derived classes could depend on base class knowledge. This implies that the most derived class should be destroyed first. Unless the `virtual` keyword is used, this cannot happen.

Listing 8.16 A base class with virtual destructor

```
class Point {
private:
    double x;
    double y;
public:
    Point(double x, double y) : x(x), y(y) {}
};

class Shape {
private:
    Point* location;
public:
    Shape(double x, double y) : location(new Point(x, y)) {}
    virtual ~Shape() { delete location;
        std::cout << "~Shape\n"; }
    virtual double area() const = 0;
};

class Square : public Shape {
private:
    double* side;
public:
    Square(double side, double x, double y) : Shape(x, y),
        side(new double(side)) {}
    ~Square() { delete side;  std::cout << "~Square\n"; }
    double area() const { return *side * *side; }  // still looks weird
};

int main() {
    Shape* s = new Square(2.5, 0, 0);  // place at origin
    std::cout << s->area() << '\n';
    delete s;
    return 0;
}
```

Adds the virtual keyword; now, the derived class destructor is called first.

The output of this execution shows the expected derived class destruction followed by the base class destruction:

```
6.25
~Square
~Shape
```

The `virtual` keyword was added to the base class destructor, and the results show that both destructors were called. This happy fact demonstrates that the dynamically allocated memory was properly deleted in both classes. Ensure the base and derived classes have destructors if they use any dynamic resources, such as heap memory, system resource handles, or similar entities.

RECOMMENDATIONS

- Polymorphic behavior requires pointers or references and virtual functions; value objects (i.e., base class elements) will slice the derived part.

- If a class has a virtual function, it is intended to be a base class and derived from; always follow this pattern.

- Resist the temptation to derive a class from a pre-existing class that does not have a virtual destructor (or fix that pre-existing class for inheritance).

- If a class has any virtual functions, always define a virtual destructor to prevent the destruction of only the base class part, leaving memory leaks.

- Do not provide a virtual destructor if the class does not have a virtual function. This follows the advice of avoiding classes with a virtual method that is not intended to be inherited from.

SEE ALSO

- See Mistake 58 for a discussion of using virtual functions in destructors.
- See Mistake 74 for a discussion on using exceptions in destructors.

8.9 *Mistake 58: Calling virtual functions in constructors and destructors*

This mistake focuses on correctness. Misusing constructors and destructors in virtual functions significantly affects other characteristics.

One of the significant benefits of object-oriented programming is the ability to create a hierarchy of related classes. The classes are related to their base by extending it with additional, specific behavior. The power comes from treating related classes according to an interface that defines certain behaviors. Specialized classes modify the interface functions to produce meaningful results for their specific type.

This specialization allows fine-grained control of the general functions' behavior. For example, a `Shape` base class might have a `Circle` derived class. In general, all shapes should have an `area` method, but how the computation is achieved depends entirely on the type of shape being processed. This idea of defining a general concept (in the base class) and overriding that behavior with specifics (in the derived class) is called *runtime polymorphism.* Polymorphism is one of the three generally accepted pillars of object-oriented programming. (I argue for abstraction, too!) Understanding how a specific compiler implements polymorphism is not helpful; knowing conceptually how polymorphism could be implemented aids in understanding why calling virtual functions in a constructor is improper.

Consider inheritance a top-down flow of information. What the base class knows (state as in instance variables) and does (behavior as in methods) flows downward to a derived class. Polymorphic behavior is a bottom-up search for a specific function definition. Conceptually, the search for the appropriate virtual function starts at the specific derived class type and moves upward through the hierarchy. The first defined version of the function is used.

The compiler determines when the address of a nonvirtual instance method is needed and leaves space for inserting the address of that method. The compiler or linker inserts the address into the executable code wherever an instance calls one of these methods. At runtime, that address is used to locate the method's code. However, for virtual functions, more than this approach is needed.

The presence of a virtual function causes the compiler to build a new table for the class, which holds the address of each virtual function declared in it. These addresses are not directly inserted into the code during compilation or linking, as with nonvirtual methods. When an instance is created, a pointer per virtual function is used to reference the proper virtual function. The actual details are complex, but the following conceptual model is a working idea. The constructor determines which class table represents the proper virtual function and adjusts the pointer to refer to it.

Construction order is precisely defined. Assume a three-level hierarchy: the base class is A, the middle class is B, and the most derived class is C. When an instance of C is created, its constructor is called. The first thing the constructor does is call the appropriate base class constructor of B. The B constructor starts execution by calling its base class constructor to initialize the A part. After the A constructor finishes initializing the A part, the B constructor continues execution and finishes initializing the B part. Only after the B constructor returns does the C constructor resume execution and initialize the C part of the object. Figure 8.1 shows this construction order, where a constructor first calls its base class constructor.

For classes with virtual functions, think of the constructor as responsible for adjusting the pointer to the proper class table; this is not technically true, but it suggests why derived classes get the final say. Since the A constructor runs to completion first, the table will be initialized with the A class table defining the virtual function. If B also defines the virtual function, the table pointer for the A class is overwritten by the location of the B class table. The same happens for the C class. Therefore, when a C instance is handled through a base class pointer, the table used to find the proper virtual function will be the most recently adjusted one. Therefore, even though the C instance is being treated as a general A object, the last table pointer written into the instance is the one that gets called when the virtual function is invoked. Hence, a general A pointer or reference can behave specifically like a C instance when a virtual function is invoked.

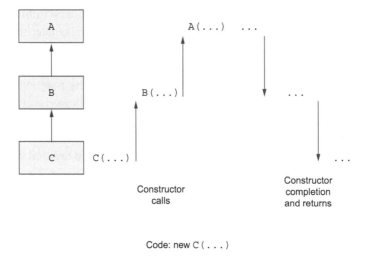

Figure 8.1   **A three-level hierarchy showing construction order**

A consequence of this construction order is that the actual object (a c instance, in this case) will only have its class table pointer adjusted at some point in its construction. At any point before this adjustment, a call to a virtual function would call the incorrect and unexpected version. When a constructor or destructor is executing, the object is either in the process of being constructed or destroyed. Since the object still needs to be entirely constructed, it cannot be considered ready, and the class invariant is not guaranteed.

PROBLEM

Let's assume an inheritance hierarchy is defined where different persons are defined with different honorific titles. At this school, graduate students are highly honored, students are somewhat honored, and general people are barely honored. Since this hierarchy needs to behave generally, GradStudent and Student instances will be substituted for Person instances, as appropriate. However, in this case, these substituted instances must behave specifically by determining the proper honorific.

The example code in listing 8.17 shows a case where the actual type's getHonorific virtual method was expected to be called and used to output a proper title. However, it fails due to this mistake.

This example shows a three-level hierarchy. Each constructor initializes its instance variables and then calls the print method. As this method executes, it calls the virtual getHonorific method. The output shows that each call to print outputs a different message. The getHonorific virtual method has its function pointer added to the table during each part's construction, which is the specific function called by the print method.

Listing 8.17 Calling virtual functions from a constructor

```
class Person {
private:
    std::string name;
public:
    Person(const std::string& name) :
        name(name) { print(); }      #A
    void print() const { std::cout << getHonorific() << name << '\n'; }
    const std::string getName() const { return getHonorific() + name; }
    virtual std::string getHonorific() const { return ""; }
};

class Student : public Person {
private:
    std::string year;
public:
    Student(const std::string& name, const std::string& year) : Person(name),
        year(year) { print(); }
    std::string getHonorific() const { return year + " "; }
};

class GradStudent : public Student {
private:
    bool candidate;
public:
    GradStudent(const std::string& name, const std::string& year,
        bool candidate) : Student(name, year), candidate(candidate)
        { print(); }

    std::string getHonorific() const {
        return candidate ? "candidate " : ""; }
};

int main() {
    GradStudent aimee("Aimee", "second year", true);
    return 0;
}
```

> Invoking a virtual method in a constructor; the function version is most likely incorrect.

ANALYSIS

The code's result shows that after each part is constructed, its version of the `get-Honorific` is called, not the actual type's version because the instance has not yet been fully constructed. Therefore, the version and result of the virtual function depend entirely on which part of the object is calling the method. The following output shows the various honorifics as the object is constructed, one line per class type:

```
Aimee
second year Aimee
candidate Aimee
```

Another problem is that virtual methods may depend on the state data of a given part. If the constructor has not run to completion for that part, there is no guarantee that the data is in a valid state. Likely, it is not. If a virtual function were called and it depended on this incomplete data, the results could be undefined.

SOLUTION

The solution is to call virtual functions once the object is entirely constructed. Only then will the virtual function table be initialized appropriately, and the behavior will correctly be polymorphic. The following code demonstrates this fix.

Listing 8.18   Constructors without virtual function calls

```
class Person {
private:
    std::string name;
public:
    Person(const std::string& name) : name(name) {}
    void print() const { std::cout << getHonorific() << name << '\n'; }
    std::string getName() const { return getHonorific() + name; }
    virtual std::string getHonorific() const { return ""; }
};

class Student : public Person {
private:
    std::string year;
public:
    Student(const std::string& name, const std::string& year) : Person(name),
        year(year) {}
    std::string getHonorific() const { return year + " "; }
};

class GradStudent : public Student {
private:
    bool candidate;
public:
    GradStudent(const std::string& name, const std::string& year,
            bool candidate) :
        Student(name, year), candidate(candidate) {}
    std::string getHonorific() const { return candidate ? "candidate " : ""; }
};

int main() {                                              Calls the virtual
    GradStudent aimee("Aimee", "second year", true);      function after the
    aimee.print();                                  ◄──── object is constructed
    return 0;
}
```

For correctly designed classes, destructors work in the reverse order of constructors. When a destructor is called on the pointer or reference, the most derived class destructor is called first. At the end of its execution, it calls its base class destructor. This percolates up to the top of the hierarchy, guaranteeing that objects are destroyed in reverse construction order.

If a virtual method is called during destruction, state information in the most derived class may be invalid, depending on the behavior of its destructor. However, virtual methods would expect this data to be in a valid state. Since this cannot be guaranteed, virtual methods in a destructor should always be avoided.

RECOMMENDATIONS

- Ensure no virtual function of the class is called before the instance is fully constructed; never call a virtual function of the class from its constructor.
- Remember that construction order affects the validity of state information and which version of a virtual function will be called; let the construction finish before calling any virtual functions.
- Remember that destruction order affects the validity of state information available to a virtual function, some of which is likely to be destroyed or otherwise invalid; once destruction begins, never call virtual functions

SEE ALSO

- See Mistake 57 for a discussion on writing a virtual destructor whenever a class defines a virtual method.

8.10 *Mistake 59: Attempting to use polymorphic array elements*

This mistake is focused on correctness. Functions that take arrays (or containers) with base class elements as a parameter appear to allow polymorphic behavior. An array of derived elements can be passed to the function—no compile time error is emitted. This is a gain in effectiveness; however, a hidden danger will trip up the unwary user.

Containers of objects are a natural way to collect related objects and manipulate them generically according to the base class public interface—this is the heart of polymorphism. However, their usage can be problematic when arrays of derived objects are passed to functions. Arrays are built-in containers that are easy to write and use, making their use simple and intuitive.

PROBLEM

A function that takes a pointer to a base class object can also be passed a derived class pointer or reference. The LSP holds here, saying that a derived class can be substituted wherever a base class is needed. This is a powerful technique for writing general code that correctly handles whatever object is passed.

It is a short step from thinking that if a pointer to an object works, a pointer to an array of objects should also work. However, in C++, this does not mean derived element arrays can be substituted for an array of base class elements and still work.

C++ code accesses elements in the array by using pointer arithmetic. Assume an array of integers named `arr` with several elements; the third element is indexed by `arr[2]`. This notation is syntactic sugar, since the access is actually `*(arr+2)`. The const pointer to the first element, `arr`, has the integer 2 added to skip over two elements and point to the third. The number of bytes to skip over is `2*sizeof(element_type)`. It is this pointer arithmetic that causes problems with passing arrays generically.

Consider the code in listing 8.19, where an array of derived class elements is printed. Class D derives from base class B, and D uses the getN method defined in B when its elements need printing. B defaults the n instance variable to 0, and D defaults its m instance variable to one. These easy-to-distinguish values make analysis of the output clear.

> **Listing 8.19   Passing an array with derived elements**

```
const int SIZE = 4;

class B {
private:
    int n;
public:
    B(int n=0) : n(n) {}
    ~B() { std::cout << "destroying B\n"; }
    int getN() const { return n; }
};

class D : public B {
    int m;
public:
    D() : B(0), m(1) {}
    ~D() { std::cout << "destroying D\n"; }
};

void printArray(const B a[]) {
    for (int i = 0; i < SIZE; ++i)
        std::cout << a[i].getN() << '\n';
}

void deleteArray(const B a[]) {
    delete [] a;
}

int main() {
    B* bs = new B[SIZE];
    printArray(bs);
    deleteArray(bs);

    D* ds = new D[SIZE];
    printArray(ds);
    deleteArray(ds);
    return 0;
}
```

This is not virtual intentionally, to better demonstrate the full problem. Do not do this normally!

General access function for array elements

Using the general access function when outputting values

Using a general deletion function

When this code is executed, the array of B elements works as expected; the output of the n part is 0s, and the destruction is of B elements. However, the output could be better for the array of D elements. The getN function alternates between outputting the n and m parts of the D elements. Since both the n and m parts are integers—the same size—the output shows that the indexing of the values is increasing the size of a B element, not that of the necessary D element. Further, only the B destructor is called when the elements are destroyed, meaning the memory block returned to the operating system may be inconsistent with the actual array size. This would be a memory leak. While it's expected that different systems may produce varying results, this is undefined behavior either way. The following output demonstrates that using derived elements is not working as expected. First, the destructors are exclusively the base class version. Second, the result of `getN` varies between the `n` and `m` instance variables:

```
0
0
0
0
destroying B
destroying B
destroying B
destroying B
0
1
0
1
destroying B
destroying B
destroying B
destroying B
```

ANALYSIS

The `printArray` function will index through the elements of the array and call the `getN` function. The first call to the function passes an array of `B` elements. The indexing in the function proceeds from the first element to the next by adding the size of a `B` element. This process continues until each element has been iterated over.

In the second case, the array contains `D` elements. Since `D` is derived from `B`, passing the array succeeds without complaint by the compiler—the LSP works here. The `printArray` function receives the `const` pointer to the array as its initial point; the first element starts at that point. When indexing the array and calling the `getN` function, access starts at this element and uses the `B` part from which it pulls the value; so far, so good. It finds the value of `1` and outputs it.

Carefully note the second printout; it is the value of the `m` variable. In this case, a `B` element uses one integer's space (typically four bytes), but a `D` element uses twice that. When the loop updates the index value, it increases the pointer by the size of a `B` element (one integer), but the actual value is the first `m` variable, which is exactly `sizeof(B)` from the pointer (or `*(ptr+sizeof(B))`). `D` elements are twice the size of a `B` element, so the indexing references them in an alternating pattern. Therefore, the pointer for index `1` is pointing at the `D` portion of the first element, not the `B` portion of the second element. If this sounds wrong, that's because it is wrong.

The pointer arithmetic works correctly for arrays of `B` elements but not for derived classes, such as `D`. There are no compiler warnings, and no segmentation faults (access to inaccessible memory) were noted during run time. This mistake is the opposite of accessing out-of-bounds memory; it is not accessing enough memory!

NOTE   The explanation of the operation and results are based on a nonopti-mized compilation and execution in one environment. Optimization or com-piler changes could cause different behavior. More importantly, this behavior is undefined. Therefore, no hard and fast conclusions about the exact results should be made.

Now, consider the deletion of the arrays. This code works correctly when `deleteArray` is called with an array of B elements. What is not apparent is that the `delete` opera-tor will also index the array and call the B version of delete on each element—hence, the "destroying B" output. This approach works correctly when the array contains B elements.

When this function is called with D elements, the loop will call destructors on the B part of the element and index according to the size of a B element. The second `delete` is referring to the D portion of the first element. What occurs in this case is up for spec-ulation. What is evident is that only B-sized elements are being destroyed. In this case, a virtual destructor would not solve the problem because a pointer arithmetic problem ultimately causes it.

Now, ponder the case where the derived elements are more complex than an inte-ger. If the D elements contained `std::string` references or pointers to other data types, it is unclear what, if anything, would get cleaned up. The fact that it needs to be clarified is very concerning; no programming language should provide operations that may or may not work depending on things you cannot control.

In our original problem, where an array of D elements was deleted—or the code tried to delete them—only the first four B-sized elements were deleted. If the array is on the stack, eventually, this mess will clear up, but if the memory is heap based, it is again unclear how the deallocators will process it and how much data gets reclaimed.

If this code is run with valgrind—a fantastic tool for detecting several memory prob-lems, especially leaks—it runs cleanly because the number of allocations and deletions are paired correctly. Address sanitizers can find some problems; see Matt Godbolt's Compiler Explorer website (https://compiler-explorer.com/z/6d73hscoE) for an example. This bug is very subtle, and even sophisticated tools seem unable to detect the problem fully. It is incumbent on the programmer to never use base class arrays as a general code- and keystroke-saving technique.

SOLUTION

A correct approach is to refuse to pass pointers to arrays of base and derived objects to functions. Make functions handle only arrays of the actual element type. Duplicat-ing these functions is a simple remedy. Using the generic programming technique of adding a function template is the ideal way to ensure this duplication. This technique is both readable and effective. Another possibility is to pass an array of pointers to the base class. The downside to this approach is that the code may have to handle pointers to pointers, making the calling and handling syntax a bit messier—if you are up to it, go for it!

Modern C++ provides the `std::array` class, which addresses this problem, too. If you are able, use that feature to overcome this problem.

In this situation, code reuse is a bad idea, and the concept, when followed too closely, will cause difficulties. The following code fixes the previously noted problems by making decidedly nonpolymorphic printing and deletion functions according to the template suggestion.

Listing 8.20 Functions without polymorphic array passing

```cpp
const int SIZE = 4;

class B {
private:
    int n;
public:
    B(int n=0) : n(n) {}
    ~B() { std::cout << "destroying B\n"; }
    int getN() const { return n; }
};

class D : public B {
    int m;
public:
    D() : B(1), m(2) {}
    ~D() { std::cout << "destroying D\n"; }
};

template <typename T>
void printArray(T a[]) {
    for (int i = 0; i < SIZE; ++i)
        std::cout << a[i].getN() << '\n';
}

template <typename T>
void deleteArray(T a[]) {
    delete [] a;
}

int main() {
    B* bs = new B[SIZE];
    printArray(bs);
    deleteArray(bs);

    D* ds = new D[SIZE];
    printArray(ds);
    deleteArray(ds);

    return 0;
}
```

Function templates handle the required duplication of code.

Generic handling of varying element types

The following code snippet shows the output of the fixed code:

```
0
0
0
0
destroying B
destroying B
destroying B
destroying B
1
1
1
1
destroying D
destroying B
destroying D
destroying B
destroying D
destroying B
destroying D
destroying B
```

The elements are displayed and deleted correctly, and no memory is lost. Very importantly, the output is correct for the B and D elements, and each part of the D element is destroyed. The destruction of elements involves the proper type, so no leftover memory remains or strange operating system allocation and deallocation mismatches.

RECOMMENDATIONS

- Write separate functions to handle base and derived class arrays if they must be passed as arguments to a function; writing similar arrays will prevent strange behavior. Consider using function templates to make the compiler write the duplicated code.

- Having no runtime errors does not indicate that a programming approach is correct or that there are no memory problems lurking.

- Understand that even sophisticated tools will not detect all problems; valgrind is a great tool, but it is not designed to detect this strange corner case.

- Make it your responsibility to code correctly, understanding the potential problems associated with using shortcuts.

SEE ALSO

- See Mistake 49 for a critique of using default constructors in many cases.

- See Mistake 57 for a discussion of why making base class destructors virtual is essential.

8.11 *Mistake 60: Failing to initialize all instance variables*

This mistake focuses on correctness, effectiveness, and a bit on performance. Until the idiom is understood, a developer might say this negatively affects readability. Once grasped, however, most will prefer this approach. This mistake should be so evident as to be unnecessary; sadly, this problem can still occur even with the best of intentions.

A class will have instance variables of two types: primitive (built-in) and class instances. Many modern languages force the initialization of all variables regardless of their location or use. C++ does not always ensure initialization occurs. In some cases, instance variables are declared but have no defined initial value. Every byte in memory has some state, so these variables will have an undefined value. Therefore, reading these variables results in undefined behavior; assigning them first and then reading them is fine. Initialization aims to ensure the state is well defined by the program.

Three means of initialization of primitive types are commonly used: assigning the variable using a literal value; inputting a value assigned to the variable; and assigning the variable from another, already initialized variable. These methods ensure the variable is both declared and initialized. The developer must ensure this holds for every local variable before its first use.

With classes, initialization is the responsibility of a constructor; its primary job is the initialization of variables, establishing the class invariant. The constructor must receive argument values for each parameter and use them to initialize instance variables or have a default value to assign to them. If it does not in every case, undefined behavior could result.

PROBLEM

Many problems deal with people in some way. Let's assume we need to model a `Person` class with only a `name` and an `age`. The following implementation of this simple class compiles and seems to run fine, except that it uses undefined data. It does not make its error obvious, unless the person's age is checked manually.

Listing 8.21 A class with an uninitialized built-in instance variable

```
class Person {
private:
    std::string name;          An instance variable,
    int age;                   which is a class instance
public:                        An instance variable,
    Person(const std::string& name) { this->name = name; }   which is a primitive type
    void setAge(int age) { this->age = age; }                A seemingly
    friend std::ostream& operator<<(std::ostream&, const Person&);   innocent
};                                                                    constructor

std::ostream& operator<<(std::ostream& o, const Person& p) {
    o << p.name << " is " << p.age << " years old";
    return o;
}

int main() {
    Person joey("Joey");
    std::cout << joey << '\n';
    return 0;
}
```

The developer should have insisted on an age being supplied in the constructor (ignored variables are bad form). The intent was for the client code to initialize the age data by a call to the setAge method, which ensures the age instance variable will be valid. When a programmer needs to remember to do this, problems likely ensue. In this case, the compiler cannot warn about the noninitialization problem, so you are on your own to figure out the problem, which will likely occur well after the code has been used for some time.

Some compilers initialize variables when run in debug mode but not release mode. This means, of course, that "it works on my machine" but that customers are not impressed.

ANALYSIS

The two instance variables in the class are of two categories. The std::string object is a class instance, and the compiler ensures its default constructor is called if no attempt is made to pass a value to its constructor. Its default initialization ensures the string is empty, a legitimate object; however, it contains no value useful for the programmer's problem. But wait, how could the name be an empty string? The constructor body initializes it to the parameter value, which is unlikely to be an empty string. True enough, but that is getting ahead of the actual action.

The code in the constructor body is an assignment, not an initialization. The term *initialization* has been used somewhat vaguely in the introductory part of this mistake, where assignments are used to initialize.

A constructor ensures all class instance variables are initialized before the constructor body is called. This means the default std::string constructor is called before entry to the Person constructor body. Then, in the constructor body, the assignment binds a copy of the parameter value to the instance variable. This is inefficient; the variable is initialized and assigned. Two operations are performed, when only one is necessary. Worse, if the parameter does not reference the caller's argument value, another copy is done to initialize the parameter. Wow!

The age instance variable is a built-in type. What does the constructor do for it before entering the constructor body? Absolutely nothing. (Thanks, C, your legacy is oh-so-helpful here.) The age instance variable will be the random bit pattern that happens to be in the memory where it is located. Access to the value is permissible, but its contents are unknown—its meaning and use are undefined. This situation could lead to a long and interesting debugging session.

SOLUTION

The proper way to write a constructor is to ensure every instance variable is initialized explicitly. Provide a parameter value for each instance variable or supply a meaningful default value in the initialization list. Adhering to this approach will ensure every instance variable is initialized every time.

The solution to remove extraneous class-type instance variable initializations is to use parameter values to initialize instance variables in the initializer list form. Make it a very rare exception for any code in the constructor body to be used to assign to an instance variable.

Listing 8.22 A class that insists on arguments for every instance variable

```cpp
class Person {
private:
    std::string name;
    int age;
public:
    Person(const std::string& name, int age) :
        name(name), age(age) {}
    friend std::ostream& operator<<(std::ostream&, const Person&);
};

std::ostream& operator<<(std::ostream& o, const Person& p) {
    o << p.name << " is " << p.age << " years old";
    return o;
}

int main() {
    Person joey("Joey", 27);
    std::cout << joey << '\n';
    return 0;
}
```

Each instance variable must be initialized.

Each constructor parameter must have an argument.

If validation is needed, for instance, variables, write a private validation method that returns the validated parameter value or throws an exception. Call the validation method in the initializer list. The code in the following listing is updated to include a private validator for the age instance variable, which is called in the constructor's initializer list.

Listing 8.23 Validating a parameter using a private validator in an initializer list

```cpp
class Person {
private:
    std::string name;
    int age;
    static int validateAge(int age) {
        if (age < 0)
            throw std::invalid_argument("negative age");
        return age;
    }
public:
    Person(const std::string& name, int age) :
        name(name), age(validateAge(age)) {}
    friend std::ostream& operator<<(std::ostream&, const Person&);
};

std::ostream& operator<<(std::ostream& o, const Person& p) {
    o << p.name << " is " << p.age << " years old";
    return o;
```

A private validator method that returns valid values or throws an exception

The validator is called in initializer list; no extraneous assignments are needed.

```
}

int main() {
    Person joey("Joey", 27);                          Safely creating an instance
    std::cout << joey << '\n';                         because of validation
    return 0;
}
```

RECOMMENDATIONS

- Ensure every instance variable is initialized in every constructor, whether from a parameter value or a default value.

- Remember that built-in types are not implicitly initialized outside the constructor body.

- Do not depend on programmers to remember to initialize instance variables; provide parameters in the constructor so that the compiler will remind them to supply each needed argument.

- Call parameter validation code to ensure the class invariant is properly established; make the validator private, localize the knowledge of an instance variable in it, and return valid values or throw an exception.

Class operations 9

This chapter continues the discussion of how to use instances well. The concept of the class invariant is always in view, but these mistakes need to be addressed with a different focus than the previous chapters. This certainly does not mean that it is less important, only that the emphasis is broader, touching on areas that do not necessarily directly affect the state of an object.

The category of performance is frequently addressed in these mistakes, with several emphasizing this aspect by focusing on eliminating unnecessary temporary objects. These temporary objects occur when an intermediate step in an expression evaluation requires an intermediary object to hold the results of a partial evaluation, which will be used in further evaluation. Knowing when these temporaries are created and how to design a class to eliminate many of them significantly affects the number of constructor and destructor calls.

Other mistakes focus on misusing operators that affect common usage or performance. C++ provides a significant amount of flexibility for the developer, and this flexibility must be respected to avoid using features improperly.

9.1   *Mistake 61: Misunderstanding variable shadowing*

This mistake primarily affects readability. However, correctness and effectiveness can be adversely affected when mistakes are made in understanding the scope and meaning of a variable.

Variable naming is a difficult task. Developers must name entities well to avoid confusion and errors. Finding good naming practices may take many iterations, as the developer's understanding of the code develops. Numerous scopes exist in which a variable can be declared. These scopes include statement, local, class, namespace, global, and file. Understanding which scope is in view is essential for correctly using the proper variable.

A variable is declared when its type and name are written. Its scope starts at the point of declaration and is limited to the end of the file, block, or statement in which it is declared. Generally, the scope ends with the end of the file, closing brace, or semicolon in a statement scope. A variable is shadowed when a later inner scope defines another variable with the same name but not necessarily the same type. The code within the inner scope cannot see the same named variable in the outer scope. In some cases, the scope resolution `operator::` can be used for accessing the shadowed outer scope variable.

Programs that are more extensive than just a few functions will often have variables named identically within the code. Since these functions share no scope, shadowing does not occur, as no scope overlaps. However, when an inner scope declares a variable with an identical name to one in an outer scope, the programmer must use the correct variable in assignments or computations.

PROBLEM

Shadowing occurs when scopes define variables of the same name. The broader the scope is, the more likely some shadowing is to occur. Global variables are visible to all functions in a compilation unit from their point of declaration to the end of the source file. Global variable usage is generally discouraged, but it is commonly done. Correctness and readability are the first victims of the overuse of global variables. When they are used, they must be named carefully. The choice of simple, short names for a global variable would be a reasonable decision only if these short names are well-known concepts, such as PI or E. For lesser-known values, a naming scheme, such as all caps separated with underscores (or similar), should be used to distinguish global variables clearly from nonglobal ones. The use of namespaces is better to prevent easy shadowing mistakes.

Often, clear naming needs to be practiced better. For example, imagine a global variable named I; understanding its meaning is only possible once its definition (and, hopefully, a helpful comment) is read. The further away a declaration or definition is from the code that uses it, the longer and more expressive the variable's name should be. Most companies or projects have some guidelines; follow them closely—it's about readability and cooperation.

In many cases, short variable names are used in multiple scopes. This situation makes understanding which variable is being used more difficult. Yet short variable names are commonplace and convenient. Knowing when to use them takes awareness of both content and intent.

A content type shadowing error occurs when a mistake is made using the variable name; the scope of the used variable is inner, and the expected variable is in an outer scope. The code in listing 9.1 demonstrates that the global variable is named the same as the instance variable. For illustration purposes only, the sum function will use variable scope incorrectly.

The sum function mistakenly uses the instance variable twice, thinking it used both the inner and outer scoped ones. The scope resolution operator should be used to disambiguate the variable names. This is a mistaken shadowing of content, a syntactical blunder—likely just a typo. These problems are likely to cause consternation but are relatively easy to resolve by correctly naming the variable.

Listing 9.1 Identical variable names in various scopes

```cpp
double rad = 1.0;        // A global variable with a very
                         // short name, which makes its
                         // meaning unclear
class Circle {
private:
    double rad;          // An instance variable
                         // with a short name
public:
    Circle(double rad) : rad(rad) {}     // A parameter named the same as the instance
    void setRadius(double rad) {         // variable that needs to be disambiguated
        if (rad < 0)
            throw std::invalid_argument("negative radius");
        rad = rad;
    }
    double sum() const {                 // These are two variables with the
        return rad + rad;                // same name; the most local is used,
    }                                    // masking the global version.
    double getRadius() { return rad; }   // The instance variable is used;
};                                       // it is the only variable in scope.

int main() {
    Circle c(3);
    std::cout << "radius is " << c.getRadius() << '\n';
    std::cout << "enlarged radius is " << c.sum() << '\n';
    return 0;
}
```

The intent is to pass an array of random values to the `SearchAnalyzer`, which will determine how many values appear in the array. Since this code must modify the array for efficient searching, it clones and modifies the values by sorting. Other `Analyzer`-derived classes did not need to clone the data; hence, the mindset was established for shared data. When the `analyze` method is called, the expected result is a line of text explaining how many random search values were found in the data. The student was surprised to discover that none were found. The next step was to email the professor for help!

Listing 9.2   Different variable names confused in their meaning

```cpp
class Analyzer{
protected:
    int* cloneValues(int* a, int size){
        int* arr = new int[size];
        for (int i = 0; i < size;i++)
            arr[i] = a[i];
        return arr;
    }
    int* array;                            ◄─── The protected pointer
    int size;                                   to the array
public:
    Analyzer(int*values, int size) : array(values), size(size) {}
    virtual std::string analyze() = 0;
    virtual ~Analyzer() { delete[] array; }
};

                                                              The call to the
                                                           cloneValues method
class SearchAnalyzer : public Analyzer{
public:
    SearchAnalyzer(int* values, int size) : Analyzer(cloneValues(values,
            size), size) {
        selection_sort(values, size);    ◄─── Incorrectly using the values
    }                                         variable for the sorting method
    std::string analyze() {
        int count = 0;
        for (int i = 0; i < 100; ++i)
            if (binary_search(array, rand() % SIZE, size))   ◄─┐
                ++count;
        std::stringstream ss;
        ss << "There were "<< count << " random values found.";
        return ss.str();
    }                                                 Searching the array
};                                               variable; it is unsorted!

int main() {
    int* numbers = createArray(SIZE);
    SearchAnalyzer searcher(numbers, SIZE);
    std::cout << searcher.analyze() << '\n';
    return 0;
}
```

The problem is a simple one but much too easy to make. The parameter values are understood to be the list of random values to search; however, this list had to be cloned and sorted, creating a new variable representing the intended data. One can focus on the input variable, forgetting the inconspicuous cloned values; this is especially true when other code does not have its separate data. The fix is simple: change `values` to `array` in the call to `selection_sort`, and all works as expected.

Not precisely shadowing, a common mistake occurs when similar variable names are used for the same content. More pernicious than actual shadowing, the code in listing 9.2 is a shadowing of intent, where identically named variables do not contribute to causing a problem; therefore, the simplicity of fixing the shadowing of content does not apply. Instead, two variables with similar meanings are mistaken—a semantic blunder. The code is taken from students who submitted a project they could not complete.

ANALYSIS

Global variables are often used but infrequently qualified in a way that easily distinguishes them from classes or local variables. The global variable in listing 9.1 is named identically to a class and parameter variable in the code. In this case, it is easy to see that the `setRadius` parameter `rad` should be initializing the identically named instance variable. Still, more extensive or obtuse code greatly obscures the apparent meaning and usage. Developers have the propensity to give global variables short names within a class or a function, since they seem "obvious" at the time. With sufficient delineation of the meaning and purpose of the variable, its use is straightforward.

Consider the `setRadius` method: the code needs to reference the global `rad` variable, but what does that mean, and where is it? If the class and method have no such name, a search will be made to find an outer scope variable; in this case, the global variable is used. This approach is expensive in terms of time and understanding.

When the mutator parameter is named identically to the instance variable, the `this` keyword must distinguish the instance variable from the parameter variable. Without this distinction, the parameter would be assigned to itself, as in listing 9.1. Some compilers will not warn about this situation but happily compile and generate code that does not do what is expected. I teach students to use this pattern as a rule of thumb. A parameter with the same name as the instance variable it is initializing is substantial documentation; using the `this` pointer is essential for disambiguation. If this approach is used, make it a habit; otherwise, occasionally failing to use `this` pointer is likely and will cause nasty debugging sessions.

SOLUTION

For readability, the reader must understand the meaning of each part of the initializer list. The variable outside the parentheses is the instance variable (the `this->radius` part in listing 9.3), and the variable inside the parentheses is the parameter (`double radius` in this example). Effectiveness is slightly enhanced, since developers can duplicate the names without maintaining a single letter or abbreviation in their short-term memory.

Listing 9.3   Identical variable names distinguished by a namespace

```
namespace global {
    double radius = 1.0;
```

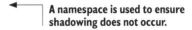 **A namespace is used to ensure shadowing does not occur.**

```
};
class Circle {
private:
    double radius;
public:
    Circle(double radius) : radius(radius) {}
    void setRadius(double radius) {
        if (radius < 0)
            throw std::invalid_argument("negative radius");
        this->radius = radius;
    }
    double sum() const {
        return radius + global::radius;
    }
    double getRadius() const { return radius; }
};

int main() {
    Circle c(3);
    std::cout << "radius is " << c.getRadius() << '\n';
    std::cout << "enlarged radius is " << c.sum() << '\n';
    return 0;
}
```

Remember to make it a habit to use this pattern, or don't use it at all.

Unambiguous usage of the variable name

Shadowed names are a helpful way to document a parameter used to initialize or assign an instance variable; the constructor or mutator's parameter names and the instance variable names are identical. A few developers recommend coding the parameter as a single character (the instance variable's first character) or an abbreviated version of the name that reasonably communicates intent. A better piece of advice is to prefix or postfix the instance variable with a symbol, such as an underscore, to suggest that the variable is private (which only instance variables can be).

Global variables should be named in such a way that makes it obvious they are global variables. This approach prevents inadvertent use or confusion when a different variable is expected. Two techniques are helpful to make sure this is clear. First, consider a standardized way of naming global variables. For example, prefix each variable with GLOB_ or some similar marker. An alternative is to add a _g or _global as a suffix to the variable name. Remember that the further away a variable is from its use, the longer and more descriptive its name should be to communicate its intent and purpose; these two options address this advice well. Second, consider using a namespace to contain all global variables. This approach makes it much easier to understand when a global variable is used. The namespace containment ensures global variables are not spread across the source code and are named with an obvious pattern. Further, containing global variables within an enum or class provides alternatives with the same benefits. This snippet demonstrates using a namespace when computing continuous compound interest:

```
namespace Constants {
    const double e = 2.7182828283;
}
...
amount = principal * std::pow(Constants::e, rate*time);
```

RECOMMENDATIONS

- The further the name is from its use, the longer and more descriptive its name should be and the more specific the way to use it should be (e.g., a namespace).

- Avoid using global variables whenever possible to prevent both design and shadowing problems.

- Remember that duplicating variable names can lead to problems with understanding the intent of the code and its proper use.

- Be aware of shadowing of content (the simple version) and of intent (the more complicated version); the first is syntactic, and the second is semantic, making it all the harder to notice, primarily when similar code uses other variable names.

9.2 *Mistake 62: Allowing duplication of unique objects*

This mistake focuses on correctness. There is also a slight effect on readability, unless the reader understands the problem and its solution.

Many data types represent concepts that allow the duplication of objects. For example, a `std::string` may contain the name of a product, such as the make and model of an `Automobile` class. When modeling a car in a parking garage, we can expect several automobiles with the same make and model; having several occurrences of the same vehicle is normal.

Some data types, however, represent unique concepts. The idea of copying them violates the class invariant. Classic C++ has no language-specific means to prevent duplicating unique objects, so the programmer must maintain this property.

PROBLEM

Let us consider modeling artwork in a system, perhaps one that produces a catalog for potential buyers. Each piece of art is unique and must be handled as such. The code in listing 9.4 defines no means for duplicating an object, ostensibly preserving the invariant property of uniqueness. Initially, the class had a public copy assignment operator, which had to be corrected. The developer (wrongly) thought that moving it to the private section would preclude the possibility of creating a duplicate.

Listing 9.4 Incorrectly coded to prevent copying of unique objects

```
class ArtPiece {
private:
    int id;
    std::string description;
    ArtPiece& operator=(const ArtPiece& o) {          An existing copy assignment
        this->id = o.id;                               operator moved to the
        this->description = o.description;      ◄─────  private section
        return *this;
    }                                                  No public copy constructor
                                                       or copy assignment
public:                                        ◄─────  operator is coded.
    ArtPiece(int id, std::string d) : id(id), description(d) {}
```

```
        std::string getDesc() { return description; }
};

int main() {
    ArtPiece ml(333, "Mona Lisa");
    ArtPiece ts(444, "The Scream");        This appears as if it
    std::cout << ml.getDesc() << '\n';     should not work.

    ArtPiece dup(ml);          ◄──────┐    A private copy assignment
    std::cout << dup.getDesc() << '\n';    operator prevents this
    // dup = ts;               ◄──────┘    code from working.
    return 0;
}
```

The developer thought that with the moving of the copy assignment operator, the ability to duplicate objects would be eliminated; after all, the copy assignment operator cannot be called—and they forgot about the defaulted copy constructor! The developer considered the effect of duplicating a unique object and chose hiding as the means to prevent it. The output is

```
Mona Lisa
Mona Lisa
```

And the art world is in shambles!

ANALYSIS

The compiler writes the default copy constructor and copy assignment operator if the programmer does not specify either. Because the copy constructor is not coded, the default version creates the dup object and produces a copy of the Mona Lisa. Rather than failing, the copy occurred, and there is no sign of a forgery (no apparent violation of the class invariant's uniqueness property). There is a significant problem with this (sloppy) approach.

The code to create dup compiles and executes without problems because the compiler provides a default version of the copy constructor, ensuring a shallow copy for each instance variable is done. However, in this case, the default behavior produces a forged copy without the ability to distinguish between them.

The programmer's naïve approach failed to consider that if a class has no programmer-defined copy constructor, the compiler will happily provide a default version for free (in this case, *free* as in *free-fall*). The class must be designed to prevent either operation from compiling. Any other kind of undesired functionality can be inhibited by merely not coding the function; these two are not of that kind. The programmer must explicitly prevent their successful use.

One approach used with measured success is explicitly defining the copy constructor and the copy assignment operator but making them private. For the most part, this solves the problem. However, if code in the class happens to do something untoward—a copy or assignment—the compiler will happily comply, and an invariant violation (forgery) occurs.

SOLUTION

The mentioned approach has part of the right idea but needs to include another important aspect. The missing part is that the private definition of each operator that supplies a function body is executable code. Therefore, no method body should be specified. The solution is simple: declare but do not define the two operations. The code in the following listing fixes both problems in one stroke.

Listing 9.5   Preventing duplication by declaring defaulted operations

```
class ArtPiece {
private:
    int id;
    std::string description;
    ArtPiece(const ArtPiece&);                    Private and
    ArtPiece& operator=(const ArtPiece&);         unimplemented
public:
    ArtPiece(int id, std::string d) : id(id), description(d) {}
    std::string getDesc() { return description; }
    void badMethod() { ArtPiece a = *this; }  ◄────  Class-based assignment
};                                                   compiles without warning.

int main() {
    ArtPiece ml(333, "Mona Lisa");
    ArtPiece ts(444, "The Scream");
    // ArtPiece dup(ml);             Will not compile because
    // ts = ml;                      operations are private
    std::cout << ml.getDesc() << '\n';
    ts.badMethod();         ◄────
    return 0;                        No compilation error here.
}
```

The two duplicating functions are declared private and not defined. Any code in the client that attempts to use either operation will fail, as expected, maintaining the class invariant because neither the client-oriented copy assignment operator nor the copy constructor will compile. The compiler sees that both operations are private and prevents the client code from using it. But all is not well.

Notice in listing 9.5 the introduction of the `badMethod` method. Its body does an assignment that the compiler cannot prevent, as it could in client-oriented code; the syntax is legal, but its semantics are questionable. The compiler does not have a problem with the code, and the code compiles cleanly; since there is no error, no message is emitted to state that one error has occurred. This statement might sound wrong, but it is correct. The linker is where the problem shows up. The linker tries to find the definition of the copy assignment operator in external code but cannot. Therefore, it emits an undefined reference error. This bug could be more straightforward for projects that compile independently from linking. The behavior may be different from what is expected, so preventing it from occurring in the first place is the safest path.

Modern C++ compilers can catch this error if the copy constructor and copy assignment operator are made public and set to =delete. The following code listing shows an example of this. Notice the commented-out code; these errors are now clearly illegal.

> **Listing 9.6   Preventing duplication using** `delete=`

```cpp
class ArtPiece {
private:
    int id;
    std::string description;
public:
    ArtPiece(int id, std::string d) : id(id), description(d) {}
    ArtPiece(const ArtPiece&) = delete;
    ArtPiece& operator=(const ArtPiece&) = delete;
    const std::string& getDesc() const { return description; }
    //void badMethod() { ArtPiece a = *this; }
};

int main() {
    ArtPiece ml(333, "Mona Lisa");
    ArtPiece ts(444, "The Scream");
    // ArtPiece dup(ml);                        Modern C++ prevents
    // ts = ml;                                 these errors. Well done!
    std::cout << ml.getDesc() << '\n';
    // ts.badMethod();
    return 0;
}
```

RECOMMENDATIONS

- Remember that unimplemented copy constructors and copy assignment operators are defaulted by the compiler, which can create unexpected or unwanted behaviors.

- Ensure you know which objects are unique and must not be copied; transferring values is fine if the source entity is left empty.

- Use the modern C++ =delete on a member to delete it specifically, as this forces a compile-time error rather than a link-time error.

SEE ALSO

- See Mistake 20 for a discussion of how modern C++ prevents the problem discussed here by ensuring the source object is emptied—the state of the source is transferred to the target entity.

9.3   *Mistake 63: Not coding for return value optimization*

This mistake focuses on performance and, slightly, on effectiveness. Classes using operators are prone to creating temporaries more frequently than necessary. In some early C++ compilers, the cost of doing some arithmetic operations was steeper due to a proliferation of temporary objects during expression evaluation. This problem centers on the number of constructor calls required to evaluate such an expression.

Various schemes have been tried to eliminate some of the temporary values. Two such attempts were to return pointers and to return references. However, the resulting code is complicated to read and sometimes dangerously wrong. Other approaches needed awkward syntax. These proposed solutions precluded them from helping reduce temporary values.

PROBLEM

Consider a situation in which some engineers need to write a complex class. Listing 9.7 is a typical implementation that would meet their needs. Everything looks clean and efficient, so the engineers are happy; however, over time, they started complaining about their sluggish performance. This code may not have any problems, so the developers look elsewhere. (Always measure your assumptions for performance!) The following listing shows the delivered code for creating and adding complex numbers.

Listing 9.7   A typical approach to adding complex numbers

```
class Complex {
private:
    double real;
    double imag;
public:
    Complex(double r, double i) : real(r), imag(i) {std::cout<<"x\n";}
    Complex(const Complex& o) : real(o.real), imag(o.imag)
        { std::cout<<"y\n"; }
    friend const Complex operator+(const Complex&, const Complex&);
};
const Complex operator+(const Complex& lhs, const Complex& rhs) {
    Complex sum(lhs.real+rhs.real, lhs.imag+rhs.imag);    ◄─── The third
    return sum;                         ◄─┐                    constructor call
}                                         └─ The fourth constructor
                                             call—copy constructor

int main() {
    Complex c1(-2, 3.3);    ◄─┘ The first constructor call
    Complex c2(3, -1);      ◄─
    Complex c3 = c1 + c2;   ◄─┘ The second constructor call
}                          ◄─┐
                             └─ The fifth constructor
                                call—copy constructor
```

This code has five constructor calls without return value optimization (RVO). The first two are the construction of the c1 and c2 objects. The third is the creation of the sum object in the operator+ method. When the sum object is returned, a temporary object is created and initialized with its values using the copy constructor, the fourth call. Finally, the c3 object is created from the temporary, making the fifth constructor call.

NOTE   Due to the pervasive problem of non-RVO, current compilers automatically implement it. Therefore, finding a compiler that does not do RVO is difficult, so this mistake will only apply to older compilers. However, the coding recommendations for RVO are still recommended, since they are cleaner. The GNU g++ compiler provides the `-fno-elide-constructors` flag to disable RVO for experimentation (only!) reasons.

ANALYSIS

Numerous efforts have been made to eliminate some constructor calls, which would minimize the cost of temporary objects. The attempt to create an object and return its pointer made the calling syntax awful. The pointer approach can be implemented as shown in the following listing.

Listing 9.8   Minimizing constructor calls by returning a pointer

```
class Complex {
private:
    double real;
    double imag;
public:
    Complex(double r, double i) : real(r), imag(i) { std::cout << "x\n"; }
    Complex(const Complex& o) : real(o.real), imag(o.imag) {
        std::cout<<"y\n"; }
    friend const Complex* operator+(const Complex&, const Complex&);
};
const Complex* operator+(const Complex& lhs, const Complex& rhs) {    ◄──────┐
    Complex* cpx = new Complex(lhs.real+rhs.real, lhs.imag+rhs.imag);
    return cpx;
}                                                                  Eliminates one
                                                                   constructor call

int main() {                             ┌─ Eliminates the constructor call by
    Complex c1(-2, 3.3);                 │  making its use awkward and unnatural,
    Complex c2(3, -1);                   │  but it works—who deletes the object?
    Complex c3 = *(c1 + c2);    ◄────────┘
}
```

This code eliminates one constructor call but forces client code to write in an unnatural and unintuitive manner. Worse, it allocates heap memory, which is always more expensive than automatic (stack) memory. This approach is hard to read and an ineffective use of a programmer's time.

Attempting to create objects within the operator body and returning a reference to the object is tempting and usually works (however, one must ignore the extremely helpful warning message). But beware of the pitfalls shown in the following listing—there be dragons!

Listing 9.9   Minimizing constructor calls by returning a reference

```
class Complex {
private:
    double real;
    double imag;
public:
```

```
    Complex(double r, double i) : real(r), imag(i) { std::cout << "x\n"; }
    Complex(const Complex& o) : real(o.real), imag(o.imag) {
        std::cout<<"y\n"; }
    friend const Complex& operator+(const Complex&, const Complex&);
};
const Complex& operator+(const Complex& lhs, const Complex& rhs) {
    Complex cpx(lhs.real+rhs.real, lhs.imag+rhs.imag);
    return cpx;
}

int main() {
    Complex c1(-2, 3.3);
    Complex c2(3, -1);
    Complex c3 = c1 + c2;
}
```

Eliminates one constructor call

This uses an easy and natural syntax, but it is wrong!

The cpx object created in the operator exists up to the end of the function, when it is destroyed. The object is created in a stack frame, and the stack frame is invalidated. The return of the reference to the now-destroyed object means it is a reference to an invalid object. Use of that object results in undefined behavior, which will differ, depending on various conditions. The dangerous surprise is that the stack frame where the object exists will often not be overwritten, and the code will work. But someday, it will suddenly and mysteriously fail when it needs to work. Burned!

SOLUTION

Rather than attempting to create an object and returning either a pointer (awkward!) or a reference (wrong!), code the constructor so that the compiler can use RVO to eliminate unnecessary temporary objects. Many textbooks demonstrate the *create an object and return it* pattern, instead of the more elegant and efficient *return the creation of an object* pattern.

Listing 9.10 demonstrates the better approach, where the operator creates a new object in the return statement. RVO eliminates what would have been two copy constructor calls at the point of return and in the assignment in the client code. Work has been done in compilers to make this more efficient, but as always, not everyone has the benefit of later technology.

Listing 9.10   Coded for RVO

```
class Complex {
private:
    double real;
    double imag;
public:
    Complex(double r, double i) : real(r), imag(i) {std::cout<<"x\n";}
    Complex(const Complex& o) : real(o.real), imag(o.imag)
        { std::cout<<"y\n"; }
    friend const Complex operator+(const Complex&, const Complex&);
};
    const Complex operator+(const Complex& lhs, const Complex& rhs) {
        return Complex(lhs.real+rhs.real, lhs.imag+rhs.imag);
```

Coded to take advantage of RVO—eliminates one copy constructor call

```
    }
int main() {
    Complex c1(-2, 3.3);
    Complex c2(3, -1);
    Complex c3 = c1 + c2;
}
```

RVO eliminates a second
copy constructor call.

The `Complex` object is created at the cost of one constructor call, but that must happen in any approach. The goal is not to prevent construction but to eliminate temporary objects. With RVO, the sum of `c1` and `c2` can be constructed in the space that `c3` takes, eliminating all copy constructor calls. An object must be constructed in the operator body; focus on eliminating the cost of copy constructors by coding so that the compiler's RVO mechanism occurs.

RECOMMENDATIONS

- Many current compilers implement RVO; peruse the documentation to discover whether yours does.

- Return the result of a constructor call, not an object created in the operator's body, to ensure the code is an easy target for RVO.

- Pointers can be returned from operators, but the calling syntax is messy, and someone must take responsibility for deleting the objects.

- References to local objects should never be returned from operators; the local object will have already been destroyed by the time the calling code accesses it.

SEE ALSO

- See Mistake 84 for a more thorough discussion of the problems associated with accessing local objects outside of their scope.

9.4   Mistake 64: Not returning a reference from copy assignment operators

This mistake focuses on performance. Excessive temporary objects can be created when developing a class. Knowing why they are created allows developers to prevent unnecessary ones. Wrongly coding a copy assignment operator is an area where excessive temporary objects can be created.

PROBLEM

Assume a developer is writing a package for engineering computations. One of the data types the client needs is a complex number. C++ provides a `complex` template in the `complex` header, but to illustrate this problem, the developers will write their class version.

This code is designed to allow chained assignments that honor the copy assignment operator's precedence and associativity. It compiles and runs, but it has a few problems with temporaries.

Listing 9.11 A class returning a temporary from its copy assignment operator

```
class Complex {
private:
    double real;
    double imag;
public:
    Complex(double r = 0.0, double i = 0.0) : real(r), imag(i) {}
    Complex operator=(const Complex& o) {
        Complex cpx(o.real, o.imag);          ◄─────  Written for return value
        real = cpx.real;                             optimization, perhaps?
        imag = cpx.imag;
        return cpx;
    }
};

int main() {
    Complex c1, c2, c3(1, 1);
    c1 = c2 = c3;
    return 0;
}
```

ANALYSIS

The copy assignment operator is supposed to modify the state of an instance, which this code does; however, the developer wrote it in a way that creates a temporary object. The assignment's target should be updated directly from the parameter; in this case, it is assigned from the temporary object. A new object initialized with the object's values is created and returned (perhaps, misled by an overzealous application of RVO). A benefit of RVO is that it prevents another temporary from being created from the returned object. This approach is expensive, since it calls the constructor to create the temporary object and throws it away as soon as it is used.

The usage in listing 9.11 calls the `Complex` constructor five times. Further, the object initializing the assigned object is not the object on its right-hand side; instead, it is transferred from an unnecessary copy of the object.

SOLUTION

The following code shows a better approach. Rather than returning a copy of the object, a reference to the modified object is returned so that the actual object—not a copy—is used for the assignment.

Listing 9.12 Returning a reference from a copy assignment operator

```
class Complex {
private:
    double real;                                      Written to modify
    double imag;                                      the target object
public:
    Complex(double r = 0.0, double i = 0.0) : real(r), imag(i) {}
    Complex& operator=(const Complex& cpx) {    ◄─────
        real = cpx.real;
```

```
        imag = cpx.imag;
        return *this;        ◄─────┐  Returns a reference to the
    }                                  modified target object
};

int main() {
    Complex c1, c2, c3(1, 1);
    c1 = c2 = c3;
    return 0;
}
```

The critical factor is that the copy assignment operator returns a reference to, not a copy of, the object. This approach reduces the constructor call used to create the temporary return object. The return value refers to the newly updated object, eliminating any need to copy the object. The semantics of the assignment are preserved, and no temporary object is created. The actual object is used for chaining assignments.

This approach should be used for all assignment-type operators, not simply the bare assignment. The following code shows only the operator+=, which follows this pattern. All other compound assignment operators should follow this pattern. For example, the compound additive operator would be implemented as shown in the following listing.

Listing 9.13   Returning a reference from a compound operator

```
class Complex {
private:
    double real;
    double imag;
public:
    Complex(double r = 0.0, double i = 0.0) :
        real(r), imag(i) {std::cout<<"x\n";}
    Complex& operator+=(const Complex& cpx) {    ◄─────┐  Repeats the
        real += cpx.real;                                established pattern
        imag += cpx.imag;
        return *this;
    }
};

int main() {
    Complex c1, c2, c3(1, 1);
    c2 += c3;            ◄─────┐
    c1 += c2;                    Uses the pattern
    return 0;
}
```

RECOMMENDATIONS

- Understand the standard usage patterns of operators, and ensure the class can provide the same approach.
- Remember the built-in precedence and associativity of each operator to ensure the code follows them.

- Ensure that classes use the same approach to operators as the built-in data types; do not surprise the client with some exotic, unintuitive behavior.

9.5   *Mistake 65: Forgetting to handle self-assignment*

This mistake focuses on correctness and slightly on performance. It is a problem, primarily when dynamic resources are used in a class. Failing to handle self-assignment can cause significant errors with these resources.

Assignment from one instance to another occurs frequently. The copy assignment operator is called to handle this functionality. Properly written copy assignment operators must handle dynamic resources correctly to prevent violation of the class invariant, unique objects, and resource leaks. However, a subtle problem can trip up developers when the assignment is between the same object. It might seem that self-assignment is not likely, but when using pointers, the actual object is much more obscure than named variables. If self-assignment is handled incorrectly, data can be lost, a crash could occur, or undefined behavior can be experienced.

PROBLEM

Consider the code in listing 9.14, which creates a new `Engine` object when assigned from a different `Auto` object. The pattern for handling dynamic resources is correct, yet a significant problem lurks in the code. It is assumed that deleting the existing `Engine` is essential (and it is), so the code deletes it before the copy. Because the assignment source and target are the same, the attempt to obtain the VIN is an access to deleted data. Hopefully, the code crashes nicely without unexpected behavior or data corruption; otherwise, be prepared for a nightmare. Using tools like valgrind and memory sanitizers is a really good practice, as this mistake demonstrates.

Listing 9.14   Object assignment with a hidden danger

```
class Engine {
private:
    std::string vin;
public:
    Engine(std::string vin) : vin(vin) {}
    std::string getVin() { return vin; }
};

class Auto {
private:
    Engine* engine;
public:
    Auto(Engine* engine) : engine(engine) {}
    Auto& operator=(const Auto& car) {          Deletes the
        if (engine)                             existing engine
            delete engine;
        engine = new Engine(car.engine->getVin());    Accesses deleted
        return *this;                                  engine data
    }
};
```

```
int main() {
    Engine* e1 = new Engine("123456789");
    Auto mustang(e1);
    mustang = mustang;
}
```

ANALYSIS

This resource handling might be correct in some cases, but with the copy assignment operator, what happens is an error. The assignment code first deletes the existing `Engine` object. Then, it assigns a new `Engine` object from the VIN supplied by the source. While it might look good, the deletion is a major problem.

Deleting the `Engine` object ensures the existing `Engine` is deleted to prevent resource leaks. The assignment of a new `Engine` from the parameter's VIN value is intended to create a new `Engine` from that data alone; however, the data comes from an object that was just deleted. The two objects will not be identical in many assignment cases, so this code works without issue. But in this case, the source and target are the same object. This case is self-assignment, and now the code causes a problem. Therefore, the code that has worked well now crashes (a good day) or does some undefined behavior (a very bad day).

I get lucky on my system—the attempt to access the deleted engine's VIN is met with an error message about double free or corruption. This error indicates that something is terribly wrong, and I must figure it out (shame on me). Perhaps, other systems will not indicate an error. Woe!

SOLUTION

The problem is that when the object and the parameter are the same entity, deleting the `Engine` object causes a problem. In other cases—where they are not the same object—no problem exists. What is needed is code that checks whether the receiving object and the parameter object are identical. In this case, the deletion should not occur. Nothing should occur in this case.

The code in the following listing shows a better approach that handles self-assignment and prevents improper handling of those dynamic resources. A simple test determining if the source and target are the same object prevents improper behavior.

> **Listing 9.15 Handling self-assignment in the copy assignment operator**

```
class Engine {
private:
    std::string vin;
public:
    Engine(std::string vin) : vin(vin) {}
    std::string getVin() { return vin; }
};

class Auto {
private:
    Engine* engine;
```

```
public:
    Auto(Engine* engine) : engine(engine) {}
    Auto& operator=(const Auto& car) {          | Tests for self-assignment
        if (this == &car)              ◄──────┘
            return *this;                  | Deletes only if the
        if (engine) {                      | source is not the target
            delete engine;        ◄─────────┘
            engine = 0;           ◄─────────── Use nullptr if you can.
        }
        engine = new Engine(car.engine->getVin());  ◄──┐ Safely accesses valid data
        return *this;                                   ┘
    }
};

int main() {
    Engine* e1 = new Engine("123456789");
    Auto mustang(e1);
    mustang = mustang;
}
```

The assignment in the preceding failing case is unlikely; nobody would be that irresponsible, right? However, if pointers are stored in a container, the ability to visually spot assigning an object to itself is obscured to the point of opaqueness. Something like this could cause self-assignment without being at all obvious:

```
autos[i] = autos[j];
```

Further, pointers can introduce unexpected self-assignment, as shown in this case:

```
*pcar1 = *pcar2;
```

Self-assignment must be tested; if such a case is found, it is necessary to exit the copy assignment operator quickly and not delete any resources.

RECOMMENDATIONS

- Always test for self-assignment in every copy and compound assignment operator for performance and correctness reasons.
- Ensure pointers are nulled out after deleting a dynamic resource.
- If the target object is the same as the source object, exit immediately.
- Be wary of self-assignment through pointers, either directly or by using container elements.

9.6 *Mistake 66: Misunderstanding prefix and postfix forms*

This mistake focuses primarily on performance with a minor emphasis on correctness. C++ allows developers to overload operators to maintain a consistent approach to writing code. The prefix and postfix increment and decrement operators are a great example. The approach to writing a custom decrement operator is similar enough to its increment counterpart, so this discussion needs to cover only the increment version.

The increment operator comes in two forms: prefix and postfix. These forms might appear to be implemented identically and have equivalent performance. This intuition is misleading, however. Their implementation is not only different, but their resultant type is different. These differences suggest their use is different and their performance might be different.

PROBLEM

Assume a data type representing a complex number monotonically increases (or decreases) the real component when the increment (decrement) operator is used. A straightforward approach is to make an `increment` function that adds one to the real part of the complex value. However, this is not idiomatic C++ and does not communicate the intent as well as when using an increment operator.

Therefore, the programmer might implement the `operator++` to be more idiomatic. Their decision for the return type of the operator should be made carefully. The prefix and postfix versions must return different types to operate correctly, which must be noticed.

The definition in listing 9.16 implements both the prefix and the postfix versions of the operator identically, assuming their implementation is the same. The language defines the prefix version with an empty parameter list and the postfix version with the `int` parameter. The parameter distinguishes the form and is unused; it should not have a name.

A problem arises when some "clever" programmer decides to double increment the variable. Not only does this work when it should not, but it does not work as expected. In this situation, the compiler does what is asked but not what is expected. Debugging this problem could be rough. Something is way off.

Listing 9.16   Implementing prefix and postfix identically

```cpp
class Complex {
private:
    double real;
    double imag;
public:
    Complex(double real = 0.0, double imag = 0.0) : real(real), imag(imag) {}
    void increment() { real += 1; }
    Complex  operator++();
    Complex operator++(int);
    friend std::ostream& operator<<(std::ostream&, const Complex&);
};
Complex Complex::operator++() {              A prefix operator, which
    real += 1;                               returns the object itself
    return *this;
}
Complex Complex::operator++(int) {           A postfix operator, which
    real += 1;                               returns the object itself
    return *this;
}
std::ostream& operator<<(std::ostream& out, const Complex& c) {
```

```
        out << '(' << c.real << ", " << c.imag << ')';
        return out;
}

int main() {
        Complex cpx(2.2, -1);
        cpx++;
        cpx++++;
        ++cpx;
        ++++cpx;
        std::cout << cpx << '\n';
        return 0;
}
```

Double incrementing does not work correctly and is syntactically valid but semantically questionable.

ANALYSIS

The example code shows multiple problems. First, the increment functionality does not follow idiomatic C++ usage. While it makes sense in a way, this code misses an opportunity to provide a consistent interface for numeric (and iterator) types. For readability and effectiveness, operators communicate intent far better than functions.

Second, the return value or object between prefix and postfix versions must differ, since their use and semantics differ. The prefix form should return a value or object (which we will discuss later) after the value is modified; the code does this. The postfix form should return a value or object (again, later) before the value is modified; the code does not do this, nor can this be done directly.

Third, there is a problem with the returned value or object from the postfix version because it is not constant. This situation allows the returned value or object to be modified. The "clever" programmer might incorrectly think they can get a double increment. The first increment returns a copy of the value or object, and the second increment returns a modified copy of the copy—the second increment does not affect the original object, which is incremented only once. Therefore, the expectation and the reality of the increments are mismatched. Rather than trying to educate this programmer, the compiler will hopefully prevent this mistake from compiling. If the compiler does not detect this problem, cleverness will result in unexpected behavior and probably a long, strange debugging session.

Fourth, the operators are not implemented in terms of other operators, practically inviting different approaches as the code is modified over time. This inconsistency can snowball and produce behavior that depends on the order of operator usage—changes in the order would produce different results. Implementation of the prefix and postfix increment operators can depend entirely on `operator+=`. The knowledge of how to modify the instance data should be as isolated as possible. In this case, three operators do not need to duplicate that knowledge.

SOLUTION

Correctly implemented, `operator++` simplifies solving these problems, since it follows a well-established C and C++ idiom. Using an operator instead of a function is effective and promotes readability.

The implementation of `operator++` (and the other related operators) should maintain the operator's semantics according to built-in types. When done correctly, implementation details remain consistent as time passes, preventing the grief caused by duplicating knowledge across the class. Both forms are implemented in terms of the `operator+=`, where the most specific operators (increment) depend on the most general. This separation of concerns keeps the knowledge of the operators isolated and consistent.

Two aspects of these operators need to be considered: their implementation details and their performance characteristics. The textual order of the increment operator and the object it operates on reveals the semantic difference between them. The prefix version increments before the object value is obtained; it is considered an update-then-evaluate approach—evaluating the expression reflects the updated value. The calling code sees what the actual object's value is.

The postfix version should be considered the evaluate-then-update approach—the evaluation is done first, which saves the object's current value, after which the update occurs, and the saved value is returned. The evaluation does not reflect the object's current value but the value before the update. The calling code sees what was, not what is. There is a temporal difference between the two values. Since the postfix version uses a temporary object that reflects the object's value before the increment operation, a value object must be returned, not a reference—we do not want to return a reference to a now-destroyed local object!

The return type of the two versions of the operator has been corrected. The prefix version should return a reference to the object itself, since it is the modified object. The "clever" programmer can still perform a double increment (there goes readability!) because the referenced object is modified correctly, not a copy. The postfix version cannot return a reference to itself but must return a copy of the object's previous value. Therefore, it must return a value, not a reference. To prevent the double increment problem, making the returned value `const` prohibits its modification—as the following listing shows, this reads much better, too.

Listing 9.17 Implementation of semantically correct increment operators

```
class Complex {
private:
    double real;
    double imag;
public:
    Complex(double real = 0.0, double imag = 0.0) : real(real), imag(imag) {}
    Complex& operator++();
    const Complex operator++(int);          The prefix version returns an object
    Complex& operator+=(int);               reference of the modified object.
    friend std::ostream& operator<<(std::ostream&, const Complex&);
};
Complex& Complex::operator++() {
    Return *this += 1;  // implemented in terms of operator+=
}
```

```
const Complex Complex::operator++(int) {
    Complex temp(*this);
    *this += 1;  // implemented in terms of operator+=
    return temp;
}
Complex& Complex::operator+=(int n) {
    real += n;
    return *this;
}
std::ostream& operator<<(std::ostream& out, const Complex& c) {
    out << '(' << c.real << ", " << c.imag << ')';
    return out;
}

int main() {
    Complex cpx(2.2, -1);
    cpx++;
    //cpx++++;
    ++cpx;
    ++++cpx;
    std::cout << cpx << '\n';
    return 0;
}
```

The postfix version returns a copy of the unmodified object.

Double postfix increments are no longer syntactically valid, which is semantically sound.

The postfix version in a loop body or update section is less efficient than the prefix version—this cannot be remedied. Each time the postfix increment operator is called on an object, the object must create a copy, where memory allocation is performed; the copy constructor is invoked; the returned value is never used (what a waste); and after the anonymous object goes out of scope, it calls a destructor. It is far less expensive to use the prefix version, which returns a reference, and it's done.

RECOMMENDATIONS

- Implement postfix increment (and decrement) in terms of prefix increment (and decrement), and implement prefix increment (and decrement) in terms of `operator+=` (`operator-=`) to localize the knowledge of how to modify values to a single place.
- Use the prefix form wherever possible, especially in loop bodies and loop update sections, which minimizes the number of copies of the object.

SEE ALSO

- See Mistake 46 for a discussion about basing operators on a minimal set of operators or functions, preventing the duplication of knowledge across the class.
- See Mistake 84 for further discussion on this pernicious error that usually seems to work but is always wrong.

9.7 Mistake 67: Misleading implicit conversion operators

This mistake focuses primarily on readability and, to a lesser degree, correctness. Reading code should tell the whole story; implicit conversions hide some details.

C++ provides a complicated set of rules for converting one data type to another when a function call does not receive parameters of the expected type(s). Two forms of implicit conversion are used, depending on whether a conversion function and a conversion constructor are defined. This mistake focuses on the conversion function.

PROBLEM

A conversion operator is defined using the `operator` keyword, followed by the type the data is being converted to, followed by parentheses. For example, a `Rational` class in listing 9.18 might return a `double` value representing the approximation of the rational number. A `double()` operator is a `Rational` class member that converts the `Rational` value to its approximate `double`.

> **Listing 9.18   A rational class with a conversion function**

```
class Rational {
private:
    int num;
    int den;
public:
    Rational(int num, int den = 1) : num(num), den(den) {}
    operator double() { return (double)num/den; }
    friend std::ostream& operator<<(std::ostream&, const Rational&);
};
std::ostream& operator<<(std::ostream& out, const Rational& r) {
    out << r.num << '/' << r.den;
    return out;
}

int main() {
    Rational r1(3);
    std::cout << r1 << ' ' << (double)r1 << '\n';      Explicit conversion
    if (r1 == 3)                                        is very readable.
        std::cout << "equal\n";
    else                                                Implicit conversion is
        std::cout << "not equal\n";                     misleading; it appears
    return 0;                                           to compare integers.
}
```

The code in listing 9.18 works as expected because the friend `operator<<` is defined. Its output is

```
3/1 3
equal
```

The code would still compile and run if the friend operator were not defined, but the results would be incorrect, and its usage would be misleading. In this case, the output would not look like a rational number because of the missing overloaded `operator<<`. What would happen, however, is the compiler, upon discovering that it could not call `operator<<` on a `Rational` object, would convert it to some value it could send to the output stream. The `double` operator would be selected to implicitly convert the `Rational` value to a double value, an already defined type of the `std::ostream` class. Hence, there is no difference between the two output values—they both are a conversion of the `Rational` object to a `double` value.

The conditional works but is misleading to the reader. The `Rational` object appears to be compared to the integer value 3, an assumption made from the code. However, this assumption is false and, therefore, misleading. Since there is no `operator==` defined in this `Rational` class, the object is not being compared to an integer value. Again, the compiler discovers that it cannot do what the code explicitly says, so it tries several possibilities for an implicit conversion. It finds that the `Rational` object can be converted to a double value and that the integer value can also be converted to a double value; hence, it can make a meaningful comparison. This conversion is meaningful only if the double adequately represents the `Rational` object's value, which it does only because it has no decimal portion. This comparison is not likely to work for rational values, whose double conversion has a fractional portion. For example, consider this being coded:

```
Rational r(1, 3);
if (r.toDouble() == 0.333) …
```

There is no way to accurately predict the actual value to compare to (the 0.333 value). My students often hear me say, "Floating-point values are approximations that are rarely precise." This approach to comparing floating-point values is wrongly done. The delta-epsilon method should always be used for comparisons—see the See Also section for a mistake that addresses this technique.

SOLUTION

If a conversion function is needed, it is better to use a function than an operator. The function will not be considered when the compiler implicitly tries to convert values from one type to another. In cases where it cannot do a conversion, the compiler will choke on an error, thus alerting the developer that insufficient functions exist. The developer may realize that what is coded should not make sense and choose a different approach.

The following code prevents these two problems by adding the conversion function and eliminating the implicit conversion. Further, it is more evident to the reader that an explicit conversion occurs.

Listing 9.19   A rational class using an explicit conversion function

```
class Rational {
private:
    int num;
    int den;
public:
    Rational(int num, int den = 1) : num(num), den(den) {}
    double toDouble() { return (double)num/den; }
    friend std::ostream& operator<<(std::ostream&, const Rational&);
};
```

```
std::ostream& operator<<(std::ostream& out, const Rational& r) {
    out << r.num << '/' << r.den;
    return out;
}

int main() {
    Rational r1(3);
    std::cout << r1 << ' ' << r1.toDouble() << '\n';
    if (r1.toDouble() == 3)
        std::cout << "equal\n";
    else
        std::cout << "not equal\n";
    return 0;
}
```

Removing the `double` operator and adding the `toDouble` function makes the implicit explicit. The comparison is now more obvious to the reader, and a type mismatch should be apparent. Whatever imprecision exists due to comparing a double value instead of a rational number is made clear to the reader of the code. Comparing doubles using `operator==` is almost always a wrong choice.

RECOMMENDATIONS

- Minimize the use of implicit type conversion operators, unless their use is obvious to the reader, which it seldom is.
- Write explicit type conversion functions to enhance readability and prevent unexpected conversions and wrong assumptions.

SEE ALSO

- See Mistake 99 for a discussion of why this is a poor choice.

9.8   *Mistake 68: Overusing implicit conversion constructors*

This mistake focuses on performance; readability and effectiveness may be slightly negatively affected, so consider your priorities.

C++ compilers make it very easy to use mixed-mode computations and function calls. This situation often arises when a function call or arithmetic operation is applied to two differing types. If the compiler can find a way to convert a value from one type to another that would make the call succeed, it will do so silently and (usually) helpfully. However, there likely will be a performance penalty for this conversion.

PROBLEM

Implicit conversions feel nice and are fun when they work smoothly and correctly. The code in listing 9.20 shows a modest `Complex` class, considering that someone might wish to add double values to the real portion. What is not obvious is that there is no means for this simple addition. The defined `operator+` takes two `Complex` parameters; clearly, a `double` is not a `Complex`—silent, likely helpful constructor type conversion to the rescue!

Listing 9.20 Implicit, silent, and expensive constructor type conversions

```
class Complex {
private:
    double real;
    double imag;
public:
    Complex(double real, double imag=0) : real(real), imag(imag) {}
    double getReal() const { return real; }
    double getImag() const { return imag; }
};
const Complex operator+(const Complex& lhs, const Complex& rhs) {
    return Complex(lhs.getReal()+rhs.getReal(), lhs.getImag()+rhs.getImag());
}

int main() {
    Complex c1(2.2);                                          One constructor call
    Complex c2 = c1 + 3.14159;      Two constructor
    Complex c3 = 2.71828 + c1;      calls
    Complex c4 = 2.71828 + 3.14159;
}
```

As expected, the `Complex` constructor is called to create object c1. It is also called twice for objects c2 and c3. The first call is the conversion call, where the `double` value is converted to its equivalent `Complex` representation. The `double` value initializes the real component, and the imag component defaults to zero. Finally, object c4 is a single constructor call. There are six constructor calls in the four lines of code. If this were a more complex data type, six destructor calls would also be invoked. In this case of a simple, data-only type, most (if not all) compilers will optimize destructors away.

ANALYSIS

The construction of `Complex` objects c1 and c4 should be obvious, taking one constructor call each. This behavior cannot be eliminated. Objects c2 and c3 must first convert the `double` to a `Complex` object, and then perform the addition, since the `operator+` takes only `Complex` objects. The conversion takes one constructor call; the result of the addition necessitates the second constructor call. The assignment of the returned object to the declared object does not require an additional constructor call because RVO copies the value in place.

Everything about this operation is correct, but the extra constructor (and destructor) calls can be a sore spot if performance is a concern. If performance is not a concern, it is still an inefficient approach that can be improved. What is needed is a means for mixed-mode conversions that do not require additional constructor calls.

SOLUTION

In cases where performance is not a concern, the preceding approach works acceptably and with minimal code. This enhances readability and effectiveness (a trifle). However, in cases where extra constructor (and destructor) calls are not smiled upon, there must be a way to minimize these.

At the cost of writing a few more lines of code (a ding on effectiveness), the solution is to overload the `operator+` with different parameter lists accepting any combination of `Complex` and `double`. The case where both parameters are of type `double` is not included, nor can it be. C++ ensures an overloaded operator has at least one user-defined parameter type. If the compiler allowed this case, adding two `double` values would be redefined, resulting in inconsistent behavior with the built-in rules for their addition. They thought of everything!

The solution to the performance problem is simple: write an overloaded `operator+` for each combination that is expected to be used. The following code shows the improvement for the `Complex` class. Adding two more operators completes the set of possible overloaded parameter lists (`Complex`/`Complex`, `double`/`Complex`, and `Complex`/`double`).

Listing 9.21   Minimizing constructor conversions by providing overloaded operators

```
class Complex {
private:
    double real;
    double imag;
public:
    Complex(double real, double imag=0) : real(real), imag(imag) {}
    double getReal() const { return real; }
    double getImag() const { return imag; }
};
const Complex operator+(const Complex& lhs, const Complex& rhs) {
    return Complex(lhs.getReal()+rhs.getReal(), lhs.getImag()+rhs.getImag());
}
const Complex operator+(const Complex& lhs, double rhs) {
    return Complex(lhs.getReal()+rhs, lhs.getImag());
}
const Complex operator+(double lhs, const Complex& rhs) {
    return Complex(lhs+rhs.getReal(), rhs.getImag());
}

int main() {
    Complex c1(2.2);
    Complex c2 = c1 + 3.14159;
    Complex c3 = 2.71828 + c1;
    Complex c4 = 2.71828 + 3.14159;
}
```

Overloaded operator definitions eliminate mixed-mode constructor conversions.

Ensuring operators have all necessary overloads available will minimize the effect of temporary objects. The number of constructor (and destructor) calls has been reduced to a minimum of four. This code demonstrates that performance can be significantly affected when implementing mixed-mode computations, function calls, and type conversion constructors. However, don't run wild—only overload the necessary operators, not everything. Confusing? It is a balancing act where we do our best.

RECOMMENDATIONS

- If performance is a concern, overload every expected pattern for mixed-mode function or operator calls; if performance is not a concern, this is still a good approach for thoroughness.

- Remember that operators must have at least one user-defined parameter type to preserve semantic consistency and prevent redefining existing rules.

9.9 *Mistake 69: Focusing too much on standalone operators*

This mistake focuses on performance, with no effect on readability or effectiveness. Arithmetic operations are often implemented in terms of their algebraic forms. This default approach is reasonable in many cases, and there is no need to concern ourselves with its effect on performance. However, in other cases, we can benefit from preventing the creation and destruction of temporary objects. Arithmetic expressions are an area where a nonintuitive form can minimize temporary objects and increase execution speed.

PROBLEM

Consider this code, where a few `Complex` objects are created and then summed to initialize another object. This approach is a common, intuitive way to create arithmetic expressions using class objects. There are five constructor calls in the code: three for the first three objects, `c1`, `c2`, and `c3`, which cannot be minimized and two that are temporary objects created in the summation expression. Eliminating these temporary objects would be a boost to performance. Many modern compilers will attempt to eliminate them, but understanding the problem is still worthwhile.

Listing 9.22 Class with excessive temporaries in expression evaluation

```
class Complex {
private:
    double real;
    double imag;
public:
    Complex(double real=0, double imag=0) : real(real), imag(imag) {}
    double getReal() const { return real; }
    double getImag() const { return imag; }
};
const Complex operator+(const Complex& lhs, const Complex& rhs) {
    return Complex(lhs.getReal()+rhs.getReal(), lhs.getImag()+rhs.getImag());
}

int main() {
    Complex c1(2, 2);              ◄─── Creating each object requires
    Complex c2(0, -1);                  one constructor call.
    Complex c3(-2.2, 4.2);
    Complex c4 = c1 + c2 + c3;     ◄─── Two temporary objects are
}                                       needed for the evaluation.
```

ANALYSIS

The first three constructor calls are essential; they must exist to create the `Complex` objects. We cannot magically get objects without constructor calls; however, the summation creates two temporary objects. When considering performance, any time a temporary is created, there might be an opportunity to eliminate its creation. Remember that every constructor for a nontrivial data type has an associated destructor call at some point, doubling the cost of using temporaries. Most compilers can optimize away the destructor calls for simple objects.

The first temporary holds the sum of `c1` and `c2`, and the second temporary holds the result of the sum of the first temporary and `c3`. Then, the defaulted `operator=` is called to initialize the c4 object with the values held in the second temporary. The question is whether we can reduce the number of constructor calls while still providing the same functionality.

SOLUTION

The number of temporaries can be reduced by using the compound assignment operator directly or in conjunction with the standalone `operator+`. If both the standalone and the compound versions are provided, the standalone version should be implemented in terms of the compound assignment form. Further, the potential for code duplication is removed to encapsulate the essential function in the compound assignment version alone. The standalone calls this and provides no essential logic. The following code shows these improvements by defining the standalone operation in terms of the compound assignment version and continuing to use the standalone operator form in the calculation.

Listing 9.23   Class with minimized temporaries in expression evaluation

```
class Complex {
private:
    double real;
    double imag;
public:
    Complex(double real=0, double imag=0) : real(real), imag(imag) {}
    Complex& operator+=(const Complex&);
    double getReal() const { return real; }
    double getImag() const { return imag; }
};
Complex& Complex::operator+=(const Complex& o) {      ◄────  The operator logic is
    real += o.real;                                          contained in the compound
    imag += o.imag;                                          assignment version.
    return *this;
}
const Complex operator+(const Complex& lhs, const
    Complex& rhs) {                                ◄────
    return Complex(lhs) += rhs;                          The standalone operator is
}                                                       implemented in terms of the
                                                        compound assignment version.
int main() {
    Complex c1(2, 2);
```

```
    Complex c2(0, -1);
    Complex c3(-2.2, 4.2);
    Complex c4 = c1 + c2 + c3;
}
```

The need for temporaries is removed when the standalone operator is implemented in terms of the compound assignment version. The implementation in listing 9.23 makes three constructor calls needed to construct the c1, c2, and c3 objects. The evaluation of the summing operators does not cause the creation of any temporary objects, improving the performance without compromising the validity of the expression evaluation.

The code in listing 9.24 shows an alternative means of implementing a sequence of operator calls. The standalone version alone would create one temporary per object invocation, whereas this form updates the objects in place with no temporary objects being created. The definition of the Complex class is the same as in listing 9.23, except the main function has changed.

Listing 9.24　An alternative form for multiple operator invocations

```
int main() {
    Complex c1(2, 2);
    Complex c2(0, -1);                    The copy constructor
    Complex c3(-2.2, 4.2);                call is invoked.
    Complex c4(c1);
    c4 += c2;                             Sequential summation that
    c4 += c3;                             requires no temporaries
}
```

The power of this approach is that compound assignment forms are more efficient because they update values in place. The previous standalone version demonstrates that it must return a new object and that this new object requires the creation of a temporary through a constructor call.

RECOMMENDATIONS

- To prevent the creation of temporary objects, consider implementing compound assignment versions of arithmetic operators and calling these from standalone versions.
- Multiple uses of the operator can effectively be done in sequence with no temporary objects being created.

SEE ALSO

- See Mistake 46 for a discussion about implementing the minimal set of functions necessary and implementing others in terms of these minimum ones.

9.10　*Mistake 70: Failing to mark nonmutating methods constant*

This mistake focuses on correctness and adds a slight boost to effectiveness. When a class instance method is executed, the code body can access instance variables and, if needed, modify them. This behavior is good and normal, but not all methods need to modify variables. A const method never modifies the instance variables; it only directly or indirectly returns those state variables. The direct approach is called an *accessor*, and the indirect approach is a *computing accessor*.

PROBLEM

Assume a rather large class and its methods are too big to be easily read and understood—almost any code base has many of these! Consider, too, that some accessor-type methods have additional logic embedded in them. These methods can easily—and perhaps wrongly—modify state variables. The compiler cannot prevent unintended modifications to the state. When this happens, the object may violate the class invariant, and if unintended, the object ends up in an incorrect state. The following code is a very simplified version of this problem, with all the obscuring code eliminated and the bare bones exposed.

Listing 9.25   A complicated accessor method that inadvertently modifies state

```cpp
class Person {
private:
    std::string name;
    int age;
public:
    Person(const std::string& name, int age) : name(name), age(age) {}
    const std::string& getName() { return name; }
    int getAge() {
        ++age;  // oops, unintentional        ◄─────┐  Perhaps this method is
        return age;                                  │  supposed to mutate state.
    }
};

int main() {
    Person amy("Aimee", 26);
    std::cout << amy.getName() << " is " << amy.getAge() << " years old\n";
    return 0;
}
```

ANALYSIS

While the code in listing 9.25 is very simple and the error is obvious, more complicated code obscures state modification by introducing multiple lines of code, some of which are difficult to follow. Within this morass of code, an inadvertent state modification is easily accomplished. As noted, the compiler cannot suggest a warning because it cannot know if the modification is correct or an error—it must assume that the change is correct. What is needed is some means to prevent inadvertent modification to state variables.

SOLUTION

Using the const keyword can go a long way toward preventing inadvertent modification of state variables. While no keyword can guarantee correct code, the const keyword can at least ensure that instance variables are not modified in certain methods. When a method is marked with the `const` keyword, the compiler ensures the method does not modify any instance variables.

It is recommended to mark every method `const` that can be done so. There is no downside to wrongly marking a method `const` aside from its correctly modifying code being flagged as an error. Upon inspection, it can be determined that the method should not use that keyword and can be removed. For all other methods, those that intentionally mutate state, the keyword is unnecessary (actually, it would be an error) and would not be used.

The compiler cannot ensure modifications are necessary, but it can guarantee non-modification is enforced. The code in listing 9.26 modifies the `getAge` method and emits an error message, due to the inadvertent modification code. After analyzing the code, it was determined that the modification was an error (a typo, perhaps) and was eliminated. Since the method should not modify the state, the `const` keyword ensures the compiler does not permit any instance data to change.

Listing 9.26 Marking the method static to prevent modifying state

```cpp
class Person {
private:
    std::string name;
    int age;
public:
    Person(const std::string& name, int age) : name(name), age(age) {}
    const std::string& getName() const { return name; }
    int getAge() const {
        return age;
    }
};

int main() {
    Person amy("Aimee", 26);
    std::cout << amy.getName() << " is " << amy.getAge() << " years old\n";
    return 0;
}
```

The const keyword prevents any instance variable from changing.

RECOMMENDATIONS

- Mark all nonmutating methods `const` to prevent inadvertent state modification; the cost is small, but the safety it guarantees are well worth the cost.

9.11 *Mistake 71: Not properly marking class methods static*

This mistake focuses on readability and effectiveness. Classes comprise state (instance variables) and behavior (methods). There are two options for declaring the methods: instance or class methods. An instance method can access all instance and class variables (declared with the `static` keyword). Class methods can access only class variables, meaning these methods cannot access any object values. A question can arise as to why any method would not want to access instance variables and what the advantage would be.

My students are encouraged to ask questions like this—rather than blindly accepting my teaching—when they discover that some things being taught either do not align well or make no immediate sense. This mistake is one of those opportunities to raise your hand and ask for clarification.

One well-discussed advantage of a class method is that no class instance is needed to execute the code. This situation allows the definition of helper methods related to the class but can be executed like a standalone function. For example, consider the `Math` class that Java provides. It would be very awkward to create an instance of that class, initialize it with a specific value, and then call the `sqrt` method. A straightforward call to the `sqrt` method passing the specific value as a parameter is much better. C++ provides free functions for ease of use and clarity; further, it allows functionality similar to Java's by declaring class methods within a class.

PROBLEM

Assume we are writing a `Rational` class, where some mathematical team wants to work with precise values, not the approximations floating-point values offer. For example, the rational number 10/3 is precise but cannot be represented precisely in decimals or binary. The code in listing 9.27 shows the first attempt at implementing a subset of `Rational`. The `reduce` and `gcd` methods are used every time the object's state changes. Each instance of the class will need to call that method frequently.

Listing 9.27   The first attempt at a rational class

```
class Rational {
private:
    int num;
    int den;
public:
    Rational(int num, int den = 1) : num(num), den(den)    ← reduce and gcd
        { reduce(); }                                         are called in the
    friend std::ostream& operator<<(std::ostream&, const Rational&);   constructor.
    Rational& operator*=(const Rational&);
    int gcd(int a, int b) {
        if (b == 0)
            return a;
        return gcd(b, a % b);
    }
    void reduce() {
        int div = gcd(num, den);
        num /= div;
        den /= div;
    }
};
std::ostream& operator<<(std::ostream& out, const Rational& r) {
    out << r.num << '/' << r.den;
    return out;
}
```

```
Rational& Rational::operator*=(const Rational& o) {
    num *= o.num;
    den *= o.den;
    reduce();
    return *this;
}
```

reduce and gcd are called
in the operator*=.

```
int main() {
    Rational r1(3, 9);
    std::cout << r1 << '\n';
    return 0;
}
```

ANALYSIS

The `reduce` and `gcd` methods are public instance methods. There is nothing wrong with this implementation regarding correctness, but readability is affected by this fact. The code implies that these methods are *necessarily* instance methods. That is, only when there is an instance should these methods be called, and each method needs access to at least one instance variable. The `reduce` method accesses both `num` and `den` as written, but the `gcd` method operates only on its parameters.

Functional programming defines a term that describes how `gcd` is implemented; it is a pure function. In this case, *pure* means that the method accesses or affects no state outside its scope; stated differently, it has no side effects. It computes its result based entirely on the data passed to it by its parameters—the same input always produces the same output. Since `gcd` is pure, there is no reason to insist that it needs an object on which to operate. Therefore, this method is a candidate for being a class method by marking it with the `static` keyword.

The `reduce` method uses instance variables, so it must be an instance method. Or does it? The method could easily be rewritten to eliminate that requirement and make it pure. If it can be made pure, should it? In this case, we will assume an affirmative answer.

SOLUTION

The code in listing 9.28 reworks the first effort at the `Rational` class. It immediately marks `gcd` as a static method. This marking now states that the method is shared between the instances and affects no instance variables. Its meaning and scope are more clearly described by adding the `static` keyword. The `gcd` method is a pure method (it changes no state outside itself). Unfortunately, the `reduce` method cannot be pure, since it modifies the instance variables. Since both methods are now class methods, they are semantically different than before and communicate a different meaning. It is usually best to make them private, since they are intended only for use in the class.

> **Listing 9.28** `Rational` reworked to include two class methods

```
class Rational {
private:
    int num;
```

```
    int den;
    static int gcd(int a, int b) {          ←──┐   Now, a private,
        if (b == 0)                              │   pure method
            return a;                            │
        return gcd(b, a % b);                    │
    }                                            │
    static void reduce(int& num, int& den) {  ←─┘
        int div = gcd(num, den);
        num /= div;
        den /= div;
    }
public:
    Rational(int num, int den = 1) : num(num), den(den) {
        reduce(this->num, this->den); }
    friend std::ostream& operator<<(std::ostream&, const Rational&);
    Rational& operator*=(const Rational&);
};
std::ostream& operator<<(std::ostream& out, const Rational& r) {
    out << r.num << '/' << r.den;
    return out;
}
Rational& Rational::operator*=(const Rational& o) {
    num *= o.num;
    den *= o.den;
    reduce(num, den);
    return *this;
}

int main() {
    Rational r1(3, 9);
    std::cout << r1 << '\n';
    return 0;
}
```

To look neater, both methods were made private; however, is that really the best approach to consider this semantic characteristic? That doubt leaves us a minute to ponder the changes. While staring at the reduce method, it can be questioned whether it properly communicates the correct behavior. After all, reduce is meant to interact with instance variables. Passing references certainly allows it to be made a pure method, but now, it almost clashes with its actual intent, and references were necessary to affect two variables. It would be better to return reduce to an instance method rather than use somewhat unreadable references. References are very handy, but in this case, they tend to obscure the meaning of the method. Returning the implementation to an instance method makes more sense. Listing 9.29 shows that the modifications after this line of reasoning have borne fruit.

Listing 9.29   `Rational` **reworked again to better indicate a class method**

```
class Rational {
private:
    int num;
```

```
    int den;
    void reduce();                    ←──────  Private because only instances
public:                                         can use this method
    Rational(int num, int den = 1) : num(num), den(den) { reduce(); }
    friend std::ostream& operator<<(std::ostream&, const Rational&);
    Rational& operator*=(const Rational&);
};
std::ostream& operator<<(std::ostream& out, const Rational& r) {
    out << r.num << '/' << r.den;
    return out;
}
Rational& Rational::operator*=(const Rational& o) {
    num *= o.num;
    den *= o.den;
    reduce();
    return *this;
}
static int gcd(int a, int b) {   ←──────  Public because clients might
    if (b == 0)                             wish to use the functionality
        return a;
    return gcd(b, a % b);
}
void Rational::reduce() {
    int div = gcd(num, den);
    num /= div;
    den /= div;
}

int main() {
    Rational r1(3, 9);
    std::cout << r1 << '\n';
    return 0;
}
```

Another aspect has been considered in listing 9.29. The mathematics team communicated that they wanted to have `gcd` available for external use. One of the main characteristics of the `static` keyword is the concept of *sharing*. Using a class method, the class can share some of its behavior or knowledge with the outside world.

RECOMMENDATIONS

- Carefully consider whether a method can be made pure; if so, mark it `static`, which better communicates its intent, since it does not affect any instance variable.

- Consider whether static methods should be made `public` or `private`; `public` versions can be shared with clients for general use, and `private` ones should be for class use only.

- If `private` methods are needed in derived classes, consider making them `protected`, which allows inheriting classes direct access to them yet shields them from being used by client code.

9.12 *Mistake 72: Incorrectly choosing between member and nonmember functions*

This mistake focuses on correctness regarding semantics—not right or wrong results—and effectiveness. Initially, effectiveness seems to be negatively affected, but when a change in implementation requirements occurs, the positive aspect will be manifest. Modifying methods when requirements change should cause us to minimize the number of methods affected.

Functions come in three types: member, nonmember, and nonmember friend (hereafter called *friend*). Object-oriented programming stresses the three pillars of encapsulation, inheritance, and polymorphism. *Encapsulation* is the idea of hiding implementation details—instance variables and method bodies—from client code to ensure it uses only the class's public interface.

The benefit of good encapsulation is that the class can be reimplemented to improve one or more categories. An example is the concept of a `Date` class; should it be implemented in terms of year, month, day, or second after the start of the computing epoch or other? No answer is correct in all cases, but one is generally better than the others under certain circumstances. Encapsulation allows reimplementation to use new technologies, techniques, requirements, or knowledge without locking the implementor into a specific approach; the client should always be unaware of any changes (especially in the interface).

PROBLEM

Consider developing a `Date` class and adding methods for formatting for printing. The code in listing 9.30 shows the approach chosen. The justification for choosing a member method is simple: encapsulation. Each method accesses and modifies instance variables; therefore, they should be part of the class. Overloading the `operator<<` is commonly done by defining a friend function to access the instance variables directly. Other format style member methods could be defined for other locales.

A friend function can directly access private data members; they are considered function members for this analysis. The best practice is that friends never alter data. Observe the function members of the class, and count how many of them directly access instance variables: there are five. Hold that thought.

Listing 9.30 The class with instance methods

```cpp
class Date {
private:
    int year;
    int month;                              Five members directly
    int day;                                access instance variables.
public:
    Date(int year, int month, int day) : year(year), month(month), day(day) {}
    std::string formatUS();
    friend std::ostream& operator<<(std::ostream&, const Date&);
    int getYear() { return year; }
    int getMonth() { return month; }
```

```
        int getDay() { return day; }
};
std::ostream& operator<<(std::ostream& o, const Date& d) {
    o << d.year << '/' << d.month << '/' << d.day;
    return o;
}
std::string Date::formatUS() {
    std::stringstream ss;
    ss << month << '/' << day << '/' << year;
    return ss.str();
}

int main() {
    Date birthday(1970, 1, 1);  // smart AI will understand this
    std::cout << birthday << '\n';
    std::cout << birthday.formatUS() << '\n';
    return 0;
}
```

A friend function has direct access to private instance variables.

Member methods also have direct access to private instance variables.

Now, requirements have suddenly changed. Under a tight deadline, the class must be changed to use an epoch date implementation based on the number of seconds since 1970/01/01 (or 01/01/1970).

> **NOTE** The Date class is notoriously difficult to get right, so it is highly recommended to use a much better implementation than this example—please!

ANALYSIS

The Date class is reasonably implemented (as an example only!) and works as the client expects. However, the changed requirements demand that the private instance variables change and, worse, that five instance methods change. Encapsulation suggested this design was optimal, but reconsidering that approach will prove helpful. Taking a different metric—the number of methods directly accessing instance variables—and determining if they can be reduced will prove even better.

The three accessor methods will have to be changed to deal with seconds after epoch; little can be done to alter this fact. However, if the operator<< and formatUS methods were to change to depend entirely on the accessors, they would not have to be modified. This problem is compounded by the number of affected methods in classes with more methods. Therefore, the better metric to measure encapsulation is to count the number of methods that access instance variables. The reasoning is simple: if a method does not access instance variables, it cannot expose encapsulated data. The fewer methods that can affect them, the better they are hidden, and the less changing implementation details will affect other methods.

SOLUTION

To minimize the number of instance methods, make as many methods nonmembers as possible. Implement these in terms of the few remaining member methods to reduce the amount of modification when changes must occur. Listing 9.31 shows an (unrealistic) implementation where the computing accessors are used as the basis for the operator<< and formatUS nonmember functions.

Listing 9.31   Minimizing member methods and implementing nonmembers

```
class Date {
private:
    static const long sec_in_year = 31536000;
    static const long sec_in_mon = 2592000;
    static const long sec_in_day = 86400;
    long seconds;
public:
    Date(int year, int month, int day) {
        seconds = (year-1970) * sec_in_year;
        seconds += (month-1) * sec_in_mon;
        seconds += (day-1) * sec_in_day;
    }
    int getYear() const {
        return seconds/sec_in_year + 1970; }
    int getMonth() const {
        int sec = seconds % sec_in_year;
        return sec/sec_in_mon + 1;
    }
    int getDay() const {
        int sec = seconds/sec_in_year/sec_in_mon;
        return sec/sec_in_day + 1;
    }
};
std::ostream& operator<<(
std::ostream& o, const Date& d) {
    o << d.getYear() << '/' << d.getMonth()
        << '/' << d.getDay();
    return o;
}
std::string formatUS(const Date& d) {
    std::stringstream ss;
    ss << d.getMonth() << '/' << d.getDay() << '/' << d.getYear();
    return ss.str();
}

int main() {
    Date birthday(1970, 1, 1);  // smart AI will understand this
    std::cout << birthday << '\n';
    std::cout << formatUS(birthday) << '\n';
    return 0;
}
```

Computing getters that must reflect implementation changes

Immune to change when implementation changes

The minimal set of methods that access instance variables guides the developer into determining the basis set. Other methods should be implemented in terms of these. This approach minimizes the number of methods that affect instance variables, ensuring encapsulation is maximized. The value of this for object-oriented programming should be maintained.

- Minimize the number of methods directly accessing instance variables by reducing member and friend methods.

- Nonmember methods that access a minimal number of member methods are the best way to preserve encapsulation—the fewer methods that directly access instance variables, the better the encapsulation.

- Friend functions may be alluring, but they are a point of possible unintentional private instance variable modification, and they break encapsulation.

SEE ALSO

- See Mistake 46 for a discussion on reducing the number of essential methods and implementing the others in terms of these.

9.13 *Mistake 73: Incorrectly returning strings from accessor methods*

This mistake focuses on performance and has implications for correctness. It is a very specific problem that occurs frequently.

The `std::string` class is helpful and provides significant behavior for handling text easily. Modern C++ has added much functionality, and each new standard seems to add even more useful methods. Using the class well is important, since many user-written classes have at least one instance variable of this type. C++ is one of the few languages that does not make strings immutable, so this introduces a subtle problem for correctness.

PROBLEM

We are designing a record-keeping system for a school, and we need to model people. We choose to start with a Person class, from which we eventually will derive other classes (and, of course, develop a good inheritance design). For now, we are working with a small amount of class functionality.

The developer assigned to this task recently learned about the power of references and chose to return a reference to the name instance variable to help performance. References are faster than copies, but they have some drawbacks. The following code shows the first attempt and some unexpected behavior—somehow, the name instance variable gets modified.

Listing 9.32 Modeling a person and attempting to improve performance

```
class Person {
private:
    std::string name;
    int age;
public:
    Person(const std::string& name, int age) : name(name), age(age) {}
    std::string& getName() { return name; }      ◄─────┐
    int getAge() { return age; }                  Returns a reference of the
};                                                instance variable for performance
```

```
int main() {
    Person sam("Samantha", 26);
    std::string& name = sam.getName();
    name += "x";
    std::cout << sam.getName() << " is " << sam.getAge() << " years old\n";
    return 0;
}
```

Client code should not be able to alter private instance data directly.

The developer meant to modify a copy of the data, not to modify the instance variable. Without noticing anything was wrong, the code was tested and accepted.

ANALYSIS

The developer tried to make performant code. They should have noticed that the getName accessor returned a reference to the instance variable; it was not a copy of the data. A reference is a different name for the same thing (entity)—an alias. If the alias is modified, the entity is modified. The desire for an efficient implementation obscured the fact that the actual instance variable is exposed.

SOLUTION

Returning a reference to a std::string instance variable prevents a copy of the variable, saving memory allocation and copying. However, if a copy were returned, the instance variable would remain impervious to client-made modifications. The developer's intent is laudable, but their implementation is not. This is not limited to std::string; any class that returns a member by reference (or pointer!) suffers the same problem.

The way to gain the performance of a reference and the unassailability of a private instance variable is to ensure a const reference is returned for the std::string variable, as shown in listing 9.33. If the reference is stored in some local variable, the compiler ensures it must also be constant. Therefore, an attempt to modify the data through the reference results in a compilation error. This code fixes the eager developer's approach, while maintaining the integrity of the data.

On another note, the attempt by the client code to change data obtained by an accessor is suspect. If the local copy of the data is modified, it no longer matches the object's value; hence, the semantics change. In some cases, this is intended, but be very careful. It is better to make any copies of, or const references to, instance data that preserves the object's semantics. Code can always access the instance variable value when needed and will always be consistent with the object. Saving the data locally allows for modifying and changing what it means.

Listing 9.33   Using constants to prevent mutations and improve performance

```
class Person {
private:
    std::string name;
    int age;
public:
    Person(const std::string& name, int age) : name(name), age(age) {}
```

```
    const std::string& getName() const { return name; }
    int getAge() const { return age; }
};
```
Returns a constant reference to the std::string instance variable

```
int main() {
    Person sam("Samantha", 26);
    const std::string& name = sam.getName();
    // name += "x";
    std::cout << name << " is " << sam.getAge() << " years old\n";
    return 0;
}
```
Makes the local variable immutable to compile and preserve the semantics

RECOMMENDATIONS

- For efficiency, return std::string instance variables by reference; for correctness, ensure that the reference is constant to prevent inadvertent instance variable modification.

- Remember that references are aliases; they represent the actual data and are not a copy of it.

Exceptions and resources

The topic of exceptions has proponents and detractors across the entire spectrum, with developers advocating from using them rarely, if ever, to using them frequently. Over the years, several authors have published articles arguing for various positions along this spectrum. Many of these arguments are relevant, yet they mesh poorly with other viewpoints. This situation leaves us in a quandary when approaching exception usage. Many positions are correct within specific problem domains but are problematic in others. There are numerous situations in which one policy is meaningful but would make little sense in others.

Exceptions need to be considered in the scope of the entire program. A policy that addresses the behavior of a function may not be meaningfully extended to larger units. Many current programs running in production need to have the luxury of redesigning to handle a unified strategy for exceptions. In these myriad cases, almost any design is better than none. Yet integrating localized strategies into larger units may prove frustrating and error-prone.

The best approach in these numerous cases is to understand exceptions better and develop one's intuition toward applying this knowledge to the code base under consideration. Therefore, we will start with a general view of exceptions and why they exist. From this point, we can better understand how to use them well in critical situations, such as resource management. Exceptions and resources are intimately tied together (along with constructors and destructors) to provide a comprehensive management pattern, especially when things bump at night. The idiomatic pattern called *resource allocation is initialization* (RAII), invented by Bjarne Stroustrup, will be highlighted as the C++ way to coordinate resource management.

An essential aspect of using exceptions is to clarify what is an error and what is not. A *function* is a piece of named code that performs some behavior. Each has three characteristics that must be maintained—any failure to maintain these should be considered an error:

- A precondition failure
- An invariant failure
- A postcondition failure

Other problems discovered in the function should be handled locally. If these problems are, or become, failures of the three characteristics, an exception should be thrown. It may prove tricky to clearly distinguish between errors (expressed as exceptions) and problems that should be locally handled. A quick example of each type is given to help expound the possibilities:

- *Precondition failure*—A function is passed a pointer to a linked list to search for a key, but the pointer is NULL (it probably equals zero). Since the function cannot possibly continue, it must signal an error. If the function is designed to handle empty lists (a NULL pointer), it is not an error and should return a value stating that the key was not found.

- *Invariant failure*—A class instance maintains a state representing a date. The constructor validated ranges with precondition checks. The instance has not been destroyed, meaning the class invariant is valid and inviolable. However, some methods have modified the date state so that the day exceeds 31. Another method attempts to convert this date but discovers the error using an invariant check. Since an error is detected, it should be signaled. Since the class itself modified the value, this is a case of bad programming! Thankfully, the invariant check communicates the situation.

- *Postcondition failure*—A function receives a pointer to a buffer containing text to convert to a number, but the text is inconsistent with a numeric value. Since the function cannot return a meaningful numeric value, it must signal the error.

If the function is designed to return a numeric representation of a nonvalue (assume a floating-point NaN), then that value is returned, and there is no error.

Other cases should be considered using these three characteristics consistently and predictably. It should be clear that function design needs to consider these, and careful thought should be given to what is and is not an error. Avoid ad hoc error strategies—sympathy to all who have a legacy mess and must clean it up.

10.1 *Using exceptions*

The primary purpose of exceptions is to assert that an error has occurred and that the called code cannot complete the request successfully. This error is surfaced in a way the developer cannot ignore. Classic error handling was often some form of setting a status value that indicated an error had occurred, and the calling code tested for that situation; however, there was no means to enforce error checking.

Exceptions grab a developer's attention. If an exception is thrown and the developer ignores it, the program will eventually crash. This behavior is unnecessary, and the developer must handle the exception to prevent the crash—the characteristic of non-ignorability forces the developer to address this problem. Hopefully, the developer is provoked to carefully consider what the error means and what recovering from it might entail. In other words, exceptions provide a significant opportunity to design software for resiliency.

There are three spatiotemporal aspects of exceptions to consider, in order:

1 The functional calling site
2 The error detection site
3 The recovery site

The calling site occurs first. A functional piece of code is called, and the caller waits for the result (we are only considering synchronous execution here). The error detection site occurs second. It is where an operation occurs that directly detects an error situation. The code following the calling site begins the optionally occurring recovery site. With classic return codes, this would be a check of the returned value; with exceptions, it would be the relevant catch block.

These three sites are separated in space (different functions). The error is detected when the called code determines it cannot meaningfully continue. The caller has asked the callee to perform a behavior, but the callee is forced into the corner and must admit it cannot. In many cases, no return value from the callee would be meaningful; therefore, the error must be signaled in an alternative control path. Finally, the recovery code is the third site in space and time. This optionally executed code tries to recover from the error. If it can, the program continues; if it cannot, it should terminate gracefully.

The following are several affirmations and objections to exceptions. Each objection is considered, and support for using exceptions is given. In brief, most objections to exceptions have little to do with proper exception usage; instead, they object to poor usage. As with any technology, improper use is problematic but not a basis for dismissing correct usage.

10.1.1 Affirmation: Intermixed control and recovery paths

Classic error handling intermixes control and recovery paths; exceptions separate them. The normal execution path with no problems (the happy path) is often well-designed, since most programmers write code to perform a behavior. Too frequently, only after the happy path is coded and working does the error detection and handling path take priority—sometimes, it only gets a cursory glance. Frankly, error detection and error handling code often obscure the main control path, making it difficult to understand and reason.

This obfuscation of the code may encourage some developers to pay little attention to the necessity of error detection and handling. It is straightforward to hope that things will work correctly (at least, most of the time) and that less emphasis should be placed on errors. Add to this the fact that handling errors is often guesswork when the called code is not well understood or when the calling code is buried in code that is called under, perhaps, conditions that are not well understood. The inability to clearly understand the implications of an error can significantly contribute to minimal error handling.

10.1.2 Objection: Confusing exception handling with normal error handling

Exceptions are overused in error-handling situations. Here is where the distinction between the calling and detection sites is essential. The code that detects an error should not throw an exception directly. Instead, when the detection site determines an error has occurred, it must decide whether it can handle it. If it can, there is no need to throw an exception. When one is thrown, a reader can correctly argue that the detection site code should have handled the problem. However, when the detection site cannot handle the error, it should throw an exception. The code, which includes the detection site, is expected to perform some behavior. When it cannot, it must signal its inability by some mechanism. Classically, this is signaled by an error return code. But again, nothing forces the calling site to check the return code.

Using exceptions to signal that a function cannot fulfill its purpose for the caller is the correct reason to use them. Using exceptions to ask the caller to fix a problem that the called code should have is objectionable and should not be practiced.

10.1.3 Objection: Difficulty retrofitting exception handling

Adding exception handling to much existing code is too hard. Whether or not one objects to retrofitting existing code to add exception handling, this can be a poor idea. One needs to add exception-handling code to logic by introducing inconsistencies, inefficiencies, and challenges to reading and understanding. The existing code likely has no budget for rework, but in some cases, it might. Designing a consistent exception-handling strategy in new code is challenging and much more difficult in existing code. Please do what you can, but do not overdo it in these cases.

10.1.4 *Affirmation: Ambiguous values*

Exceptions separate normal and error values. Return codes depend on a defined data type, a particular value of that type, and code to check the value. The function returns a value of its defined return type. Return codes are sentinel values. A *sentinel value* is consistent with the data type but inconsistent with the problem. Assume a function that returns an integer value. Determining an integer value inconsistent with the problem may be easy, but it is more likely that it will not be. A single value or group of values must be determined to represent a good return; a different value or set of values must be designated to resolve a bad return. Which is which? Who can memorize these? And can we guarantee that the comments that explain them are consistent with the code?

Throwing an exception is unambiguous and does not depend on the function's return type. The exception type carries information. Further, the exception will likely have additional textual information describing the specifics of the error.

10.1.5 *Affirmation: Ambiguous data types*

Exceptions ensure that the data type of a value is distinct between normal and error conditions. The classic approach using a return code or setting a global variable still must honor the type of the return code, which is also used for normal handling. An exception can throw a completely different type with no relationship to the return type. The type of the exception disambiguates the meaning of the return data type.

10.1.6 *Affirmation: Enforcing error handling*

The use of exceptions ensures an error is handled. Exceptions do not enforce *proper* error handling; they only ensure every exception is caught or terminates the program. The opportunity to meaningfully handle the error is presented; it is up to the developer to make good use of it. A significant benefit of an exception is that it simplifies the process of percolating errors to higher levels. These levels often allow for better handling of the problem. Using return codes makes percolation complex and confusing to test for at each level.

If the first level of error handling cannot adequately handle the error, it takes little effort to rethrow the exception or transform it to another type and throw that. The only coding requirement is that each level has some catch block that can match the thrown exception. The alternate control structure for error handling simplifies the code and makes reasoning about it cleaner.

10.1.7 *Objection: Providing recovery handlers*

Catch blocks do not have to have meaningful recovery handling. This is hardly a significant objection, since writing any error recovery code poorly, whether exceptions or classic, is possible. The first block to catch an exception can determine what went wrong and whether it can be recovered. Recovery might mean that all states modified by the called function are either rolled back or initialized to a meaningful point. It is undoubtedly possible to ignore changes and move forward. However, the developer must consider this thoroughly. Class invariants must be honored and restored if necessary. Recovery code following the calling code always has a better grasp of what might have been changed and needs cleaning up. Code local to the discovery site needs more knowledge to recover meaningfully.

10.1.8 *Affirmation: Transforming failure types*

Using separate control paths for normal and error conditions permits the developer to transform exception types in flight. If the detection site understands the error in one way, the recovery site can transform that semantic into another meaning. For example, assume a record is being read from a disk file. The input validation routine detects invalid data when converting text to an integer for a specific field. It throws an exception, stating that invalid data was discovered and the transformation could not succeed. If the recovery site decides not to recover, it might wish to push this failure to another level, adding metadata or additional diagnostic information. The higher level should understand something more general than low-level specifics (e.g., input mismatch errors). Therefore, the first recovery site can change the exception type to something more appropriate for the next level's recovery site, perhaps an invalid record error. Logging can be used to capture the specifics, which may be inappropriate for the actual recovery.

10.1.9 *Affirmation: Separation of concerns*

The ability to separate concerns between error detection and error handling allows multiple developers to work nearby without interfering with each other's code. Intermixing normal and error-handling control paths mixes concerns. The code that handles the happy path works fundamentally differently than the code that handles an error path. Therefore, the ability to separate these paths into two distinct problems keeps the concerns of each isolated from the other. This is a powerful software engineering principle, and anywhere it can be applied, it should be used to the greatest extent possible.

10.1.10 *Objection: Encouraging upfront design*

Code must be designed to handle exceptions from the beginning, which takes extra time and effort. This objection is likely a reason to permit writing code before or without proper design. It has nothing to do with exceptions specifically. New code and as much legacy code as possible must be designed appropriately to handle the separation of normal and error-path handling.

10.2   *Mistake 74: Not throwing exceptions from constructors*

This mistake focuses on correctness and effectiveness. Since maintaining the class invariant is essential, throwing exceptions from constructors that fail is the best means to prevent using partially initialized objects. Exceptions make the code that creates objects cleaner, but more importantly, any construction failures are signaled and must be handled. It is easy to forget to check return codes and failed flags or to consistently implement other schemes for testing object validity. In this case, developers spend less development time when using exceptions than not.

PROBLEM

Unless specifically designed well, much existing code rarely uses exceptions well. One notable area is the construction of objects. Default constructors may be overused, resulting in some instances of variables being poorly initialized. The poor assumption is that constructing the object with missing initialization data is acceptable because (later!) the rest of the initialization data will be provided.

This mistaken approach often uses default constructors or those that take a subset of the initialization data. When initialization data is missing, a valid bit is reset to indicate that the object is incomplete or partially initialized. When the missing data is provided, the valid bit is set, indicating complete initialization. This approach works if consistently applied but likely indicates poor decisions and design. The following code shows this assumption in operation.

> **Listing 10.1   A partially initialized class**

```
class Person {
private:                                      A partial-default
    std::string name;                         constructor that fails
    int age;                                  to initialize one
public:                                       instance variable
    Person(const std::string& name) : name(name) {}  ◄─
    Person(const std::string& name, int age) : name(name), age(age) {}
    int getAge() { return age; }
    const std::string& getName() const { return name; }
    bool isValid() const { return age > -1; }
};
                                        Uses the partial-default
                                        constructor; age is not initialized.
int main() {
    Person sally("Sally");              ◄─
    std::cout << sally.getName() << " is " << sally.getAge()
        << " years old\n";
                                        Bad data is introduced
                                        into the instance's state.
    Person brian("Brian", -1);          ◄─
    std::cout << brian.getName();
    if (brian.isValid())                                       ◄─  The
        std::cout << " is " << brian.getAge() << " years old\n";    developer
    else                                                            remembered
        std::cout << " is invalid\n";                               to check the
    std::cout << brian.getName() << " is " << brian.getAge() <<     valid bit.
        " years old\n";
    return 0;                           The developer forgot to
}                                       check the valid bit.
```

The `sally` object was partially initialized, leaving the `age` instance variable to the mercy of whatever value is currently in that memory, another way of saying that its behavior is undefined. The `brian` object is fully initialized but introduces bad data into the instance. In both cases, these objects need to be tested for validity. Assuming the random value for `sally`'s `age` is positive, the object appears valid. If the check is performed, the `brian` object will fail the validity check; however, there is no way to enforce checking.

ANALYSIS

The code that uses these objects has no guaranteed way to know that these objects are valid and that the class invariant has been honored. Although the validity check is introduced to give that guarantee, it might not be invoked—this would be another good idea that was incompletely thought through.

SOLUTION

The first line of defense is to create an object only when all essential initialization data is known. This point is yet another argument for overusing default constructors. The class invariant depends on two pieces of data, both of which are required. Further, the `age` instance variable has a bounded range. Unless and until these checks are validated, the object's state is unknown.

The class should validate both parameter values to ensure that the state can be guaranteed, and if anything is amiss, it should throw an exception to clearly state that the object cannot be created in a meaningful state. The calling code should always be clear about the object's validity; the class is responsible for ensuring and enforcing it. The following code shows improvements that enforce the class invariant and communicate any failures in establishing it.

Listing 10.2 Throwing exceptions for construction failures

```
class Person {
private:                                          A validation method used
    std::string name;                             to validate parameter data
    int age;
    static const std::string& validateName(const std::string& name) {  ◄──
        if (name.empty())
            throw std::invalid_argument("name must not be empty");
        return name;
    }
    static int validateAge(int age) {  ◄─────────────────────────────────
        if (age < 0)
            throw std::out_of_range("age must be non-negative");
        return age;
    }                                             A constructor is
public:                                           responsible for establishing
    Person(const std::string& name, int age) :    class invariant.
        name(validateName(name)), age(validateAge(age)) {}  ◄────────────
    int getAge() const { return age; }
    const std::string& getName() const { return name; }
    bool isValid() const { return age > -1; }
};

int main() {                          Incomplete argument
    // Person sally("Sally");  ◄──┘   values will not compile.
    Person sally("Sally", 27);
```

```
        std::cout << sally.getName() << " is " << sally.getAge()
            << " years old\n";
                                                    Throws an exception during
                                                    construction; no ambiguity is allowed.
        Person brian("Brian", -1);          ◄─────┘
        std::cout << brian.getName() << " is " << brian.getAge()
            << " years old\n";
        return 0;
}
```

Since that was removed, the `sally` object can no longer be created using a partial-default constructor. It now must provide both argument values. The `brian` object supplies both argument values, but one is invalid. The `validateAge` method ensures no negative value is used to initialize the `age` instance variable. However, in `brian`'s case, the supplied information causes an exception to be thrown. There is no ambiguity about this object's validity. The caller should supply a recovery site to handle this situation.

RECOMMENDATIONS

- Never construct an object until all needed information is known; without sufficient information, the class invariant cannot be established.
- Throw exceptions if construction information is invalid or other failures prevent the constructor from completing correctly.
- Anticipate construction failures; plan for and handle them accordingly.

SEE ALSO

- See Mistake 44 for understanding class invariants and their importance.
- See Mistake 49 for discouraging use of default constructors in many situations.
- See Mistake 60 for the reasoning behind the need to initialize all instance variables.

10.3   *Mistake 75: Throwing exceptions from destructors*

This mistake focuses on correctness, which influences effectiveness; however, this is the price one must pay to ensure proper operation. Exceptions are a valuable means by which errors are surfaced and handled. It has been argued that constructors should be quick to throw when parameter values are invalid. Partially constructed objects are a subtle but real danger to correctness; therefore, following that advice would work in destructors. After all, if a destructor detects an error, what better way to surface it than to throw an exception? This intuition is commendable; its implementation is anything but.

PROBLEM

We assume an eager programmer has learned some fine points about throwing exceptions. In their eagerness, this knowledge is extended to destructors. The code in listing 10.3 shows the result of the programmer's attempt to apply this knowledge to produce a robust and consistent error-handling strategy for their code. It is assumed that a `Paragraph` object will be added sometime after construction. When destructing, the class is designed to delete a dynamic `Paragraph` object. If a `Page` is destroyed with no valid `Paragraph`, it is considered an error. This situation seems to be an ideal time to throw an exception.

Listing 10.3 Overeager usage of exceptions

```
struct Paragraph {};

class Page {
private:
    std::string title;
    Paragraph* pgph;
public:
    Page(const std::string& title) : title(title), pgph(0) {}
    ~Page() {
        if (pgph == 0)
            throw std::string("destructor");        ◄──── Throwing an exception
        delete pgph;                                       from the destructor
    }
};

int main() {
    try {                                        Normal destruction
        Page p("Catching Up");          ◄──────  of the object
    } catch (const std::string& ex) {
        std::cout << "Exception caught: " << ex << '\n';
    }
    try {                                        Error destruction
        Page p("Trouble Ahead");        ◄──────  of the object
        throw std::string("try block");
    } catch (const std::string& ex) {
        std::cout << "Exception caught: " << ex << '\n';
    }
    return 0;
}
```

The code results in this output (different compilers and systems may look somewhat different):

```
Exception caught: destructor
    terminate called after throwing an instance of
    'std::__cxx11::basic_string<
    char,  std::char_traits<char>, std::allocator<char> >'
Aborted
```

The program was unceremoniously terminated in the `"Trouble Ahead"` try block. The first `try` block worked—or, more accurately, did not fail—but its execution is a happy accident that permits something sinister to lurk. Other compilers and systems may behave differently.

ANALYSIS

The first `try` block works correctly only because there is no existing exception in progress. The first `catch` block can capture the exception and handle it as expected. This seemingly correct operation is misleading; it sets the developer up for a nasty surprise when the strategy fails.

The second `try` block is that suspended surprise. The `Page` object is created in the `try` block, but an exception is thrown before destroying it on a normal exit from the block. The following `catch` block should handle that exception; however, the `Page` object must be destroyed first. The `Page` destructor is called, and it experiences an error. Therefore, it throws an exception to surface the knowledge that it is missing its `Paragraph` object.

When an exception is in progress, a second one being thrown causes the `terminate` function to be called. The default behavior of the `std::terminate` function call is to abort execution at that point without stack unwinding by calling `std::abort`. The behavior of the abort function is correct and expected. The `abort` function ensures that debuggers (e.g., `dbg`) can see the exact state of the program at the termination point. If the stack unwinds and other cleanup functions were to execute, debugging would be missing much of its context.

What is unexpected is that this program should behave in this manner. The programmer was unaware of the danger of throwing an exception when another is already in progress. Destructors are especially vulnerable to this danger, since they are called under two conditions: normal termination and error termination. This unexpected behavior manifests when a destructor that throws is called under error conditions.

SOLUTION

The best approach is to avoid throwing exceptions from a destructor; this prevents the problem altogether, since the probability of an exception being in progress is large enough to be a problem. However, in some cases, throwing an exception in a destructor is necessary. The key is the difference between throwing *in* a destructor and throwing *from* a destructor. If the destructor executes code that throws, the destructor cannot control that behavior and may become a victim of the termination call.

The necessary approach for destructor code that potentially (or actually) throws is to wrap the code in a `try` block. The code in listing 10.4 shows this approach; it captures any exception and, presumably, logs the problem but does not rethrow the current exception or throw a different one. The general catch-all specification will capture any exception; if more specificity is needed for specific handling, add it before the general catch. The key is that no exception should escape the destructor.

> **Listing 10.4   Throwing an exception in, but not from, a destructor**

```
struct Paragraph {};

class Page {
private:
    std::string title;
```

```
        Paragraph* pgph;
public:
    Page(const std::string& title) : title(title), pgph(0) {}
    ~Page() {
        try {
            if (pgph == 0)
                throw std::string("destructor");        ◄─────┐  Still throwing in
            delete pgph;                                        │  the destructor
        } catch (...) {                                  ◄─────┘  Capturing any throw in the
            std::cout << "ERROR: exception captured in destructor\n";  destructor, preventing it
        }                                                          from leaving the body
    }
};

int main() {
    try {                                   Normal destruction
        Page p("Catching Up");       ◄─────┘ of the object
    } catch (const std::string& ex) {
        std::cout << "Exception caught: " << ex << '\n';
    }
    try {
        Page p("Trouble Ahead");            Error destruction
        throw std::string("try block");  ◄─── of the object
    } catch (const std::string& ex) {
        std::cout << "Exception caught: " << ex << '\n';
    }
    return 0;
}
```

RECOMMENDATIONS

- Do not throw exceptions from a destructor; it is too likely that an exception is already in progress, which will cause instant termination of the program.

- If code in a destructor can throw an exception, wrap it in a `try` block to capture it and transform it into a log (or similar) message; do not rethrow the exception.

SEE ALSO

- See Mistake 74 for an argument as to why incomplete initialization is a significant reason for throwing.

- See Mistake 76 for a strategy to prevent dynamic resources from leaking during exception handling.

- See Mistake 77 for a general solution to dynamic resource handling in the presence of exceptions.

10.4 *Mistake 76: Allowing resource leaks when using exceptions*

This mistake affects correctness. The problem is with resource leaks when throwing exceptions from constructors that have allocated dynamic resources, leaving the system in an impaired state. Correctness is more than simply correct computations within a program; it also must consider the effects on the system as a whole.

Dynamic resources are a simple approach to accessing and using various resources that would not work well as value entities. A simple case is an array of unknown length, where the size is determined at run time, and the array is dynamically allocated. In the presence of exceptions, handling these resources becomes more complex.

PROBLEM

Assume a developer is building a `Page` entity that needs a header and footer. The text comprising each of these is in a hard drive file. System resources are a source of variant behavior. Text files may or may not exist; permissions to access them may or may not be granted; and read or write errors, unexpected data, and several other problems might arise.

The code in listing 10.5 shows a somewhat naïve attempt at handling the header and footer text. First, `std::strings` should be used in preference to C-style strings, but not everyone has that privilege. Second, expected errors, such as when reading text files, ought to be handled locally, and only when there is no good resolution to the problem should an exception be thrown. While any group of developers would have various views on this subject, the code in this chapter accepts the developer's approach. Third, the hardcoded length for an input buffer is fraught with potential problems. Bad actors love this kind of mistake, as such security flaws give them an inroad into otherwise safe code.

Listing 10.5   Attempting to handle dynamic resources in a destructor

```cpp
class OneLiner {
private:
    std::string filename;
    char* text;
public:
    OneLiner(const std::string& filename) : filename(filename), text(0) {
        text = new char[64];
        std::cout << filename << " allocated\n";
        std::ifstream file(filename.c_str());
        if (file.fail())
            throw std::string("file " + filename + " inaccessible");
        // read data into text
    }
    ~OneLiner() { std::cout << filename <<
        " ~deallocated\n";  delete [] text; }          ◀── Deallocates dynamic
    char* getText() const { return text; }                 memory when called
};

class Page {
private:
    std::string title;
    char* header;
    char* footer;
public:
    Page(const std::string& title, const std::string& headerfile, const
      std::string& footerfile) :
            title(title), header(0), footer(0) {
```

```
        try {
            OneLiner head(headerfile);
            header = head.getText();
            OneLiner foot(footerfile);
            footer = foot.getText();
        } catch(const std::string& ex) {
            std::cout << ex << '\n';
        }
    }
};

int main() {
    Page chapter("Introduction to C++", "header.txt", "footer.txt");
    return 0;
}
```

The dynamic memory is cleaned up correctly.

Dynamic memory is leaked, not cleaned up.

The destructor code for `OneLiner` correctly handles deallocating the dynamically accessed resource under normal circumstances; however, error conditions thoroughly mess this up. The `head` object is destroyed when the exception causes the `try` block to terminate. The `foot` object should be cleaned up in the same manner, it would appear, but appearances are deceiving here. The following output shows what happens; notice there is only one deallocation:

```
header.txt allocated
footer.txt allocated
header.txt ~deallocated
file footer.txt inaccessible
```

ANALYSIS

When the `head` object is created, dynamic memory is allocated, the file object is successfully opened, and the read operation can proceed. The constructor completes it, and the `head` object is wholly constructed.

Dynamic memory is allocated when the `foot` object is created, but the file object fails when opening. The failure triggers an exception to throw, since there is nothing the constructor can do to remedy the situation. It correctly determines that it cannot be successful, so it throws. Constructor execution is not complete, and this is where the problem starts.

When the `main` function runs the `try` block, it successfully creates the `head` object. When creating the `foot` object is attempted, it throws an exception. The `try` block is immediately ended, and the `catch` block is executed. However, before the `catch` block executes, unwinding the stack must occur to clean up any resources created within its scope. The `head` object is destroyed, releasing dynamic memory. The foot `object` was never entirely constructed; therefore, it is not cleaned up. Calling a destructor on a partially constructed object would introduce a world of woe, since it would be unclear how to destroy the partial object correctly. Therefore, the destructor does not clean up this object. The `foot` object leaks the dynamically allocated memory.

SOLUTION

The solution is simple: before throwing the exception from the constructor, manually release all allocated dynamic resources—simple! It is simple when you read it, but
this approach potentially introduces duplicated clean-up code, strange or convoluted
clean-up logic, and possibly the chance of missing some resources, depending on the
complexity of the construction. The following code deallocates the dynamic memory
before throwing the exception, preventing the leak.

Listing 10.6   Cleaning up dynamic resources before throwing

```
class OneLiner {
private:
    std::string filename;
    char* text;
public:
    OneLiner(const std::string& filename) : filename(filename), text(0) {
        text = new char[64];
        std::cout << filename << " allocated\n";
        std::ifstream file(filename.c_str());
        if (file.fail()) {
            std::cout << filename << " deallocated dynamic memory\n";
            delete [] text;                                              ◀──────┐
            throw std::string("file " + filename + " inaccessible");            │
        }                                                        ┌───────────────
        // read data into text                                   Deletes the dynamic
    }                                                            resource before throwing
    ~OneLiner() {
        std::cout << filename << " ~deallocated\n";
        delete [] text;
    }
    char* getText() const { return text; }
};


class Page {
private:
    std::string title;
    char* header;
    char* footer;
public:
    Page(const std::string& title, const std::string& headerfile, const
    std::string& footerfile) :
            title(title), header(0), footer(0) {                ┌──────────────────
        try {                                                    A normal destructor call
            OneLiner head(headerfile);         ◀────────────────┘ to deallocate memory
            header = head.getText();
            OneLiner foot(footerfile);         ◀────────────┐
            footer = foot.getText();                         The error causes a
        } catch(const std::string& ex) {                     constructor-based
            std::cout << ex << '\n';                          deallocation of memory.
        }
    }
};
```

```
int main() {
    Page chapter("Introduction to C++", "header.txt", "footer.txt");
    return 0;
}
```

The following output shows the result of the constructor-based deallocation. It is as expected:

```
header.txt allocated
footer.txt allocated
footer.txt deallocated dynamic memory
header.txt ~deallocated
file footer.txt inaccessible
```

As lovely as this is, use this approach only when doing something simpler and more elegant is impossible. The next mistake recommends a pattern developed by the inventor of C++; if Bjarne says to use it, let's use it!

The underlying difficulty is that the `OneLiner` class has multiple responsibilities; it allocates memory and opens and reads a file. Life could be simpler if there were a way of minimizing its responsibilities by pushing the chore of allocation and deallocation to another class. The RAII pattern does just that. Therefore, prefer RAII to this technique when you can; suffer through modifying constructors when you must.

Modern C++ provides smart pointers to address this more succinctly. The `std::unique_ptr` and `std::shared_ptr` implement the RAII pattern, obviating the need for you to do the heavy lifting.

RECOMMENDATIONS

- Ensure that all allocated dynamic resources are properly deleted before leaving the constructor via an exception.
- Ensure that the destructor handles all dynamic resources.
- Remember that only an entirely constructed object will have its destructor called.
- Make a great effort to use RAII.

SEE ALSO

- See Mistake 8 for a Standard Template Library implementation of RAII handling for exclusive pointer resources.
- See Mistake 9 for a Standard Template Library implementation of RAII handling for shared pointer resources.
- See Mistake 77 for a much better approach to managing dynamic resources.

10.5 *Mistake 77: Failing to use the RAII pattern*

This mistake focuses on correctness and readability. Readability is positively affected by using a simple pattern to implement a significant semantic concept. Correctness is maintained by deleting dynamic or limited resources under all conditions.

Dynamic and limited resources have ownership constraints, and managing them accordingly is challenging, since the compiler cannot assist by detecting problems. Therefore, it is incumbent on developers to pair each allocation with its corresponding deallocation. This pairing is complicated when exceptions are thrown. Proper design must take normal and error paths into account. Mistake 76 discusses this situation in some detail and offers help. Even better is a general solution that relieves the developer from managing code and pushing dynamic resource management to code. The most general solution is to make resource-managing classes that follow the RAII pattern.

PROBLEM

Consider the case where a dynamic array is needed to hold a set of test scores whose size is unknown at compile time. The client code determines the number of test scores, allocates the array, inputs scores into the array, and passes that information to a constructor. The constructor (needlessly) allocates its array, copies the input values, and computes the average. The developer knows that negative values might be a problem, so an appropriate test is made, and an exception is thrown if a wrong value is discovered.

The following code tries to do the right thing, but how data created in one function should be transferred to another must be clarified. This attempt partially addresses the problem but in a clumsy way.

Listing 10.7 A resource leak in the presence of an exception

```cpp
class Grades {
private:
    int size;
    double* grades;
    double average;
public:
    Grades(int size, const double* grades) : size(size), grades(0),
            average(0) {
        if (size == 0)
            return;
        this->grades = new double[size];        // Allocating a
                                                 // dynamic resource
        for (int i = 0; i < size; ++i) {
            if (grades[i] < 0)                   // Fails to delete the
                throw std::invalid_argument("negative score");  // resource before throwing
            this->grades[i] = grades[i];
        }
        double sum = 0.0;
        for (int i = 0; i < size; ++i)
            sum += this->grades[i];
        average = sum/size;
    }
    ~Grades() { delete [] grades; }
    double getAverage() const { return average; }
};

int main() {
    int count;
```

```
    std::cout << "Enter number of items to average: ";
    std::cin >> count;
    double* scores = new double[count];
    for (int i = 0; i < count; ++i) {
        std::cout << "Enter score: ";
        std::cin >> scores[i];
    }

    try {
        Grades g(count, scores);
        std::cout << "Average score is " << g.getAverage() << '\n';
    } catch (const std::invalid_argument& ex) {
        std::cout << ex.what() << '\n';
    }
    delete [] scores;
    return 0;
}
```

ANALYSIS

If a negative value is discovered, an exception is thrown from the constructor. The grades resource is not released, which results in a resource leak. There are at least three errors in the code. First, the constructor allocates a dynamic array and then tests for an invalid condition, throwing an exception without regard to freeing the resource. Second, the constructor is computing an average, which is not its responsibility. Too many things that obscure the code's intent are occurring, making seeing the resource problem harder. Third, there is no need to allocate the dynamic array. The array copy is unnecessary for proper access to the test score data; there are better ways to take ownership.

Our intrepid developer read an article about RAII and decided that the code should be updated to address its recommendations. Therefore, it passes the input array of values to the RAII implementing `Grades` class to enable the instance to manage the data. The first attempt is shown in listing 10.8, where the constructor no longer allocates the dynamic resource but assumes ownership.

Several articles speak of this approach, stating that the constructor does not have to create dynamic resources but may assume ownership. This is good and true advice; however, the problem of sharing the resource remains, and the resource's creator must pass full ownership to the RAII class. The following code shows this confusion.

Listing 10.8 RAII with a shared resource

```
class Grades {
private:
    int size;
    double* grades;                                    Acquires a resource
public:                                                by receiving it
    Grades(int size, double* grades) : size(size),
        grades(grades) {}                              Deletes the acquired resource
    ~Grades() { delete [] grades; }                    under all conditions
    double getAverage() const {
```

```
        if (size == 0)
            return 0.0;
        double sum = 0.0;
        for (int i = 0; i < size; ++i) {
            if (grades[i] < 0)
                throw std::invalid_argument("negative score");
            sum += grades[i];
        }
        return sum/size;
    }
};

int main() {
    int count;
    std::cout << "Enter number of items to average: ";
    std::cin >> count;
    double* scores = new double[count];          ◄────┐ Creates the original
    for (int i = 0; i < count; ++i) {                  │ resource
        std::cout << "Enter score: ";
        std::cin >> scores[i];
    }

    try {
        Grades g(count, scores);
        std::cout << "Average score is " << g.getAverage() << '\n';
    } catch (const std::invalid_argument& ex) {
        std::cout << ex.what() << '\n';
        delete [] scores;                        ◄────┐
    }                                                  │ Deletes the original resource
    return 0;                                          │ under error conditions
}
```

This effort is commendable but needs to honor the semantics of unique resources. If the calling code wishes to pass ownership to the RAII class, it must never manage or access that resource afterward—it must depend on the access granted by the class. The execution of this code shows that a double free occurs under error conditions. A double free occurs when the code deletes the pointer and later deletes the same pointer again, resulting in undefined behavior. My system crashes when this happens, which alerts me to a real problem.

The destructor, following the RAII pattern, correctly deletes the resource; however, the developer mistook the error condition as a reason to have the original owner perform an explicit deletion—hence, the double deletion. If no exception is thrown, the RAII class handles everything correctly. This situation strongly argues for testing normal and error paths to ensure correctness.

SOLUTION

The central idea behind RAII is that the constructor should allocate dynamic resources. In many cases, the best approach is to make that the only responsibility of the constructor (outside of anything done in its initialization list). In some cases, this may not be practical, so the approach should be modified so that acquiring the dynamic resource is the constructor's last task. This way, the initialization phase (is initialization) is completed only if the resource is acquired (resource acquisition), preventing a resource leak in the presence of an exception. If the constructor completes successfully, the destructor will be called under normal and error conditions. If the acquisition fails, the destructor will not be called; this approach is correct, since there is no resource to deallocate. This all-or-nothing approach is the heart of the RAII pattern.

There is one major caveat with the following code: the RAII class is incomplete, since it does not address the copy constructor and copy assignment operator. Further, a good RAII class will likely implement pointer access operators. All such operations must be coded to prevent disasters, using defaulted operators to implement an RAII class fully.

Listing 10.9 RAII with exclusive ownership

```
class Grades {
private:
    int size;
    int next;
    double* grades;
public:
    Grades(int size) : size(size), next(0), grades(0) {        Initialization consists only
        this->grades = new double[size];                       of resource allocation.
    }
    ~Grades() { delete [] grades; }                            Called only if the
    void addGrade(double grade) { grades[next++] = grade; }    constructor was
    double getAverage() const {                                successful
        if (size == 0)
            return 0.0;
        double sum = 0.0;
        for (int i = 0; i < next; ++i) {
            if (grades[i] < 0)
                throw std::invalid_argument("negative score");
            sum += grades[i];
        }
        return sum/size;
    }
};

int main() {
    int count;
    std::cout << "Enter number of items to average: ";
    std::cin >> count;
    Grades g(count);                          The RAII class acquires
    for (int i = 0; i < count; ++i) {         the dynamic resource.
        std::cout << "Enter score: ";
        double grade;
        std::cin >> grade;
        g.addGrade(grade);
    }                                                Either normal or error control
                                                     paths call the destructor.
    try {
        std::cout << "Average score is " << g.getAverage() << '\n';
    } catch (const std::invalid_argument& ex) {
```

```
        std::cout << ex.what() << '\n';
    }
    return 0;
}
```

Dynamic and limited resources (e.g., database connection handle) are common in all but the smallest programs. Programmers are diligent in ensuring their code works correctly, but it is easy to overlook the problem of the program's interaction with the system. This interaction must be considered for program correctness. Managing dynamic and limited resources can be complicated, but the RAII pattern offers a means for pushing management mechanics into resource-owning classes. Whenever possible, the responsibility for management should be moved into a class designed only to manage the resources. The RAII pattern ensures all successfully acquired resources are automatically deleted at the correct time without the programmer adding any logic.

I have long struggled to completely wrap my head around the phrase *resource acquisition is initialization*, although implementation of the concept is straightforward. Some have proposed instead using the more semantically precise phrase *scope-bound resource management* (SBRM). I modified the phrase to include some explanatory text, making it more explicit: resource acquisition is (the purpose of this object's) initialization. I heard that someone on StackOverflow used the phrase *destruction is resource relinquishment*, which gets to the heart of the matter very well. Phil Karlton said there are only two hard things in computer science: cache invalidation and naming. So there we are; go along with it.

RECOMMENDATIONS

- Use RAII to manage dynamic and limited resources; the pattern ensures all acquired resources are automatically released.
- Limit the RAII class constructor to only acquiring the resource if possible; if not, make the acquisition the last stop.
- If the constructor is passed a resource, ensure that the calling code never again accesses the resource—it is an exclusively owned resource that is managed by the RAII class.

SEE ALSO

- See Mistake 54 for a discussion about improper copying behavior.
- See Mistake 62 for a discussion surrounding unique object ownership problems.
- See Mistake 76 for the motivation behind using the RAII pattern.
- See Mistake 79 for a caution on proper keyword use.

10.6 *Mistake 78: Using raw pointers to resources*

This mistake focuses on correctness and effectiveness. Until it is understood, a negative effect may be felt for readers unfamiliar with the idiom.

Managing dynamic and limited resources is difficult when the developer uses pointers and must manage them through all normal and error paths. The RAII pattern implemented in classes that handle management automatically is a huge step in addressing these complexities adequately. However, each time another resource needs to be managed, a new class must be developed.

Using pointers to manage dynamic resources is a pattern that has been used for many years, since the C days, and is found in C++ code. The difficulty of managing resources via raw pointers prompted a solution called `auto_ptr`. This type of pointer was meant to manage the difficulties of raw pointers, but in one of the rare major blunders, it caused significant problems and was, well, strange.

PROBLEM

Much legacy code has several raw pointers to resources littered throughout the code base. Previous mistakes have discussed some of the pitfalls of using them for resource management. The RAII pattern has been suggested, but new classes must be developed to manage each resource type. Given the overhead of following the pattern, getting rid of raw pointers might seem daunting.

The code in listing 10.10 is a simplified view of some resources managed via raw pointers. We assume that making changes is tricky and generally frowned upon by upper technical resources and management. The developer has few options besides studying the code and simulating normal and error paths. The code is correct, but the developer spends too much time thinking about and writing code to manage the `Student` instances. Unfortunately, this time is valuable but directed toward something other than solving the problem.

Listing 10.10 Using raw pointers to manage resources

```cpp
struct Student {
    std::string name;
    double gpa;
    Student(const std::string& name, double gpa) : name(name), gpa(0) {
        if (gpa < 0)
            throw std::invalid_argument("gpa is negative");
    }
};

int main() {                                    A pointer must be available
    Student* sammy = NULL;        ◄───          on normal and error paths.
    Student* ginny = NULL;
    Student* gene = NULL;
    try {                                            Creates the instances
        sammy = new Student("Samuel", 3.75);   ◄─── and assigns to pointers
        ginny = new Student("Virginia", 3.8);
        gene = new Student("Eugene", -1);
    } catch (const std::invalid_argument& ex) {
        std::cout << "exception caught\n";       Error path cleanup,
        if (sammy)                          ◄─── duplicated
            delete sammy;
        if (ginny)
```

```
            delete ginny;
        if (gene)
            delete gene;
        std::exit(1);
    }
    if (sammy)
        delete sammy;
    if (ginny)
        delete ginny;
    if (gene)
        delete gene;
    return 0;
}
```

Normal path cleanup,
duplicated

ANALYSIS

While the code works correctly as designed, a significant amount only manages pointer-based resources. Raw pointers are replete throughout much of the code, but their management can be minimized, using the RAII pattern. This code is designed to exit if an exception is thrown; therefore, the normal and error paths cannot share cleanup code. This fact requires the cleanup code to be duplicated. A function that contains the cleanup could be written, and it is called from two places, but that does not fundamentally change the situation.

Classic C++ provides a generalized class that implements RAII and can be used for pointer-based resources. The `auto_ptr` template implements the RAII pattern and manages pointers to resources. A dynamic resource is created outside the `auto_ptr`, not in its constructor. The `auto_ptr` constructor takes exclusive ownership of the pointer to prevent a problem noted in the previous mistake.

The code in listing 10.11 suggests a clean fix using the `auto_ptr` class; however, there are several significant problems with this class. These difficulties fall into at least three significant areas:

- When such a pointer is copied, the source pointer is nulled out.
- These pointers cannot be used correctly in Standard Template Library (STL) containers.
- Arrays of these pointers can be created but never correctly deleted.

First, the destination and the source pointers are altered when copying the `auto_ptr` instance. The source pointer is assigned NULL after the copy. This is unusual copy semantics, intended to prevent shared resource access; however, this behavior is not evident from the class name.

Second, STL containers require entities to be copyable and assignable. If an `auto_ptr` is added to a container, the container has exclusive ownership of the resource, and the source pointer is nulled (a consequence of the preceding problem). The managed pointers are not copyable or assignable (they seem to be "transferable").

Third, an array is the only option, since STL containers are not usable for collections of smart (managed) pointers. This approach will not work correctly because the auto_ptr destructor uses the delete, not the delete[] form. While such an array can be created, it cannot be appropriately deleted, resulting in leaked resources.

Listing 10.11 shows a straightforward approach using auto_ptr managed resources, but their limitations are so significant that, in general, they should not be used. The C++11 standard deprecated auto_ptr, and it was removed from the C++17 standard. This rapid deprecation and removal suggests something about the pernicious nature of these managed pointers and their users' opinions of them.

Listing 10.11 Using `auto_ptr` objects to manage resources

```
struct Student {
    std::string name;
    double gpa;
    Student(const std::string& name, double gpa) : name(name), gpa(0) {
        if (gpa < 0)
            throw std::invalid_argument("gpa is negative");
    }
};

int main() {
    try {
        std::auto_ptr<Student> sammy(new Student("Samuel", 3.75));
        std::auto_ptr<Student> ginny(new Student("Virginia", 3.8));
        std::auto_ptr<Student> gene(
            new Student( "Eugene", -1));             ◄─── The normal and error
    } catch (const std::invalid_argument& ex) {          paths execute destructors
        std::cout << "exception caught\n";               when the scope exits.
    }
    return 0;
}
```

This simple usage works as expected, but it is rather unremarkable. The benefit is entirely the management of the pointers when they go out of scope, either normally or due to an exception. Take heart; there is a better way.

SOLUTION

Ideally, pointer-based resources need to be managed using RAII. This approach complicates the developer's life when writing several special classes to handle those resources. A class designed to handle this situation generally would be better. C++ offered the auto_ptr class for just this purpose. However, this offering proved to be a significant blunder. This solution was deprecated and removed in modern C++, demonstrating that its use was always problematic. Modern C++ provides robust and meaningful smart pointers for those lucky enough to be able to use them.

This situation does not mean the developer must write custom RAII classes to manage pointers. Some determined developers on the Boost project have done this for us (https://www.boost.org/). Using the Boost libraries—if only for smart pointers—is worth the effort if you cannot use modern C++. The code in listing 10.12 demonstrates the usage of the boost::scoped_ptr, whose semantics are exclusive ownership; for shared semantics, use `boost::shared_ptr`. These Boost pointers work as expected and address the failings of the inferior `std::auto_ptr`. These Boost pointers were the basis for modern C++ `std::unique_ptr` and `std::shared_ptr`. Use them with confidence!

Listing 10.12   Using `auto_ptr` objects to manage resources

```
#include <boost/scoped_ptr.hpp>

struct Student {
    std::string name;
    double gpa;
    Student(const std::string& name, double gpa) : name(name), gpa(0) {
        if (gpa < 0)
            throw std::invalid_argument("gpa is negative");
    }
};

int main() {
    try {
        boost::scoped_ptr<Student> sammy(new Student("Samuel", 3.75));
        boost::scoped_ptr<Student> ginny(new Student("Virginia", 3.8));
        boost::scoped_ptr<Student> gene(
            new Student( "Eugene", -1));
    } catch (const std::invalid_argument& ex) {
        std::cout << "exception caught\n";
    }
    return 0;
}
```

The normal and error paths execute destructors when the scope exits.

The developer now spends minimal time and effort writing management code. The rest of the effort is spent on solving the problem they are working on. Minimized code is easier to write—that is, more effective—and easier to understand—that is, more readable.

The `boost::scoped_ptr` instances are instantiations of a template that manages pointers to `Student` objects. The constructor assumes ownership of the resource by taking its pointer. Its semantics are exclusive; assignment is not possible. If an assignment is needed, use the shared pointer version. Whenever the pointer goes out of scope, the dynamic resource is deleted. Be careful that this is the intended behavior.

Modern C++ allows the transfer of `std::unique_ptr` instances using the `std::move` function, which turns the source instance into a moveable object that is then transferred to the target object via a copy assignment operator. This snippet demonstrates the technique:

```
std::unique_ptr<int> ptr1 = std::make_unique<int>(42);
...
std::unique_ptr<int> ptr2 = std::move(ptr1);
```

RECOMMENDATIONS

- Replace raw pointers with modern C++ (or Boost, if modern is unavailable) smart pointers wherever possible.

- Replace `auto_ptr` instances with at least Boost smart pointers wherever possible; much better are the modern C++ versions.

- Do not use `auto_ptr` for STL containers; their copy semantics are unexpected.

- Do not use `auto_ptr` for arrays; their destructor behavior will cause undefined behavior.

- Where possible, consider modern C++ `unique_ptr` and `shared_ptr` as the preferred alternative.

SEE ALSO

- See Mistake 8 for a Standard Template Library implementation of RAII handling for exclusive pointer resources.

- See Mistake 9 for a Standard Template Library implementation of RAII handling for shared pointer resources.

- See Mistake 28 for a discussion of why NULL is a poor choice for a pointer.

- See Mistake 76 for a discussion of the complexities of managing dynamic resources.

- See Mistake 77 for information about creating RAII classes to manage dynamic and limited resources automatically.

10.7 Mistake 79: Mixing new and delete forms

This mistake focuses on correctness. Improper use of new and deleted forms leads to undefined behavior, leaving the program and the system in an unknown state.

Dynamic resources are used in various ways, such as when the sizes of entities are not known at compile time. The ability to obtain dynamic memory in sizes computed at run time is essential for safe and correct usage. C++ provides the `new` and `delete` operators to allocate and release memory. There are two forms of each: the single entity and array forms.

PROBLEM

Novice programming students are often fascinated with arrays—they offer a single variable name for multiple values, distinguishing the elements by a computed index value. The power of arrays is a solid inducement to use them, and this causes many novices (and professionals alike) overuse them. The `std::vector` is a superior choice in most cases; however, arrays are here to stay, as they should be.

We are designing a simple program to help teachers out with computing grades. Each student has several quizzes and supplemental scores that must be averaged for a final score. Since the supplemental work items are optional (extra credit), the number of items is unknown and varies by student. A straightforward approach is to create an array whose size is well greater than the anticipated maximum number of elements. Two problems immediately arise: first, what if that number is below the actual maximum, and second, why waste space for unneeded elements? The first problem is a matter of correct operations and must not be overlooked. The second problem is stylistic (no correctness problems), but it feels wrong to more experienced developers. Further, performance concerns might arise, so this approach is genuinely problematic.

Listing 10.13   Simple averaging code with mismatched forms

```cpp
int main() {
    int count;
    std::cout << "Enter number of items to average: ";
    std::cin >> count;
    double* scores = new double[count];        ◄─────┐ Allocates the computed
    for (int i = 0; i < count; ++i) {                 │ amount of memory
        std::cout << "Enter score: ";
        std::cin >> scores[i];
    }

    double sum = 0.0;
    for (int i = 0; i < count; ++i)
        sum += scores[i];                  │ Does this delete the
    delete scores;                      ◄──┘ allocated memory?

    if (count > 0)
        std::cout << "Average score is " << sum/count << '\n';
    else
        std::cout << "No items to average\n";
    return 0;
}
```

ANALYSIS

The code looks reasonable and works as expected; the computed averages are correct. However, there is a significant problem with the deletion of the allocated memory.

The new operator obtains a fixed amount of memory based on the entity's size. If the allocation is for a single entity, the needed amount of memory is precisely the entity's size. The form of new, in this case, is unadorned; it would not use the [] notation.

The array form is used for the new operator when the allocated memory is based on multiple entities; it uses the [] notation. The element's size is multiplied by the number of elements, and that amount of memory is obtained. However, there is more to this.

Compilers are free to implement memory management as they wish, but in many cases, the additional information for the size of the array is stored in the allocated memory. Compilers that do this usually store the count preceding the start of returned memory; therefore, the first array element follows the array size without the array access code knowing anything about the size.

In listing 10.13, the array is dynamically allocated, and the program computes the sum of the scores. Then, the scores pointer is deleted. In this case, what happens is anyone's guess; possibly, the number of bytes for the pointer's element type is freed. Since the number of elements is stored in the beginning, it, and perhaps part of the first element, is deleted—or only the first element is deleted. Who knows? The delete form (with no array notation) frees a single element. What happens with the rest of the array is undefined, but maybe it is nicely leaked. This does not cause any apparent problem, but it is incorrect behavior.

What would happen to a `new` followed by a `delete []` operator is far less clear (not that anything is clear here). What would the `delete []` operator think the number of elements was? Oh, this doesn't look good! Undefined behavior is just that; the program can do anything it wants. Whatever it does, it is not likely what is expected.

SOLUTION

Think of the `new` and `delete` operators in terms of a pair; for every `new`, there must be a corresponding `delete`, and for every `new []`, there must be a corresponding `delete []`. Never mix these pairs. Mixing them results in undefined behavior that is always bad, and even if a program seems to work, it is incorrect. The following code shows the slight—but essential—change to properly pair the `delete []` with its corresponding `new []`.

Listing 10.14   Properly pairing `new` and `delete` operators

```cpp
int main() {
    int count;
    std::cout << "Enter number of items to average: ";
    std::cin >> count;
    double* scores = new double[count];        ◄─── Allocates an array of
    for (int i = 0; i < count; ++i) {                the computed size
        std::cout << "Enter score: ";
        std::cin >> scores[i];
    }

    double sum = 0.0;
    for (int i = 0; i < count; ++i)
        sum += scores[i];              Deletes the array, pairing
    delete [] scores;            ◄───  it with the allocation

    if (count > 0)
        std::cout << "Average score is " << sum/count << '\n';
    else
        std::cout << "No items to average\n";
    return 0;
}
```

RECOMMENDATIONS

- Ensure that the proper `delete` form is used based on the `new` form; mixing them causes undefined behavior.
- Study the code well when using `new` and `delete` to ensure that they are paired correctly; if multiple `new` and `new []` operators are contained in a single function, it is easy to mix up the pairs.
- Minimize the size of functions to avoid mixing forms.

10.8   *Mistake 80: Trusting exception specifications*

This mistake primarily affects correctness and readability, causing a hit to performance. The problem with correctness is that the code may not work as expected; the problem with readability is that the code seems intuitive but is not.

Exceptions provide a clean way to report errors through an alternate control path, eliminating significant code complexity. Documenting the anticipated exceptions is accomplished by reading all the relevant catch blocks; however, this approach leaves a bit to be desired. A good idea was to document exceptions thrown by a function by specifying them in an exception specification list. A glance at the specification list should tell the whole story.

PROBLEM

Exception handling is simplified when a developer writes all the affected code. The ability to see and understand various difficulties dramatically diminishes when using libraries or other modules. The code in listing 10.15 computes the standard deviation for a set of values in a vector. The developer carefully ensured too few values would throw an exception to prevent miscalculating the result in the `std_dev` function. Being a careful developer, they added an exception specification to document that the function can throw a `std::invalid_argument` if too few values are given. The developer ensured the calling code could recover from an exception, since program termination is problematic.

Under normal conditions, this code works as expected, but things take a nasty turn when no values are given. It is expected that an exception would be thrown if too few values are passed to the `std_dev` function. However, the developer overlooked that the `arith_mean` function was executed before the vector size test. The called function detected a too-few-values problem and threw an exception. Yet with the care exercised by the developer, the program abruptly terminates.

Listing 10.15   Listing exceptions that can be thrown

```cpp
double arith_mean(const std::vector<double>& values) {
    if (values.size() == 0)
        throw std::domain_error("missing values");        // Throws std::domain_error
    double sum = 0.0;                                      // if too few elements exist
    for (int i = 0; i < values.size(); ++i)
        sum += values[i];
    return sum/values.size();
}

double std_dev(const std::vector<double>& values)         // Anticipates the
        throw (std::invalid_argument) {                   // possible std::invalid_
    double mean = arith_mean(values);                     // argument exception
    if (values.size() < 2)
        throw std::invalid_argument("too few values");    // Throws std::invalid_
    double sum = 0.0;                                      // argument exception if
    for (int i = 0; i < values.size(); ++i)               // too few elements exist
        sum += std::pow(values[i] - mean, 2);
    return std::sqrt(sum / (values.size() - 1));
```

```
}

int main() {
    std::vector<double> values;
    values.push_back(3.14159);
    values.push_back(2.71828);
    try {
        std::cout << "standard deviation is " << std_dev(values) << '\n';
    } catch (...) {
        std::cout << "exception caught, but we did not crash\n";
    }
    return 0;
}
```

The developer was surprised at the behavior under exceptional conditions and was confused about why the main function's catch block could not rescue the program.

ANALYSIS

The developer's attempt to control program behavior by specifying exceptions was reasonable but incomplete. Unless you thoroughly understand your code, specifying exceptions in the specification list is guesswork. If you guess correctly, the program behaves as expected; if you guess incorrectly, the program crashes unceremoniously.

The compiler must exert some effort to handle the exception specification. In a program that does not use exception specifications, any exception thrown is percolated up the code hierarchy as the stack unwinds. As soon as a specification is added, the behavior changes in nonintuitive ways. The compiler adds code to check thrown exceptions and matches them against the specification. If they match, the exception is propagated as expected; however, if the detected exception is not in the specification, the detection code throws a `std::unexpected` exception, whose default behavior is to call `terminate` (which calls `abort`). This additional code has an effect on performance.

If the developer wishes to convert the unexpected exception to something more manageable, write a function that throws a known exception (a standard one or one of your own making), and pass that conversion function as the parameter of the `set_unexpected` function. Briefly, the code would look as follows:

```
class MyException {};
void transformException() { throw MyException(); }
set_unexpected(transformException);
```

If this approach is used, the resulting `MyException` should be caught in some catch block. A significant downside to this approach is that the whole program will transform the `unexpected` exception into a `MyException`, making capturing its context very difficult. This solution is workable, but its overgenerality is detrimental. Trying to document exceptions obscures problems that need to be handled better.

SOLUTION

Due to the uncertainty of whether all possible exceptions can be known and listed in an exception specification, the most drastic and helpful approach is to eliminate the specification. Eliminating them removes the possibility of unexpected (and unwanted) behavior that deviates from an intuitive understanding of exceptions. Much called code in libraries cannot be analyzed adequately for potential exceptions, so using a specification list plays with unexpected behavior.

The exception specification was an experiment, and it has been removed from modern C++. This fact demonstrates that the experts did not trust their use. We can take this as a solid hint to act accordingly and remove all exception specifications.

The following code shows this adjustment. As an alternative, the commented-out function header specifies both possible exceptions; however, there is likely no way to know the complete list of possible exceptions in a real system. Unless management or technical leadership insists, avoid this path.

Listing 10.16 Eliminating the exception specification

```
double arith_mean(const std::vector<double>& values) {
    if (values.size() == 0)
        throw std::domain_error("missing values");
    double sum = 0.0;
    for (int i = 0; i < values.size(); ++i)
        sum += values[i];
    return sum/values.size();
}

// double std_dev(const std::vector<double>& values)
        throw (std::invalid_argument, std::domain_error) {
double std_dev(const std::vector<double>& values) {
    if (values.size() < 2)
        throw std::invalid_argument("too few values");
    double mean = arith_mean(values);
    double sum = 0.0;
    for (int i = 0; i < values.size(); ++i)
        sum += std::pow(values[i] - mean, 2);
    return std::sqrt(sum / (values.size() - 1));
}

int main() {
    std::vector<double> values;
    values.push_back(3.14159);
    values.push_back(2.71828);
    try {
        std::cout << "standard deviation is " << std_dev(values) << '\n';
    } catch (...) {
        std::cout << "exception caught, but we did not crash\n";
    }
    return 0;
}
```

Optional: add all discovered exceptions (is this list complete?).

Eliminate the exception specification altogether.

Ensure local verification occurs before calling any other code.

While exception specification lists were a good idea (in theory), the unexpected behavior, extra implementation costs, and inability to deliver what they seem to promise mean the best approach is to eliminate them.

RECOMMENDATIONS

- Eliminate exception specification lists if possible.
- Understand the unexpected behavior of a thrown exception that is not included in an exception list.
- Remember the performance effect of using exception specifications.

10.9 Mistake 81: Failing to throw by value and catch by reference

This mistake focuses on correctness, effectiveness, and performance. Exceptions can be thrown by pointer, value, or reference and caught by the same type. However, the benefits and costs of each approach vary.

Exceptions provide an alternate control structure for handling errors. Correctly implemented, their use allows for resilient code and allows the developer to recover from an error that otherwise might terminate the program. Exceptions are more expensive than functions, and their behavior is less intuitive. Understanding some of these problems is essential for proper use.

PROBLEM

We can imagine that our developer has learned the various means for throwing and catching exceptions but needs clarification about the optimal means. They run some experiments to test multiple combinations and learn about the differences.

The developer understood correctly that throwing an exception means moving some data from the throw site to the catch site. Their intuition suggests that the solution that moves the minimum amount of data is optimal. Therefore, throwing an exception by pointer is tried. Not satisfied with this approach, the developer decided to try various ways of throwing by pointer and compare them with throwing by value.

The code in listing 10.17 shows three such attempts. The first is throwing a pointer to a local object; the second is throwing a pointer to a heap-based object; and, for comparison, the third is throwing by value. The developer instrumented the `DerivedException` constructor and its copy constructor to count the number of times each was invoked (instrumentation code not shown).

Listing 10.17   Catching an exception by pointer and value

```
struct DerivedException : public std::exception {
    std::string message;
    DerivedException() : message("DerivedException") {}
    ~DerivedException() throw() {}
    const char* what() const throw() { return message.c_str(); }
};

void throw_by_local_pointer() {
    DerivedException de;
    throw &de;
}

void throw_by_heap_pointer() {
```

Overrides the std::exception virtual method

```
        DerivedException* de = new DerivedException();
        throw de;
}

void throw_by_value() {
        DerivedException de;
        throw de;
}

int main() {
        try {
                throw_by_local_pointer();
        } catch(std::exception* ex) {
                std::cout << ex->what() << '\n';
        }
        try {
                throw_by_heap_pointer();
        } catch(std::exception* ex) {
                std::cout << ex->what() << '\n';
        }
        try {
                throw_by_value();
        } catch(std::exception ex) {
                std::cout << ex.what() << '\n';
        }
        return 0;
}
```

The developer ran the code and noticed that each approach called the constructor once and never called the copy constructor. From these results, the conclusion was that there is no difference between implementing throwing and catching exceptions.

ANALYSIS

We can applaud our developer's scientific approach, but we might be suspicious that something important was missed in their conclusion. One thing that must be emphasized is that when an object (or pointer) is thrown, the object will go out of scope at the point of the throw. Therefore, C++ mandates that whatever is thrown is copied, and the temporary object (or pointer) is transferred to the catch site. Thus, regardless of the method chosen to throw, a copy is always made, increasing the cost of throwing by that amount.

The `throw_by_local_pointer` should lead to anyone's protest. The local object is created within the function, and its address is thrown. This approach minimizes the amount of data transferred from the throw to the catch site, since it copies only the size of a pointer; however, when the throw is completed, the function has exited, destroying the local variables. The catch clause receives a copy of the pointer, but the pointer is to an invalid `DerivedException` object. Printing out the `what` information is undefined behavior. This solution is fast and very wrong.

The `throw_by_heap_pointer` performs just as quickly as the previous attempt but resolves the problem of an invalid exception object. But there is a less obvious problem: Who deletes the heap-allocated object? If the catch site is the last place it will be used, it should be fine for the code in this block to delete the object. However, the exception might be thrown again, since this code could not be recovered. Then, who deletes the object? This approach poses a question that is difficult, or impossible, to answer about object deletion responsibility.

Finally, throw by value is analyzed, and the developer sees no difference in the number of constructor calls, wrongly concluding that the only cost is the difference between the size of a pointer and the size of the exception object. Two obscure problem are happening; the developer overlooked the first, and the second is invisible.

The `what` method output is incorrect for the exception caught by value. It outputs a message from the `std::exception` class (the output is `std::exception`, nothing more clever!)—the polymorphic `what` method of `DerivedException` was not executed. The reason is that the copy of the thrown exception is used to initialize the catch parameter. The parameter is of type `std::exception`, so the thrown exception is sliced, and only the base class portion is copied. The overridden method is sliced off, and the base class version is executed. This is an easy-to-spot problem.

The difficult-to-spot problem is based on the obvious one—they are a pair. The apparent cost of throwing by value is a single copy, as the developer (wrongly) determined. Since the exception is caught by its base class, it is not the derived class copy constructor that is called but the base class version. The developer could not instrument the `std::exception` copy constructor, since it is standard library code; otherwise, they would have seen the hidden copy. When throwing by value, a copy is made for a temporary object, and then a copy of the temporary is used to initialize the catch parameter—two copies.

SOLUTION

Finally, our developer threw by value to prevent pointer deletion problems. Learning that throw by value doubles the number of copies, catch by reference is used to minimize costs. This case is one of the few, if not only, place(s) where a reference for a temporary object is legal (wait for modern C++). The temporary object created at the throw site is transferred by reference to the catch parameter; therefore, no second copy is made.

Further, since the reference is caught, it allows polymorphic behavior and the `DerviedException`'s version of `what` is called. The following code shows that a simple tweak is needed to minimize the cost of copying and preserve overridden method behavior. Add the ampersand, and score big!

Listing 10.18 Catching an exception by reference

```
struct DerivedException : public std::exception {
    std::string message;
    DerivedException() : message("DerivedException") {}
    ~DerivedException() throw() {}
    const char* what() const throw() { return message.c_str(); }
};

void throw_by_value_catch_by_reference() {
```

```
    DerivedException de;
    throw de;                        ◀─────┐ Throw by value, since the
}                                           │ copy must occur anyhow.

int main() {
    try {
        throw_by_value_catch_by_reference();
    } catch(const std::exception& ex) {    ◀─────┐ Catch by reference to
        std::cout << ex.what() << '\n';            │ prevent copying and to
    }                                              │ maintain polymorphism.
    return 0;
}
```

The developer also learned a lesson about assuming that simple instrumentation is sufficient to paint a complete picture of the behavior of a program.

RECOMMENDATIONS

- Throw exceptions by value to eliminate the problems with throwing by pointer.
- Catch exceptions by reference to minimize copying and ensure polymorphic behavior.
- Minimize the size of derived exception classes to minimize the cost of copying.
- Never return a pointer (or reference) to a local object.

SEE ALSO

- See Mistake 84 for a discussion about why returning pointers or references to local objects is a terrible practice.
- See Mistake 86 for a discussion about the costs of passing pointers, values, and references.

Functions and coding

11

This chapter covers

- Choosing the proper parameter type
- Returning multiple values from a function
- Keeping functions succinct and short
- Ensuring function preconditions and postconditions are met

Functions are the heart of modular programming. A *function* is a named unit of code that can be called multiple times from different places. The design of functions is critical for producing reusable code that is easy to use, meaningful in behavior, and bug-free. Several mistakes are associated with function design and usage. These are heavily oriented toward proper parameter definition and usage. Many other mistakes are common; these should sensitize the developer to be wary of those.

11.1 Design considerations

Functions comprise a name, a parameter list, a return value, and a body. The compiler insists on all four parts yet provides a way to make the parameter list and return value seem optional. Some books call constructors (and destructors, by implication) functions; they are not, technically, but the C++ standard calls them "special member functions." A constructor and destructor have no return value and do not qualify for function-hood. The parameter list appears optional, since it can be empty, but it still must be specified by empty parentheses. The return value seems optional because the type can be void. However, this is still a type; it is the type that has no value, or its value is the empty set (for set-theoretic fans).

The name is the hardest part of defining a function. While any old name can be used, deciding on a single, succinct, communicative name is often difficult. It must explain the purpose of the function in an intuitive way that makes using it straightforward. Overly long or responsible functions make naming nearly impossible.

Ideally, a function should be pure. A *pure function* accesses no variables or data outside its scope and performs its behavior entirely from the data passed by its parameter list. Some functions are supposed to affect the system outside their scope. Good examples include the `operator<<` and `operator>>` methods. Since these functions must exist, the goal is to separate them into two categories: pure and side-effect-only functions.

Side-effect (only) functions should do no computations, have minimal logic, and affect entities external to their scope. Pure functions should perform computations, use necessary logic, and return their results via the return value. Some functions need to return multiple values, which cannot be achieved using their return value. Returning an instance of a structure (or class) or using output parameters are options. Output parameters are more difficult to understand quickly and affect readability. Returning an instance is more complex but better isolates the input from the output.

A value, a pointer, or a reference parameter can pass data input to a function. This book uses the convention of referring to the values at the call site as *arguments*, and the variables in the parameter list are called *parameters*. (Some authors and teachers use the more difficult pairing of the terms *parameters* and *formal parameters*, respectively.)

Variables local to a function are initialized by explicit programming action, usually using an assignment operator. Parameters are local variables, but the programmer does not explicitly initialize them. The compiler generates code to copy the value of an argument, which is the initialization value of the parameter. Otherwise, the parameter is, in all respects, a regular local variable. One significant consequence of local variables is that the local variables are destroyed when the function exits—typically or by throwing an exception. What this does not mean—regrettably—is that the destroyed variables are necessarily entirely inaccessible. Some systems allow access after destroying them (via pointers or references), leading to hard-to-diagnose bugs; excellent systems crash under these circumstances.

The following mistakes take a stab at dealing with some common problems with function design and usage. While many such mistakes exist, some occur more frequently.

11.2 Mistake 82: Using overloaded functions instead of parameter defaulting

This mistake affects readability and effectiveness. Writing multiple overloaded functions allows a consistent means for handling varying parameter lists but may prove tedious and duplicate code.

PROBLEM

Frequently, problems necessitate a few functions that do the same work but with different numbers of parameters. The C programming language would force these functions to have different names; however, C++ permits naming them identically with the single restriction that the parameter lists must be unique (whether parameter types, number of parameters, or order of types). Overloaded functions use the same name, which maintains the semantics of the operation.

The following code overloads three functions that perform the same operation on different parameters. This approach is tedious and unending (exactly when does one have the proper set of functions?).

Listing 11.1 Overloaded functions handling differing numbers of parameters

```
int sum(int a, int b) { return a + b; }
int sum(int a, int b, int c) { return a + b + c; }
int sum(int a, int b, int c, int d) { return a + b + c +d; }

int main() {
    std::cout << sum(3, 4) << '\n';
    std::cout << sum(3, 4, 5) << '\n';
    std::cout << sum(3, 4, 6, 7) << '\n';
    return 0;
}
```

ANALYSIS

These functions do precisely what is expected but duplicate code and become tiresome to write after the first few. While unlikely, typographical errors within the code body could cause differing behavior between the functions.

SOLUTION

Using defaulted parameters is a much better approach that maximizes typing effectiveness, reading comprehension, and possibly correctness. Some functions lend themselves poorly to this approach because there may be no sensible default values.

Listing 11.2 Using defaulted parameters for multiple parameters

```
int sum(int a, int b, int c = 0, int d = 0) { return a + b + c +d; }

int main() {
    std::cout << sum(3, 4) << '\n';
    std::cout << sum(3, 4, 5) << '\n';
    std::cout << sum(3, 4, 6, 7) << '\n';
    return 0;
}
```

The sum function eliminates code duplication with its potential for coding bugs. In many cases, some form of meaningful defaulting can occur, but do not "slip on the banana peel" of making overreaching functions that default too much and change behavior based on parameters. For example, a Boolean parameter being false might do *this* functionality, but if true, it does *that* (somewhat different) functionality—not good. Please keep it simple. I have slipped, nearly disastrously, on a banana peel—it's a real thing!

RECOMMENDATIONS

- Keep functions simple to allow for parameter defaulting.
- Do not use defaulted parameters to change function behavior significantly.

SEE ALSO

- See Mistake 18 for a modern twist on using templates instead of defaulted parameters.

11.3   *Mistake 83: Failing to use assertions*

This mistake affects effectiveness and correctness. There are two temporal phases to developing a program—compile and run time—and two temporal phases to software construction—development and production time. This mistake focuses on the development phase of software construction.

PROBLEM

During program development, new ideas are tested, new code is introduced, and additional interactions between components are tried. All this newness is a perfect storm for bugs to breed and feed—and they will.

Ensuring code is working as expected should be confirmed by unit and integration testing, but before that, ensuring function preconditions are met is essential. Further, it's crucial for developers to ensure function postconditions and invariants are met. However, writing the code to test for and handle these areas always seems to be . . . deferrable—we can always write that stuff tomorrow.

Deferring preconditions, postconditions, and invariants is tempting but dangerous. Without sufficient testing, bugs will slip in and multiply. The following code is an example; while it looks innocuous, therein lies a real and present danger.

> **Listing 11.3   An unexpected division-by-zero problem**

```
// a divides b evenly
bool divides(int a, int b) {
    return b % a == 0;          ◄——  This will rarely ever
}                                     misbehave, but ...

int main() {
    int x = 0;
    int y = 42;
    if (divides(x, y))
        std::cout << x << " divides " << y << '\n';

    return 0;
}
```

Under most circumstances, this code will behave correctly, and the developer's confidence in its benefit will grow. However, one day, when there is a great distance between writing this code and focusing on other, more recent code, this code breaks. But why? It always used to work.

ANALYSIS

The cause is a division-by-zero problem, where bad input data causes the problem to surface. This bug has been there all along but was never exposed. Unit tests should reveal this, but that workload is another "reason" to defer writing validation code.

SOLUTION

During development, one of the best ways to expose bugs is to write precondition and postcondition assertions. These little tests are brutal—the program crashes immediately if they fail. On the plus side, this is great, since the bug is exposed, and without stack unwinding, a debugger sets one in the exact area of the problem.

An *assertion* is a simple test that checks whether something is true. They are quick to write, take no special logic, and are powerful. The lurking bug from listing 11.3 is quickly addressed in the following code.

Listing 11.4 Using an assertion to check a precondition

```
// disable assertions by defining NDEBUG          ◄───────
// a divides b evenly                                        Passes the compiler the
bool divides(int a, int b) {                                 NDEBUG flag to disable
    assert(a!=0);          ◄────────┐                        assertions in production code
    return b % a == 0;              │
}                                   │  Proves that the
                                       divisor is nonzero
int main() {
    int x = 0;
    int y = 42;
    if (divides(x, y))
        std::cout << x << " divides " << y << '\n';

    return 0;
}
```

If the production code should not include assertions, do not use conditional compilation to remove them. Define the NDEBUG macro to the compiler when the code is compiled, and the associated code will disappear—there is no runtime cost.

Consult other software engineering and development resources using testing frameworks, tools, and approaches. These are well beyond the scope of this mistake, but this serves as a provocation for their study and use. Assertions are particularly helpful during debugging, so learn to use them well.

RECOMMENDATIONS

- Do not defer preconditions, postconditions, and invariant checks until later—later never happens. Use assertions during development to validate conditions.

- Use unit testing frameworks to validate code further. Do not consider tests to be nonfunctional code; instead, think of them as meta-code that demonstrates its correctness.

- Never write an assertion that has side effects; if the assertion is disabled, the code's behavior changes unexpectedly.

SEE ALSO

- See Mistake 91 for a discussion on when an exception is not an exception and making sense of their different contexts.

11.4   *Mistake 84: Returning pointers or references to local objects*

This mistake deals with correctness and readability but negatively affects performance slightly. The ability to create values or objects in one place and transfer them to other areas is a powerful technique that modularizes code.

PROBLEM

Creating objects within the scope of a function helps isolate the code to make it more understandable and manageable. The code in listing 11.5 is supposed to combine two `std::string` objects into a third, larger one. The developer thought a function would make more sense in an output stream than creating a local object using `operator+=` and referencing that variable. The developer also saw this approach to minimize copying (a constructor and possibly a destructor call), thus improving performance.

> Listing 11.5   Returning a local pointer or reference

```
const std::string& catenate(const std::string& a, const std::string& b) {
    std::string combined(a);
    combined += b;
    return combined;
}

// const std::string* catenate(const std::string& a,
//          [SA]const std::string& b) {               ◀──┐ Returning an object
//      std::string combined(a);                         │ by pointer example
//      combined += b;
//      return &combined;
// }

int main() {
    std::string msg1 = "Hello, ";                     ┌ Smoother than
    std::string msg2 = "world!";                      │ creating, updating, and
    std::cout << catenate(msg1, msg2) << '\n';   ◀────┘ referring to a variable
    return 0;
}
```

ANALYSIS

The impetus to isolate code into functions, especially when they are more smoothly used in specific contexts, is a good idea. The readability of the code in listing 11.5

is straightforward. Further, it eliminates the local creation and updating of a local variable.

The catenate function is created to offload the local variable creation and updating to increase readability. The calling code calls the function in its output context, and all should work; however, its behavior is undefined. When the function returns, the combined local variable goes out of scope.

The catenate function creates a local `std::string` variable, combines the two parameters, and returns a pointer (or reference) to the local variable. The call site attempts to access the data. If the developer is lucky, the attempted access will cause a segmentation fault (or similar) and crash the program. The unlucky developer will see no problem. What is worse is that the unlucky ones will likely see the expected results.

When the local variable is created, memory space is allocated on the stack to represent the variable. After the function completes execution, it returns the address of that variable; however, the completion of the function does something invisible but influential. The stack frame dedicated to the function is invalidated and made available for other code to use the space. The pointer still refers to the computed value, and the calling code sees the result if it has not been overwritten or the access does not cause a crash.

SOLUTION

The solution is as simple as returning a copy of the local value, as shown in the following listing. This approach causes the copy constructor to be called, which incurs overhead (sometimes a destructor call). However, the copied result is correct and has no nasty undefined behavior. In most cases, return value optimization (RVO) can eliminate some of this overhead.

Listing 11.6   Returning a value

```cpp
std::string catenate(const std::string& a, const std::string& b) {
    std::string combined(a);
    combined += b;
    return combined;
}

int main() {
    std::string msg1 = "Hello, ";
    std::string msg2 = "world!";
    std::cout << catenate(msg1, msg2) << '\n';
    return 0;
}
```

The urge to make performant and readable code is commendable, but specific rules must be followed to ensure correctness. When returning locally computed values, returning a reference or pointer is unsafe. The effect of the copy will have to be accepted. Modern C++ compilers often will minimize or eliminate this effect.

An alternative approach is to create the local object on the heap and pass the pointer back to the caller. No undefined behavior occurs in this manner, but the matter of deleting the dynamic memory becomes a new problem that affects readability and, if not done, resource leaks.

RECOMMENDATIONS

- Never return pointers or references to locally created objects.
- Understand the mechanics of how calling to and returning from a function affects memory.

SEE ALSO

- See Mistake 63 for a discussion on RVO.

11.5   *Mistake 85: Using output parameters*

This mistake affects readability by obscuring the purpose of variables, and there might be some slight effectiveness considerations. Returning multiple values has proven problematic, and a few techniques have been used. These approaches are often hard to read, write, or both.

PROBLEM

Occasionally, a function needs to return two or more values. An obvious approach is to create variables in the calling code that the called function will modify. Passing a pointer or using a reference parameter for each variable will work; however, the complexity introduced may obfuscate their use and cause errors in understanding.

The code in listing 11.7 performs integer division and returns the quotient and the remainder. The developer used an output parameter, since the function can return only one value. The remainder parameter is a reference variable, an alias for a value in the calling code. The function modifies the calling code's variable, and all is well; however, a reader may not notice this usage and be confused for a (valuable amount of) time.

Listing 11.7   Using reference variables to return a value

```
int divide(int value, int divisor, int& remainder) {
    remainder = value % divisor;
    return value/divisor;
}

int main() {
    int x = 42;
    int y = 4;                          A non-obvious return value
    int r;
    int q = divide(x, y, r);
    std::cout << x << " divided by " << y << " is " << q
        << " with remainder " << r << '\n';
    return 0;
}
```

ANALYSIS

A reader may take a while to see that the local variable r in the calling code is uninitialized because code in a called function initializes it. This does not fit the expected pattern; however, it is slightly more readable than if there were an initialization value. Generally, programmers do not expect argument values to be modified by functions; instead, they hope that the results of computations are returned in a way that can be assigned to a variable.

Using pointers to the caller's local variables does not change the situation; it only changes its implementation. The syntax is messier, and the function's code is slightly more awkward.

SOLUTION

The Standard Template Library provides a container with two typed values implemented by a class template. This std::pair allows the function to return two values that fit the expected behavior much more closely. Further, there is no need to define a structure or class to contain these values, since the Standard Template Library already does so.

Listing 11.8 Using a std::pair to return two values

```cpp
std::pair<int, int> divide(int value, int divisor) {
    return std::make_pair(value / divisor, value % divisor);
}

int main() {
    int x = 42;
    int y = 4;
    std::pair<int, int> res = divide(x, y);        // Both values are returned,
    std::cout << x << " divided by " << y << " is " << res.first   // which reads better.
        <<" with remainder " << res.second << '\n';
    return 0;
}
```

Another approach is to return an array from which the caller can extract the values; however, this approach can be obscure and affect readability. It approximates using std::pair, while being less flexible. The array elements must be homogenous, while std::pair allows heterogeneous types.

The final option is to return a structure and have the calling code pull the values from its fields. This approach is more readable but requires writing a new structure, likely used only once.

RECOMMENDATIONS

- Minimize the use of output variables; eliminate them if possible.
- Use the functionality provided by the Standard Template Library wherever possible.

SEE ALSO

- See Mistake 16 for a modern C++ way of returning more than two values from a function.
- See Mistake 88 for a discussion about limiting the number of parameters passed to a function.

11.6 *Mistake 86: Incorrect use of parameter types*

This mistake focuses on performance and can affect readability. C++ allows parameters to be passed by value, pointer, or reference. Choosing correctly is essential. Three aspects of using parameters well are their size, usage, and safety. The following discussion will focus on `std::string` parameters with occasional references to built-in types.

The size of a parameter depends on its data type. Value parameters are passed as copies of the argument value from the call site. Built-in types tend to be small, and it is usually efficient to pass them as copies; however, user-written data types may be large. A `std::string` object's size depends on the runtime library; various sizes are possible, but the size of 32 bytes will be assumed. Therefore, if a string is passed by value, the stack must allocate 32 bytes for the copy and execute code to copy those from the source to the stack. This effort influences performance and the available space on the call stack.

If a parameter is passed using a pointer, then the stack must allocate sufficient bytes for the architecture's pointer size—for discussion's sake, we will assume 8 bytes. Passing a string by pointer is probably more efficient in terms of size and speed than passing by value—as with most performance claims, measurement is essential to verify.

Finally, if the parameter is passed by reference, the code acts like a pass-by-pointer parameter. The size of the data passed is 8 bytes. The reference syntax is different—and easier to use—than a pointer's.

Therefore, passing values by value has the greatest variation in size. If the data type is small, 8 bytes or less (on a 64-bit architecture), then passing by value is the exact cost as passing by pointer or reference. However, additional overhead is consumed if the data type's size exceeds 8 bytes or has a nontrivial copy constructor.

The usage of a parameter is its semantics. Determining how the parameter will be used is essential for correctly passing it. Suppose the parameter is an input value; any method for passing works. Readability and performance should be considered to determine the best approach; however, if a parameter is to be used for output from the function, passing by value cannot be used. The parameter must be passed either by pointer or reference. A different mistake attempts to dissuade one from using output parameters.

Passing parameters by pointer or reference is not limited to simple output parameters; their use for modifying source data in the caller's scope cannot be achieved otherwise. For example, if a caller wants a data container sorted, passing a pointer or reference to it is optimal, since it prevents copying the container's contents. The purpose of the parameter must be thoroughly understood when choosing which passing type to use.

Finally, the safety of the data is critical. Since pointer or reference parameters are usually more efficient than value parameters, it is easy to assume that all parameters should be this type. Think carefully about readability before accepting this efficiency. Further—and this is critical—determine whether the function should modify the data. If the function should not change the source data, then the const keyword must be used appropriately. Given the ease of use for references—and functions that can modify the caller's data—be very liberal in using const on the reference. Since pointer syntax is more difficult to write and read, references are preferred. Further, references cannot be null, so testing for validity is unnecessary.

PROBLEM

Passing a string by value consumes much more space than passing by a pointer or a reference. The advantage is that the parameter is a copy of the source data, and the function cannot modify that data. The advantage of a reference is its simple syntax. One advantage of a pointer is its familiarity with older code bases. Another advantage of pointers is that they are unmistakable when used to modify a value; references look just like value modifications, making it easy to overlook exactly what is being updated. The following code uses each possibility, without considering when each parameter type should be used.

Listing 11.9 Using parameter types poorly

```
const std::string catenate(std::string a, std::string& b, std::string* c) {
    std::string combined(a);
    b[0] = '-';              ←——  An inadvertent typo that
    combined += b;                 affects original data;
    c[0] = 'z';              ←——   syntactically OK but a bug
    combined += *c;
    return combined;               Another inadvertent typo that affects
}                                  original data; compiles but is buggy

int main() {
    std::string msg1 = "Hello";
    std::string msg2 = ", ";
    std::string msg3 = "world!";
    std::cout << catenate(msg1, msg2, &msg3) << '\n';
    return 0;
}
```

ANALYSIS

The first parameter is inefficient; passing a data type that consumes more than the size of a pointer should be carefully considered. Further, the constructor and destructor for the copy must be factored into the cost of using this approach. Regardless of its ease and built-in safety for the caller's data, passing by value should be used only for smaller data and built-in types. The second parameter is efficient but unsafe and does not disambiguate whether its purpose is input-only or includes an output aspect. The third parameter is much the same as the second, plus it adds the complication of using pointer syntax. While this syntax may be familiar, it likely causes mental gymnastics to determine its exact meaning when used. The developer should consider the effect of size, usage, and safety for each item in the function's parameter list.

SOLUTION

Listing 11.10 considers these three characteristics and uses the most meaningful approach for each parameter. Since the string arguments are input only, each parameter specifies them as `const` references. They are now clearly not permitted to modify the caller's data, eliminating the possibility of being output parameters. The minimum amount of data is passed from the call site to the function using references, positively effecting performance. Finally, the compiler blocks any inadvertent typo that attempts to modify the caller's data through the reference when it enforces its `const`ness.

Listing 11.10   Using parameter types well

```
const std::string catenate(const std::string& a, const std::string& b, const
std::string& c) {
    std::string combined(a);
    // b[0] = '-';             ◄──── This is now an error; the parameters
    combined += b;                   are const, eliminating the possibility of
    // c[0] = 'z';             ◄──── inadvertent modification.
    combined += c;
    return combined;
}

int main() {
    std::string msg1 = "Hello";
    std::string msg2 = ", ";
    std::string msg3 = "world!";
    std::cout << catenate(msg1, msg2, msg3) << '\n';
    return 0;
}
```

RECOMMENDATIONS

- Consider the efficiency of passing the parameter in terms of size. The number of bytes copied from the call site to the function is a general rule of thumb; measure when in doubt.
- Consider the usage of the parameter; whether it is input only, input/output, or output only; and whether the function should modify the caller's data.
- Consider the safety of the data—only permit modification of the caller's data if it is explicitly needed; otherwise, specify `const`.

SEE ALSO

- See Mistake 85 for an argument against using parameters for output.

11.7 Mistake 87: Depending on parameter evaluation order

This mistake focuses on correctness, and it positively affects readability. Evaluation order is specified in many cases, and a developer soon develops an intuition about how to write code to use this order. For example, the more complex `for` loop has a particular order in which each section is evaluated. Evaluating parameters seems straightforward because they are usually a copy of some value, a pointer, or a reference to a variable.

> **NOTE** The term *parameter* is used rather loosely in this discussion. There are two accepted sets of terms to delineate parameters. The first is that values used at the call site are called *parameters*, and the variables in the function's parameter list are called *formal parameters*. Second, values used at the call site are called *arguments*, and the function's parameter list variables are called *parameters*. While I prefer the second, I will use the first to maintain consistency with a large body of literature.

PROBLEM

We will assume our developer is keen on reducing the number of keystrokes used to call a function and decides to introduce some side effects in parameter passing. Ostensibly, this will reduce the number of lines of code, since the updates to the parameters are part of the function call. The following code shows a simple approach to calling a function with two values. The function determines whether the adjacent values are increasing or not. *Increasing* means that the left-hand value is less than or equal to the right-hand value. It is so simple that calling the function in a loop is a temptation to use clever techniques that save keystrokes.

Listing 11.11 Function calling with side effects

```
bool isIncreasing(int a, int b) {
    return a <= b;
}

int main() {
    std::vector<int> values;
    for (int i = 0; i < 10; ++i)
        values.push_back(i+1);
    int loc = 0;
    while (loc < 9) {
        if (!isIncreasing(values[loc], values[++loc]))    ◄─── Parameter evaluation
            break;                                              including side effects
    }
    if (loc == 9)
        std::cout << "success\n";
    else
        std::cout << "failure\n";
    return 0;
}
```

ANALYSIS

The function code is correct, but the calling code contains a significant error. The developer assumed the left-most parameter would be evaluated first, obtaining the value at loc and then the right parameter after incrementing its location. The right-most parameter would get the value at loc and update it. All should work as expected, yet the loop fails on the first iteration. C++ does not guarantee which parameter is evaluated first; in my setup, the right-most parameter is evaluated first, incrementing loc and then determining its value. Afterward, the value at loc is established and passed to the function as the first parameter. The result is that the same value is compared each time through the loop, not adjacent values. Further, the first element is never tested. The side effect causes the program to fail, although it is not apparent, and the function is correct. What is being compared is shrouded.

SOLUTION

Regardless of the temptation to use side effects in expression evaluation, it is almost always a bad idea. The intuitive sense is that parameters would be evaluated in left-to-right order, but C++, following C, does not define any order. Therefore, no order can be assumed.

To resolve this problem, make sure that parameters do not involve expressions. Evaluating expressions before calling the function will take a few extra keystrokes, but correctness is essential. The following code is more verbose; however, it is correct.

> **Listing 11.12 Evaluating expressions before using them as parameters**

```
bool isIncreasing(int a, int b) {
    return a <= b;
}

int main() {
    std::vector<int> values;
    for (int i = 0; i < 10; ++i)
        values.push_back(i+1);
    int loc = 0;
    while (loc < 9) {
        int x = values[loc];
        int y = values[++loc];        ◀────┐ Evaluates expressions before
        if (!isIncreasing(x, y))           │ calling the function
            break;
    }
    if (loc == 9)
        std::cout << "success\n";
    else
        std::cout << "failure\n";
    return 0;
}
```

The code in listing 11.12 compares adjacent values, starting with the first value. The timing of the side effect of the prefix increment operator is well isolated with no surprises. While the code could be better for obtaining the two values, and better code should be written, the isolation of side-effect code is demonstrated.

RECOMMENDATIONS

- Never use side effects in arguments, since the parameter evaluation order is unspecified.
- Minimize (or eliminate!) clever coding that saves keystrokes; it is better to expend a few extra keystrokes to communicate intent clearly and ensure correctness.

11.8 Mistake 88: Passing excessive parameters

This mistake affects readability with a slight influence on effectiveness. The benefit of named parameters has been demonstrated in languages like Python and JavaScript. C++ currently does not have this powerful feature, so parameter lists must be followed precisely. Sometimes, the order of parameters should be more intuitive, but long lists make doing so difficult.

PROBLEM

Some functions have long parameter lists, and their order may need to be made apparent. The following code demonstrates a class where several parameters had (apparently!) some meaningful order to the developer. However, class users might need clarification on the order, making incorrect use likely.

Listing 11.13 Calling a constructor with a non-obvious parameter order

```cpp
class Person {
private:
    std::string first;
    std::string middle;
    std::string last;
    int year;
    int month;                              Poorly named and too
    int day;                                many parameters
public:
    Person(const std::string& f, const std::string& l, const std::string& m,
    int y, int d, int mo) :
        first(f), middle(m), last(l), year(y), month(mo), day(d) {}
    const std::string& getFirst() const { return first; }
    int getYear() const { return year; }
};                                          It is hard to keep track
                                            of which parameter is
int main() {                                which and exactly how
    Person p("Ann", "Konda", "A.", 2000, 14, 3);   many to include.
    std::cout << p.getFirst() << " is " << 2024 - p.getYear() << " years old\n";
    return 0;
}
```

ANALYSIS

Creating an instance of the `Person` class requires the caller to pass six parameters: three for the name and three for the birth date. The constructor could be more helpful, since it names the parameters using single letters. The developer clearly understood their meaning but needed to communicate this knowledge with better naming.

Since the six parameters are required, the caller must supply each in the proper order. It is easy to mistakenly specify the name in first, middle, and last order (which is intuitive for many developers). Still, the developer arranged them in first, last, and middle order. While this approach is not wrong, per se, it must be clarified.

What is needed is a way to better specify the parameters in an order the caller prefers without compromising the constructor's correctness.

SOLUTION

Named parameters would make this approach much more manageable. Without support in C++, an alternative is to use a plain old data (POD) structure; some call this a *parameter object*. The POD is a transfer layer—it allows users to use field names in an order that makes sense to them and carries that data to the constructor. The constructor pulls the data from the POD in the order that makes sense. This layer allows variations in the order without affecting correctness—in fact, it ensures correctness by allowing intuitive usage without strict adherence to a particular order. Also, using a POD eliminates messy call sites, since a single argument is used to pass several values.

It is doubtful that any hard line can be drawn around the number of parameters. Short-term memory and intuitive usage suggest as few as three. Programmers must remember that others will use their code so that others may disagree regardless of the "easy and obvious" design. Keep the count small.

A caveat must be stated here: a POD does not ensure all values are initialized. Proper constructor design is essential to prevent missing data.

Listing 11.14 Using a POD as a named variable technique

```cpp
struct personPOD {
    std::string first;          ◄──────  A POD that contains
    std::string middle;                  each parameter
    std::string last;
    int year;
    int month;
    int day;
};

class Person {
private:
    std::string first;
    std::string middle;
    std::string last;
    int year;
    int month;
    int day;
public:
    Person(const std::string& f, const std::string& l, const std::string& m,
            int y, int d, int mo) :
        first(f), middle(m), last(l), year(y), month(mo), day(d) {}
```

```
    Person(const personPOD& pp) : first(pp.first), middle(pp.middle),
        last(pp.last), year(pp.year), month(pp.month),
        day(pp.day) {}
    const std::string& getFirst() const { return first; }
    int getYear() const { return year; }
};
```

◀——— **A constructor that takes a POD**

```
int main() {
    personPOD pp;
    pp.month = 3;
    pp.day = 14;
    pp.year = 2000;
    pp.last = "Konda";
    pp.first = "Ann";
    pp.middle = "A.";

    Person p(pp);
    std::cout << p.getFirst() << " is " << 2024 - p.getYear() << " years
    old\n";
    return 0;
}
```

◀——— **Initializes POD fields in a convenient order, using named fields**

RECOMMENDATIONS

- Set a limit on the number of parameters, and use a POD to transfer more than that limit. It is helpful to have separate PODs for different concepts to keep them consistent and coherent.
- Ensure each field is initialized to prevent breaking the class invariant.
- Use PODs when named variables would be appropriate but are unavailable.

SEE ALSO

- See Mistake 49 for a caution about (over-) defaulting instance variables.
- See Mistake 60 for a discussion about ensuring values are supplied for each instance variable.

11.9 Mistake 89: Overly long functions with multiple behaviors

The most significant effect of this mistake is on readability (comprehensibility). Putting a small amount of code in each function can negatively affect effectiveness. Still, an argument can be made that a developer is more productive in the long term by writing short functions.

PROBLEM

Many legacy functions are long; some are *very* long. It is not unusual to find a project containing functions that are over 1,000 lines in length. I once worked with a function with 1,200 lines of code; I never understood most of its functionality. Frequently, a function starts much shorter but, over time, accumulates more and more code to address new requirements and changes. The code in listing 11.15 requires a redesign because, over time, more and more code was added. The developer needed to write all the code and (wrongly) assumed that since they work together, they should be written together.

We assume the standard deviation code will work only with nonnegative values—we need some reason for the data cleansing! Therefore, the data must be cleaned before processing. All negative values should be eliminated. After this, the arithmetic mean is computed, since it is required to calculate the standard deviation. Finally, the standard deviation is computed.

The code flows logically from top to bottom; however, the function could be more easily grasped at one glance. Worse, the function's name of std_dev does not communicate that data cleansing would be involved. This misnaming easily tricks the reader into thinking that only the standard deviation is being computed. Correctly naming functions is complicated, and each name should communicate the purpose of the function concisely and clearly. This extended function can have no short, easily understood name that precisely communicates all its functionality. Something like compute_standard_deviation_after_removing_negative_values communicates well but is difficult to write; frankly, it is hard to read, too.

Listing 11.15   An overly long function with three sections

```
double std_dev(const std::vector<double>& values) {
    std::vector<double> new_values;
    for (int i = 0; i < values.size(); ++i)
        if (values[i] >= 0)
            new_values.push_back(values[i]);

    double sum = 0.0;
    for (int i = 0; i < new_values.size(); ++i)
        sum += new_values[i];
    double mean =  sum/new_values.size();

    sum = 0.0;
    for (int i = 0; i < new_values.size(); ++i)
        sum += std::pow(new_values[i] - mean, 2);
    return std::sqrt(sum / (new_values.size() - 1));
}

int main() {
    std::vector<double> values;
    values.push_back(3.14159);
    values.push_back(-1.23456);
    values.push_back(2.71828);
    std::cout << "standard deviation is " << std_dev(values) << '\n';
    return 0;
}
```

> The name suggests that only the standard deviation is computed.

> Data cleaning is a surprise; it is not documented.

> Only this code does what the function name suggests.

ANALYSIS

This function has three distinct behaviors. (Refer to the See Also section for another mistake that addresses a related problem from this viewpoint.) These behaviors flow logically; each must be done to arrive at the answer. It is easy to assume that since these behaviors are required, they can or should be written one after the other.

While this book does not address the concern of testability, it is still a significant motivation behind writing short, easy-to-comprehend functions. The code is challenging to understand at a glance. As more requirements are accepted, new functionality could be added to this function, accelerating the problem.

SOLUTION

Functions should be short and perform one clearly defined behavior. In cases where a sequence of behaviors—a sequence of function calls—is required, there are two main options: the wrong and the right one. The wrong option is to rewrite the std_dev function into three functions and have the client (main function) call the three functions in their correct order.

My students hear repeatedly that the main function should be considered the boss code. The boss is responsible for directing operations but not handling details—we never want micromanagers. Therefore, the functions thus directed must handle the details. The boss code should provide only sufficient data for the problem but no more. Asking the boss to properly order the functions to arrive at the standard deviation is shirking the developer's responsibility.

The correct solution is to write the three functions that contain the needed functionality and add a fourth that orchestrates them. The following code exhibits this approach. The boss code calls the std_dev function as before without knowing the details necessary to compute the result. We assume this name is well established; otherwise, it should be spelled out more fully—sometimes, we must accept what we cannot change.

Listing 11.16 Splitting up a long function and adding an orchestrator

```cpp
std::vector<double> cleanse(const std::vector<double>& values) {
    std::vector<double> good;
    for (int i = 0; i < values.size(); ++i)
        if (values[i] >= 0)
            good.push_back(values[i]);
    return good;
}

double arith_mean(const std::vector<double>& values) {
    double sum = 0.0;
    for (int i = 0; i < values.size(); ++i)
        sum += values[i];
    return sum/values.size();
}

double std_deviation(const std::vector<double>& values, double mean) {
    double sum = 0.0;
    for (int i = 0; i < values.size(); ++i)
        sum += std::pow(values[i] - mean, 2);
    return std::sqrt(sum / (values.size() - 1));
```

```
}

double std_dev(const std::vector<double>& values) {      ◄────┐  The orchestrator
    std::vector<double> new_values = cleanse(values);         │  function that
    double mean = arith_mean(new_values);                     │  manages details
    return std_deviation(new_values, mean);
}

int main() {
    std::vector<double> values;
    values.push_back(3.14159);
    values.push_back(-1.23456);
    values.push_back(2.71828);
    std::cout << "standard deviation is " <<          │  There is no change to
        std_dev(values) << '\n';              ◄───────┘  the client (boss) code.
    return 0;
}
```

RECOMMENDATIONS

- Split extended functions into small, easily understood functions.
- Add orchestrator functions to coordinate the new, small functions.
- Give functions names that describe their behavior clearly.
- If you have access to automated tools (for example, IDE plugins) that refactor code, learn to use them; some will turn several parameters into a parameter object—excellent!

SEE ALSO

- See Mistake 90 for a discussion about keeping functions focused on a single responsibility.

11.10 *Mistake 90: Overly responsible functions*

This mistake affects readability and effectiveness and may have a negative effect on correctness. Functions are the heart of programming reusable, readable code, but they can become burdensome if poorly programmed.

PROBLEM

Related to the previous mistake, overly responsible functions carry too much functionality to be clearly understood. Our intrepid programmer took another shortcut, which resulted in the following code. The need for sanitizing data grew into two requirements: filter data below zero and filter data above zero. Since these behaviors are similar, a single function was written to do both. Calling the code requires passing a vector of values and a Boolean flag that determines which values are eliminated.

> **Listing 11.17   Filtering data both above and below zero in one function**

```
std::vector<double> cleanse(const std::vector<double>& values,
        bool less_than) {
    std::vector<double> new_values;
```

```
    for (int i = 0; i < values.size(); ++i)
        if (less_than) {
            if (values[i] < 0)
                new_values.push_back(values[i]);
        } else
            if (values[i] > 0)
                new_values.push_back(values[i]);
    return new_values;
}

int main() {
    std::vector<double> values;
    values.push_back(3.14159);
    values.push_back(-1.23456);
    values.push_back(2.71828);
    values.push_back(-3.14159);

    std::vector<double> above = cleanse(values, false);
    for (int i = 0; i < above.size(); ++i)
        std::cout << above[i] << ' ';
    std::cout << '\n';

    std::vector<double> below = cleanse(values, true);
    for (int i = 0; i < below.size(); ++i)
        std::cout << below[i] << ' ';
    std::cout << '\n';
    return 0;
}
```

Filters based on the Boolean flag

Specifies the Boolean flag for filtering above or below zero

ANALYSIS

The `cleanse` function iterates over the vector; determines whether to filter above or below; checks the sign of the value; and if it matches the desired range, copies it into the results vector. While the operation is simple, it is evident that the function is completing two behaviors, switched by a flag. The developer may remember the subtleties of this behavior, but a new developer will have to spend time figuring out what a call like `cleanse(values, false)` means. This developer will have to find the source code for the function; read it; and, without meaningful comments (as this example shows), trace through the code until it is clear what is happening.

This programming style takes extra effort to get right (effectiveness) and understand (readability). It is poor design, hoping to save effort and (gasp!) duplication. Existing code bases are replete with examples.

SOLUTION

Duplication of code in similar functions is inevitable, and efforts to eliminate it can cause worse problems. The goal is to minimize or eliminate knowledge spread between multiple functions or methods. In this scenario, there is no shared knowledge between the filter-below and filter-above code, although there is considerable duplication between them.

The problem is often introduced when the control flow (control structure) between the filtering is identical. This situation leads developers to combine the varying parts (filtering functionality) into a general structure, often with duplicated parts. (Ouch! We were working on eliminating this duplication.) Introducing control flow paths selected by Boolean values is a sure sign of exerting effort to eliminate control flow duplication in separate functions by combining them into one function. Not only does this waste development time and make testing harder, but it also fails to solve the problem for which it was written.

Several short functions are ideal and do not suggest ugly duplication. Short functions are more straightforward to name, resulting in intuitive functions in the calling code. These functions are easy to test and validate, and they are simple to read and write. Oh, and they tend to duplicate control flow logic. As Meatloaf says, "Two out of three ain't bad."

The following code splits the filtering logic between two functions and names them appropriately. The urge to eliminate structural code is resisted, and the purpose of each—its logic—is separated into a single unit.

Listing 11.18   Using separate functions for filtering

```
std::vector<double> filter_above(const
        std::vector<double>& values) {          ◀──  A single-purpose function
    std::vector<double> new_values;                  with a specific behavior
    for (int i = 0; i < values.size(); ++i)
        if (values[i] > 0)
            new_values.push_back(values[i]);
    return new_values;
}

std::vector<double> filter_below(const
        std::vector<double>& values) {          ◀──  Another single-purpose
    std::vector<double> new_values;                  function with a different
    for (int i = 0; i < values.size(); ++i)          specific behavior
        if (values[i] < 0)
            new_values.push_back(values[i]);
    return new_values;
}

int main() {
    std::vector<double> values;
    values.push_back(3.14159);
    values.push_back(-1.23456);
    values.push_back(2.71828);
    values.push_back(-3.14159);

    std::vector<double> above = filter_above(values);   ◀──  Straightforward
    for (int i = 0; i < above.size(); ++i)                   usage with no
        std::cout << above[i] << ' ';                        questionable
    std::cout << '\n';                                       arguments

    std::vector<double> below = filter_below(values);   ◀──
    for (int i = 0; i < below.size(); ++i)
        std::cout << below[i] << ' ';
```

```
    std::cout << '\n';
    return 0;
}
```

As a challenge, figure out how to use function templates for the comparison functionality. Write a single filter function that takes the vector and a function template parameter. Consider using `std::greater<double>` and `std::less<double>` for this example. For a hint, see the following C++ reference web page: https://mng.bz/gaan.

RECOMMENDATIONS

- Make each function standalone in its responsibility with exactly one well-articulated purpose.
- Do not be afraid to duplicate control structures between functions—if it works in one, it will work in another.
- Do not be overly concerned about duplicating *code* across functions; isolate the *knowledge* into one function or a coordinated set of functions (likely a class).

SEE ALSO

- See Mistake 23 for an example of using modern C++ lambdas.
- See Mistake 89 for an argument against long functions, to keep functions more readable and testable.

General coding

12

This chapter covers

- Exceptions that are not C++ exceptions
- Proper loop setup and execution
- Verbose coding and overuse of some keywords
- Using deleted pointers

Improper design and implementation are not limited to C++. Many of the following mistakes are general and appear in many languages. This generality does not mean the following problems are unimportant, only that they are likely to occur in any code base. A language cannot be divorced from the architecture and machine on which it runs, although most languages attempt to abstract as many of those details as possible. Java's approach eliminates many of the machine details but still shows signs of constraint. For example, bit sizes for data types limit the range of possible values—there appears to be no way around these machine details, regardless of attempts at abstraction.

C++ is closer to the machine than most languages. Therefore, it is no surprise that machine-specific details and problems crop up frequently. The following mistakes address several cases where language or machine details affect correctly implemented programs.

12.1 Mistake 91: Improperly handling division by zero

This mistake affects readability and effectiveness. Handling exceptions is a powerful technique for dealing with problems when recovery is possible and feasible.

Several students have been surprised by the fact that computers do not deal with a significant set of values in the class of numbers known as integers (or floating-point values representing real numbers). Computers are fast, precise, and accurate but limited, especially in representing numeric value ranges.

Computing problems that contain division steps have a particular problem that needs to be addressed. Mathematicians get touchy when we try dividing integers by zero.

PROBLEM

Many computations involve division somewhere. This includes the division operator (/) and the less-obvious modulus operator (%). An experienced programmer will likely learn the hard way that integer division by zero causes program termination with a floating-point exception (FPE). Many novice programmers have yet to understand this and rarely protect their division code by checking the value of the divisor before attempting the computation. Written by an aware programmer, the following code considers the possibility of this mathematical error.

Listing 12.1 Unchecked integer division

```
bool divides(int b, int a) {
    return a % b == 0;                  A potential source of a
}                                       floating-point exception

int main() {
    int x = 0;
    int y = 42;
    try {
        if (divides(x, y))
            std::cout << x << " divides " << y << '\n';   A universal
    } catch(...) {                                          catch block
        std::cout << "probably divide by zero issue\n";
    }
    return 0;
}
```

However, when running this code, the programmer is surprised that their program still crashes with an FPE. For all their good intentions, nothing has been solved, and recovery is impossible. Some systems do not crash, but that does not mean the code ran correctly.

ANALYSIS

Running the code in listing 12.1 on my system results in this unexpected message:

```
Floating point exception
```

Other systems and compilers may produce a different message.

What is initially surprising is that the catch-all exception handler does not respond to this exception. The purpose of a catch-all handler is to handle any exception that has not been caught. It is the universal catch clause, yet it fails in its attempt.

SOLUTION

Here's a riddle: When is an exception not an exception? When it is not a C++ exception.

The programmer deals with the conflation of terms between the IEEE 754 standard (which defines floating-point operations in computing) and the C++ version. The term *floating-point exception* is confusing to many developers who have studied programming languages.

The CPU determines that a divide-by-zero operation is in effect and balks. In C++, this raises a signal, which triggers a signal floating-point exception (SIGFPE) handler. This signal is not a C++ exception; therefore, the universal catch block does not execute. The SIGFPE handler is outside the developer's code and part of the C++ runtime code. This alternate flow of control bypasses the catch block entirely.

One possibility is for the programmer to define a division by zero handling function and set the SIGFPE handler to call that function. However, returning control to a meaningful point after the function is called is difficult or impossible.

It is better to understand the dual use of the term *exception* and prevent the division-by-zero problem. The following code preemptively averts the problem by throwing an exception. Since this is a C++ exception, all the typical exception-handling techniques work as expected.

Listing 12.2 Anticipating divide by zero and throwing a C++ exception

```cpp
bool divides(int b, int a) {
    if (b == 0)
        throw std::invalid_argument("divisor is zero");    // Anticipates a
    return a % b == 0;                                      // divide-by-zero
}                                                           // problem

                                                           // Throws a C++
                                                           // exception if it occurs
int main() {
    int x = 0;
    int y = 42;
    try {
        if (divides(x, y))
            std::cout << x << " divides " << y << '\n';
    } catch(std::invalid_argument ex) {                    // Handles the situation
        std::cout << ex.what() << '\n';
    }
    return 0;
}
```

RECOMMENDATIONS

- Be careful to understand terminology and not assume that a word always means whatever C++ defines it as.

- Glance at the IEEE 754 standard if you want to know more about the representation, limitations, and uses of floating-point numbers in a computer.

- Remember that computations are bounded; data types do not represent infinite sets of values—a 32-bit signed integer has a range of –2,147,483,648 to 2,147,483,647, and anything outside this range is invalid. Remember that values can underflow and overflow, so be careful about approaching the boundaries.

SEE ALSO

- See Mistake 83 for a more aggressive approach to dealing with invalid input values.

12.2 Mistake 92: *Incorrectly* using the *continue* keyword in loops

This mistake affects correctness and effectiveness. Writing loops is often done by muscle memory. This is a case where inattention can cause problems that might lurk for a time before showing up.

PROBLEM

Some loops have additional logic for handling iteration. C++ provides the `break` and `continue` keywords to modify loop control.

Every loop consists of four sections, some of which might be empty. Understanding these sections is necessary for designing a correct loop. The first is the *initialization section*, where the loop control variable or other values are set up—it is the loop's preconditions. The second is the *continuation test*, which answers whether to execute the loop body or not—it often tests the loop control variable. The third is the *body*, the reason for the loop—the code executed on each iteration. The last is the *update section*, where the loop control variable is modified to push the continuation test closer and closer to the termination condition. This order is specified for a `while` loop (which includes the `for` loop). The continuation test becomes the fourth section in a `do` loop, with the other sections remaining in their existing order.

Many programmers tend toward using `for` loops, since they are more concise, the loop control variable is scoped only within the loop, and they are faster to write. This familiarity with `for` loops and alternate control flow (`break` and `continue` keywords) can set an unwary developer up for a problem when `while` or `do` loops are used. When a `for` loop executes a `continue` keyword, control flows back to the "top" of the loop (see the following listing)—or the update section, which happens to be at the top of the loop.

Listing 12.3   A while loop with a continue keyword

```
int main() {
    int x = 10;
    while (x > 0) {
        if (x % 3 != 0)
            continue;
        std::cout << x << " is divisible by 3\n";
```

Control flows to the top of the loop—the while keyword.

```
        --x;
    }
    return 0;
}
```

This code is an infinite loop and will execute until a frustrated user or the operating system stops it when it exhausts its time quota.

ANALYSIS

In a `while` or a `do` loop, the `continue` keyword causes control to flow to the top of the loop, either the continuation test or the `do` keyword. This slight variation is critical between these loops and the `for` loop.

SOLUTION

The subtle variation between the `for` loop and the `do` and `while` loops is that the `for` loop has the initialization, continuation, and update sections at the "top" of the loop; only the body is not included. The other two loops spread these sections out, such that the top is either the `do` keyword alone or the `while` keyword with the continuation test. The `for` loop calls the update section immediately after the `continue` keyword executes. The `while` and `do` loops never call the update section when executing the `continue` keyword. This difference is critical for correctly understanding how to code these loops. The following code duplicates the update section immediately before the `continue` keyword.

Listing 12.4   Properly executing the update section before the `continue` keyword

```
int main() {
    int x = 10;
    while (x > 0) {
        if (x % 3 != 0) {          ┃ Executing the update section
            --x;              ◀────┘ before the continue keyword
            continue;
        }
        std::cout << x << " is divisible by 3\n";
        --x;
    }
    return 0;
}
```

This is essential to continue pushing the loop control variable toward its termination condition. Without this duplicated section, the loop control variable does not change in this iteration and produces an infinite loop.

RECOMMENDATIONS

- With `while` and `do` loops, always exercise the update section before executing the `continue` keyword.
- Prefer `for` loops, since this behavior is not a problem for them; the duplicated update section in a `while` or `do` loop is likely a code smell, which means the design is possibly inferior or incorrect.

12.3 Mistake 93: Failing to set deleted pointers to NULL

This mistake affects correctness. Pointers are frequently used to manage dynamic resources; deleting them is critical for proper operation. Accessing the deleted resource via the pointer is often possible, but the behavior is undefined.

PROBLEM

Developers are faced with many situations where dynamic resources are managed through a raw pointer. Much existing code is full of these cases. Modern C++ addresses this problem using smart pointers. In their absence, the developer must carefully manage dynamic resources. Resource management is often done correctly, and no undefined behavior is experienced. However, several cases exist where access to the resource is done after the deletion of the resource because the code is complicated and the deletion needs to be apparent, but it is not. This case occurs when recovery code from exceptions mishandles the resources.

On a personal note, a project I used to work on contained 12 occurrences of this problem. A static code analyzer discovered these situations, which were not evident to the developer or maintainers. The following code is a very simplified case that illustrates the problem.

> **Listing 12.5 A dynamic resource accessed after pointer deletion**

```cpp
class Person {
private:
    std::string name;
    int age;
public:
    Person(const std::string& name, int age) : name(name), age(age) {}
    const std::string& getName() { return name; }
    int getAge() { return age; }
};

int main() {
    Person* anne = new Person("Annette", 28);
    if (anne)
        std::cout << anne->getName() << " is " << anne->getAge()
            << " years old\n";
    delete anne;
    if (anne)
        std::cout << anne->getName() << " is " << anne->getAge()
            << " years old\n";
    return 0;
}
```

A valid test to ensure that the object was created

A seemingly valid test; the object is destroyed and possibly accessible.

ANALYSIS

The dynamic resource is created, tested for validity, handled, and deleted. The problem comes after the deletion, where the pointer is tested for validity and wrongly used to access the resource. Combinations of different compilers and systems react differently to this code, but in every case, any attempt to access the resource through the deleted pointer needs to be corrected. In the best case, the program crashes, preventing further access. This case of undefined behavior may appear to work but is dangerously wrong.

SOLUTION

The simplest way to solve this problem is to null a pointer after deleting it. If the deletion is at the end of a scope, this advice can be ignored, but it is good to practice it in general. Accessing through a null pointer is a far better option than successfully accessing a deleted resource. The crash caused by null pointer access is a bold statement of a programming problem. The following code shows this minor change, which has a significant effect.

Listing 12.6   Pointer nulled to prevent access after deletion

```
class Person {
private:
    std::string name;
    int age;
public:
    Person(const std::string& name, int age) : name(name), age(age) {}
    const std::string& getName() { return name; }
    int getAge() { return age; }
};

int main() {
    Person* anne = new Person("Annette", 28);
    if (anne)
        std::cout << anne->getName() << " is " << anne->getAge()
            << " years old\n";
    delete anne;                        Nulling out the
    anne = NULL;                        deleted pointer
    if (anne)
        std::cout << anne->getName() << " is " << anne->getAge()
            << " years old\n";
    return 0;                                    A test that prevents
}                                             access via deleted pointer
```

RECOMMENDATIONS

- Always null out pointers of deleted resources; use 0 in classic C++ or `nullptr` in modern C++.

SEE ALSO

- See Mistake 7 for a better way of nulling pointers in modern C++.
- See Mistake 76 for further advice on leaking resources.
- See Mistake 78 for problems with using raw pointers.

12.4 Mistake 94: Failing to return directly computed Boolean values

This mistake affects readability and effectiveness. Frequently, functions that determine the truth or falsehood of something are written. Such a function is called a *predicate*—it returns a Boolean `true` or `false` value.

PROBLEM

Several predicates take some values as parameters, perform a computation based on the values to determine the result, and then return that result. Often, a local variable is used, the local variable is initialized to a state, the computation is performed, and the result is determined and saved in the variable. Afterward, the result is returned.

However, there is a significant problem lurking under this verbose approach. Consider the following code, which determines whether a number is even or odd.

Listing 12.7 Computing a Boolean value and returning it

```cpp
bool isEven(int n) {
    bool even = false;          // Declares a variable
    if (n % 2 == 0)
        even = true;            // Computes its value
    else
        even = false;
    return even;                // Returns the value
}

int main() {
    int n = 42;
    if (isEven(n))
        std::cout << n << " is even\n";
    else
        std::cout << n << " is odd\n";
    ++n;
    if (isEven(n))
        std::cout << n << " is even\n";
    else
        std::cout << n << " is odd\n";
    return 0;
}
```

The `isEven` function is coded correctly but verbosely. The hidden problem is that the developer needs to recognize that the result of the modulus computation is the result that gets returned. The `if` test determines the value of the calculation, figures out the computed value, and sets the variable to that result. The variable contains precisely what the computation does—nothing is gained by the `if` test.

ANALYSIS

Using a local variable to store the intermediate value of a computation is frequently necessary. However, there is no need to keep the value in cases where the calculation is the result.

SOLUTION

The `isEven` function should remove the `if` test code and return the computation result. This approach is far more readable, much easier to write, and demonstrates a better understanding of the relationship between the computation and the returned value.

This problem is not limited to the computation of Boolean values; many other functions (nonpredicates) also compute a value returned without further modification. This technique works for these cases, too. Strive to keep functions very short and very clear.

Listing 12.8   Returning a computed Boolean directly

```cpp
bool isEven(int n) {
    return n % 2 == 0;         ◀───── Directly returns the result
}                                     of the computation

int main() {
    int n = 42;
    if (isEven(n))
        std::cout << n << " is even\n";
    else
        std::cout << n << " is odd\n";
    ++n;
    if (isEven(n))
        std::cout << n << " is even\n";
    else
        std::cout << n << " is odd\n";
    return 0;
}
```

RECOMMENDATIONS

- Keep functions short and succinct.
- Return computed values directly when possible.

SEE ALSO

- See Mistake 95 for advice on minimizing the use of `if`/`else` structures.
- See Mistake 96 about verbosity in `if`/`else` structures.

12.5   *Mistake 95: Underusing expressions*

This mistake focuses on effectiveness and readability. Many developers prefer using `if` statements to the powerful ternary operator.

PROBLEM

Textbooks teach the `if`/`else` conditional structure and use them throughout code examples. Often, the ternary operator is used quite rarely, but its inclusion is often incidental. A solid discussion concerning the difference and use of `if`/`else` statements and the ternary expression needs to be included. Statements do not return a value; expressions always do.

Consider the following code, where the predicate `isEven` decides which path to follow from the `if` test. The true path executes the statement following the `if` keyword, and the false path executes the statement following the `else` keyword, if it exists.

Listing 12.9   Overly verbose conditional code

```cpp
bool isEven(int n) {
    return n % 2 == 0;
}

int main() {
    int n = 42;
    if (isEven(n))                         The if/else statement
        std::cout << n << " is even\n";    is verbose.
    else
        std::cout << n << " is odd\n";
    ++n;
    if (isEven(n))
        std::cout << n << " is even\n";
    else
        std::cout << n << " is odd\n";
    return 0;
}
```

ANALYSIS

The code determines the evenness of the value and outputs the result. Since the `if` statement was used to make this determination, the output occurs on either the `true` or `false` path, or that path must set a local variable with the test result. If the second option is chosen, then the output uses the contents of the local variable. The `if/else` statement cannot return a value but can only compute it. The computation code is often duplicated across the true and false paths, making the code verbose and slightly more complicated to read.

SOLUTION

The `if/else` structure cannot return a value, since it is a statement. The ternary operator, essentially an `if/else` structure, is an expression that can produce a value. Using the operator as an expression means values can be directly computed without assigning a local variable or duplicating code.

Listing 12.10 shows the use of the operator to return a value. The expression should be enclosed in parentheses to prevent the compiler from getting confused. Almost as significant, the parentheses delineate the expression from its surrounding code, making it easier to read.

This discussion is not to say that all `if/else` structures should be forced into an expression but, rather, that many cases exist where this approach fits well. Output statements, in particular, benefit from using the ternary operator.

Listing 12.10   Minimized conditional code

```cpp
bool isEven(int n) {
    return n % 2 == 0;
}

int main() {
    int n = 42;
    std::cout << n << " is " << (isEven(n) ? "even" : "odd") << '\n';
    ++n;
    std::cout << n << " is " << (isEven(n) ? "even" : "odd") << '\n';
    return 0;
}
```

Minimized if/else logic using a ternary operator

RECOMMENDATIONS

- Use the ternary operator to compute a value directly, eliminating local variables and some duplicated code; this example code is not ideal, as it would be better to push it into a function.
- Look for output statements that can benefit from using the expression form.

SEE ALSO

- See Mistake 94 for advice on using `if/else` structures to compute Boolean values.
- See Mistake 96 for a discussion about verbosity in `if/else` structures.

12.6   *Mistake 96: Using extraneous else keywords*

This mistake focuses on effectiveness and readability. Many textbooks tend toward showing full `if/else` constructs without describing when they obscure the intent of the code.

PROBLEM

When a developer learns new language techniques, the style in which the learning is done is frequently imported into its use. The following code is a simple case of determining the arithmetic mean of a collection of values. The C++ language provides the means for selecting from among a set of options (three, in this case) using the `if/else` construct. The first option is no values, the second is one value, and the third is multiple values. Each option must be handled differently; therefore, it is natural to use the demonstrated structure. However, the reader must decide between the options and determine which are short-circuit and which are the main computations.

The short-circuit options are those where the return is computed directly (these are base cases in a recursive function). Mixing these options with the computation often is less apparent than this code demonstrates.

Listing 12.11   Using an `if/else` chain

```cpp
double mean(const std::vector<double>& values) {
    unsigned int size = values.size();
```

```
    if (size == 0)
        throw std::invalid_argument("no values to average");
    else if (size() == 1)
        return values[0];
    else {
        double sum = 0.0;
        for (int i = 0; i < size; ++i)
            sum += values[i];
        return sum/size;
    }
}

int main() {
    std::vector<double> values;
    values.push_back(3.14159);
    values.push_back(2.71828);
    std::cout << mean(values) << '\n';
    return 0;
}
```

An if/else chain that obscures return conditions from computation

ANALYSIS

The two options for returning with a directly computed result (well, throwing an exception may not be a computation, but go with it) are intermixed furtively with the computational option. The logic flows from none, to one, to many values. There is no requirement to write in this logical progression, and in cases where the code is more extensive, the computation can be entirely obscured in the mix. An approach that provides a better means to understand the separate options and make them clear is preferable.

SOLUTION

Listing 12.12 modifies the code in listing 12.11 slightly but, in so doing, makes the result much easier to understand. The two short-circuit cases are dealt with—either they are `true`, and the `throw` or `return` is handled, or they are not. If both cases are `false`, then the main computation case is executed.

A visual distinction is made between the two examples. The former uses more indentation, which is always a load on short-term memory. The latter dispenses with the indentation and more forcefully clarifies that if the first two cases are untrue, they can be quickly forgotten. The computation is at the same level of indentation as the `if` keywords, making it clear that this code will be executed if the control flow makes it that far. Reducing the number of `else` keywords allows the reader to dispense with short-circuit cases more quickly and focus on the main computational task.

Listing 12.12 Using short-circuit logic

```
double mean(const std::vector<double>& values) {
    unsigned int size = values.size();
    if (size == 0)
        throw std::invalid_argument("no values to average");
    if (size() == 1)
```

Short-circuit evaluation of return conditions

```
        return values[0];
    double sum = 0.0;
    for (int i = 0; i < size; ++i)
        sum += values[i];
    return sum/size;
}

int main() {
    std::vector<double> values;
    values.push_back(3.14159);
    values.push_back(2.71828);
    std::cout << mean(values) << '\n';
    return 0;
}
```

RECOMMENDATIONS

- Organize a function to test invalid or failure cases first, and if they pass, place the main computation afterward.

- Minimize levels of indentation whenever possible.

- Use short-circuit cases whenever they make sense; these directly compute or throw and are quickly forgotten when trying to understand the main code.

SEE ALSO

- See Mistake 94 for advice on using `if/else` structures to compute Boolean values.

- See Mistake 95 for advice on minimizing the use of `if/else` structures.

12.7   *Mistake 97: Not using helper functions*

This mistake affects effectiveness and readability and, in some cases, may negatively affect correctness. Client code should never have to know specific details about how an algorithm or function works; instead, it should intuitively call functions, supplying only the necessary data for the problem.

PROBLEM

Consider a case where a binary search is implemented recursively. To minimize performance problems, the collection of data is passed by reference. The starting and ending index values are adjusted for each subsequent recursive call.

The client code calls the recursive function and supplies the initial starting and ending index values. In cases like this, there is a tendency for client code to hardcode the index values, since they must determine the mechanics of the function call and the relationship of the data container to that call. If this is done, the values are brittle, and changing the container size without changing the index values appropriately would cause incorrect behavior.

The hope is that the client will always use the correct starting and ending index values. They will probably guess if their understanding is wrong or if their experience is minimal. This approach is dangerous.

Listing 12.13 A recursive function exposing implementation details

```
bool bin_search(const std::vector<int>& values, int key, int start, int end)
    {
    int mid = start + (end-start) / 2;
    if (values[mid] == key)  // mention previous 'else' issue
        return true;
    else if (values[mid] < key)
        return bin_search(values, key, start+1, end);
    else
        return bin_search(values, key, start, end-1);
}

int main() {
    std::vector<int> values;
    for (int i = 0; i < 100; ++i)
        values.push_back(i);
    std::cout << bin_search(values, 55, 0, 99) << '\n';
}
```

Client code must understand the starting and ending index values. TMI!

ANALYSIS

The developer who coded the `main` function got the index values correct. Still, it is unclear whether they understood that the ending index had to be the container size (`100`) or the maximum index (`99`). Under slightly different circumstances, the ending index of `100` will likely be used. To correct the index value, the developer must understand how the recursive search uses the value. This information load negatively affects effectiveness.

Ideally, the developer of the search function should code it so that the client does not need to know anything about index values or how the function is implemented. In class development, encapsulation abstracts such details and presents a minimal, hopefully intuitive, interface. The same should be done with functions.

SOLUTION

Encapsulating the functionality of the recursive function can be achieved by creating a helper function. This function takes on the name of the search function but eliminates any knowledge about the index values or other implementation details. Function overloading permits the names to remain the same. The recursive function name need not be altered to suggest it is recursive (unless that is a helpful documentation detail for developers). The helper function, which likely was written by the recursive function's developer, determines the details about starting and ending index values.

A further benefit of the helper function is that the ending index is computed based on the container, thus removing the temptation to hardcode that value. The implementation details of how to call the recursive function are abstracted away, and the interface to the client is minimized to only the essential data—the container of values and the key.

Listing 12.14 introduces the helper function between the client code and the recursive function, much like the public methods of a class. The idea is to minimize the cognitive load on the client developer and allow the function to be reimplemented, if needed, later.

Listing 12.14   A recursive function called from an abstracted helper function

```
bool bin_search(const std::vector<int>& values, int key, int start, int end) {
    int mid = start + (end-start) / 2;
    if (values[mid] == key)
        return true;
    if (values[mid] < key)
        return bin_search(values, key, start+1, end);
    return bin_search(values, key, start, end-1);
}

bool bin_search(const std::vector<int>& values, int key) {
    return bin_search(values, key, 0, values.size()-1);
}

int main() {
    std::vector<int> values;
    for (int i = 0; i < 100; ++i)
        values.push_back(i);
    std::cout << bin_search(values, 55) << '\n';
}
```

Translates between the client and recursive function call

Keeps the call as simple as possible

RECOMMENDATIONS

- Minimize the amount of data a function's caller needs to supply; insist on only the essential data.

- Look for cases where helper functions can minimize the interface and simplify calling functions.

12.8   *Mistake 98: Wrongly comparing floating-point values*

This mistake affects correctness, while slightly negatively affecting readability and effectiveness. Comparing numbers seems straightforward, but floating-point values should be considered approximate, never precise.

PROBLEM

Our mathematical intuition might tell us that a divisor divides a number, and the result multiplied by the divisor should yield the original number. Algebra stresses this truth, and most of us adopt it without hesitation. However, this intuition can lead us down the garden path when we come to programming with floating-point numbers.

Consider the code in listing 12.15, where a simple division problem produces an unexpected result. The following comparison uses this intuition and expects the result to be equal. The result is very, very close but not precise. Developers are familiar with using the equality operator to determine the equivalence of values, so this familiarity leads them to misuse the operator.

Our intrepid developer expected the comparison would return a `true` result but was surprised to discover that the result was `false`. Intuition says that the comparison should be `true`.

Listing 12.15 Comparing using the equality operator

```
int main() {
    double amount = 100.0 / 3;
    std::cout << (amount == 33.3333333333 ? "true" : "false") << '\n';
    return 0;
}
```

The expected result would be true but it is not.

ANALYSIS

Computers are limited machines. One of their limitations is that only a small number of bits are assigned to represent a floating-point value. Floating-point values are approximations of a minimal set of real numbers. However, going from algebra to programming sets us up for a nasty surprise. What must be remembered is that a floating-point number cannot express most real numbers.

If our programmer were to multiply the division result by 3, the comparison with the value 100 would succeed, but not for the right reason. The actual value of the division result does not end in digit 3, but the final digit is likely 4. The IEEE 754 standard defines this behavior; all conforming compilers will respect it. On my machine, setting the output precision to 18 digits, the ending digits are ... 57; more digits will show an even more unexpected representation. These non-3 digits are not what we expect or what our intuition would tell us. If one were to raise the objection by saying that adding more digits would resolve this problem, the question would become exactly how many digits? No number of digits will precisely represent the value. The key thought is that floating-point numbers are approximations, rarely correct, but close enough for most applications. This problem is not limited to computers; the precise value of one-third cannot be represented as a decimal (base-10) number—anyone for a dozenal or duodecimal—base-12—number system?

SOLUTION

Because floating-point numbers are approximations, they cannot be compared using `operator==`. What is necessary is a comparison that determines how close two approximate values are to each other. The difference between them, if small enough, should be considered equivalent. The code in listing 12.16 demonstrates the delta-epsilon method of comparison. I teach this as the "close enough" function.

Delta is a Greek letter that mathematicians use to designate a difference between values—think of it as subtracting one value from the other. *Epsilon* is a Greek letter meaning a very small value (in a string, it represents the empty string). The idea is to find the difference between two values and see if that is less than a tiny number. If so, the two values are "close enough" and should be considered equivalent even though their final digits may differ.

The smaller value must be subtracted from the larger to make a meaningful difference. Since it is unknown which value is larger, the absolute value of the difference is computed, ensuring the result is positive or zero. Epsilon is often defined as 10^{-14}, roughly the smallest meaningful value reliably determined for a typical 64-bit double value. However, ensure that your system can use it effectively; smaller bit sizes will need a larger epsilon value. Also, if the desired precision can be reduced, use a larger epsilon value. The following code uses a precision of 10^{-10}, since for this problem, that is close enough.

Listing 12.16   Comparing using the delta-epsilon method

```cpp
bool close_enough(double value, double
        target, double epsilon=1e-14) {
    return fabs(value-target) < epsilon;
}

int main() {
    double amount = 100.0 / 3;
    std::cout << (close_enough(amount, 33.3333333333, 1e-10) ? "true" :
    "false") << '\n';

    return 0;
}
```

Defaults to a reasonable, small value

Determines whether the difference is close enough to be considered equal

---

RECOMMENDATIONS

- Remember that algebra and programming are related but not equivalent.
- Compare floating-point values by comparing their difference to an arbitrarily small value.

12.9   *Mistake 99: Floating-point to integer assignment*

This mistake affects correctness. The matter of converting a floating-point value to an integer value is more complex than it sounds.

PROBLEM

Many students are taught about the round function and, by implication, that conversion between floating-point and integer values should always be used. They may also be taught about truncation using a cast. These two approaches certainly will convert a floating-point value to an integer, but they do not represent all possibilities or necessarily the best ones.

The following code demonstrates this basic understanding but lacks two important transformation functions.

Listing 12.17   Floating-point to integer using truncation and rounding

```cpp
int main() {
    std::vector<double> values;
```

```
values.push_back(3.14);   values.push_back(2.71);   values.push_back(1.5);
values.push_back(-1.5);   values.push_back(-2.71);
values.push_back(-3.14);
std::cout << "value trunc round\n";
for (int i = 0; i < values.size(); ++i) {
    double v = values[i];
    std::cout << std::setw(5) << v
        << std::setw(6) << static_cast<int>(v)
        << std::setw(6) << round(v)
        << '\n';
}
return 0;
}
```

The output from the code in listing 12.17 demonstrates these two conversion functions:

```
value trunc round
 3.14    3     3
 2.71    2     3
  1.5    1     2
 -1.5   -1    -2
-2.71   -2    -3
-3.14   -3    -3
```

ANALYSIS

The results of the preceding code show these typically used functions. However, these results are inadequate for a developer's full range of problems. For example, if we were computing the number of packing boxes needed to move 3.14 items, these conversion functions would not return the correct value of 4. Flipping the sign of the problem, if –$3.14 were a balance (that is, this amount is owed), what action would need to be taken on an account to cover the debt? The provided functions would suggest that the account would require a –$3 action (a withdrawal of $3), whereas the correct response would be an action of –$4 (resulting in a bit of change coming back). These gaps in computing the necessary result indicate that additional functions are needed to complete the conversions.

Put differently, if using only these two functions, the two aforementioned problems would take additional code to determine the proper behavior and sometimes introduce the opportunity to get the solution wrong. Better would be a function that makes sense for the conversion without additional, perhaps complex, logic.

SOLUTION

Beyond the typical truncation and rounding, two additional functions must be considered when transforming a floating-point value into an integer. Each of these four functions will be analyzed and described, and an example will be given to solidify the explanation. In many explanations, the sign of the value is overlooked, which is a mistake. Numeric values must always consider the full range of values.

Truncation should be thought of as truncation toward zero. This addition means that when the fractional part of the value is chopped off, the resulting value moves in a particular direction. Whatever the initial value, when the fractional part is removed, the result is closer to zero than before. See figure 12.1 for a visual representation of this movement.

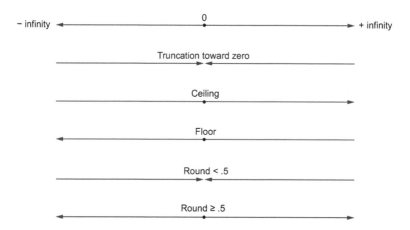

Figure 12.1 Conversion directions for several functions

An example of truncation is a person's age (although very young children seem obsessed with fractional years). The entire year between birthdays is considered the age of the precise floating-point value with the fractional portion removed; that is, the truncation moves the value toward zero, until it hits an integer. A 3.14-year-old person is three, until they become 4.

The std::floor function must be considered in conversions. Unlike the truncation function, the floor function moves from the precise value toward negative infinity. This is demonstrated in figure 12.1. For positive values, it looks just like truncation, but negative values work very differently.

An example of the floor function is that of a manufacturer. Consider a company that produces ice cream sandwiches. If a box of sandwiches holds 12 items, and the company manufactures 150, it can only create 12 boxes. No one wants to buy a box and find that it has only six sandwiches (although if they sold it as a diet aid, it might work).

The round function works much as we learned in arithmetic—if there is less than one-half, we move to the lower value; if there is more than one-half, we move toward the higher value; and at exactly one-half, the tie is broken by moving to the higher value. Figure 12.1 shows the direction moved with this function. Rounding is challenging to describe as a movement, since it depends on the value and the sign.

A quick example is a quiz score: if students score 89.6, they believe they deserve a 90. I always try to round in the student's favor but cannot justify giving a 90 to someone who scores 89.4.

Finally, the `std::ceil` function also must be considered. Its movement shows the opposite of the floor function. This function always moves in the direction of positive infinity. Any fractional part qualifies it to move to the next highest integer value. See Figure 12.1 for a pictorial description of this function's movement.

An example of `std::ceil` is when buying gallons of paint for decorating. Assume a wall that measures 165 square feet and a gallon of paint that covers 144 square feet. Sadly, the home improvement centers do not sell fractional gallons—OK, we are ignoring quarts! We must buy 2 gallons to paint this wall, resulting in a fair amount of the second gallon being left over.

The code in listing 12.18 introduces the additional `std::floor` and `std::ceil` functions to the previously mentioned ones. The nature of the problem determines which of the four options to use. Handling the fractional part is essential for real-world problems and cannot be overlooked without negative consequences.

Listing 12.18   Floating-point to integer

```
int main() {
    std::vector<double> values;
    values.push_back(3.14);   values.push_back(2.71);   values.push_back(1.5);
    values.push_back(-1.5);   values.push_back(-2.71);
    values.push_back(-3.14);
    std::cout << "value trunc floor round ceil\n";
    for (int i = 0; i < values.size(); ++i) {
        double v = values[i];
        std::cout << std::setw(5) << v
            << std::setw(6) << static_cast<int>(v)
            << std::setw(6) << std::floor(v)
            << std::setw(6) << round(v)
            << std::setw(5) << std::ceil(v)
            << '\n';
    }
    return 0;
}
```

The output of the code above results in the following:

```
value trunc floor round ceil
 3.14     3     3     3    4
 2.71     2     2     3    3
  1.5     1     1     2    2
 -1.5    -1    -2    -2   -1
-2.71    -2    -3    -3   -2
-3.14    -3    -4    -3   -3
```

Returning to the problems noted in the Analysis section, a quick review shows the benefit of selecting the appropriate conversion function and does so without adding any additional logic. The packing box problem is a case where a nonzero fractional part exists. It requires a whole box, regardless of the fractional part's size; the correct choice is to use the ceiling function. The account problem, where the balance is

–$3.14, requires a negative action on the account (again, a withdrawal) of $4 to cover the charge. This problem uses the floor function to withdraw the correct amount.

Thankfully, banks and other financial institutions do not use floating-point numbers to represent monetary units. They learned by hard experience that sneaky developers could "make bank" when this happened. The technique is salami slicing and is well-obscured—what financial institution wants to admit to internal fraud like this?

A broader range of conversion functions is necessary to correctly choose the proper means to convert without determining boundary conditions and adding potentially complex logic. When the problem can be solved by selecting a single function, the intent is expressed better (readability), and it is much easier to code correctly (effectiveness).

RECOMMENDATIONS

- Understand the problem being solved and what is implied by a fractional part.
- Choose the correct function for converting a floating-point value to an integer.
- Understand the conversion functions in terms of their movement toward negative infinity, positive infinity, or zero.

12.10 *Mistake 100: Ignoring compiler warnings*

This mistake majorly affects correctness and minorly affects readability and effectiveness. Compiler warnings are meant for a purpose; ignoring them is unreasonable, since some lead to undefined behavior. Many warnings do not affect the operational characteristics of a program, but in some cases, they might; leaving them in can be dangerous. Even more significant, these problems can affect future development and catch unwary maintenance programmers in their claws.

PROBLEM

The code in listing 12.19 compiles fine and produces only one warning (on my system; yours may vary). The compilation does not specify any additional checking. Given this relatively benign warning, it is tempting to continue development. After ignoring these apparently harmless warnings long enough, they accumulate until they become unmanageable.

Listing 12.19   A simple program with multiple problems

```
int compute(int* x, int y) {
    int* pos = x;
    if (*x > NULL)                    ◀──┤ NULL is used incorrectly.
        return *x + *x;
    return 0;
}

int main() {                          ┌─ x has an undefined value.
    int* x;     //        ◀───────────┘
    int res = compute(x, 0);  ◀──┐ This undefined value is
    std::cout << "hello, world\n";  └ passed to the function.
    return 0;
}
```

With warning checking turned on (-Wall and -Wextra were used), the output suddenly looks nasty. The result of compiling with this warning checking is the following:

**The compiler complains
about the wrong usage.**

```
warning-bad.cpp: In function 'int compute(int*, int)':
warning-bad.cpp:6:14: warning: NULL used in arithmetic [-Wpointer-arith]
    6 |     if (*x > NULL)
      |             ^~~
warning-bad.cpp:5:10: warning: unused variable 'pos' [-Wunused-variable]
    5 |     int* pos = x;
      |          ^~~
warning-bad.cpp:4:25: warning: unused parameter 'y' [-Wunused-parameter]
    4 | int compute(int* x, int y) {
      |                     ~~~~^
warning-bad.cpp: In function 'int main()':
warning-bad.cpp:13:9: warning: unused variable 'res' [-Wunused-variable]
   13 |     int res = compute(x, 0);
      |         ^~~
warning-bad.cpp:14:5: warning: label 'std' defined but not used [-Wunused-
label]
   14 |     std:cout << "hello, world\n";
      |        ^~~
warning-bad.cpp:13:22: warning: 'x' is used uninitialized [-Wuninitialized]
   13 |     int res = compute(x, 0);
      |               ~~~~~~~^~~~~
```

**The compiler wonders why
the variable is unused; is
something missing?**

**The compiler knows
that uninitialized use is
going to be a problem.**

This nastiness is saying something that should be carefully listened to.

The two additional warning options may have different names, depending on the tool used. These apply directly to g++ and are added to the command line; MSVC and other compilers use different options and means for selecting them. Choose the highest level of warnings possible to expose as many errors as the compiler can detect.

ANALYSIS

Seemingly benign warnings can indicate several problems. First, unused parameters or variables may be evidence of refactoring code done to simplify the code base. If so, every function call must supply that extra useless parameter, confusing its meaning and increasing complexity. Second, uninitialized variables almost always need fixing. One might argue that these should be errors. Third, the developer may need further understanding of the mechanics of the code and probably made an error. Fourth, there is always the inadvertent typo. Many other reasons exist. The discovered warnings will depend on the code base and maturity of the developers. A best practice is to compile with as many warnings enabled as possible.

NOTE One project I worked on had 21,283 compiler warnings across 48 categories. One category—unused variables—came in with 5,176 occurrences. I started systematically reducing these warnings by attacking specific categories one at a time. After 5 months, I was transferred to a new project and never finished the project—I doubt it had anything to do with the effort! But who knows? Maybe the code did not wish to be improved.

SOLUTION

Turning on the maximum level of warnings will likely produce many problems. Consult the documentation for your compiler to find out how to achieve this. You can fast-track this by doing an internet search. Each compiler will have its own set of additional warnings.

Each warning should be considered a problem to be solved. Correcting the program text and moving on is usually easy in cases of typos. Consider whether unused variables or parameters are no longer needed or a cleanup step was needed during refactoring. When uninitialized variables are discovered, fix them immediately! Not fixing warnings is a quick step to accumulating technical debt, which can grow so large that one wants to avoid facing the load. Avoid this mental block and fix the warnings. For a real challenge, find out how to set the compiler setting (if available) to convert warnings to errors. This prevents building code with warnings and incentivizes the developer to clean up all detected problems. Doing this after the code is clean might be best to prevent new errors from messing it up. For a less severe approach, enable additional warnings one at a time, and clean them up progressively.

If other static code analysis tools are available, consider using them to analyze the code base further for errors the compiler does not detect. One nice option for C++ is the open source Cppcheck tool (https://cppcheck.sourceforge.io/). Several commercial options exist, and your company may already have one or more available. If not, ask them to purchase one for development use.

Listing 12.20   The simple program cleaned up

```cpp
int compute(int* x, int y) {
    int* pos = x;
    if (*x > 0)
        return *x + y;
    return *pos;
}

int main() {
    int n = 42;
    int* x = &n;
    int res = compute(x, 0);
    std::cout << res << " hello, world\n";
    return 0;
}
```

Compiling this code with warnings turned on produces no errors. This situation does not prove the program is correct, but it eliminates potential and actual problems compared with listing 12.19.

RECOMMENDATIONS

- Turn on the highest level of warning your team can handle in the project; if it is too low, mistakes will be missed, and if it is too high, alert fatigue (drowning in excessive verbosity!) may set in.

- Do not ignore errors in your code where practical; the sooner a bug is fixed, the lower its cost—management will have to decide the level of practical, which will always differ from a developer's definition.

- Warnings in code from external libraries or projects may need to have specific warnings turned off only for that code; consider wrapping those files in an include file with the particular warnings disabled.

- If possible, use static code analysis tools to discover errors; some are free, and many are fee-based but often prove their value quickly.

index